Radical Thought
in Central America

Latin American Perspectives Series

Ronald H. Chilcote, Series Editor

† Available in hardcover and paperback.

Also by Sheldon B. Liss

Roots of Revolution: Radical Thought in Cuba

Marxist Thought in Latin America

Diplomacy and Dependency: Venezuela, the United States, and the Americas

Man, State, and Society in Latin American History, coeditor with
P. K. Liss

The Canal: Aspects of United States–Panamanian Relations

A Century of Disagreement: The Chamizal Conflict, 1864–1964

Radical Thought in Central America

Sheldon B. Liss

Westview Press
Boulder • San Francisco • Oxford

Latin American Perspectives Series, Number 7

Published in 1991 in the United States of America by Westview Press, Inc., 5500 Central Avenue, Boulder, Colorado 80301, and in the United Kingdom by Westview Press, 36 Lonsdale Road, Summertown, Oxford OX2 7EW

Library of Congress Cataloging-in-Publication Data
Liss, Sheldon B.
  Radical thought in Central America / Sheldon B. Liss.
    p. cm. — (Latin American perspectives series)
  Includes bibliographical references (p.) and index.
  ISBN 0-8133-8208-4 (hc) — ISBN 0-8133-8209-2 (pb)
  1. Central America—Politics and government. 2. Central America—
Intellectual life—20th century. 3. Radicalism—Central America—
History—20th century. 4. Self-determination, National.
I. Title. II. Series.
F1438.L74 1991
320.9728—dc20   91-21144
                                                                      CIP

Printed and bound in the United States of America

The paper used in this publication meets the requirements
of the American National Standard for Permanence of Paper
for Printed Library Materials Z39.48-1984.

10   9   8   7   6   5   4   3   2   1

Contents

Acknowledgments

Numerous coworkers in the antiinterventionist movement and academic colleagues encouraged me to examine the history of radical thought and action in Central America and to present my findings. For over a quarter of a century, countless people from all walks of life in Latin America have imparted their wisdom to me and graciously facilitated my explorations into inter-American relations and radical thought. In the years since the Vietnam War, with the hope of averting similar disasters in the Americas, Central American friends and acquaintances have invited me to analyze the obstacles to, and vehicles for, progress in their region. They have also asked me to convey to the people of my country their ideas, fears, beliefs, and aspirations for a brighter future.

In one way or another, through their assistance, insights, or advice, Nora Astorga, Fernando Cardenal, Susan Chester, James Cockcroft, Lisa Freeman, Richard Harris, Felipe Ixcot, Frank LaRue, Uriel Molina, Tommie Sue Montgomery, Lauren Osborn, Helen Ryan, Gary Ruchwarger, Janet Shenk, Edelberto Torres, Edelberto Torres Rivas, Philip Wheaton, Jaime Wheelock, and Rubén Zamora contributed to this work. Donald Ramos read the entire manuscript and offered extremely thought-provoking suggestions that helped me to reshape its contours. Scholarly and activist friends corrected my errors, and their ideas enabled me to clarify my thoughts, write more precisely, and present a more cohesive book. Sarah Lorenz efficiently processed hundreds of my interlibrary loan requests. Mia O'Connor and Edie Richeson typed the manuscript from my quasi-legible longhand draft, handled three sets of "final" revisions, and probably wondered why I have not entered the modern age of computers and word processors. My Westview Press editors, Barbara Ellington, Alice Colwell, and Jane Raese, turned what is generally the aggravating part of the publication process into a pleasurable experience. A final note of thanks goes to Central America's radical thinkers and writers, especially those about whom I have written. They continually make personal sacrifices to sustain others in the struggle for human dignity and social justice and are an ever-present source of inspiration.

Sheldon B. Liss

Acronyms

AF of L	American Federation of Labor
AID	U.S. Agency for International Development
AIFLD	American Institute for Free Labor Development
APRA	Popular American Revolutionary Alliance
CACM	Central American Common Market
CIA	Central Intelligence Agency
CIO	Congress of Industrial Organizations
CONDECA	Central American Defense Council
CSUCA	Higher Council of Central American Universities
CTAL	Confederation of Latin American Workers
CTG	Confederation of Guatemalan Workers
EGP	Guerrilla Army of the Poor (Guatemala)
ERP	Revolutionary Army of the People (El Salvador)
FAR	Rebel Armed Forces (Guatemala)
FDR	Democratic Revolutionary Front (El Salvador)
FMLN	Farabundo Martí Front for National Liberation (El Salvador)
FSLN	Sandinista National Liberation Front (Nicaragua)
MR-13	Revolutionary Movement of November 13
OAS	Organization of American States
ORIT	Inter-American Regional Organization of Workers
ORPA	Organization of People in Arms (Guatemala)
PGT	Guatemalan Workers' party
PLI	Independent Liberal party (Nicaragua)
PLN	National Liberation party (Costa Rica)

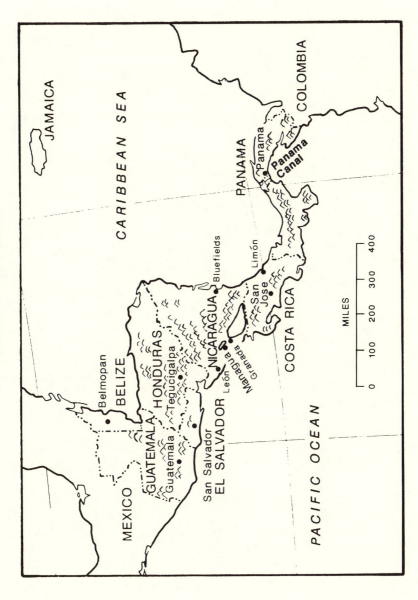

CENTRAL AMERICA

JAMAICA

CARIBBEAN SEA

COLOMBIA

PANAMA

Panama

Panama
Canal

MEXICO

BELIZE

Belmopan

GUATEMALA

HONDURAS

Tegucigalpa

Guatemala

NICARAGUA

Bluefields

León

Managua

Granada

San Salvador
EL SALVADOR

Limón

San
Jose

COSTA RICA

PACIFIC OCEAN

MILES

0   100   200   300   400

1

Introduction

The Fruit Company, Inc. reserved for itself the most succulent, the central coast of my own land, the delicate waist of America. It rechristened its territories as the "Banana Republics" and over the sleeping dead, over the restless heroes who brought about the greatness, the liberty and the flags, it established the comic opera.
—Pablo Neruda

Radical Intellectuals

This volume deals with the radical segment of Central America's intellectual elite. These radical intellectuals contemplate, discover, clarify, or bring new ideas or theories to the attention of the intelligentsia. They challenge and question a wide range of ideals and ideologies, both abstract and concrete, as they analyze the development of society.

Intellectual life in the five Central American nations is based upon Western traditions. The term *intellectuals* first became widely used in France in 1898 as a consequence of the *manifeste des intellectuels* that protested the imprisonment of Alfred Dreyfus. The word referred to individuals with scholarly reputations, outstanding professors, or writers who allegedly represented a national political conscience. In later years intellectuals were often thought of as educated people who aspired to political influence by seeking office or influencing officeholders.[1]

Italian thinker Antonio Gramsci called those who play a directive role in society intellectuals. His definition included managers, bureaucrats, administrators, politicians, and organizers of culture such as journalists, artists, and scholars. Gramsci believed that social structures undergo perpetual change, and he viewed intellectuals as mobile within those structures. To him intellectuals always reflected their social connection and were not rootless or classless. Gramsci, whose thinking has enjoyed

1

considerable acceptance among Central America's Marxist *pensadores* (profound thinkers) since World War II, reasoned that each major social group creates its own intellectuals who are organically tied to it. He also believed that there exist traditional intellectuals tied to older groups. As each new social group emerges, he felt, its organically linked intellectuals endeavor to conquer the minds of the traditional intellectuals. Thus intellectuals are involved in a continuous dialectical process. He concurred with Karl Marx that intellectuals deal with ideas as a part of human activity. Gramsci searched for a creative system of societal restructuring, or revolution, and urged radical intellectuals to do likewise and to analyze ideas on a nonsectarian basis.

As we examine Central America's radical intellectuals, we will note that, as Gramsci indicated, they exhibit class ties. They generally perceive themselves as separate from the ruling class. They believe that they put their knowledge of history and understanding of class and social relations at the disposal of the masses to help them build a new state, whereas the establishment intellectuals use their skills to serve the existing state. Radical intellectuals, more than their establishment counterparts, adhere to the need to blend theory with practice.

Radical thought has antecedents in ancient Greece, where the philosopher Heraclitus (ca. 510 B.C.) advanced the idea that materialism affected social relations. It also has precursors in the humanist tradition of the Renaissance and in eighteenth-century rationalism. The word *radical* has evolved over the centuries. During the late seventeenth century, epistemologists used it to refer to advocates of progress. By the late eighteenth century in England, it also connoted social attitudes. The word radical began to replace the term *radical-reformist* in France shortly after 1830, when it designated people who struggled against a government that rejected popular sovereignty and individual freedom. Radicalism as a political movement probably began during the French Revolution and was championed by the French syndicalists of the 1890s, who espoused the transferal of the ownership and control of the means of production to trade unions, not to the state.[2] Ideas about class conflict, worker solidarity, national liberation, social revolution, imperialism, and the justification of violence to remove tyranny abound in nineteenth-century history.

This book, for the most part, deals with twentieth-century radicalism. On the following pages I use the term *radical* broadly to refer to socialist and nonsocialist advocates of left-of-center progressive social, political, and economic thought and action. The radicals I discuss here have critical minds and understand that all issues have many sides. They do not always possess the same ideology but are linked by an abhorrence of injustice, and by a common recognition of their political and social roles in society. The socialists oppose the capitalist system. The non-socialist radicals, exemplified by those primarily interested in antiimperialism and antidictatorship, do not usually seek systemic change but want to terminate political and economic subordination.

Radicals question motives as well as judgments, and they often see value in tension and conflict, which they perceive as vehicles for creativity. Those who think dialectically believe that knowledge emanates from crises and contradictions. In reference to advanced industrialized societies, they agree with Francis Bacon's adage that "knowledge is power." They think that the ability to deny people knowledge is power in underdeveloped Central America, where a few can reduce the freedom of the majority. Most Central American radicals seek to transfer power to the people.

The radical goes beyond mere espousals of militance and independence and seeks social justice, equality, and a more even distribution of wealth. To attain these objectives, radicals are daring, often courageous, and willing to experiment and risk failure. Their actions are not irrelevant to established social and political concerns, but they do not always treat such matters conventionally. They often respond negatively to the idea of respect for authority simply because it exists. One must not equate their willingness to forcefully renounce the established order with a penchant for authoritarianism. The overwhelming majority of Marxist and non-Marxist radicals prefer electoral and participatory democracy and constitutionalism. The Marxist radicals examined in this study know that by "dictatorship of the proletariat," Marx did not mean something undemocratic but rather majority or working-class rule. These Marxists view Marxism as a theory of class struggle, and they regard it as an analytical tool and a revolutionary doctrine that urges people to take action. Non-Marxist radicals discussed on the following pages reject historical materialism and Marx's notion that all systems evolve through a dialectic of contradictory negations. But they generally concur with anthropologist Marvin Harris's concept of cultural materialism based on the premise that human social life is a response to the practical problems of the world.[3]

Praxis

Central America's radical intellectuals usually combine theory and praxis. Before we proceed it would be useful to examine some general elements of praxis. The Greek word *praxis* means action. In contrast to theory, whose objective is wisdom or knowledge, praxis is oriented toward doing. Aristotle used the term to connote activities that characterize a person's political and ethical life.[4] During the 1840s, among young Hegelians, praxis had an almost magical appeal. To this group, which included Karl Marx, praxis meant the ability to put theory into action while confronting problems.

Marx eventually developed his own theory of praxis, one that many of Central America's radical thinkers have adopted. He also warned intellectuals not to plunge into action without a systematic theoretical analysis of existing institutions and their contradictions. To Marx, praxis encompassed a broad range of human activity including consciousness, production, labor, criticism, alienation, and revolutionary practice,[5] the factors that shape history. He believed that theoretical contradictions could be resolved only through practical action and that the world could be altered through conscious activity. He understood that all activity was not praxis. In other words, he construed as praxis only objective activity directed toward the transformation of the natural and social world and designed to satisfy human needs.[6] He sought liberation through praxis and searched for knowledge to guide praxis.

Marx reasoned that the human condition resulted from historical events caused by human activity. He contended that by analyzing the roots and forms of alienation and exploitation we discover the possibilities for restructuring society. By examining past praxis we understand that new praxis can foster revolution and create a society free of alienation, one in which creative and rational development of human individuality exists.[7]

Marx laid the concept of praxis as a foundation block of socialist thought. Lenin reasserted the notion of the unity of thought and action and partially achieved, in the Russian Revolution, what Marx had predicted. From Marx and Lenin, Gramsci learned that theory and practice constantly teach and influence each other. Gramsci saw praxis as the unity of theory, practice, and action. He viewed revolution as a rational-cognitive activity and believed that radical theorists had a passionate emotional commitment rooted in political struggle.[8] In Gramsci's philosophy of praxis the thinker understands historical contradictions, sees himself as an element of them, and strives to gain knowledge and institute revolutionary action.[9]

Marx and His Major Interpreters

No examination of radical thought in Central America would be complete without some explanation of Marx's ideas and those of his major interpreters from whom the region's radical thinkers have extrapolated.[10] First let us look at Karl Marx, who created an entire movement by the force of intellect. The German humanist–social scientist never considered his ideas valid for all times and places. He changed his mind, made mistakes, and his thinking contains contradictions and inconsistencies. His writings are so broad that one can find in, or read into, them almost anything beyond what he meant.

Marx said that he applied scientific tools of analysis to complex situations in order to develop new understandings. He demonstrated that phenomena previously believed to be incomprehensible, or a direct result of some act of God, could be understood in terms of scientific principles. He believed that what will occur is not determined by natural laws, independent of humans, but by how humans perceive situations and what they do about them. He considered society as constantly developing and tried to categorize its specific stages. To him, history represented a continuous struggle for human freedom and the economic, social, and political conditions to attain it. He predicated his theory of history on the principle of social dynamics (the dialectic), class struggle, the mode of production, and how ideas are derived.[11] By using these analytical tools, he concluded that history could be evaluated and used as a rational guide to create a new order.

Marx stated that he could not postulate a methodology for interpreting a continuously changing society, and thus his ideas needed constant revision. He gave future generations of thinkers a model, one that even non-Marxists could use as a heuristic device. He focused primarily on capitalism, with its belief in progress, the function of science and technology, and production. He felt that capitalism carried the seeds of its own destruction, that as its classes destroyed each other in struggle, either barbarism would result or civilization (socialism) would emerge. He believed that modern capitalism dated from the sixteenth century—the time of the conquest of Central America.

Marx saw capital as generated by labor, and labor controlled by greedy capitalists. He criticized capitalism because its purpose was profit, not the betterment of humanity. In his view, capitalists chose what and how much to produce and competed for markets without regard to society's needs.[12] He saw workers and capitalists in a symbiotic relationship, creating more wealth for the latter and greater poverty for the former. He preferred a classless society devoid of exploitation and misery.

Marx depicted the capitalist stage of societal development as dominated by the bourgeoisie. He believed that the proletariat would support the bourgeoisie only until the time was ripe to end capitalism by a socialist, worker-led, revolution. In constructing his theory of capitalist development, Marx demonstrated that economics do not function in a vacuum but within a social structure that supports the economic structure. He did not believe that the economic base determined every aspect of society's institutions but claimed that the mode of production was the most vital aspect determining social and legal systems, ideology, and how they changed. He disclaimed being an economic determinist.

Marx strove to build class consciousness, which included a distinct ideology, a worldview, and a program of action to maintain, or alter, the established system. He thought that class analysis enabled one to locate and comprehend power relationships. He saw the state as an organ of class domination, one that protects the ruling class or those who own the means of production, and he wanted to see the state subordinate to society.

To develop his thoughts on revolution, he studied capitalism and class relations. His writings were intended to be a guide to action, to free workers from ruling-class domination, not a program for revolution per se. He never specified how the proletariat would achieve its revolutionary role. He abhorred bloodshed and did not view violence as the most important function in revolution. He concerned himself mainly with social revolution, which he believed evolved from conflicts in the mode of production that created anatagonisms expressed in class conflict—which ultimately led to the overthrow of the state. He affirmed that the seizure of power by one class from another necessitated force, that historically ruling classes do not yield control without violence, but that once power has been acquired new institutions must be constructed and based on proletarian democracy.

Laypeople commonly associate Marx with revolutionary thought and often erroneously attribute to him some theories on imperialism. He expressed an interest in imperialism and pointed out its harmful effects on humanity, but all of the so-called Marxist theories of imperialism have been the work of his interpreters. The most well-known theoretician who dealt with imperialism was V. I. Lenin, the twentieth-century Russian revolutionary. His book *Imperialism: The Highest Stage of Capitalism* (1916) noted the supremacy achieved by capitalism by 1900. He asserted that monopoly capitalists investing abroad caused imperialism, which enabled them to sustain themselves by extracting profits from foreign areas through economic and political control. He predicted correctly that this situation would ultimately lead to war between major capitalist powers. Germany and the United States, he believed, were the primary capitalist nations spreading monopoly capitalism throughout the world. Lenin made Marx's ideas pertinent to nonindustrialized, underdeveloped areas affected by foreign investment, and he gave nationalism revolutionary respectability by directing it against Western imperialism. Lenin referred to the Latin American republics as dependent countries, meaning that although they were technically independent, economic dependence caused them to lose political sovereignty. His ideas formed the foundation upon which were built the dependency theories that became popular among some radical Central American scholars in the late 1960s and 1970s.

Lenin never admitted having revised Marx's thought, but he did so by successfully adapting it to Russian conditions, thereby creating a theoretical model for revolutionary thought and action in backward societies. His ideas concerning the subjective conditions for revolution and his belief in preparing socialists for assuming power through the simultaneous use of parliamentary means and armed insurrection have had considerable influence in Central America.

Lenin spent his life trying to attain Marxist socialism, which he believed consisted of public ownership of the means of production, exchange, and distribution, as well as popular democracy that enabled each worker to participate in state management. He strove to make Marx's theory of dictatorship of the proletariat a reality. He included in the category of proletarian the intelligentsia. He felt that distinctions between manual and mental workers should be abolished, that all workers must have access to every type of culture and the opportunity to develop fully his or her talents, ideas subsequently embraced by Central American socialists.

Lenin emphasized the role of the political party in raising proletarian consciousness and in becoming the vanguard of the revolution. Although he believed in forming coalitions and cooperating with bourgeois political parties when necessary, he opposed subordination to them. Unlike Marx, who saw social revolution as the basic act, Lenin believed social and political revolution to be synonymous. With no tolerance for reform, he saw the bourgeoisie as incapable of completing its revolution. He thought that the peasantry was backward but that it had potential for revolution. He made Marx's thinking more relevant to Central America by demonstrating that the decisive factor in revolution is the nature of the political organization rather than the existing stage of social or economic development. By emphasizing that the proletariat could seize power during, instead of after, a bourgeois-democratic revolution, Lenin refined Marx. He also warned of the dangers of state control exercised by elitist bureaucracies after a victorious revolution.

Another Russian interpreter of Marx who influenced Central American radical thought was Leon Trotsky. His followers in the region generally have rejected Josef Stalin's contention that the revolution would pass through a bourgeois stage, and then through a socialist stage. They have accepted Trotsky's theory of "permanent revolution," which held that Russia would lead the world revolution while socialist revolution could go on simultaneously in backward countries, and in which he depicted the revolution as a single, not a two-stage, process. Central American followers of Trotsky share his desire for a world revolution in which the productive workers would constitute the ruling class. They stress his belief in the need to combat bureaucracy, which tends to lead from above and thus usurps the power of the people. Trotsky also claimed that the revolution had to transcend national boundaries, that proletarian support from other nations was essential to revolution. He advocated incorporating the peasantry into the socialist system rather than permitting it to remain as a petit bourgeois opponent. Central American Trotskyists also share his distaste for U.S. imperialism. Like he did, they constantly remind socialists about the dangers of pursuing peaceful coexistence with capitalism.

In recent decades, in their quest for revolutionary models, some Central American thinkers have added the thought of China's Mao Zedong to that of Marx, Lenin, and Trotsky. Mao's humanism, his stress on the importance of people, and his ability to adapt Marx critically to a nonindustrialized society have especially appealed to Central American intellectuals and students. Mao accepted Lenin's contention that Marxism must be molded to historical conditions and must adopt a specific national form before it can be implemented. He shifted the focus of revolution from urban to rural areas by maintaining that world revolution did not have to start in proletarian centers but could begin in colonies or the agrarian sector. He developed a peasant-based Communist party, believed in alliances between peasants and urban workers, and emphasized peasant guerrilla warfare. Mao felt that Asia, Africa, and Latin America stood at the forefront of world revolution. They were the earth's countryside, and whoever controlled them could thwart the world's imperialists by closing off their access to raw materials and markets.

Mao called imperialism the major instigator of revolution in semi-colonial nations, and he added to Lenin's theory of imperialism the idea that certain classes in dependent states are united by a common desire to eliminate foreign exploitation. He maintained that a politically aware, armed, and dedicated people could not be defeated, that human beings, not machines, can overcome strong imperialist powers. Unlike Lenin, Mao saw no insurmountable contradiction between being a nationalist and an internationalist. Central American thinkers, with their deep national heritages, can identify with his programs designed to radically transform China, and with his belief that only national liberation would enable the workers to free themselves. Mao also repudiated the Leninist concept of the party leadership's giving the people a revolutionary program. He held that the people have to make the program, that they are the intellectuals who teach, not vice versa.

Although Mao's name is not often invoked by current Central American radical thinkers, they frequently refer to Italian newspaperman, theoretician, and Communist party leader Antonio Gramsci. Gramsci contended that the study of history superseded all other intellectual activity by relating the past to the present and the present to the future, making the position of historian a high calling. He stressed development of the popular creative spirit, culture, and understanding Marxism. He challenged the dominant Marxist view that changing the economic base was the initial step toward revolution and viewed class struggle as the first move toward radical change. Rejecting the idea of waiting for the inevitable revolution, he urged the party to develop a revolutionary consciousness among the masses to prepare them for social, economic, political, and cultural revolution. Revolution, he contended, alternated between active and passive phases, thus causing slowdowns in what Trotsky called "permanent revolution." Gramsci stated that revolutionary movements could endure even though capitalism had not been destroyed as Marx predicted. He thus provided new hope for socialism in areas like Central America.

Central American radical thinkers appreciated Gramsci's intellectual rigor. They agreed with his view that positivism, the major philosophy of the region's ruling classes, strove to develop only the privileged sectors of society. They approved of his refusal to follow slavishly strategies and tactics used elsewhere and his belief that policies must conform to local historical conditions. They shared his conviction that fascism, so prevalent in Central America, represented the violence inherent in capitalism, that fascism was the only way that capitalists could preserve their economic system. His ideas increased Central American socialists' sense of urgency in their quest to eliminate capitalism.

Gramsci labored to create a citizen militia through which the large Italian peasantry, which in some ways resembled that of Central America, could enter political life. He believed that a worker-peasant alliance was indispensable to the struggle for socialism. He emphasized the need to organize in the countryside to break traditional holds on the peasants, such as those put into place by the efficient propaganda of the church. Overall, his approach to the study of the development of Italian society, especially his thinking on the peasantry and his ideas on the role of intellectuals in the battle for hegemony, provided useful models for those interested in effecting change in Central America.

Taking off from Italian humanism, Gramsci built a bridge for liberal intellectuals to cross to socialism. Central American Marxists regarded the bridge as vital if they were successfully to appropriate liberal and domestic institutions and turn them toward eliminating the problems that the bourgeoisie could not solve. Gramsci also showed how to create a new cultural consensus, with intellectuals leading the way by fostering historical awareness and interpreting it for others.

The Writers' Approaches

The writers examined in this book are almost all radicals. They include populists, antiimperialists, anticapitalists, those who use Marxist tools of analysis as heuristic devices, and those who adhere to one form or another of Marxism. By examining and interpreting the ideas of these radicals, we can illuminate the problems that they have confronted.

Studies of ideas by Central America's radical thinkers generally take the external approach, which traces the relationship of ideas to events rather than to one another and primarily views ideas as catalysts for change. The thinkers usually reject the internal approach, which analyzes ideas apart from questions of social origin and assumes that ideas have lives of their own and do not fit a particular scheme. Most of the writers also belong to the plebeian school of intellectual history that believes ideas originate in all sectors of society, not the aristocratic school that sees ideas and opinions originating in an intellectual elite and flowing downward.

Although all of the writers whose words are examined in this volume have a philosophy, conscious or otherwise, they are not all philosophers who explain the relationships of ideas. They believe that ideas must be explained by their historical roots, otherwise they acquire a mystical quality. As theorists, these writers express interest in programs and interpretation of ideas. As exponents of praxis, they are concerned with mobilizing forces around those ideas, thereby giving them legitimacy.

Central America's radical thinkers recognize the role of language in transmitting historical tradition from generation to generation and in binding together compatible social groups. Like Gramsci, they construe this as a means of maintaining cultural hegemony. They believe that language serves as a repository of history and has a liberating effect. They have great reverence for language and contend that those who use it well to dissect the social fabric will, in the long run, serve the best interests of society.

Many of the region's radical intellectuals have no university base and come to research and writing through necessity and their passion for politics rather than through conventional schooling or scholarly training. They want to convey their thoughts to as large an audience as possible but generally do not write articles and books with recognition or remuneration uppermost in their minds.

The area's Marxist radicals are referred to interchangeably as socialists throughout this book. For the most part, the Marxists, whose works are examined on subsequent pages, fall into two categories outlined by the late C. Wright Mills: Those he called "sophisticated" Marxists I prefer, for the sake of accuracy, to label "rigid" Marxists. They see Marxism as a model of society, mold Marxist ideas to fit new situations, find Marxist answers for everything, and their inflexibility sometimes hinders their analysis and leads them to substitute dogmatism for inquiry and reflection. Those Mills called "plain" Marxists I designate "critical" Marxists. They work openly and flexibly, believe that Karl Marx's ideas can be applicable to present situations, but reject forcing realities to conform to hard-and-fast rules.[13]

In addition to the classifications noted above, some Central American writers and thinkers merit the designation "Christian-Marxist." Others discussed in this book are non-Marxist radicals. By no means are the distinctions between the categories of radicals always clear. At various times in their lives some of the *pensadores* have occupied different places on the political-ideological spectrum. These unique individuals reside in a dialectical world and thrive on revolutionary dialogue, and their ideas change. They always adhere to, and strive to instill in their fellow citizens, a belief in progress. They are willing to project society into temporary upheaval to reshape traditional institutions. All feel an obligation to delegitimate conventional wisdom, search for solutions to social problems, and provide intellectual leadership.

Non-Marxist radical intellectuals are idealists for whom thought takes precedence over material reality. For the socialists, material reality is more important than ideas. Both groups reject metaphysical analysis in favor of historical analysis. They subscribe to the almost universal Latin American concept of humanity moving toward social justice through radical reform or revolution. They share a belief in human malleability and realize that striving for high goals can bring substantial gains to society. They generally abhor bloodshed but acknowledge that it is occasionally necessary in order to forge a more just world.

Central America's radical writers do not pursue thought for its own sake. They deal with problems emanating from human situations. They are humanists who want to know how people can utilize their potential and overcome weaknesses to gain control of the world. They seek to understand how power works in society and try to comprehend the relationship of individual liberty to central authority and the state's capacity for social control. They look for ways to build their nations and effect national sovereignty and democracy.

The radical thinkers would generally agree with Immanuel Wallerstein's assertion that all history is based on social science, that one cannot discuss any event without using concepts that imply generalizations or theories about recurrent phenomena.[14] They reject the "mainstream" belief in value-free social science. To them, all choice of concepts implies a political option and all thoughts have an ideological quality. They concur with Wallerstein that all good scholarship is polemic but not all polemic is good scholarship.[15] As they see it, objectivity always operates in an ideological framework. Almost all of them participate in political life, have an activist bent, and view themselves as a part of social relations.

Radical intellectuals in Central America express little concern about their social standing. They believe that writers who care primarily about their positions and careers are more interested in adding to or modifying slightly the existing corpus of knowledge than in changing it radically. But we must not construe the polemical aspect of their writing and their disinterest in climbing social ladders as disregard for quality. They demand unity of politics and art, generally believing that their writings, no matter how politically progressive, are powerless if they lack artistic quality and intellectual rigor.

The Author's Approach

Although this book stands on its own, it also serves as a companion volume to my *Marxist Thought in Latin America* (1984), which did not include Central America. Unlike that volume, this one includes the thinking of non-Marxist radical intellectuals. As in the earlier volume, I use both internal and external analyses, with stress on the latter. Where possible, I attempt to establish each writer's relationship to the means of production, personal ideology, social and political goals, unique theories of society, and views on the state, institutions, and power. I also examine the writer's ideas on social and workers' movements, views on imperialism and the role of the United States in the Americas, and beliefs about his or her nation's struggles for independence. In addition, I try to analyze each thinker's attitudes on ethics, social mobility and control, esthetics, and the quality of life. Where possible, I examine each *pensadore*'s search for community, views on reform or revolution, relationships to social and political movements, and role in national and regional intellectual life and discuss how the thinker's ideas were implemented and whether they endured.

The following chapters explore the relationship of nationalism to imperialism. They examine the evolution of anticommunism in Central America and the manifestations of the cold war in the region. They address the question of how Central American radicals have challenged bourgeois institutions and explore how some have sought to supplant the capitalist ethic with diverse socialist beliefs. The book shows how Central America's *pensadores* have interpreted and implemented Marx's thoughts in diverse ways, but it is not a critique of Marxist theories. It posits no sectarian definition of Marxism.

This book treats most of the questions examined by radical intellectuals in Central America. To avoid repetition, some problems characteristic of the area and dealt with by more than one thinker are handled in connection with a single nation and one writer. In one place or another the book touches most bases. For example, the reader interested in recent progressive developments in the Roman Catholic church, and specifically liberation theology, which affects all five Central American republics, will find it mentioned throughout the book, but a detailed analysis of it appears only in the chapter on Nicaragua. Many of the writers whose works I examine express opinions on Central America as a whole, but for the sake of expediency I cite their views in individual chapters on the countries in which they were born or that they have adopted. Their beliefs are often compared with those of their compatriots before being scrutinized in a wider context.

Because of space limitations, I have tried to select only those thinkers I consider to have made the greatest contributions, those whose critical intelligence has best clarified the objectives of Central America's radical movements. On occasion, I have included writers such as Nicaragua's poet-essayist Rubén Darío, whose radical credentials are questionable but whose ideas constitute part of the foundation upon which subsequent generations of radicals built. Women do not receive much space on the following pages because historically they have been discouraged from entering political and intellectual circles in male-dominated Central America. I hope that situation will be different twenty years from now, after a generation of increased radical activity has altered the area's consciousness and eliminated some of its prejudices.

The reader will find that, following a selective historical overview in Chapter 1, this book contains country chapters, which stand on their own and can be read individually or out of sequence. Each chapter begins with a brief historical introduction emphasizing the rise of radical activities, thought and organizations, and intellectual development and is followed by essays on specific thinkers. The essays on individual thinkers can also be read independently. Where appropriate, references to the thinkers are made in the historical introductions. Because many of the writings of the radical thinkers pertain to the United States and imperialism, I have also included background material on U.S. involvement in the various Central American nations. Each author examined here could be the subject of a full biography, and I hope that this work will encourage others to pursue such studies.

This book synthesizes the ideas of Central America's major radical intellectuals. Most of it is based on their published articles and books, some of it on interviews with them or on others' analyses of their works. I have tried to interpret what the writers said and to present it in language that the reader can understand, a task made difficult because many of the works examined were written in idiomatic Spanish. I have tried to retain the unique characteristics of the writers' thoughts and at times use their phraseology. I have also attempted to capture a sense of the ideological climates of the historical periods in which they lived and worked. The observant reader, especially one who pays attention to the notes, will find it easy to separate the ideas and opinions of Central America's radicals from my analyses and comments. I do not always concur with the beliefs of the writers, but I endeavor to convey their ideas precisely. I am well aware that my margin for error is great.

This book focuses primarily on political and social analysis and theory and intellectual history, not military strategy, political party tactics, or specific guerrilla insurrections. What follows is not a history of contemporary Central America but essays that provide historical and historiographical background material vital to an understanding of recent events.

Historical Backgrounds

The following pages provide background material and historical perspectives not touched upon in subsequent chapters and necessary to an understanding of Central America as an entity. They also introduce a few points that will be elaborated upon later.

After Christopher Columbus reached Central America in 1502 on his fourth voyage to the Americas, wealth-seeking, class-conscious Spaniards with orders to expand Spain's empire colonized the region. This expansion coincided with the beginning of modern capitalism, thus lending credence to our use of Central America as a laboratory for radical historical analysis.

Spain established the Captaincy General of Guatemala in 1543 as an administrative subdivision of the Viceroyalty of New Spain (Mexico), which had authority to govern Central America. Guatemala City became the hub of a region that developed unevenly. In Costa Rica and Honduras the colonists primarily worked the land as subsistence farmers. Guatemala, with some agricultural exports, became a commercial center, and in El Salvador and Nicaragua there existed a combination of subsistence and cash crops and commerce. The early conquerors found no great mineral wealth in Central America, and few natives to form work forces. Spain introduced capitalism, new relations of production, a different class system, *mestizaje* (racial mixing), Roman Catholicism, religious intolerance, disease, forced labor, and subordination.

The French Revolution of 1789 sent new patterns of thought to Central America, including liberalism and ideas about economic independence, political democracy, and local control over businesses. After independence from Spain in 1821, primarily because of the efforts of class-conscious Creoles (whites born in the New World), 1.25 million Central Americans, half of them Indians, lived in what historian Louis Hartz would call a fragmented society, a former colony where the body politic was immobilized as it could not transcend its conservative origins.[16] Independence did not bring ideas or institutions appropriate to the needs of the majority of Central Americans. The advanced political ideas of Europe were unsuited to backward areas. By 1823, Central America broke ties to Mexico and formed the Central American Federation, a loose confederation of states. Obstacles to intellectual and cultural development, or what one writer called "mental immobility," existed in Central America.[17] The five provinces contributed little to political, social, or economic thought. Government leaders and the region's tiny intelligentsia looked to Europe and the United States for ideological support and inspiration while building their respective nations. Oligarchs and *caudillos* (strongmen) rendered lip service to individualism, liberalism, personalism, conservatism, democracy, and authoritarianism.

The five provinces promulgated a constitution for a new federal republic of Central America in 1824, an arrangement that failed by 1838. But the concept of Central American unity never disappeared totally from the Central American mind. Throughout the first half of the nineteenth century, Central America continued the intellectual habits of the colonial era and added a few ideas from England, France, and the United States, such as Jeremy Bentham's utilitarianism and Montesquieu and Jefferson's concepts of parliamentary and republican democracy. The region's political elite divided into liberal and conservative groups. The liberals opposed political power for the church, advocated the abolition of slavery, and favored economic development. The conservatives wanted privileges for the church and very incremental economic change. Meanwhile, Great Britain began to fill the economic vacuum in the area left by the departure of Spain. The weak but forward-looking United States issued the unenforceable Monroe Doctrine in 1823 to warn European powers not to pursue further colonization in the Americas.

By the 1840s, the rapid expansion of coffee production in El Salvador, Costa Rica, and Guatemala caused some of the peasants to be forced off their land, curtailed the production of food, and strengthened the landholding class. Regional unity returned in 1844 under the banner of the United Provinces of Central America but rapidly fell victim to border conflicts, commercial rivalries, and distrust. Instability ensued as Central American leaders had no experience with constitutional republicanism and had no tradition or understanding of political compromise or the concept of peaceful transferal of political power. Power resided in the hands of a series of *caudillos* and their armies, and violence became the midwife of Central American history.

Agricultural exports made Central America an integral part of the world economy by the 1850s. Large plantations began to dominate the economies of Costa Rica, El Salvador, Guatemala, and Honduras. After midcentury Central America fit the world systems analysis hypothesis that economy is basically a world structure, that political acts take place primarily within narrower boundaries, and that world supply is fundamentally a function of market-oriented "individual" production decisions, whereas world demand is basically a function of "socially" determined decisions.[18] Although Central American states participated in the international economy, their economic activities did not help develop their political or educational systems.

By the 1860s most of the Central American states had embryonic universities staffed by clergy or part-time faculty from upper- or middle-class backgrounds. Poor nations cannot afford the luxury of intellectuals, and authoritarian states do not encourage the free flow of ideas.

Intellectuals were few and far between, radical thinkers virtually nonexistent, and only a few progressive individuals espoused faith in automatic progress and evolutionary reform. Increased foreign contacts brought new philosophies to Central America, and a few leaders realized that their societies had not progressed as had that of the United States. This led to a resurgence of liberalism, with its emphasis on free enterprise and free trade and talk about civil and political liberties.

Liberals took control of the Central American nations, except Nicaragua, during the 1870s and remained in power for over a half century, during which they achieved some material progress but not general prosperity. Foreign economic and political ideas penetrated the region throughout the remainder of the nineteenth century, the church lost some of its power, agricultural exports grew, and foreigners were encouraged to invest in the area. Landholdings consolidated, landowners sought economic progress through strong governmental action. Through collaboration, the politicians and landholders grew wealthy. Coffee plantations, generally native-owned, and banana lands, almost totally under foreign control, dominated Central America's economy.[19] Export capitalism expanded without a middle-class revolution. Foreign funds entered Central America without basically changing its precapitalist economic and social structure. A local clientele class, or comprador bourgeoisie, arose and owed its position to the foreign enclaves to which it was subordinate.[20]

Throughout much of the last quarter of the nineteenth century, entrepreneurs placed a premium on order and progress. The positivism of Auguste Comte (1798–1857), who disagreed with the utopian socialist contention that public was superior to private ownership of property, came to dominate Central American thought. Comte's philosophy, based on determinism and stressing science and reason, promised to foster the desperately needed order and progress. Positivism would henceforth guide the thinking of Central America's ruling class.

Anticapitalist thinking was not in vogue in Central America during the final decade of the nineteenth century. *Das Kapital* was not published in Spanish in Latin America until 1895. Marx's ideas about achieving social justice through class struggle attained no popularity among Central America's intellectual elites, most of whom belonged to the groups that governed their respective countries and whose major objectives were political control and economic growth.[21]

Central America entered the twentieth century with essentially a two-class structure. An aristocracy existed, based upon ownership of land and mines, the professions, and new or inherited wealth. Political, social, or economic connections generally determined a person's rank within the upper class. The majority, the lower class, had no political, social, or economic influence. With the rise of mestizo (those of mixed Indian and white blood) groups in the nations with large Indian populations, a three-class society developed. As the twentieth century progressed, a nonlaboring sector of middle-class bureaucrats and managers emerged. It was frequently difficult to distinguish between members of the upper and middle class because they often allied in support of common interests.

Politically sovereign Central America remained economically dependent. The plantation economies of the early twentieth century, sustained by foreign capital and administered by outsiders, required large work forces. The social and political consciousness of workers rose, and they explored the possibilities of organizing formally. Simultaneously, U.S. interests in the region expanded. The United States intervened in the Cuban-Spanish War in 1898, established a virtual protectorate over the island, and occupied Puerto Rico in 1901. Theodore Roosevelt sent forces to Panama in 1903 as a prelude to constructing and operating an interoceanic waterway there.

As a consequence of U.S. interventions, Latin American intellectuals rediscovered a sense of Spanish-American fraternity and continental unity. Intellectuals identified with the antiimperialist ideas of Nicaraguan poet Rubén Darío, explored in Chapter 6, as well as the thoughts of Uruguayan writer José Enrique Rodó, whose seminal *Ariel* appeared in 1900. Rodó appealed to Latin American youth to cultivate sentiment, beauty, reason, and thought—the attributes of the Shakespearean sprite Ariel rather than the instincts of the bestial Caliban, which he equated with the self-interest and material values of the United States.

Mexico's nationalistic revolution of 1910, with its dreams of social, economic, and political reform and democratic government, and the egalitarian promise of the Russian Revolution of 1917 evoked some fascination in Central America and increased awareness of imperialism among workers and intellectuals. Utopian, anarchosyndicalist, and Leninist ideas slowly filtered into the region. World War I diverted Central America's trade away from Britain and Germany and toward the United States. U.S. investment expanded considerably in the area and would do so until the Depression. Central America's few socialists viewed the war as a result of capitalist competition for markets and urged their fellow citizens to take a pacifist stance. After the termination of hostilities, Central American *pensadores* began to interpret Marx and Lenin in terms of the area's problems, especially those caused by expanding productive forces combined with a retrograde socioeconomic system based on latifundia and foreign control of basic resources. In particular, Lenin's harsh denunciations of U.S. imperialism struck a responsive chord in Central America.

The University Reform Movement, started in Argentina in 1918, advocated placing higher education within the reach of the poor and eliminating the division between the educated and the uneducated classes. It pressed for full discussion of all ideologies in the universities and an end to the aristocratic scholastic tradition in education and the plutocratic form of government held over from the colonial era. Reinforcing Latin America's tradition of connecting intellectual activity with political and social concern, it spread to Central America, where a few young radicals demanded democracy in education and condemned authoritarianism in public life. The movement eliminated some elitism in the universities, raised the level of scholarship, and encouraged scientific studies of social problems that enabled students and professors to identify crises caused by semicolonial economic domination. The University Reform Movement, socialism, and radical politics nourished and reinforced one another. Consequently, the intelligentsia developed a deeper interest in how class domination perpetuated the status quo and contributed to the plight of the workers. Student leaders of the University Reform Movement often became, or influenced, radical intellectuals who directed movements for social change in subsequent decades.

U.S. gunboat diplomacy in Cuba, the Dominican Republic, Haiti, Mexico, Nicaragua, and Panama led Central American thinkers to make connections between imperialism and the steadily deteriorating social and economic conditions in their nations. They assailed the greed of the foreign capitalists and the human exploitation that accompanied it and criticized the U.S. notion that Central America was its sphere of influence.

During the 1920s, new modes of thought, such as the liberal reformist *Aprismo* of Peru's Víctor Raúl Haya de la Torre, concurred with the antiimperialism of Rodó and Darío, and added to it new beliefs about Indianism, solidarity of the oppressed peoples of the world, and nationalization of industry and land. At the same time, interest revived in the Partido Unionista Centroamericano (Party of Central American Unity), an antiimperialist organization established in Guatemala City in 1899 to combat governmental brutality and corruption. Founded as a result of the Cuban-Spanish-American War, which placed the United States in control of Cuba and Puerto Rico, the organization worked to prevent a similar occurrence in Central America. It attributed regional disunity to U.S. and European origins, strove for Central American independence, and sought to eliminate rivalries between the five Central American nations. The party's unique program also supported a socialist economy, political democracy, class collaboration, government run by scientific principles, education for all, regional judicial powers, and internationalism.[22]

While Central America's radical intellectuals inveighed against imperialism, organized labor emerged during the 1920s. Heretofore, labor was not oriented toward class struggle but existed mainly in the form of mutual benefit societies, which did not threaten the area's ruling elites. Class-conscious unions, whose development had been thwarted for decades by the ruling oligarchs, began to emphasize the connections between low wages and foreign ownership of the means of production.

In 1925 the Communist party of Central America was formed. It lasted until 1929, when its leaders decided that it was more convenient for each country to have its own Communist party. Socialist parties formed in El Salvador, Guatemala, and Honduras and often allied with the Communists. The Communists followed the Comintern policy of turning Latin America's proletariat against imperialism; supported strikes aimed at U.S.-owned banana companies in Honduras, Nicaragua, and Guatemala; and backed trade union activities in El Salvador and Costa Rica. During the late 1920s and early 1930s, the Comintern broke alliances with the Socialists, the Communists criticizing them as petit bourgeois and rejecting their stand that Latin America was still semi-colonial. This occurred as the Depression caused socialism to gain adherents among those who envisioned the collapse of capitalism and sought to replace it with the system that appeared to be solving social and economic problems in the Soviet Union. Relatively strong Communist parties arose in Costa Rica and El Salvador as the result of solid organizing and party platforms emphasizing economic independence and political democracy.[23] Meanwhile, the strength of the Socialist parties in the region declined because of theoretical weaknesses and their failure to develop ties to the peasantry.

The Depression damaged Central America's foreign-controlled oligarchies and gave rise to dictatorships that could maintain order and contain the demands of an increasingly volatile working class. By the 1930s Central America's liberal era ended, but the social and economic problems that liberalism had promised to eliminate persisted. Under strongmen Maximiliano Hernández Martínez (1931–1944) in El Salvador, Jorge Ubico (1931–1944) in Guatemala, Tiburcio Carías Andino (1932–1949) in Honduras, and Anastasio Somoza (1932–1956) in Nicaragua, military control increased. Only in Costa Rica did a more reformist government exist.

Fascism gained strength in Europe, and militarism tightened its grip on Central America. The area's radical intellectuals organized against both currents. Left-wing sectarianism broke down. Socialists, and Communists responding to Comintern policy, formed "popular fronts" and even allied with liberal capitalists to oppose fascism and dictatorship. As the Roosevelt administration's Good Neighbor policy unfolded during the 1930s, some radicals believed that it was intended to unify the Americas under U.S. hegemony; others felt that it signified the waning of imperialism. Roosevelt established excellent rapport with the Central American governments, and by the time World War II began, all five nations responded favorably to U.S. political and economic overtures.

Throughout World War II, Central America's radicals generally curtailed their criticism of U.S. policies and supported Pan-American solidarity. The notion of fighting the war to preserve democracy provided grist for the radical mill. The altruism of the Atlantic Charter and the United Nations, together with the defeat of European fascism, gave greater impetus to antidictatorial attitudes in Central America. The organized Left, strengthened by the Soviet-U.S. alliance during the war, pushed for constitutional democracy and stressed the links between the enormous poverty of the region and the inability of its dictators to foster economic development.

World War II increased the United States' demand for primary products from Central America. Incomes from sugar, tobacco, cotton, coffee, bananas, and cattle raising enriched the landowners who sought foreign credits to improve technology to expand their businesses. Peasants were driven from their subsistence lands, and the latifundia grew.[24]

Central American universities improved, and scholars began to analyze the modernization process taking place in their countries. Their studies stressed growth, change, and development. This new trend, in conjunction with the economic progress of the Soviet Union and the revolutionary upheaval in China, brought about a new interest in Marx's vision of a modernized society operated by its people for their benefit. Radicals,

Marxist and non-Marxist alike, agreed that imperialism was the greatest impediment to modernization that benefits the masses.

Between 1944 and 1954, Central America experienced growth in nationalism, bourgeois economic development, industrialization, concessions for U.S. firms, trade unionism, progressive political parties, Marxist influence among intellectuals, antiimperialist sentiment, and cold war anticommunism. Social democratic political parties, composed primarily of middle-class reformers, promoted state capitalism and encouraged class cooperation. Marxists related the region's problems to class factors and made appeals to the growing working class. Some deviated from the orthodox revolutionary theory of the necessity of developing capitalism followed by a protracted bourgeois democratic revolution before beginning a socialist revolution. They discussed the possibility of a Marxist revolution in the area without passing through the stages outlined by Marx, and before attaining full-scale industrialization. During this period Central America's first University Congress created the Higher Council of Central American Universities (CSUCA) based on the elements of the 1918 University Reform Movement, including concern for social change. With a permanent secretariat in Costa Rica, the CSUCA consortium, which included all of Central America's national universities, became a source of radical studies in the social sciences.

From the CIA-sponsored overthrow of Guatemala's reformist government in 1954, described in detail in Chapter 2, until the victory of the revolutionary movement in Cuba in 1959, Central America underwent a reaction to radical change. The United States promoted economic development and integration and spread the cold war by interpreting demands for popular sovereignty as the advance of communism. Social reforms that could lead to nationalization of industry were attributed by the United States to Soviet instigation, as were attempts to build a viable trade union movement. The ability of the United States to influence political decisions grew in the region as Central America's dominant native classes lost control of their nations.

U.S. private and government financing expanded Central America's infrastructure, its exports, and its marketing facilities. The cost of imported goods rose and trade deficits burgeoned. Development created underdevelopment as the middle class grew and prospered and lower-class poverty increased. New industries arrived, and the proletarian labor base spread. The lure of employment brought the rural poor to the cities and created a plethora of new urban problems. In response to growing social and economic difficulties, mass political and labor organizations evolved and provided a new constituency for the area's radical intellectuals.

After the military phase of the Cuban Revolution and Fidel Castro's takeover, the United States, fearing additional moves to the left in Latin

America, increased its support for some of the area's dictators who helped provide the political stability and security necessary for foreign investment. Radical nationalist sentiment against U.S. incursions focused the attention of intellectuals and workers on the ways that international capitalism contributed to underdevelopment. China and Cuba demonstrated that aggressive, unorthodox Marxist approaches to revolution could succeed in nonindustrial nations. Third World revolution became a possibility for Central America. Under the guidance of intellectuals and activists radicalized in the 1930s and 1940s, a new generation of radical thinkers reached maturity in the 1950s and 1960s and began to apply theory and praxis to the problems of their respective nations. The majority of writers examined in succeeding chapters belong to that generation.

Industrialization and modernization, together with the economic boom of the 1960s, led to the formation of a more united and vocal proletariat. Simultaneously, Central America's bourgeoisie fought for a greater share of profits, and a prerevolutionary situation evolved.[25] The United States initiated the reform-oriented Alliance for Progress (1961–1971) to defuse potential revolutionary situations and to increase its economic and political influence in Latin America. Washington supported the Central American Common market (CACM), designed to foster industrialization without land reform and stimulate regional economic integration. Because of U.S. influence, the CACM, originally conceived to replace imports with regionally produced goods, changed its philosophy from that of state control of economies to laissez-faire capitalism, which eventually benefited foreign (mostly U.S.) agribusiness. Landholdings increased, production was geared increasingly to exports, and the number of impoverished landless peasants grew.

Central America's governing elites and their U.S. partners feared the loss of power and wealth as social reform and revolutionary movements grew in Central America. They subscribed to Washington's national security doctrine predicated on the Hobbesian belief that reason alone will not restrain human behavior, thus government must use force to do its bidding. The doctrine visualizes a permanent warfare situation pitting the "free world" against communism and asserts that subversion can only be controlled by the military. In 1964 the United States supported the establishment of the Central American Defense Council (CONDECA) to coordinate action to maintain the security of the respective states.

During the 1970s Central America's dependent capitalist economic system faltered. In response to the effects of increased industrialization, militarization, and economic problems, in the 1970s and 1980s new radical political parties and guerrilla groups formed, organized labor grew, and elements of the Roman Catholic church took more progressive, and even revolutionary, social, political, and economic stances. Liberation theology emerged, explaining poverty as a result of the organization of society, criticizing the ideology that created—and the church that permitted—deprivation and inequality, and declaring the people's right to fight for a better life. Practitioners of liberation theology established Christian base communities where residents assumed responsibility for their own emancipation, studied socialism, and agitated for fundamental change. Central American intellectuals analyzed why the dominant class could not, or did not, solve the region's problems, and they increasingly sought radical solutions. The following pages show how they combined the theories of Marx, Lenin, Trotsky, Mao, Gramsci, Guevara, Castro, and one another with aspects of nationalism, Indianism, antiimperialism, and Christian theology to work toward effecting societies in which the working-class majority could share in and benefit by political, economic, and social power.

2
Guatemala

Kommunism with a "k" is every political and social democratic movement that tries to defend the interests of the working masses, the humble, and the exploited all over the world, or speaks of sovereignty and nationalism or dares to criticize the United States.

—Juan José Arévalo

The Spanish brought dependent capitalism to Guatemala in the sixteenth century, and over the next four centuries external colonialism created internal colonialism in the Central American republic. These themes are examined by the country's most distinguished social scientist, Edelberto Torres Rivas. In the nation with cities named La Libertad (liberty) and El Progreso (progress), historically 2 percent of the people have constituted a ruling class based on economic standing and inherited position. The country has traditionally been besieged by dictatorships that have terrorized its large Indian population. Class and racial discrimination have prevailed in this land where the majority are mestizos or ladinos (Westernized Indians) and the latter term connotes an economic, social, and psychological escape mechanism. *Ladino* also means subservience, cultural imperialism, and the fiction of living a white person's life, and it degrades the Indian.[1]

During the colonial era, from 1524 to 1821, the church dominated life in Guatemala. Literary production was subject to close scrutiny and censorship. The printing press entered the area in 1660. Sixteen years later Charles II founded the Royal University of San Carlos Borromeo, the first institution of its kind in Central America. Jesuits ran the school by the scholastic method and offered courses in moral theology, philosophy, astrology, medicine, native languages, and canon law. Central America's first newspaper, the *Gaceta de Guatemala* (Guatemala gazette) appeared in

1729 and existed in diverse forms through the nineteenth century.[2] It reflected the belief that only the elites needed sophisticated education and that the workers had no need for ideas. Operating on a similar philosophy, the Sociedad Económica de Amigos de Guatemala (Economic Society of the Friends of Guatemala) formed in 1794. Controlled by aristocrats, it attempted to stimulate commerce, agriculture, and the arts and promoted historical and social studies.

After independence from Spain in 1821 the University of San Carlos emphasized the training of lawyers as the new nation's links with external markets expanded and its need for legal expertise grew. Ninety percent of Guatemala's imports came from England, and local merchants became agents of British finance capital.[3] European money and ideas flowed into Guatemala by the 1830s. Torres Rivas demonstrates that the industrial revolution drew the country into international commerce, and the expansion of capitalism helped shape the nature of the Guatemalan state. Liberalism caught on at the University of San Carlos, where historical studies also attained some stature. In his *Bosquejo histórico de las revoluciones de Centro-América* (1837, Historical sketch of the Central American revolutions), Alejandro Marure, a liberal professor of law, wrote on events that occurred between 1811 and 1828. Anticlerical historian Lorenzo Montúfar y Rivera Maestre produced the seven-volume *Reseña histórica de Centro América* (1878–1888, Historical outline of Central America).[4]

The quasi-literate José Rafael Carrera commanded Guatemala from 1839 until 1865. For the most part, he protected the Indian majority and respected its opposition to Europeanization. He rejected the few ideas of the liberals, which were radical for their time, and impeded the spread of Western thought. The nation stagnated intellectually. The authoritarian Carrera advocated economic protection, nationalism, military expansion, and a rudimentary form of isolationism. He declared Guatemala a republic in 1847 and produced a constitution in 1851 but did little else to promote the exchange of ideas. Near the end of his rule, the world demand for coffee changed landholding patterns from small plots to massive estates. The Guatemalan state assumed a new role as protector and subsidizer of private enterprise. Monopoly capitalism consolidated control by extending credits to provide a new infrastructure.

Guatemala's liberal, and possibly most destructive, nineteenth-century ruler, Justo Rufino Barrios, dominated the country from 1871 to 1885. His anticlerical administration expelled the Jesuits, suppressed the clergy, and reduced the influence of the church. He put positivists, who enriched the bourgeoisie, in charge of Guatemala's development program. He imported foreign ideas, capital, goods, and middle-class values. British economic influence waned, and that of the United States grew. As a result of modernization, Guatemala encountered numerous new social, economic, and political problems, many of which Torres Rivas clarifies. The liberal government expropriated land from the church and Indian communes and distributed it to private entrepreneurs. New police and military elements emerged to enforce laws designed to keep the rural laborers tied to the new estates and to prevent the formation of workers' movements. Ironically, the liberal Sociedad Económica continued active throughout most of the nineteenth century, but its work was usurped by the government and its liberalism eroded.[5]

The government took over the University of San Carlos in 1875, and it became Guatemala's National University. Under the direction of positivist faculty it moved away from metaphysics and toward more scientific thought. Positivism provided the philosophical foundation for new legislation concerning education and became the dominant philosophy among the nation's governing and intellectual elites.

Near the end of the nineteenth century, illiteracy hovered around the 88 percent mark.[6] Few Guatemalans read books, and even fewer wrote them. Intellectual life lagged as workers' misery and U.S. influence increased. In 1894 the first workers' society, El Porvenir de los Obreros (The Future of the Workers), formed. Anti-U.S. sentiment rose, and radical thinker Maximo Soto Hall wrote Guatemala's first critical political novels. His *Problema* (1899, The problem), dealing with the building of a canal across Nicaragua, was historical fiction based on the theme of U.S. imperialism.

During Manuel Estrada Cabrera's brutal dictatorship (1898–1920), German coffee growers and the United Fruit Company expanded their Guatemalan operations. In 1904 a United Fruit subsidiary, International Railways of Central America, obtained a ninety-nine-year concession to complete the railroad from Guatemala City to the Atlantic coast and acquired 170,000 acres of prime banana land.[7] Within a quarter of a century, United Fruit would become the largest landowner, employer, and exporter in the country. While Estrada Cabrera looted the treasury and kept the Indians in peonage, an embryonic workers' organization, or mutualist society, was formed in 1914, followed by a workers' league in 1919. Major strikes by the railroad and telegraph workers took place in 1920[8] and by the dockworkers in 1924. United Fruit employees demanded wage hikes, the eight-hour working day, and an end to discrimination against black workers.[9] The United States, in the aftermath of the Russian Revolution, complained that Bolshevism was gaining adherents among Guatemala's workers. Radicals and liberals in 1921 formed the Unificación Obrera Socialista (Unification Party of Socialist Workers), which became the Communist party in 1923 and joined the Comintern in 1924. Despite governmental persecution, the Communists inspired the founding in 1925 of the Guatemalan Regional Federation of Workers, a nationalist organization that suggested socialism as the cure for Guatemala's problems.

New interest groups and political pressure groups emerged in the 1920s. The Geographical and Historical Society undertook historiographical studies but refrained from pursuing dangerous political themes. The Anti-Imperialist League established a chapter in Guatemala in 1927 as a result of U.S. intervention in Cuba, Haiti, the Dominican Republic, Mexico, and Nicaragua. The same year the Federación Obrera de Guatemala para la Protección Legal de Trabajo (Guatemalan Federation for the Establishment of Workers' Rights) formed and affiliated with the Pan American Federation of Labor.[10] The following year Juan Pablo Wainwright, a Honduran, migrated to Guatemala and revitalized the Communist party. The party, based at the National University, put forth a mild social reform program that included impeding the growth of private property in the countryside and providing the proletariat with a greater share of the wealth. But it did not call for the transfer of the means of production to the people, which it considered an impossible task at that time.[11] Although the Communists did not accomplish their objectives, the party influenced a future generation of radical writers such as Manuel Galich, whose writings and political actions I examine in depth.[12]

When the ruthless dictator Jorge Ubico (1931–1944) assumed power in Guatemala, one-third of the nation's land was controlled by foreigners. Ubico tolerated no protests against foreign intervention, and his national police supervised the workers. Those who opposed him or adopted a progressive stance, including those who simply favored democracy and rejected repression, were dubbed "Communists."[13] Ubico arrested these "Communists," executed their leaders, including Juan Pablo Wainwright, and destroyed much of the labor movement. Ubico despised writers almost as much as Communists; those who wrote from radical perspectives were special enemies, and he banned books critical of his regime. Journalists in the country practiced self-censorship; those with radical proclivities sought safety in exile. Critical scholarship barely existed in Guatemala. Manuel Galich aptly depicted the Ubico years as ones when dissidents feared to make their views known.

Student associations initiated mild protests against the Ubico regime in the late 1930s, culminating in the formation of the Generation of 1940, composed of writers characterized by militant nationalism, internationalism, and social realism and influenced by the works of Chilean Communist poet Pablo Neruda and Guatemalan radical poet Luis Cardoza y Aragón, who lived in exile in Paris.[14] The Generation of 1940, along with the student associations, actively supported the ouster of Ubico and the establishment of democracy under Juan José Arévalo. Among the leaders of the movement were Manuel Galich and Guillermo Toriello.

Democratic president Arévalo (1945–1950) governed during an era of nationalist-capitalist reform, a period not predicated on a simple coherent body of thought. "Arevalism," a romantic, pragmatic, and neoidealist movement that rejected historical materialism and communism, guided Guatemala for almost a decade. It along with its misnamed component "spiritual socialism" is examined in the section on Juan José Arévalo and amplified in the sections on Galich and Toriello, who served in the Arévalo administration.

Communists helped establish the first genuine labor union in the country, the Confederation of Guatemalan Workers (CTG), in 1944 and in 1945 supported Arévalo's candidacy. After Arévalo took office, the CTG affiliated with the Confederation of Latin American Workers (CTAL), adopted a leftist, vaguely Marxist approach, and established the Escuela Claridad (Clarity, or Understanding, School) a leadership-training institution that followed Lenin's dictum "without revolutionary theory there is no revolutionary movement." Salvadoran Communists Abel Cuenca, Virgilio Guerra, and Miguel Mármol directed the school until the government closed it in 1946 under the constitutional provisions that prohibited political organizations with foreign or international ties.[15] In the midst of this increased labor union activity, Arévalo worked for, and obtained, a new comprehensive labor code that established and protected workers' rights, a reform that significantly affected the relations of production in Guatemala and subsequently caused considerable conflict.

Arévalo granted autonomy to the National University, gave it state funds, and expanded its offerings in the humanities and sciences. Writers were encouraged to return from exile, press censorship was eliminated, book publishing flourished, and the government supported intellectual intercourse. In 1946 Miguel Angel Asturias published the antidictatorship novel *El Señor Presidente* (Mr. President), for which he subsequently won the Nobel and the Lenin prizes for literature, and he began to work on *Viento fuerte* (1950, Strong wind) and *El papa verde* (1954, The green pope), novels which dealt with the exploitation of the peasantry by the United Fruit Company.

A secret organization within Arévalo's Revolutionary Action party (PAR), the Vanguardia Democrática (Democratic Vanguard), formed in 1947. Led by José Manuel Fortuny, it viewed the Arévalo administration as part of the necessary bourgeois democratic stage of capitalism, which preceded socialism. The Democratic Vanguard subsequently provided a new nucleus for the Communist party. Also in 1947, the Grupo Saker-Ti, created by young radical Guatemalan artists and writers opposed to dictatorship in Latin America, sponsored cultural events and began publishing a magazine, *Revista de Saker-Ti*. The group merged with two labor unions and the Revolutionary Action party in 1949 to form the United Front for the Liberation of the American Peoples.[16] Simultaneously, Guatemala's Anti-Communist party worked against the progressive policies of the Arévalo government, as did the Society for the Propagation of the Faith and its offshoot, Catholic Action, supported by Archbishop Mariano Rossell y Arellano, who advised Christians to wait for the afterlife for relief from life's problems and who believed it was dangerous to educate Indians.[17]

The church and its corporate allies sustained an anticommunist crusade, and their efforts sometimes proved effective. When Communist leaders founded the Escuela Jacobo Sánchez (Jacob Sánchez School) in 1950 to replace the Escuela Claridad, it was closed down within a week. But Luis Cardoza y Aragón, home from exile, kept the radical intellectual spirit alive through Saker-Ti. Left-wing politics burgeoned. As a result of a schism in the ruling Revolutionary Action party, the Partido Socialista (Socialist party) formed in 1951. Also in 1951, the Jacobo Arbenz Guzmán administration (1951–1954) recognized the Communist party, which formerly functioned clandestinely.

Arbenz, a professional soldier, dedicated his elected government to terminating economic dependency, converting the backward economy into a modern capitalist one, and elevating the living standards of the masses. He sought to strengthen private initiative and to develop Guatemalan capital.[18] Under the Agricultural Reform Laws of 1952, which did not fundamentally alter the country's economic structure, Arbenz abolished forced labor; organized the rural workers; expropriated holdings over 273 acres, including 400,000 acres of United Fruit lands as well as land owned by his wife; and distributed plots to approximately 100,000 peasant families. Guatemala's Indians received benefits from the government for the first time. Arbenz also talked about de-Balkanizing Central America, uniting it economically and politically for the common good.

Secretary of State John Foster Dulles believed that U.S. investment was threatened by nationalization and the socialist thinking of Arbenz's friends and advisers and his wife, María Cristina Villanova. At the 1954 Organization of American States (OAS) meeting in Caracas, Venezuela, Dulles added a new wrinkle to the Monroe Doctrine by accusing the Soviet Union of ideological intervention in the Americas, and he advocated collective action to eliminate it. Guillermo Toriello, the Guatemalan thinker who represented his country at that meeting, later depicted Dulles's action as internationalizing anticommunism. While the United Fruit Company spent $500,000 a year to convince the United States that communism presented a threat in Guatemala,[19] the CIA spent even more on "Operation Success," the military adventure that overthrew the Arbenz government in 1954. The Guatemalan episode served as a model for U.S. responses to radical change, as illustrated by the 1961 Bay of Pigs invasion of Cuba, the CIA-supported ouster of Chile's Marxist President Salvador Allende in 1973, the 1983 overthrow of the government of Grenada, and attempts to topple the Sandinista-led government of Nicaragua in the 1980s.

Under the military regime established in 1954, almost all of the expropriated land was returned to its former owners, censorship reappeared, and political radicalism was eradicated. From 1954 to the present, Guatemala's ruling class has viewed the protection of private property as synonymous with keeping government out of the hands of reformers and under the supervision of the military. Leftists such as Manuel Galich inferred from the Guatemalan experience that the only way to secure change in Latin America in the future would be to mobilize and arm the people, disarm the military, and dismantle the capitalist apparatus, steps that Arbenz refused to take. Although Arbenz had built an alliance with the workers and peasants, when his regime was in jeopardy he relied on the army for support, and the latter capitulated to the will of the Guatemalan bourgeoisie and its U.S. allies.[20] In the final analysis, the counterrevolution of 1954 radicalized many Guatemalans and turned quite a few liberals into socialists. It intensified the radicalism of three of the major thinkers associated with the democratic experiment of the 1940s and 1950s: Arévalo, Galich, and Toriello, subsequently added depth to their analyses and increased their output of written social and political criticism.

After the ouster of Arbenz, the military no longer functioned as an autonomous social force but became an integral part of the dominant class, ran the state in accord with the needs of monopoly capital, and did not hesitate to use violence and terror to implement its decisions. Military leader Colonel Carlos Castillo Armas declared all peasant leagues and unions illegal and drove the Communists underground. By 1955 the number of organized workers in the country had been reduced from 100,000 to 27,000. Those who remained organized were encouraged to ally with the U.S. American Federation of Labor. Washington told the world that it had liberated Guatemala from communism, referred to the Central American republic as a showcase of democracy, and sent it military aid and advisers. Critiques of this anticommunism constitute a common theme in the writings of all of the radical thinkers featured in the essays in this chapter.

Repression in the guise of anticommunism drove Guatemalan liberals into hiding and radicals into exile. Radical thought could not be published openly in Guatemala. Only the University of San Carlos, although subjected to government attacks, retained a modicum of autonomy and produced some radical opposition to the government. Jaime Díaz Rozzotto, former secretary general of the primarily liberal and moderate National Renovation party, and author of *El carácter de la revolución guatemalteca: Ocaso de la revolución democrático-burguesa corriente* (1958, The character of the Guatemalan revolution: The case of the bourgeois-democratic revolutionary current), called for a national democratic front led by the banned Communist Guatemalan Workers' party (PGT).[21] The PGT, despite severe persecution, remained viable and strove to reorganize the masses and the progressive bourgeoisie. At its 1960 congress it accepted the idea of implementing new forms of struggle against the government, which ultimately led to the rise of an antigovernment guerrilla movement.[22]

Capitalist development in Guatemala added a new dimension during the 1960s. Agricultural exports still dominated the economy, but the Central American Common Market fostered industrialization, and economic domination shifted toward the bankers and industrialists[23] who received U.S. financial and military support. Industrialization heightened class antagonisms, and the CACM widened the gap between the rich and the poor. Guerrilla opposition to the Washington–Guatemala City alliance arose. Guerrilla (meaning "little war") tactics originally used by the Carthaginians against the Romans, modernized in the early nineteenth century by the Spanish irregulars who defeated Napoleon's army, and implemented by assorted left-wing groups in the Spanish Civil War, were well suited to Guatemala's mountainous terrain. The Cuban Revolution had proved that a small and highly mobile force, relying on the support of the civilian population, can wage a war of attrition that eventually enables the guerrilla force to defeat a regular army.[24]

In early November 1960, Lieutenants Marco Antonio Yon Sosa and Luis Turcios Lima, objecting to their government's having permitted the CIA and Cuban exiles to use Guatemala as a staging ground for the Bay of Pigs invasion, led an abortive coup at Fort Matamoros outside of Guatemala City. This uprising initiated the guerrilla movement in Guatemala. The two young officers formed the Revolutionary Movement of November 13, or MR-13, which initially developed along Trotskyist lines and split when Turcios Lima formed the Fuerzas Armadas Rebeldes (FAR, Rebel Armed Forces), a branch of the PGT.

Turcios Lima graduated from Guatemala's military academy, received ranger training at Fort Benning, Georgia, and had read the writings of Lenin, Mao, and Castro, but he felt closest to the nationalist ideas of Nicaraguan Augusto Sandino (discussed in Chapter 6). With a price on his head after the Fort Matamoros coup attempt, Turcios Lima took to the hills and became a folk hero who popularized radical ideas. He fought for human rights and for collectivization and better distribution of the land. To him, Guatemala constituted a semicolonial state with a peasant majority, where the small industrial proletariat could not carry out national liberation by itself. He viewed the peasantry as the decisive element in his guerrilla warfare. He cited U.S. imperialism and the national army as the major enemies, realized that imperialism would not relinquish hegemony easily, and foresaw a protracted war.[25] Turcios Lima predicted armed intervention by the United States as the government proved unable to maintain order. He, like Che Guevara, claimed that more U.S. interventions in Latin America were inevitable. He expected the Vietnam experience to be repeated frequently in the Third World until the United States spread itself too thin, thereby assuring guerrilla victories.[26]

Turcio Lima's comrade, Yon Sosa, who trained at the U.S. Fort Gulick in the Panama Canal zone, led M-13, which quickly adopted a socialist program. Yon Sosa and his cohorts believed that portions of the ruling class would not again, as they did in Cuba, follow a radical movement with liberal goals. He contended that to Guatemala's peasant leaders the concept of a socialist revolution appeared simple and logical.[27] He stated that fighting with the peasants made him a socialist, that the only nations to emerge from backwardness (China, Cuba, North Korea, and North Vietnam), had taken the socialist path. To him, capitalism could not eliminate backwardness, and no third alternative existed. He identified with the Chinese Revolution.[28] He claimed that the electoral path to democracy was barred in Guatemala because the bourgeoisie could not provide democratic elections and continue to remain in power and the workers had no faith in elections. Marxist analysis led him to conclude that only a united workers' movement of both factory committees and peasants could forge socialism. He advocated simultaneous strikes and demonstrations in the cities and peasant land occupations and insurrections in the countryside.[29] Yon Sosa criticized Turcios Lima and the FAR for working with the bourgeoisie. Turcios Lima complained that Yon Sosa talked about a socialist revolution, but a socialist consciousness did not exist in Guatemala.[30] For Yon Sosa, killed by a Mexican border patrol in 1970, socialism was paramount. For Turcios Lima (who died in an auto accident in 1966), when the guerrilla movement constituted a major threat to the Guatemalan government, the insurgency took precedence.

Violence escalated in Guatemala during the 1960s, further polarizing the country politically, and some intellectuals joined the guerrillas. The most noteworthy, poet Otto René Castillo, associated with the FAR in 1967, was captured by the army, tortured, and then burned alive.[31]

United revolutionary fronts formed, secret Communist party schools offered courses on economic dependency and worker-peasant alliances,[32] and the ruling class deemed it justifiable to murder Indians accused of supporting the guerrillas. Anticommunism spawned new organizations of right-wing terrorists within the ranks of the Guatemalan military. Thousands of innocent peasants died at the hands of death squads such as the Mano Blanco (White Hand), which was directed by Mario Sandoval Alarcón, who had led the overthrow of Arbenz.[33] Yet the government maintained the fiction that the deaths resulted from confrontations between left- and right-wing extremists.[34]

By the late 1960s the government unleashed a wave of terror against the University of San Carlos, a major source of radical activity. At the same time, radical priests, advocates of liberation theology, began to establish Christian base communities among the Indians, who no longer saw a contradiction between their religious views and the need to fight for liberation. U.S. Ambassador John Gordon Mein was shot and killed by the FAR in 1968, as was Colonel John Weber, head of the U.S. military mission in Guatemala. That year FAR, convinced that armed insurrection was the people's method to liberate themselves en route to a socialist revolution, broke with the PGT. Meanwhile, the Communist PGT exhibited little faith in the people's ability to take power and maintained that the bourgeoisie could direct a state capitalist regime toward socialism in a peaceful fashion.[35]

Foquismo, the theory that guerrillas could create an insurrectional center, or *foco*, from which all revolutionary activity would radiate, proved invalid by the late 1960s. The guerrilla movement was virtually destroyed by U.S.-financed counterinsurgency by 1968. Mass uprisings did not take place between 1966 and 1974. Guatemala's guerrillas suffered serious defeats but never relinquished hope. The Ejército Guerrillero del Pobre (EGP, or Guerrilla Army of the Poor), organized in 1975, solicited Indian support and by 1980 had over 12,000 members. Another popular group, the Organización del Pueblo en Armas (ORPA, or Organization of the People in Arms), made up basically of peasants, formed in 1979. The Ejército Secreto Anticomunista (Secret Anticommunist Army) responded in 1978 by assassinating the leaders of mass and peasant movements, intimidating peasants, and attacking Indian Christian base communities.

The people's victory over Somoza in Nicaragua in 1979 and the social gains of the Cuban Revolution encouraged Guatemala's radicals. From exile and clandestinely, radical writers such as Edelberto Torres Rivas inveighed against a new variety of entrepreneurs who accumulated capital by allying with the military and foreign development companies or by exploiting tourism and running the new export-oriented agribusinesses. Radical intellectuals and industrial and rural workers forged the Democratic Front Against Repression in 1979. Led by intellectuals prominent during the 1944–1954 period, such as Guillermo Toriello, Manuel Galich, and Luis Cardoza y Aragón, and younger activists such as trade unionist Miguel Angel Albízurez, architect Gilberto Castañeda, and Indian leader Rigoberta Menchú, the Democratic Front Against Repression merged in 1982 with the Guatemalan Committee of Patriotic Unity, which promoted revolutionary struggle.[36]

To curtail the growth of labor unions and halt radical activities, especially in rural areas, in the early 1980s Guatemalan businesspeople pushed the establishment of *solidarista* associations. The *solidarismo* movement, explained in Chapter 5, started in Costa Rica and stressed class cooperation in place of class conflict. Basically, workers and employers, primarily financed by employee savings, joined forces to create associations that provided social services and credit facilities. By the late 1980s *solidarista* associations had over 40,000 members, but the guerrilla movement persisted.

In an effort to terminate sympathy for radical activities, the government stepped up its Indian pacification program patterned after that used by the United States in Vietnam. In 1982 alone, in the Department of Quiché the program accounted for sixty-nine massacres and the destruction of twenty-two Indian villages.[37] Through the use of violence the minority (2 percent) who control 80 percent of Guatemala's land maintain power over the majority (83 percent) of the nation's farm workers who live on plots too small to maintain a family and sell their labor for starvation wages.[38]

Since 1954, tens of thousands of Guatemalans have been slain by state security troops because they participated in political and labor activities. By 1987, 40,000 displaced Guatemalans resided in refugee camps in southern Mexico, and during the 1980s well over 500,000 Guatemalans were forced from their homes by political violence. At the time of this writing, Guatemala's three guerrilla organizations, the Guerrilla Army of the Poor, the Organization of the People in Arms, and the Rebel Armed Forces, still struggle to end repression, to win the right of all to live in peace, to meet basic social and economic needs, to establish pluralistic democratic government, to create equality for all Indians and mestizos, and to terminate the nation's dependence upon the United States.[39] In 1989 the Central Committee of the Guatemalan Workers' party (Communist party) joined with the three guerrilla organizations to become part of the Guatemalan National Revolutionary Unity, a basically Marxist-Leninist coalition. Currently, the radical intellectual community exists in a precarious position in Guatemala, where, despite the civilian president Jorge Serrano Elías, who assumed office on January 14, 1991, political power and social control reside in the military. Freedom of expression is a myth, and writers are, as they have been for decades, the targets of right-wing death squads. But as the following pages demonstrate, the nation's radical thinker-activists continue to work, many of them from exile.

Juan José Arévalo:
The Era of Spiritual Socialism

Politician-educator Juan José Arévalo (1904–1990) has written books and essays on pedagogy, social psychology, philosophy, politics, and international relations. A prolific author, his works, generally clothed in irony and satire, range from profound and multilayered to descriptive and uncomplicated.

The son of a schoolteacher mother and a small-landowner father, Juan left the Pacific coast town of Taxisco for Guatemala City, where he graduated from the normal school in 1922. He then enrolled at the law school of the National University. While a student, he admired the thinking of Mexico's President Benito Juárez, who in the nineteenth century elevated Indian culture to a place of honor in society, believed in civilian rule, rejected foreign intervention, supported reforms, and instituted popular education.[40] Arévalo served as director of the Progressive University Student's Club, a position that enabled him to make political contacts and build a reputation that assisted him in the future.[41] He started and abandoned law studies, which lacked the philosophical foundations that interested him. At the University of La Plata in Argentina, he studied with the outstanding positivist philosopher Alejandro Korn, who taught him that liberty is a creative process in history that enables people to grow culturally. Arévalo received a doctorate of philosophy in educational science in 1934. He returned to Guatemala, where he worked for the Ministry of Education for two years, then accepted a teaching position at the University of Tucumán in Argentina. During this period he developed a strong interest in the effects of liberation upon societal development. He equated the low cultural level of his native Central America with the existence of single-crop states with little or no social mobility, no political pluralism, and aristocrats and chief executives who ruled supreme.[42]

Arévalo, the worldly scholar-activist, gained a reputation for protesting against the abuses of the Argentine military regime. In July 1944 he was asked by the young revolutionaries who had forced the resignation of dictator Jorge Ubico to return to Guatemala as a presidential candidate. Liberals as well as radicals welcomed him home.

When Arévalo assumed the presidency in 1945, he thought of Guatemala as a semifeudal country that the liberalism of 1871 had emancipated from colonialism and transformed into a neocolonial state,[43] a nation in an ideological vacuum, where no genuine political expression existed after decades of dictatorship.[44] In *Istmania, o la unidad revolucionaria de Centroamérica* (1935, Istmania, or revolutionary unity in Central America), he had written about an idealized nation in which diverse elements can function independently and collectively.[45] He perceived his presidency as an opportunity to pursue his ideals, to purify the government, to enable all classes to ally to transform the political system that had existed since 1871.[46] He hesitated to directly attack the conservatives, fearing that would alienate the military and cause his ouster. Nevertheless, his administration withstood numerous coup attempts.

He believed that government could create better conditions for the majority to express their will and develop, and he evinced great sympathy for the workers and small-business people. He admired Franklin Roosevelt's concept of safeguarding liberties unless they present a clear and present danger.[47] He felt that Roosevelt established the spirit of socialism by effecting a better distribution of wealth. Arévalo claimed that he patterned his administration after the New Deal, but he instituted less radical reforms than did Roosevelt.

To Arévalo, democracy meant more than electoral politics; it was a dynamic, a permanent series of economic and social compromises.[48] Democracy existed for all classes, and the state governed in the interests of individuals but with community goals paramount.[49] He established, under the 1945 Constitution, a unitary, quasi-parliamentary, state capitalist government. He gave private property a social function. It could be expropriated to satisfy a public need. He extended suffrage to all adults, except illiterate women, but did not provide political freedoms for members of the Communist or international parties. He gave some Communist labor leaders jobs, sent others abroad to get them out of public life, and closed the aforementioned Communist-run Escuela Claridad.

The Mexican Revolution influenced Arévalo's thinking regarding labor. He believed that "work is a right of the individual and a social obligation" and in equal wages for equal work.[50] He promulgated a progressive work code, which he considered a continuation of Simón Bolívar's dream to free people from bondage. The 1947 labor code recognized unions; established minimum wages, the eight-hour day, and labor courts; and gave preferential judicial protection to workers to compensate them for economic inequities. His policies afforded urban workers a sense of dignity but did little for their rural counterparts. During Arévalo's presidency, organized labor remained divided between unions that accepted Communist members and those that did not. Not until 1952, after his term in office, did most labor activity, Communist included, cohere around the General Confederation of Guatemalan Workers.[51]

"Arevalism," defined in the introduction to this chapter, included striving for human perfection under the direction of a popularly elected progressive government. It reflected Arévalo's preoccupation with developing individual values, but not at the expense of social progress. It involved axiology, dealing with the nature and properties of and mutual connections between values, the search for a balance between society and the individual. It combined the idealism of Kant, the classicism of Plato, the intuitionism of Henri Bergson, the humanism of Miguel de Unamuno, and neo-Kantian spiritualism.[52] Arévalo demonstrated an ability to weave the philosophies of others into a cohesive whole, which he tried to put into practice in the course of running the state.

He spent considerable time trying to come to grips with Plato's conception of the state as outlined in *The Republic,* especially his search for a more perfect nation. He appreciated Plato's dialectical approach to thought, which made people probe the depths of their minds, and regarded him as the first great systematic thinker who dealt with the relationship of education to the state and to all social classes.[53] Arévalo also identified with Peruvian political thinker Víctor Raúl Haya de la Torre, who rejected class struggle and violent revolution and supported antiimperialism. He agreed with Salvadoran *pensador* Alberto Masferrer's belief in *vitalismo* (the vital minimum), or providing everyone with minimum standards for housing, nutrition, education, health, work, justice, and rest. (*Vitalismo* is analyzed in the succeeding chapter.)

"Arevalism" also included a component called "spiritual socialism," by no means a new philosophy but a program similar to that outlined in Argentine thinker José Esteban Echeverría's study *El dogma socialista* (1846, Socialist creed), which emphasized freedom, equality, fraternity, and the idea of progress. Echeverría stood for a kind of social democratic liberalism based on equality before the law and the notion of economic equality to eliminate poverty. Arévalo's version recognized the need for a new social order and called for psychological, moral, and economic liberation.[54] He explained that it did not aim at the redistribution of material goods to make people economically equal, nor was it Communism, which he labeled totalitarian.[55] It was "spiritual" because it encompassed the psychological feeling of liberty. Unlike the liberty of liberalism, which defends the individuals who control the state, the liberty of spiritual socialism provided for collective welfare.[56] It encouraged harmony between labor and capital, which meant using the capital of the ruling classes to improve the condition of the working class.[57] "Spiritual socialism" also connoted cleansing or purifying[58] and was definitely more spiritual than socialist.

Arévalo erred in using the term *socialism.* In fact, at the time of his presidency he had little theoretical understanding of it. His early comments on it reflect negative emotional responses to some unacceptable form of Stalinism. He referred to liberals, such as writer Max Lerner, as Communists[59] and noted that "communism is contrary to human nature . . . to the psychology of man." He called the destruction of minority social classes undemocratic[60] and deemed class rule by the proletariat prejudicial to others.

Arévalo responded as negatively to positivism as he did to socialism. Viewing positivism as motivated by the drive for money and material wealth, he saw Central America as a little corner of the earth where Comte and his disciples had succeeded in inculcating a Darwinian perspective among the ruling elites.[61] He divided society into two basic sectors. The capitalist sector sees commerce as the be-all of life and believes that material interests produce political and economic currents and theories of state. The other sector, the people, do not see commerce as life's basic purpose but subordinate economic factors to other vital values such as individual liberty, dignity, and justice.

In Arévalo's view, police rulers maintain the state for the capitalists and protect them from the people who want to modify the state. The police rulers do not govern, they administer property.[62] Arévalo saw millions of people "subjected to economic servitude, surrounded by a spiritual vacuum and obliterated by political incapacity."[63] He related economic subordination to racial and social discrimination through which certain classes protect the privileges they have usurped.[64] He felt that an aura of servitude existed in Guatemala and condemned biological theories designed to make those of other races subservient. He disliked psychological servility that makes others feel inferior, sexual servility that makes men dominate women, and those who force others to be subordinate because it feels good to control them.[65] He accused the military of fostering servility as a result of Prussian attitudes that officers are the only gentlemen, the creators of culture and statesmen. He said that the military dreams of fulfilling Oswald Spengler's prediction that "the hangmen of today will be the dukes of tomorrow."[66] The church, too, he contended, taught servility and negated liberty by its condemnations to eternal hell. Arévalo, an agnostic, viewed religion as a totalitarian institution that thwarted human development, but he did not condone substituting antireligious teachings for the dogma of the church.[67] He criticized the church for persecuting freethinkers, those who believe that they can create their own spiritual life and road to salvation. He noted that historically the church abided by the theory that "the devil was the first leftist"[68] and forged the idea that freemasonry would lead to socialism. He asserted that, for the church, masonry and Communism had become the great devils that would wreck Christian civilization.[69] He ridiculed Archbishop Rossell y Arellano, who stated,

"Communism is atheism and atheism is unpatriotic." He agreed with economist Thorstein Veblen about the despicability of someone who appears a representative of God but really represents personal ambitions.[70] Arévalo did not seek to destroy the church but to get it out of politics. He resented the repeated interference of the archbishop, who wanted Catholicism to be the mandatory religion in Guatemala.[71]

Arévalo's views on the church cannot be categorized any more easily than can the various philosophies followed by his government. One writer, Jaime Díaz Rozzotto, sums up Arévalo's actions and thoughts as essentially petit bourgeois. He labels him a quasi positivist because he elevated personal autonomy and spiritual individuality; he sees him as a liberal idealist who reduced the struggle for power to political consequences of individual acts, not to economic factors or class struggle. According to Díaz Rozzotto, Arévalo believed that change could come about through high ideas such as equality but did not restructure society to effect equality.[72]

Arévalo's thinking on the political aspects of education, unlike his views on the modern state, is easy to comprehend. He appreciated nineteenth-century Argentine thinker-statesman Domingo Sarmiento's faith in the ability to foster progress through universal education. As did Sarmiento, Arévalo felt that an enlightened America could liberate itself from dictatorship. His eight books on the philosophy of education conveyed the conviction that scientific pedagogy includes teaching about social and economic relations. He claimed that pedagogy required an awareness of the goals of nationality,[73] and that education only for the privileged contributed to a fragmented society and caused economic exploitation. He believed that the state had the duty to promote educational equality.[74] Theoretically, the state should educate all people to participate intelligently in politics but, he pointed out, education had become subordinate to politics.

He noted that three categories of people existed in the history of the emancipation of the human spirit: slaves, proprietors, and revolutionaries. A revolutionary did not have to advocate violence but had to promote the proper spirit, which was guarded by the university and people with advanced education.[75] He envisioned the University Reform Movement (described in the previous chapter) as an ongoing process fostering continuous progress,[76] pointed to the effective role of the university in ousting dictator Ubico, and saw a strong autonomous university as essential to democracy.[77]

In Arévalo's opinion democracy included international sovereignty and internal sovereignty. He emphasized sovereignty by advocating the decolonization of Latin America and the curtailment of the social and economic exploitation of its people.[78] Like Bolívar, he hoped that sovereignty could be safeguarded by an international body and called for regional unity. He believed that a Central American federation could defend political independence against despotism, imperialism, and subservience to *caudillismo* (political bossism). He saw *caudillismo* as a form of male dominance—a desire to possess or control the mental, moral, and aesthetic aspects of life.[79] He wanted a regional Central American organization that would not encroach upon national sovereignty but would enhance it by keeping leaders honest, an organization that served all of the people, not like NATO, which he called a union of industrialists who manufacture arms and fabricate false reasons to get the member governments to purchase them.[80] Nor did he want a Central American body that approximated the OAS, which functions as an electoral democracy in which votes are manipulated by the United States, as a cold war apparatus in which the shark compels the compliance of the sardines.[81] Arévalo particularly deplored the way the United States used the OAS to support anticommunist dictators such as Nicaragua's Anastasio Somoza. He circumvented the OAS by backing the Caribbean Legion, a group of democrats who joined forces in 1949 in an unsuccessful attempt to oust the region's tyrants.[82]

Prior to his presidency Arévalo noted that Central America had passed from Spanish to English to U.S. control.[83] His views on the United States became more critical after 1954. He depicted the United States as a transatlantic empire extracting raw materials from Latin America and selling them in Europe. He said the United States practiced a kind of medieval primogeniture by which it reserved to itself, as the first American republic, all of the privileges granted to the firstborn.[84] He called U.S. commercialism "hard and ugly"[85] and regarded it as an aspect of a dangerous type of imperialism that is political, judicial, military, sometimes economic, and predicated on a false sense of superiority.[86] Arévalo questioned the veracity of the words *fraternity, democracy, good neighbors,* and *free world,* used so often by the United States, whose free enterprise is detrimental to Latin America.[87] To him, North American "virtuosos of gold"[88] carried out multiple exploitation with intelligence, clockwork precision, scientific coldness, harshness, and great arrogance.[89] The powerful Protestant shark devours the weak Catholic sardine under the guise of the Monroe Doctrine that implies that "America is a continent and this continent is mine because I call myself America."[90] "No shark except the Yankee shark has the right to eat purée of Latin American sardines," he wrote,[91] describing how the shark uses law and believes in law, then makes a joke of law. For example, he explained how in 1907 the United States supported the establishment of the Central American Court of Justice and how it was dissolved when El Salvador and Costa Rica protested that Nicaragua violated their sovereignty by adhering to the 1914 Bryan-Chamorro Treaty, which gave the United States rights to a future interoceanic canal route. When the court ruled against the United States, Washington assured the world that it respected international law and advised Nicaragua to ignore the court's decision.[92]

Fábula del tiburón y las sardines. América Latina estrangulada (published in Buenos Aires in 1956 and in the United States in 1961 as *The Shark and the Sardines*), represents a radicalized Juan José Arévalo, a man who questioned his earlier assumptions and often found them unsupported by precise evidence. The new Arévalo vehemently denounced the syndicate of millionaires who controlled the White House, who converted their military into the police of the hemisphere,[93] whose law is rhetoric used to justify its conduct. Arévalo wondered how the United States could prosecute a war against Hitler and Mussolini and then adopt Francisco Franco as an ally, why the Pentagon defended democracy and supported Falangists,[94] and why the United States destroyed Nazism in Europe and perpetuated it in Latin America.

According to Arévalo, John Foster Dulles, with his attacks on Guatemala, imitated Joseph Goebbels, Hitler's propaganda minister. How could the United States refer to a nation of 3 million people as a Soviet satellite when only seven Communists had positions of visibility there?[95] In *La democracia y el imperio* (The democracy and the empire), written during the 1954 invasion of Guatemala, Arévalo characterized the United States as the inventor of the cold war that victimized the rest of the world, making Latin America into a protectorate and invading Guatemala to nullify the 1947 labor code and the 1952 agrarian reform that led to the expropriation of United Fruit Company properties. He called the U.S. president at that time, Dwight Eisenhower, an ignorant man who got his information from *Reader's Digest* and who did not understand the situation in Guatemala. After 1954 Arévalo continued to identify the United States' future with democracy but felt that its "grandeur of spirit was replaced by greed."[96] He urged Latin America no longer to accept the United States as the leader of the occidental world.[97] Nevertheless, during the early 1960s he supported John F. Kennedy's Alliance for Progress, which he failed to see as an anti-Castro, proimperialist program.

Arévalo never assumed responsibility for his inability to institutionalize democracy. He viewed the abolition of democracy and installation of military dictatorship as a result of an anticommunist campaign, one that caused him to lose much of his optimism and forced him to seek a more thorough understanding of socialism. He reacted to the 1954 invasion of his country with a great deal of bitterness, analyzed what had occurred, rid himself of some shallow misconceptions, and refuted the idea that every antiimperialist was an ally of a Soviet-inspired, Stalinist variety of Communism. In *Anti Komunismo en America Latina* (1959; *Anti-Kommunism in Latin America*, 1963) he asserted that Communism with a "C" is the international movement led by the Communist party whose headquarters is in Moscow and that Kommunism with a "K" "is every political and social democratic movement that tries to defend the interests of the working masses, the humble, and the exploited all over the world, or speaks of sovereignty and nationalism or dares to criticize the United States."[98] He used the "K" to "distinguish between real Communism and fake McCarthy Communism."[99] To him, anticommunism strengthened, protected, and perpetuated dictatorial rule; served the commercial interests of the millionaires; and enabled the church to recover its monopoly on the spiritual formation of the young.[100]

He indicted the "Geese of the Capitol," the big newspapers and publicity experts who kept the anticommunist fires ablaze, who honked loudly about the leftist enemies of the Latin peoples.[101] He called the press supercapitalized, brainwashed, monopolized, and blessed with holy water,[102] and he noted that the Inter-American Press Society defended free enterprise, almost defended freedom of opinion, and decided which nations are democratic.[103] In his view, Guatemala's church viewed communism as anti-Christ, a totalitarian enemy of believers that seeks to substitute a satanic promise of terrestrial paradise for Catholicism, an advocate of atheism in which man supplants God and teaches that happiness emanates from technology and physical science.[104]

Ironically, before 1954 Arévalo represented precisely the left-of-center social reform democrats that anticommunists praised, men like José Figueres of Costa Rica. But the United States could not tolerate his nationalism and labeled him "red," or at least a Communist sympathizer. Arévalo maintained that the rumors that he was a Communist circulated "because he loved his people, suffered with them, supported the poor and the workers, refused to cooperate with the illegitimate interests of the powerful and to make deals with those who would corrupt his public function."[105] Anticommunism thwarted Arévalo's reforms and radicalized him. During his presidency he grew as a practical politician, but prior to 1954 his political thinking contained no great depth or originality. The process that he underwent while probing for answers to what curtailed the progress of his regime sharpened his powers of analysis and led him to delve more deeply into political economy; to write more creative, historically based works; and to become one of Latin America's most eloquent and effective opponents of imperialism. Arévalo's powerful indictments of U.S. expansionism so antagonized the government in Washington that when he endeavored to make a political comeback in 1963 the Pentagon inspired a military coup to prevent the development of a popular movement around him. A quarter of a century later, he remained a thorn in Washington's side by repeatedly pointing out the hypocrisy of its anticommunist policy toward Latin America, which he viewed as a conspiracy against socialism and capitalist democratic social reform that could reduce the repatriation of profits to the United States.

Manuel Galich:
Radical Analysis of Liberal Failure

A victim of persecution by the Ubico dictatorship, Manuel Galich (1913–) subsequently became the unofficial historian of the movement of intellectuals, lawyers, and university professors who fought successfully to oust the tyrant. The erudite Galich served as president of the Revolutionary Congress that prepared Guatemala for constitutional republicanism in 1944, and he served under Arévalo as minister of public education and president of the Electoral Tribunal and under Arbenz as minister of foreign relations and ambassador to Uruguay and Argentina.

The books, articles, and historical play he wrote reflect the orientation that he acquired from Cuban radical thinkers José Martí, Juan Marinello, and Emilio Roig de Leuchsenring, whose works displayed a great sense of history and the belief that revolutionaries can avoid mistakes by learning from the past.[106] Like his colleague Arévalo, Galich admired Benito Juárez, who headed Mexico's government during the late 1850s and the 1860s. In *Benito Juárez: Pensamiento y acción* (1974, Benito Juárez: Thought and action), Galich praised the Mexican leader, a full-blooded Zapotec Indian, for emphasizing native potential. Galich noted that Juárez learned about the dangers of imperialism from the 1846 war in which the United States took half of Mexico's territory and from the French invasion that put Maximilian on the throne of Mexico in 1864.

Galich construed Justo Rufino Barrios's 1885 decree proclaiming the union of Central America as a move to impede U.S. expansion, especially its desire to build and control a canal across Nicaragua, which would further divide the region and curtail Nicaraguan sovereignty. He saw Barrios as fighting an "antiimperialist war in Central America."[107] He concurred with Lenin that imperialism constituted the final stage of capitalism, one the United States entered into vigorously in the 1890–1900 era when Secretary of State James Blaine began to build an inter-American system to enhance U.S. commerce. To Galich, the inter-American system was the culmination of neocolonialism subsequently expressed in twentieth-century policies called "big stick," "dollar diplomacy," "good neighbor," and "alliance for progress," all standing for the diplomacy of dependent financing.[108] He pointed out that the inter-

American system and the OAS did not represent the Pan-American unity advocated by Bolívar. He asserted that the OAS had become a vehicle for intervention, one that sustained dependency as it placed the countries of the Americas under U.S. control. He condemned the United States for stressing the similarities between itself and Latin America when the dissimilarities are more profound. To him, the policies of the United States are anti-Bolívar and anti–Latin America.[109]

Galich discerned a pattern of native military strongmen taking over their countries on behalf of foreign, primarily U.S., interests. It began in 1922, when Guatemala's José María Orellana, the precursor of today's *"gorilas"* (right-wing military), overthrew a civilian president on behalf of a U.S. railroad monopoly. This trend continued in succeeding decades in such countries as the Dominican Republic, Nicaragua, and Paraguay under dictators Rafael Trujillo, Somoza and his sons Luis and Anastasio, and Alfredo Stroessner.[110] Also, in the 1920s and 1930s the United Fruit Company sought to curtail the growing workers' movement in Guatemala. As railroad lines and leftist thinking reached the banana plantations, unions appeared and strikes were effective. Fearing repetition of the nationalization policy of the Mexican Revolution and the spread of socialist ideology, dictator Ubico appealed to the United States for support to destroy communist ideas and organizations.[111]

In *Del pánico al ataque* (From panic to attack), originally published in 1949, Galich characterized the Ubico years as ones of silence, immobility, and death, when written criticism of the government ceased to exist. He asserted that by the 1930s there developed in the university a revolutionary trend of thought based on the need for change, not ideology. This new thinking emanated in part from the example of the 1932 political upheaval in El Salvador (detailed in the next chapter).[112] He recalled that under Ubico's misnamed Liberal-Progressive party, *Das Kapital* vanished from library shelves, official use of the word *worker* was prohibited, and terms such as *union, strike, proletariat,* and *labor justice* were blasphemies punishable by torture and imprisonment.[113] Nevertheless, activist and intellectual opposition survived and eventually overthrew Ubico in what Galich termed a French Revolution under modern conditions, led by a small middle class with the support of urban and rural labor.[114]

By 1942 the ideas of Marx, Engels, Lenin, and the anarchist Peter Kropotkin gained popularity in Guatemala among the students and faculty of law, even though these works were banned by the government.[115] Guatemala's Law Association, led by Galich, José Manuel Fortuny, and Guillermo Toriello actively opposed the dictatorship. Law students at the University of San Carlos organized and joined their mentors, and with the aid of Galich and his classmates from the 1930s, they formed the Association of University Students, which threatened Ubico with a general strike in 1944 if its demands for change were not met. This courageous act initiated the revolt.[116] For the first time in Guatemala's history, the entire intellectual element did not serve the autocracy. A new generation of intellectual-activists arose, one that perceived that the true rebellion was not merely against neocolonialism[117] but for viable political pluralism, organized labor, and respect for constitutionalism.[118]

During those years of governmental transition, Guatemalans had heard of imperialism, Galich said, but did not understand its voracity. Those who ousted Ubico harbored nebulous anti-U.S. sentiments heightened by boyhood tales of the heroic deeds of Sandino in Nicaragua. They resented U.S. military personnel stationed in Guatemala, who "swarmed over the capital on Saturday nights, like great herds of capering goats, to insult our manners and customs in drunken and obscene clashes." Guatemalans criticized the prostitutes who liked to be seen with the blond, gum-chewing, khaki-clad foreign soldiers.[119]

Galich bemoaned the fact that the junta that controlled the nation after the overthrow of the dictator did not deepen the revolutionary movement nor disband the officer corps. The old anticommunist military order existed under the façade of the new National Army of the Revolution. The "fiercely dominant class of coffee barons" remained intact, dependent on its major customer, the United States, and relied on the strong arm of the military. Not only did the landowning class survive, but it elected its members to the Constituent Assembly that prepared the new constitution.[120]

Galich stated that if the junta that ruled before the election of Arévalo had instituted land reforms, the changes would have been respected by the Roosevelt administration just as it accepted Mexico's expropriation of U.S. oil properties in 1938. He believed that the United States would not have intervened while preoccupied with World War II. But later, in the 1950s, virulent McCarthyism existed in the United States, the CIA had become the "invisible government" wielding a "big stick" in Central America. The United States had used atomic weapons and felt invincible.[121]

The triumvirate that controlled Guatemala prior to Arévalo's election established fundamental principles that guided the nation for the next decade. It abolished reelection, implemented the secret ballot, and extended suffrage.[122] But it did not construct a cohesive ideology. Its eclectic policies appeared to be predicated primarily on dislike for dictatorship and vague sympathy for the goals of the Spanish republic.

The Guatemalan people did not assume power in 1944 but started on the road to it. The Arévalo government tried to devise progressive programs quickly and in the process antagonized the United States, the church, the landed aristocrats, and the right-wing press. The press could not dissociate itself from its advertisers—the Coffee Growers' Association and the United Fruit Company (known as El Pulpo, the octopus with tentacles everywhere)—or from the Inter-American Press Association dominated by the powerful *Chicago Tribune* correspondent and communist-hater Jules Dubois, whom Galich called the "bloodhound of imperialism."[123]

The new government strove for what Galich termed "effective democracy," including written laws and respect for human rights, and "integral democracy," or political rights and economic progress for the poor.[124] The new constitution provided social guarantees and recognized, in the abstract, workers' rights. But it also consolidated the interests of the landed gentry, and the army, a self-contained entity with its own jurisdiction, became almost a fourth power in the republic. At the same time, the constitution diminished executive authority.[125]

The new labor legislation, the social guarantees, the right to unionize and to form political groups, and the free flow of ideas were depicted in the press and by the landowners and the church as the work of leftist extremists who conspired with the USSR to challenge U.S. hegemony in the Americas.[126] Counterrevolutionary political parties proliferated, the church condemned the government from the pulpit, and the Coffee Growers' Association and the railroad and banana companies subsidized newspaper campaigns against the government, called Arévalo a Communist, and turned the media in the United States against him.[127]

Guatemala formulated a new policy of not recognizing nations at variance with the democratic ideals of the OAS, and it severed diplomatic relations with dictatorships in the Dominican Republic, Nicaragua, Peru, and Venezuela. The policy unified those anticommunist allies of the United States against the Arbenz administration.[128]

Galich felt that Jacobo Arbenz in 1951 understood Guatemala's problems and sought their solution, even if it meant alienating the reactionaries. Arbenz represented the peasants,[129] proposed agrarian reform, and prepared to implement it despite powerful domestic opposition, and that of the CIA, the Pentagon, and the U.S. State Department.[130] Arbenz, Galich suggested, lost control because he did not arm the people and convert them into a revolutionary army, a move more possible in 1944 than in 1952. Galich indicated that to create a revolution you must move immediately to institutionalize and protect it, or counterrevolutionary forces will prevent it.[131] In 1954 Guatemala's army, prodded and bribed by U.S. Ambassador John Peurifoy and Papal Nuncio Gennaro Verrolino, sold out.[132]

Galich found it amazing, in 1949, that the "free world" could be suspicious of a government that implemented human rights and social guarantees, or view it as a threat to democracy.[133] By the time he wrote

Por que lucha Guatemala, Arévalo y Arbenz: Dos hombres contra un imperio (1956, What Guatemala, Arévalo, and Arbenz struggle for: Two men against an empire), he viewed the false suspicions as manifestations of powerful anticommunist propaganda.[134] The events of the Arévalo and Arbenz years intensified Galich's radicalism. He became a "critical" Marxist analyst of Guatemalan society, one who explained precisely why the reforms of 1945–1954 were not permitted to succeed. He criticized Arévalo and Arbenz for not curtailing the liberties of the counterrevolutionaries who thwarted reforms, and he castigated the revolutionary political parties for competing with one another instead of closing ranks against the reactionaries.[135] According to Galich, the 1954 overthrow of a government that did not mount a serious defense was a major disaster, but he claimed that the 1944–1954 struggle was not in vain. From it came the ability to see the need for an insurgency to liberate Guatemala from neocolonialism. Henceforth, Guatemalans would recognize their enemies and their methods, would understand why reform movements that do not completely alter the relations of production fail, and would better understand the need and method for implementing a revolution.[136]

The anticommunist victory brought the return of the public thieves, electoral frauds, and mass killings. But it spawned a new generation of revolutionaries who fought as guerrillas, worked in concert with exiled radical intellectuals such as Manuel Galich, and spurned the bourgeois reforms of 1944–1954 in favor of socialism.

Guillermo Toriello:
U.S. Response to Bourgeois Nationalism

During the Arévalo and Arbenz administrations, liberal landowner and sugarcane producer Guillermo Toriello (1910–) served Guatemala as ambassador to the United States, Mexico, the OAS, and the United Nations, and as foreign minister. In those days he repeatedly invoked the names of liberation advocates José Martí, Benito Juárez, Augusto Sandino, and Agustín Farabundo Martí. He concurred with José Martí that as long as things do not go well for the Indians, they will not go well with America, and he tried to alter Guatemala's system of white domination. He saw the Guatemalan Indians as noble descendants of the Maya who, after centuries of cruel and repressive exploitation, had to rebel against injustice.[137]

After the anti-Arbenz coup, Toriello entered exile in Mexico and wrote *La batalla de Guatemala* (1955, The battle of Guatemala), a monumental book that informed the world about what transpired between 1945 and 1954, analyzed imperialism, and interpreted Guatemalan politics. His views, which became increasingly more radical, antagonized the United

States, which has denied him a visitor's visa since the 1960s. For over thirty years, Toriello, along with Arévalo and Galich, has been a major force in the antiimperialist movement.

Toriello has dedicated himself to smashing what he called the U.S.-supported "neofascist system of domination in America."[138] Through his writing, he has kept the story of 1954 alive. He updated his *Batalla de Guatemala* with *Tras la cortina de banano* (1981, Behind the banana curtain),[139] and the title of his *Guatemala, mas de 20 años de traición* (1980, Guatemala: More than twenty years of treason)[140] is self-explanatory.

Toriello's books, like those of Galich, epitomize Guatemalan nationalism and owe a debt to Lenin's *Imperialism: The Final Stage of Capitalism* (1916). Toriello adapted Lenin's ideas to Latin America and noted that international monopoly associations acquire more importance and power than local or national companies and can in fact control a nation.[141]

According to Toriello, foreign monopolies entered Guatemala after 1871, when the liberal reform government improved rail and water transportation facilities. Dictator Manuel Estrada Cabrera (1898–1920) opened the nation to foreign businesses. At the beginning of the twentieth century, Minor Keith and the United Fruit Company received a major concession, which continued to expand.[142] Three U.S. monopolies, the United Fruit Company, International Railways of Central America, and the Electric Bond and Share Company, owned and controlled large farms; railroads; Atlantic and Pacific coast ports; telephone, telegraph, and electric power firms; and maritime transportation. Their concessions extended to the year 2009, and the companies were exempt from all taxes except ones on land.[143] This system ended prematurely in 1944.

Toriello called 1944–1954 a bourgeois nationalist, antiimperialist movement that attempted to eliminate a semifeudal, semicolonial system.[144] With Toriello's assistance, the Arévalo and Arbenz governments supported representative democracy, self-determination, nonintervention, the right of political asylum, human rights, and world peace and condemned colonialism and totalitarianism. It broke diplomatic relations with dictators, established relations with the USSR, and joined the United Nations.[145] It became a Latin American symbol of opposition to tyranny and misery.

The United States, with enormous interests in Guatemala, feared nationalization between 1944 and 1954 and embarked on a bogus anticommunist crusade to prevent it. Toriello indicated that the entire Guatemalan Communist party had only 532 registered members, 17 of whom held government positions, including 4 (out of 62) who served as national deputies (congresspeople). He illustrated how the church in collusion with the U.S. ambassador and the CIA adopted a Falangist "God, country, and liberty" point of view.[146] Archbishop Mariano Rossell y Arellano, the "Fruit Company Bishop," delivered sermons inciting the people to save Guatemala from those (Communists) who would abolish the Catholic religion.[147]

Toriello concluded that the major move that led to the 1954 coup was the expropriation of United Fruit Company land because it set a precedent for Colombia, Costa Rica, Cuba, the Dominican Republic, Ecuador, Haiti, Jamaica, Nicaragua, and Panama.[148] In addition, the transnational corporations disliked that the Guatemalan government regulated foreign monopolies and made them equal, not superior, under the law.[149]

The overthrow of Arbenz meant a return to tyranny under a U.S. satellite system with less independence for Guatemala than found in Eastern European nations under Soviet domination. Toriello noted that U.S. control was so strong that when Provisional President Carlos Enrique Díaz replaced Arbenz, the U.S. ambassador insisted that he execute a long list of revolutionaries "because they are Communists." Díaz refused and immediately lost his office.[150] The new government destroyed books, films, and records by Russian writers and artists and the works of liberals such as Jean-Jacques Rousseau. Those caught with banned texts were subject to imprisonment, or even torture, by the neofascist Committee for Defense Against Communism,[151] whose censorship also extended to the press, radio, and television. After 1954, thirty-seven formerly independent Guatemalan companies came under U.S. control. By 1983 the transnationals, with at least seventy-seven U.S. firms, ran Guatemala's economy and major industries such as mining, hydrocarbons, and agriculture.[152] The United States subsequently installed seven regimes in Guatemala that by 1983 had killed over 100,000 people, made many others "disappear," and transformed the country into a genuine colony. Toriello later noted that Fidel Castro learned from the Guatemalan episode that for a revolution to succeed it has to take a leftward turn,[153] eradicate all dependence on the United States, and resist forcefully the latter's attempts to reassert hegemony.

Worthy of mention is Toriello's personal role in the 1954 crisis that the United States precipitated in order to destroy Guatemala's reform movement. In his capacity as foreign minister, at the United Nations he questioned the U.S. attacks on Guatemala, hoping to receive better treatment than at the OAS, where the United States controlled the purse strings.[154] At the Tenth Inter-American Conference at Caracas in March 1954, Secretary of State Dulles, aiming at Guatemala, forced the passage of a "Declaration of Solidarity for the Preservation of the Political Integrity of the American States Against International Communist Intervention." Toriello responded that Guatemala was not a communist nation but favored national liberation, which affected the privileges of foreign entrepreneurs. He averred that the U.S.-sponsored anticommunist resolution meant that any Latin American state that nationalized foreign companies would be labeled "communist."[155] He predicted that if the resolution passed, Pan-Americanism would become an instrument to enable monopolies to stifle political and economic liberation. To him, the United States viewed as communist all desire for social progress, intellectual curiosity, or progressive reform.[156]

Toriello's strong defense of Guatemala elicited a positive response from the OAS delegates, many of whom voted for the Dulles resolution out of fear and without enthusiasm.[157] At the OAS, Toriello emphasized that Guatemala's capitalist government welcomed foreign investment as long as it abided by the laws of his land. He called the Dulles proposal an example of the internationalization of McCarthyism and an act that violated the OAS Charter's provision for self-determination.[158] The U.S. press denounced his speech as Moscow-inspired. He replied by excoriating the United States for undermining Guatemala's independence. He stated that the Dulles resolution would ruin the OAS by giving it the right to act collectively against undocumented foreign expansion.[159]

Toriello pointed out that in 1954 John Moors Cabot, the U.S. assistant secretary of state for inter-American affairs, and his cousin Henry Cabot Lodge, the ambassador to the United Nations, were large shareholders in the United Fruit Company, and Secretary of State Dulles and his brother, the CIA director Allen Dulles, worked for Sullivan and Cromwell, the United Fruit Company's attorneys.[160] Toriello also reported that after 1954 Guatemala's bourgeoisie divided into two groups. One group affiliated basically with U.S. capital and the U.S. market. The other, a native bourgeoisie, preferred independent local economic development. Both groups opposed revolutionary change and economic renovation.[161]

The United States reasserted control over Guatemala's army, which it equipped and modernized under the Mutual Security Acts that declared that nations that refrained from sending strategic matériel to socialist countries were eligible for U.S. economic and military aid. Guatemalan officers attended U.S. staff and command schools, where they received instruction about weaponry for sale and heavy doses of anticommunist ideology. Military operations were coordinated by the U.S. embassy and Guatemala's Committee to Defend Against Communism, an arm of the National Police that used violence against the people.[162] Guatemalan culture henceforth emanated from Washington, and the indigenous intellectual movement, which had revived for a decade, died.[163] Military-led repression eliminated many radical activities. Guatemala resumed diplomatic ties to Franco's Spain and moved closer to Latin America's anticommunist dictators.[164]

The United States maintained its policies under Kennedy, the "false democrat." Guatemala became a base for U.S. anticommunism in Central America and the Caribbean and served as headquarters for the April 1961 Bay of Pigs invasion, in which a CIA-trained and -equipped Cuban exile army failed to overthrow Cuba's revolutionary government.[165] The CIA and Guatemala's military cooperated to break down popular resistance to tyranny; to destroy armed bands of revolutionaries; and to put Guatemala's natural resources, such as nickel, copper, chrome, cobalt, and petroleum, at the disposal of the United States.[166] They joined together in 1960 and 1961 to form the Central American Defense Council that unified Central America's armed forces and tied them to U.S. methods and equipment.[167] Between 1964 and 1973, according to Toriello, the Vietnamization of Guatemala occurred. The United States used the "Operation Phoenix" plan from Vietnam to organize assassination teams to exterminate those sympathetic to antigovernment guerrillas. The U.S. Agency for International Development financed and assisted police programs in Guatemala and helped organize secret paramilitary groups such as the National Anti-Communist Movement and the New Anti-communist Organization, which initiated a bloodbath in the nation.[168]

Toriello analyzed the remilitarization of Guatemala and Latin America. He saw the 1973 CIA-engineered coup in Chile as a successor to that in Guatemala in 1954. Noting how the United States also used the International Monetary Fund, the World Bank, the Inter-American Development Bank, and the Central American Bank for Economic Integration as instruments of domination,[169] he concurred with liberal writer Max Lerner that business spirit guides U.S. foreign policy. Unlike classical imperialism, which included territorial acquisition, the U.S. variety stressed control of markets and dependent nations.[170]

Toriello also exposed the role of the United States in universities in Latin America, where exchange professors and students often work for the CIA and help destabilize traditional culture. He said that Guatemalan students and intellectuals trained in the United States returned home as *yanquimaltecos*[171] (Yankee-Guatemalans) and that imperialism had converted Guatemala's middle class into a fifth column militating against Guatemalan values. The U.S. anticommunism pervades Guatemala's radio and television,[172] and Guatemalans see U.S. cinema that glorifies the Anglo-American way of life, including its cult of violence, war, and sex. U.S. gangsters direct Guatemala's traffic in cocaine and heroin, and even properties in the colonial city of Antigua, Guatemala's national monument, are Yankee-controlled.[173]

Toriello contends that Guatemala needs to defeat imperialism and to devise a new system of life based on humane scientific socialism that includes universal justice.[174] He believes that guerrilla actions against the incumbent state are a justifiable means of opposing the aggression by the United States and its Israeli accomplice.[175] To him, because Guatemala delivered the first major blow to imperialism in the 1940s, it should be in the vanguard of the current revolution. He feels that Nicaragua's Sandinistas temporarily fulfilled Guatemala's dream of undermining the U.S. system of domination.[176] In his *Popular History of Two Revolutions: Guatemala and Nicaragua* (1985), he stated that the former nation in 1954 and the latter in 1979 introduced nationalist, democratic, pluralist, antiimperialist governments. Both were attacked by the United States, the church, and the bourgeoisie and falsely accused of being controlled by the Soviet Union.[177] The CIA toppled the Arbenz government in the 1950s. In the 1980s the administration of Ronald Reagan supported *contra* efforts to overthrow the Sandinista-led Nicaraguan government. Simultaneously, Washington buttressed the Efraín Ríos Montt (1982–1983) regime in Guatemala, which intensified repression against unarmed peasants; murdered women, children, and the elderly; established strategic hamlets (virtually concentration camps) for the rural populace; burned villages and crops; killed livestock; crucified, castrated, and beheaded citizens; and falsely blamed such atrocities on the guerrillas.[178]

In 1982 Toriello paid tribute to the Grenada Revolution that the Reagan administration subsequently destroyed, and he praised the revolutionary struggles in El Salvador and Guatemala.[179] The forceful Guatemalan "critical" Marxist pointed out that his nation's democratic experiment failed and that of Nicaragua succeeded for the moment because in 1954 the "correlation of forces" in the United Nations favored the United States, but by the 1980s they did not. Also, the Guatemalan National Army remained intact after 1954, but the Sandinistas wisely disbanded Somoza's dreaded Guardia Nacional. Perhaps most important, in 1954 Guatemala's petit bourgeois leaders had no advanced politiscientific concept of the world because for seventy years no intellectual opposition existed there, a situation that differed in Nicaragua, where the Sandinistas built a sound theoretical base for revolution and were inspired by the successful Cuban model.[180]

Edelberto Torres Rivas:
The Consummate Radical Academician

In contrast to the statesman–political activist par excellence Guillermo Toriello stands Edelberto Torres Rivas (1932–), Central America's outstanding social scientist and Guatemala's most sophisticated radical thinker. The son of Edelberto Torres, a famous Nicaraguan man of letters who has inspired radical intellectuals for over half a century, Torres

Rivas is a brilliant specialist on the formation of the Central American nation-state and a mentor to the region's leftist political economists. Torres Rivas, who lives in Costa Rica, where the atmosphere is more conducive to free academic inquiry than in Guatemala, combines the latest social science techniques with a strong sense of the history of Central America as an area and as five separate republics.

A "critical" modern Marxist, the erudite Torres Rivas has noted that socialists have often erred by believing that the European industrial revolution and its form of politics is the historical rule. His work integrates the ideas of many past and present European and non-European Marxists. Especially evident in his thinking is the influence of Rosa Luxemburg, the Polish-born theoretician of the workers' movement who propounded the idea that national objectives do not exist but that class objectives, with an international character, do. He agreed with her belief that in the process of liberating the proletariat and the people you drive toward international socialism, but in the course of doing so you must realize that problems to be resolved differ from country to country.[181] From his early research and writing of the 1960s to his more recent work of the 1980s while secretary general of the Latin American faculty of social sciences in San José, Costa Rica, Torres Rivas's perspectives on historical and social materialism and class conflict resemble those of sociologist C. Wright Mills. Like Mills, Torres Rivas believes that intellectuals do not form a class but represent a social layer with common traits.[182]

His dozens of articles and books examine Central America in terms of international social and economic changes. They stress genuine historical watersheds, not artificial periodization that simply corresponds to dates of new leaders. For example, in *Interpretación del desarrollo social centroamericano* (1981, Interpretation of social development in Central America), he analyzed when changes occurred in the social relations of production and pointed out the direct correlation between economic changes and social development in Central America. Also, his work evaluates contradictions in the historical process. For instance, he showed that the church provided a bonding element that integrated society during the colonial era, but after independence its massive material interests caused disintegration.[183]

Torres Rivas noted that following independence the expansion of capitalism shaped the nature of the five Central American states and the industrial revolution enabled them to participate in international commerce.[184] He indicated that increased industrialization produced more articulated class antagonisms. Modernization of Central America's economic, social, and political structures occurred under the hegemony of the coffee oligarchy, which expanded railroads, built factories, and developed the agro-export economy and the plantation system. Subsequently, the banana industry made similar contributions.[185] Capitalism arrived through external sources; export agriculture organized Central America's internal forces, which shaped the social relations of production that permitted higher accumulation rates for the wealthy.[186] Historically, the quest to accumulate capital has led to struggles for control of the state, which have exacerbated class conflicts in Central America.

Torres Rivas's studies have demonstrated that as the Depression (1929) initiated market crises for Central America's republics, a desire to terminate dictatorship grew, interest in industrialization increased, and society accepted new developmentalist ideas.[187] By the 1930s the Central American states functioned primarily as agrarian enclaves linked to foreign nations. World War II marked the end of the paralysis in development brought on by the Depression. Reformist and revolutionary elements sought renovation and linked social and economic questions to political answers. After the war the public sought better educational and social services. Government officials developed a new awareness of the masses, popular interest in politics and ideology grew, and state economic intervention increased. To use Gramsci's idea, laissez-faire concepts developed as a conscious expression of those who directed the economy. The state evolved as a manifestation of industrialization and political expediency.[188] The traditional social order experienced a crisis, as postwar capitalist expansion and modernization caused political and social change. A small urban working class emerged along with a larger, urban semiproletariat.

Traditional peasant forms of organization broke down; a small, middle-level peasantry evolved; and rural monopoly capital allied with that of the industrial and commercial bourgeoisie.[189] Bourgeois popular movements, such as Arévalo's in Guatemala, emerged in all Central American states except Nicaragua. Popular discontent bred middle-class national reform and desires for liberty, democracy, constitutionalism, and respect for human rights. Between 1945 and 1950, industry fostered urbanization, and new politically active unions and political parties formed. Society opened up, U.S. capital poured in, and, ironically, quests to attain autonomy through economic development often created a loss of sovereignty.[190]

Torres Rivas documented how Central American dependency deepened after World War II, how land ownership became more concentrated, and how, as export agriculture expanded, nations lost the capacity to feed themselves. Dependency was accompanied by external manipulation through credit-extending banks as well as internal repression to prevent unionization. Torres Rivas's *Processos y estructuras de una sociedad dependiente (Centroamérica)* (1969, Processes and structures of a dependent Central American society) charted the evolution of dependency from its colonial origins to the establishment of the Central American Common

Market in the 1960s, a theme expanded upon in *Interpretación del desarrollo social centroamericano* (1981). Torres Rivas depicted bourgeois dependency as a result of imperialism that made Central America peripheral to major capitalist areas, which exported industrialization. To him, dependency connoted a division of international labor, where dominant nations establish the limits within which other countries work.[191] In general his thinking corresponds to that of Latin America's other early *dependencia* theorists, Theotonio dos Santos, Aníbal Quijano, Fernando Henrique Cardozo, and Enzo Faletto. They all have agreed that under dependent capitalism, industrialization cannot absorb the entire labor force. Torres Rivas called this structural, or built-in, unemployment. He also noted that dependency is accompanied by state protection to reduce capitalists' costs by maintaining low salaries.[192] He viewed dependency, based on international class alliances, as not purely external but internal as well because dominant foreign interests align with national collaborators who, in turn, subordinate the majority.[193] According to Torres Rivas, dependency emerges in stages. During the first stage, that of the industrial revolution, capitalist manufacturing consolidates and seeks markets for goods and suppliers of raw material. The second stage includes rapid expansion of private investment in, and economic and political control over, the peripheral nations.[194]

In Torres Rivas's estimation, significant industrialization in Central America began at the end of the 1950s and was conducted within the framework of an international market system under the hegemony of U.S. corporations. In the 1960s, direction for the Central American Common Market came from corporate boardrooms in the United States. Major Central American social groups did not participate in CACM decisionmaking, and that slowed democratization in the region. Only 2 million of Central America's 18 million people had the capacity to participate in the CACM. Greater expansion of internal markets could have improved profits, wages, and living standards but would have also raised social, political, and economic consciousness and demands upon those in control.[195] Torres Rivas concluded that the CACM reduced national sovereignty, enhanced cooperation between states, and increased regional sovereignty.[196] In Guatemala, although businesspeople benefited by the CACM, it did not improve economic demands in the domestic market. While it functioned, agriculture for the export market expanded and rural poverty increased.[197]

Since the decline of the CACM, a "four-story society" has existed in the region, according to Torres Rivas. On the lowest level live the subproletariat, the unemployed or permanently underemployed. This social set has no class ascription. On the second level we find social sectors with permanent opportunities to work and receive income. The system exploits these industrial and agricultural laborers. The third level consists of an intermediate strata that has emerged in the last quarter of a century. It is difficult to classify these people, who lack the income criteria and the psychological attitudes that constitute a class. This group grows perhaps at the expense of the lower strata and to benefit the upper strata. This new middle sector is tied to expanded education and increased employment in non-value-generating jobs linked to the "hypertrophy of state apparatuses." The top floor contains a new upper class characterized by investment capital rather than by style of domination or social privileges. This floor also holds the old bourgeoisie. The new, more adventurous group "plunders the state," or uses it to its advantage through deals made possible by its power.[198]

Despite these alterations in social organization and a degree of modernization, social change has not occurred in Central America, and that militates against national autonomy. Central America is further held back because three-quarters of the region's products are produced in factories owned or controlled by U.S. capital and its market is subordinate to that of the United States, as the industrial sector depends on importing semifinished parts and technology.[199] The region's fourth-floor residents, which include those in the commercial, industrial, agricultural, and financial sectors, remain subordinate, and the foreign debts of the respective nations grow steadily.

In addition to the external factors that retard progress in Central America, Torres Rivas concluded, internal crises exist. Bourgeois elements vie for hegemony, and the masses struggle to ascend. The interbourgeois rivalry is presided over by an aura of anticommunism cloaked in rhetoric extolling the virtues of order and authority and the preservation of traditional values. Simultaneously, the military, with U.S. assistance, seizes power to ensure order and creates the counterrevolutionary state that uses terror against guerrillas, students, peasants, and clergy.[200] This confuses those on the fourth floor, who must contend simultaneously with one another and an aroused working class.[201] Thus the struggle for state power pits unevenly matched classes against one another with the survival of the protagonists at stake.[202]

Can one explain this complex situation in Marxist terms? According to Torres Rivas, one can build a Marxist analysis of the nation but not a general, coherent theory that pertains to all countries equally. For him, Marxist theory can help clarify national problems. He points out that whereas Marx and Engels were preoccupied with the question of the role of the nation in a world dominated by an international workers' movement, in a post-Marxian world we do not see the erosion of the nation-state and must think of change within national confines.[203] Torres Rivas has shown that historically the Central American nation-state has changed to conform to different modes of production, thus an ongoing dialectic exists.[204]

The dialectical process has made each Central American state, except Costa Rica, a "domestic leviathan"[205] in which denationalization takes place but internationalization does not occur. National integration in Central America, according to Torres Rivas, has emanated from the social relations of production. Thus the extant cultural integration reflects the ideology of the bourgeoisie.[206] The unity Torres Rivas sees in Central America has not come about in the independent fashion advocated by Bolívar or Arévalo but rather as a result of mutual opposition to U.S. hegemony.

Torres Rivas analyzed the relationship of the Central American countries to the capitalist world, and he recognized a need to initiate a process of national renaissance, leading to state sovereignty, to eliminate dependence,[207] which he concluded can only be achieved through class struggle. He found that historically the design of the state cannot be separated from the social and political position of the class that controls it.[208]

The instability crisis experienced by the modern Central American state has passed through three stages, according to Torres Rivas. The first stage started at the end of World War II and ended in the mid-1970s. It generated inequalities in agrarian society, increased industrial production geared to middle-class consumption, produced a surplus labor supply, and broadened popular discontent and authoritarian government. Stage two began as popular attempts at democracy failed by the early 1970s and popular, often armed, resistance occurred in Nicaragua, El Salvador, and Guatemala. Christian elements joined popular movements, as did Communist militants and radical nationalists. Social activism and revolutionary praxis grew. The state proved unable to maintain order, and state-sponsored violence ensued. By mid-1979, with the fall of Somoza in Nicaragua, stage three began. At this point antidemocratic and anticommunist actions by Nicaragua's neighbors caused Torres Rivas to posit an "antidomino" theory—that a successful revolution provokes a strong reaction in the ruling classes of neighboring countries.[209] The United States tried to control the Sandinistas who overthrew its ally Somoza, and Washington decided never to tolerate a similar revolution. In 1980 the United States opted for a policy of open intervention, massive aid to the military in El Salvador and Honduras, and counterrevolution. Torres Rivas contended that the third stage will end when solutions to the conflict are defined, national sovereignty guaranteed, and internal restructuring permits genuine participatory democracy, as opposed to electoral democracy, which has proved farcical in the past.[210]

In addition to emphasis on Central America as a region, Torres Rivas's scholarship has also included specific studies of Guatemala. As he sees it, some Guatemalans have always opposed progress. The colonial aristocracy rejected the forward thinking of the French Encyclopedists, then the conservative Creoles opposed the liberals and positivists, and now the bourgeoisie reacts against socialism, revolution, and radical reform.[211] He characterized Guatemala as a country where the idea of constitutional separation of powers existed in theory, but there emerged a strong arbitrary and personalized executive with legislative functions and a subservient judiciary.[212] He noted that representative democracy has not resulted from capitalist development, as the latter has meant domination by the ruling class. Since the late nineteenth century, despotism, progress, and modernization have gone hand in hand.[213] Considerable foreign capital penetrated the nation between 1875 and World War I, and neocolonial relations of production developed. World War II had a significant impact on Guatemala, which diversified economically. The expropriation of German plantations gave the United States more control, and the idea of combating fascism increased demands for liberty. Guatemala received its first semblance of democracy in 1945.

Torres Rivas agreed with Galich and Toriello and called the 1944–1954 era a frustrated bourgeois revolution wherein Arévalo and Arbenz wanted to convert from semicolonialism to independent modern capitalism and to destroy praetorianism.[214] When the government expropriated 100,000 hectares of land and created the illusion of a leftward move, it set off an anticommunist reaction. Although Arévalo and Arbenz stimulated new, less despotic methods for organizing the peasantry and abolished forced labor during their administrations, the inequalities of social wealth intensified in other ways.[215] The two administrations did not diminish the interests of the agricultural exporters or the bourgeois merchants but only reduced the control of the United States over those elements. The economic transformations that occurred benefited the national private sector. U.S. intervention cut short the democratization process and precluded any transformation in class control.[216]

Guatemala's current governmental crises began in 1954, according to Torres Rivas. With the victory of the CIA, the United States built a cold war model. Civil rights violations became endemic. For example, between 1954 and 1957, the government dislodged 100,000 peasants from their lands. Counterrevolution also strengthened the church, and the number of clergy in the country grew concurrently with anticommunism.[217] Guatemala's ruling class could not agree on a coherent plan to govern between 1954 and 1963. Trade union leaders, students, and politicians were assassinated. Opportunities for democracy disappeared, and popular armed struggle occurred.[218] U.S.-assisted counterinsurgency and fratricidal violence ensued. Guatemala's industrial and agricultural leaders, buttressed by the army, maintained an authoritarian form of government that thwarted political mobility and resisted reform. Torres Rivas pointed out the paradox that Guatemala, the Central American nation with the most positive trade balance, had the highest unemployment, the most unequal distribution of income, and the most anti-union violence.[219]

Torres Rivas asserted that Guatemala's revolutionaries must forge a new political order based on indigenous support and free of U.S. influence. He emphasized that armed struggle need not be a prelude to authoritarian rule. To him, the conservative, reactionary, and anticommunist thought that has prevailed in Guatemala since 1954 has no intellectual foundation, no meaning for the masses, and is mostly rhetoric supporting the national security state. Guatemala's revolutionary thinkers, such as Torres Rivas, know that their policies must be based on theory that provides logical and cohesive explanations of how capitalism has retarded progress in the past and a clear vision of how to provide for a more peaceful, democratic, and socially beneficial future.

Torres Rivas concluded that the Sandinista victory in 1979 enabled Central American citizens to understand that bourgeois solutions are unlikely and to recognize the feasibility of revolutionary solutions.[220] The Nicaraguan episode accentuated the systemic crisis in capitalism in the region.[221] He contended that the crisis resulted from the way the United States has controlled and subordinated each country. The U.S. military option eliminates democracy by restraining the rising consciousness of the oppressed classes. U.S. cold war politics have failed, and insurrection has become widespread in Central America. In the face of increased opposition, the United States changed its policy from one designed to prevent "mutually assured destruction" to one that accepts the possibility of "conventional nuclear war," and it now cites Central America as the backyard to be protected. Washington seeks to prevent reform in Guatemala, to block the consolidation of the Sandinistas in Nicaragua, to bolster the rightist military in El Salvador, and to make Honduras the major base of its Central American operations.[222]

Torres Rivas warned that the current breakdown of bourgeois hegemony and weakening of state power facilitates revolution but does not guarantee it. It reveals the difficulty of controlling the oppressed classes, the antidemocratic nature of those who govern, and the ideological poverty of their anticommunism.[223] State terrorism can neutralize popular struggle but cannot stabilize counterrevolutionary power.[224]

Torres Rivas felt that until 1975 the future for the dominated classes appeared bleak, but this turned around. The economic crises and intrabourgeois competition (described above) prevented the governing bourgeoisie from resolving the problems of the exploited masses. A new popular radicalism, led by peasants and workers, opposed the establishment. Students, who had played a major role in the fight for democracy no longer served as the primary political protagonists. The older political parties, especially the Communists, failed to lead popular struggles. They never became a vanguard, according to Torres Rivas, possibly because they permitted middle-class elements to play a leading role in the bourgeois democratic revolution. Also, the traditional leftist parties, as a result of their organic nature, had difficulty adapting their demands to the required military solutions. New movements and coalitions, including in their ranks classic Marxists, Jacobins, religious elements, and radical democrats, replaced political parties as revolutionary leaders. The state lost its power to control social dissent. Marxist-oriented political-military organizations slowly gained recognition, influence, and even territory. Today's revolutionaries represent the transition between unfinished bourgeois revolutions and incipient socialist revolutions. They reject bourgeois values and work for democracy, national independence, and economic development—goals that the bourgeoisie allegedly desired but could not achieve.[225]

For three decades, Torres Rivas has searched painstakingly for answers to exceedingly complex questions pertaining to the major problems of Central America. Through flexible Marxist analysis, he has demonstrated that political instability corresponds to the low level of legitimate power exercised by those in control in Central American countries where the popular sector does not participate in the decisionmaking process. The Cuban and Nicaraguan revolutions have shown that it is possible to establish a new equilibrium within the state, one that brings new social forces into play. In the early 1960s, Torres Rivas wondered if genuine change could be effected, given the history and dynamics of Central American society. New social science research, together with innovative Marxist theory and successful praxis, led him to conclude that it is possible to engender economic and social development, democracy, and national autonomy in Central America, but not through the reformist policies and strategies employed in the 1940s and 1950s by the Arévalo and Arbenz administrations.

Historical study, engaged in since 1954, has led Guatemala's radical intellectuals to reorient their thinking considerably. Arévalo, Galich, and Toriello all developed a broader hemispheric frame of reference. They saw Guatemala's problems emanating from an international system that has had particularly negative repercussions for the majority in Latin America. Before such studies became fashionable in academic circles in the 1970s, Arévalo, Galich, and Toriello explored the roots and consequences of dependency, which they concluded was a major contributing factor to their nation's underdevelopment. They searched for ways to eliminate dependency, which in the Guatemalan experience accompanied the imperialist stage of capitalism. Torres Rivas, as detailed above, subsequently refined their embryonic dependency analyses, examined them in light of the latest modernization theories, and showed the way for development within a socialist construct. Galich and Toriello eventually concluded that Guatemala's national bourgeoisie could not lead an antiimperialist revolution, nor was it willing to relinquish power to the rising working class. Today, they share the perspective of their countryman Edelberto Torres Rivas that history may lead us to believe that change is impossible under capitalism but recent socialist successes in the Third World provide models and hope for the years to come.

The preceding pages illustrate that Guatemalan radicalism, for the most part, did not emanate from an anarchosyndicalist or Communist party tradition but rather has liberal-reformist origins. When the Arévalo-Arbenz antioligarchic reformist experiment proved unable to withstand the onslaught of its opponents, many of the nation's outstanding liberal and social democratic leaders assumed more radical stances. Disillusioned established thinkers, as well as perspicacious young intellectuals, learned to think dialectically and adopted nonsectarian, Marxist-Leninist perspectives through which to analyze the failures of the past and to organize and plan for the future. Simultaneously, a new popular revolutionary movement evolved, one that differed significantly from others in Central America as it stressed ethnic-cultural values and sought to eliminate the racial and cultural domination that helped maintain Guatemala's oligarchy in power.[226]

3

El Salvador

For the bourgeoisie country, laws, honor and God have no meaning without private property and "free enterprise." For the proletarians the death of private property and "free enterprise" would give meaning to country, laws, honor and perhaps even to God.

—Roque Dalton

Chilean poet and Nobel Prize winner Gabriela Mistral affectionately and allegorically referred to El Salvador, Central America's smallest and least densely populated nation, as *el pulgarcito* (the little flea). Historian Thomas Anderson called it a chronically unhappy nation. To others, it is a banana republic that does not export bananas.

The nation serves an oligarchy that myth says is composed of *los catorce* (the fourteen) families. In reality, the oligarchy contains about 250 families of large landowners, merchants, and entrepreneurs. They represent about forty clans who control 80 percent of the country's coffee production, which has historically accounted for over half to more than three-quarters of its exports.[1]

Greedy oligarchies have been a major problem for El Salvador's masses since the Pipil Indians unsuccessfully tried to resist the Spanish in the 1520s. After independence from Spain, elitist natives dominated El Salvador's economy, and liberals and conservatives vied for political power. In 1833 peasants led by the Indian Anastasio Aquino in the central zone of the country rose against the white families that controlled the nation and announced El Salvador's first land distribution program. The government defeated this movement designed to effect equality among the peasants and killed its leader.[2]

The Salvadoran oligarchy closed ranks against the masses and educated its offspring to follow suit. Most Salvadorans who received higher education attended Guatemala's University of San Carlos prior to the 1840s. In 1841 the nation's politicians authorized the establishment of the Colegio de la Asunción in San Salvador, which became the National University by 1847. Education existed primarily for the sons of the elite. By the early 1850s, the periodical *El Progreso* (Progress), edited by José Francisco Barrundia, discussed the elitist positivist philosophy that began to appeal to the nation's oligarchy and guides it to this day.

At the same time, El Salvador started to build its modern state on the sale of coffee on the world market. Export agriculture grew in the 1850s, coffee replaced indigo as the primary crop, and a new, native landed bourgeoisie attained prominence in Salvadoran governmental affairs. Salvadoran entrepreneurs took measures to abolish Indian communal lands, which became coffee plantations. Public demonstrations and protests against these expropriations began in the 1870s and continued for the balance of the nineteenth century.[3]

From 1870 to the 1920s, a liberal elite ruled most of the time, developed coffee, built rail networks to ports, secured foreign loans, and outlawed vagrancy to compel the entire population to work for low wages. Meanwhile, the liberal oligarchy and its military henchmen met all dissent with repression.[4] Skilled artisans nevertheless managed to form mutual benefit societies. The Concordia Society of Artisans, the oldest organization of its kind in Central America, formed in 1872. It started an adult school to teach trade skills and in 1873 began to publish a newspaper, *El Obrero* (The worker).[5]

For the most part, intellectual life stagnated in El Salvador during the nineteenth century. The Academy of Sciences and Fine Arts opened in 1888 but disappeared by 1894. Few books were published in the nation, and *Diario Latino*, the country's oldest daily commercial newspaper, only started printing in 1890. Positivism had become the major ideology by the 1890s and, along with economic liberalism, dominated the nation's thinking.

By the turn of the century, the United States had replaced Great Britain as El Salvador's major trading partner. Primarily economic topics interested the country's oligarchs. Radical thought had not emerged in El Salvador, but some radical activism appeared by way of an embryonic labor movement. San Salvador played host to the First Central American Labor Congress in 1911. Within three years, diverse artisan guilds pooled their resources to form the Confederación de Obreros (Workers' Confederation), and by 1917 approximately fifty unions existed in the nation.[6] That year the Liga Roja (Red League), a labor-oriented organization designed by those in power to gain political control over the lower classes, was established. The league, operating with government approval, made vague socialist claims and managed to blame all political excesses on the Bolsheviks.[7] As the Russian Revolution unfolded, anticommunism appeared in El Salvador. Radicalism had barely surfaced in the nation, but weapons to combat it were already under construction.

Liberal, not radical, writers, such as the philologist, historian, philosopher, and poet Francisco Gavida (1863–1955), led El Salvador's few progressives who condemned tyranny and advocated democracy and Central American unity. A friend of Rubén Darío (Chapter 6), Gavida understood the dangers of imperialism but did not oppose it with political militance. Through his work as a university professor, director of the National Library, and minister of public education, as well as through his book *Historia moderna de El Salvador* (1917, Modern history of El Salvador), Gavida became known for his compassion for the poor.[8]

Radicals constituted a tiny minority among Salvadoran intellectuals. Just before the Russian Revolution, the country's National University began to spawn a few socialist thinkers, such as Agustín Farabundo Martí. In subsequent decades the radical tradition persisted at the university on a small scale. Noteworthy products of the university are the more contemporary radical *pensadores* Roque Dalton and Rafael Menjívar.

In the wake of the Russian Revolution, small groups of intellectuals and university students began to meet to discuss social reforms. A dominant topic was how to eliminate the widespread malnutrition that existed in the country. An underground newspaper, *El submarino Bolchevique* (The underground Bolshevik), entered El Salvador in 1918 via Panama, its writers agitating for social change.[9] Anarchist and Marxist literature began to flow into the nation from Nicaragua and emphasized abuses in the land tenure system.

By the 1920s, the *colono* system, whereby workers received plots from landowners to cultivate food crops in return for their labor, was replaced by wage labor. Peasants were deprived of their land to make it available for large coffee plantations. Coffee prices rose on the world market, *fincas* (plantations) grew, marginal lands were absorbed, food production declined, and food prices went up. The plantation owners and their government allies profited. Simultaneously, the ideas of economic and political liberalism grew. The beliefs of Jeremy Bentham, John Stuart Mill, and Adam Smith that maximum economic and political freedom enhanced progress took hold. Individual enterprise was valued above corporate or cooperative leadership, and this led to further elimination of communal lands.[10] Economic conditions for the poor deteriorated. The government reduced wages in 1921, shoemakers went on strike, and protesting market women in San Salvador were fired on by government troops.

Workers banded together to confront the landowners and the government. Permanent trade unions were established. By 1924, inspired by anarchosyndicalist and Communist ideas, workers formed the Regional Federation of Workers of El Salvador, which joined the Central American Workers' Confederation in 1926.[11] Communist cells organized in El Salvador under the direction of Mexican comrades who had been influenced by Augusto Sandino's tales of conditions in Central America.[12] Guatemala's Communists, assisted by their Salvadoran comrade Agustín Farabundo Martí, extended their activities to El Salvador and established the party there in 1925. Although illegal, the Communist party of El Salvador functioned well underground. The Guatemalan Communists also organized, in 1927, the Anti-Imperialist League, which attracted support among intellectuals.[13]

Between 1927 and 1932, the Roman Catholic church hierarchy sustained a vicious attack on socialist doctrine. According to the church, socialism was antithetical to religion, family, and state, and class struggle and the elimination of private property damaged the established way of life.[14] El Salvador's elites concurred with the views of the church and began to view the United States as a natural ally against the aspirations of the masses for radical social change. In 1929 the coffee barons formed their own protective organization, the Plantation Owners' Association of El Salvador.

The Regional Federation of Salvadoran Workers, with strong Communist party influence, joined the newly formed Latin American Confederation of Unions in 1929. El Salvador's branch worked closely with the Socorro Rojo Internacional (International Red Aid), the worldwide Communist "Red Cross," through its Salvadoran affiliate, the League for the Defense of Persecuted Workers.[15] Left-wing influence grew among the workers. The Communist party, originally organized by Mexicans and Guatemalans but directed from New York, established a local central executive committee in 1930. By then, thanks to the efforts of Mexican organizer Jorge Fernández Anaya, perhaps as many as 8,000 workers fell under the party's direction. On May Day 1930, the Communists staged a parade of 80,000 people in San Salvador.[16]

Although organized labor, with left-wing support, made considerable headway during the 1920s, the major intellectual thrust in El Salvador came from the liberal ideology of philosopher, novelist, and journalist Alberto Masferrer (1868–1932). Influenced by the humanism of Russian novelist Maxim Gorky, Masferrer broke from the social Darwinism and positivism that guided El Salvador's ruling oligarchy. Through his articles in the journal *La Patria* (The homeland), he became an apostle of hope, a national conscience who advocated social justice and peace. Among intellectuals he created a climate conducive to social change and new democratic openings.[17] His powerful writings showed him to be a reformer, an advocate of state capitalism. He admired Henry George's ideas about economic justice but distrusted class struggle, which he feared would turn people against one another. He naively believed that the wealthy could be persuaded to tax themselves to support the poor.[18] El Salvador's unconvinced aristocracy denounced him as a Communist, especially when he wrote about the need to liberate women from bondage. When he referred to the great injustices of land monopoly in El Salvador, the oligarchy claimed that his inspiration came from Marx, though it in fact emanated from nineteenth-century social Christian thought.

Masferrer espoused a vague type of economic planning, not blind obedience to a fixed ideology, as a way to rectify the problems of a monocultural nation. He realized that capitalism had not benefited most Salvadorans and understood that it could be harmful if controlled without heart or poetry, only to accumulate wealth.[19] He believed that everyone was entitled to some land. He understood that work had a collective component, that it fit into a societal schema, and that workers had to interact with one another.[20] He advocated less military spending and more social welfare programs and supported a kind of sharing of the wealth. His program, called *vitalismo* (the vital minimum), represented a combination of positivism and idealism channeled into eclectic reforms. Under *vitalismo* social justice would be attained by giving every person the minimum elements of a good life, which included an education, social equality, proper nutrition, clothing, adequate housing, health care, and a balance of work and leisure. In many ways, Masferrer advanced the "good life" concept supported by the OAS in later years. He maintained that the notion of the vital minimum existed emotionally.[21] To him, the vital minimum affected individuals but required collective agreement.[22] He wanted the state to organize, implement, and pay for it, to provide conditions to enable people to have it. He felt that it should be organized flexibly, that in various epochs and places it would be attained by different means. In the final analysis, the vital minimum was an idea rather than a plan, as Masferrer did not specify how it might be accomplished.[23] The vital minimum made a pretense of remedying class differences, but its socialist opponents, such as Martí, viewed it as an anticommunist measure, a way to outflank structural change by offering reforms as alternatives.[24] Salvadoran leftist historian-poet Roque Dalton saw Masferrer as an unwitting collaborator of the ruling class, whereas revolutionary Abel Cuenca viewed him as one who understood El Salvador's problems but not their origins.

El Salvador had virtually no middle class in the 1930s, and Masferrer's pleas for reform fell on the deaf ears of the oligarchy. Meanwhile, the Communist party recognized the urgent need for thorough change.

Unlike most Latin American Communist parties, El Salvador's did not cohere around a group of intellectuals; rather, it emerged from a movement of urban and rural workers who wanted to transform society.[25] The Communists made their demands known and elicited a strong negative response from the oligarchs, which on November 5, 1930, led *La Patria* to comment, "Communist is today a facile expression that is used to condemn any act that is approved by persons who fear the laws of God and man. It is customary in the Republic to call Communist any demand for justice. . . . If the unemployed ask for work and better wages they are immediately labeled Communists."[26]

The oligarchy unleashed a brand of anticommunist repression that included imprisonment and torture. El Salvador's International Red Aid chapter, led by Martí, defended workers persecuted by imperialist or capitalist regimes and fought to make the Salvadoran government release political prisoners. Red Aid members supported class struggle and linked El Salvador's extreme poverty to the Depression and the failure of international capitalism.

In the midst of economic and social turmoil, El Salvador held genuine elections, and Arturo Araujo took the presidency in March 1931. Masferrer advised the new president to get the oligarchy to share some of its wealth with the people and to provide a vital minimum for all. Before Araujo could implement reforms he was ousted in December 1931 by the military, which placed Vice-President General Maximiliano Hernández Martínez in control of the country, a position he held until 1944. The military claimed that it toppled Araujo because he could not curtail the unrest that pervaded the nation. Some observers assert that the Communists, who persisted in spreading dissension, shared the responsibility for the overthrow.[27]

Elections for municipal offices were held soon after Martínez took power, and for the first time in the country's history, Communists appeared on the ballot. When Communist candidates won a few seats in the west, General Hernández prohibited them from taking office. The Communist party then decided to initiate the rebellion for which it had been preparing. Among the organizers of the uprising were the Communist activist-intellectuals Martí and Cuenca. On the night of January 22, 1932, armed primarily with machetes, approximately 5,000 rural workers, including Communists, and Indian *cofradías* (brotherhoods) dissatisfied because they had lost their communal lands, attacked public buildings in the western coffee region. They captured the towns of Izalco, Juayúa, Nahuizalco, Sonzacate, and Tacuba. In other areas they were repulsed. Within three days Hernández's army recaptured all of the towns. Indians and peasants suspected of participating in the uprisings or aiding the insurgents were executed. The government-sponsored

Jan. 22, 1932 ⟶ La Matanza

rebellion - put down by gov't

matanza (massacre) took the lives of 15,000 to 30,000 people (depending upon whose figures you believe), most of them after the rebellion had been stopped. The event would forever be etched in the minds of Salvadorans. Henceforth, structural reform would be impossible in El Salvador. The coffee oligarchy consolidated its power. The military murdered dissenters, most trade unions and political organizations were banned, and government repression destroyed the Communist party, which did not reorganize until 1936. After the *matanza*, anticommunism became a major theme for Salvadoran radical writers such as Abel Cuenca, Salvador Cayetano Carpio, Roque Dalton, and Rafael Menjívar.

During the insurrection the United States placed a battleship off the coast of El Salvador until it felt that General Hernández, who said that he communicated telepathically with the White House, had stopped the uprising. Washington also offered to land troops to help Hernández, but he declined the assistance because he knew that when the United States had sent marines into the Dominican Republic, Haiti, and Nicaragua to preserve stability, they did not return home immediately. Despite the *matanza*, U.S. support for the dictator, and the oligarchy's determination to prevent what it termed "subversion," the Salvadoran masses clung to the belief that eventually another peasant rebellion would take place, one that would succeed and liberate them.

The military controlled El Salvador and, for the most part, compelled peace there throughout the remainder of the 1930s. Hernández expressed his comic-opera attitude toward fellow human beings: "It is good for children to walk around barefoot. That way they can better receive the beneficial emanations of the plants. . . . It is a greater crime to kill an ant than a man, because when a man dies he is reincarnated, when an ant dies, it dies for good."[28] Hernández's opponents and dissenters disappeared. A false calm fell over the nation. The dictator declared it illegal to express support for the Allies during the early years of World War II. The antidictatorship feelings that arose in universities in most of Central America came to a head in El Salvador in May 1943. Students at the National University, with Communist party help, led a strike against the Hernández government. At the same time, the Communists helped establish the National Workers' Union and began to create the Democratic Union party, which opposed the tyranny perpetuated by Hernández and promoted the presidential candidacy of Arturo Romero.[29]

A modicum of prosperity existed in El Salvador during World War II. Radicals such as Miguel Mármol, a well-known victim and famous chronicler of the *matanza*, resurfaced briefly. Civilian and military uprisings and pressure from the State Department forced Hernández to resign in 1944 after a U.S. citizen, José Wright, was killed by a policeman. Police Chief Osmín Aguirre y Salinas, who had played a major role in

H - M = weirdo

the *matanza*, imposed General Salvador Castaneda Castro in the presidency, and the latter immediately drove liberals and radicals into exile.

While the government closely scrutinized union activity, the Communist party agitated for legislation to legalize unions, and succeeded by 1948. But the party could not agree on how to engage the masses. It feared that self-promotion would provoke the enemy. Thus the party exercised extreme caution. For example, it distributed its newspaper only to members. It also endured a struggle between comrades who believed that it should have a labor emphasis and those who favored working through the intelligentsia.[30]

In their periodicals the Communists pointed out that as the nation's foreign trade expanded, so did the poverty of the majority of its people. The preponderance of El Salvador's trade, by 1945, was with the United States, although considerable coffee went to Germany.[31] As trade and industry increased, so did labor agitation, primarily led by Miguel Mármol and his comrades, who formed the secret Reorganization Committee of Salvadoran Workers, which sought to eliminate the nation's predominantly precapitalist mode of production and exploitation.

During the 1950s, U.S. interest in El Salvador mounted, as North American entrepreneurs encouraged modernization to expand their markets and to secure a new place to invest. Import substitution increased dependence on foreign finance capital and accelerated the cultivation of heretofore unused lands for agricultural exports. In 1958 the United States sought an investment climate free of unrest provoked by nationalists and socialists desirous of keeping profits at home. At that time the world price of coffee dropped and caused financial burdens that touched off a revolutionary upsurge and fostered a growth in Communist party membership. Revolutionaries led by Fidel Castro who took over in Cuba in January 1959 provided an attractive model for the discontented Salvadorans, and the antiimperialist struggle deepened.[32] That year, the pro-Castro Revolutionary Party of April and May, led by Roberto Carlos Delgado, formed in El Salvador and lasted until 1961. The Cuban Revolution, in which activist-intellectuals such as Che Guevara assumed a leading role in guiding the course of events and in explaining them to the masses, appealed to Salvadoran revolutionary activist and poet-historian Roque Dalton. Other Salvadoran radical thinkers, Rafael Menjívar, for instance, found that Cuba proved the efficacy of sharing the fruits of revolution rapidly, especially in terms of radical land reform, which fostered political consensus and cohesion among the peasants.

While radical disaffection grew in the nation, foreign corporations began to produce goods for export during the 1960s. Native oligarchs earned a 25 to 40 percent profit per year on their investments in export-oriented businesses. Workers' discontent grew, and the United States moved to control organized labor. Washington, together with the AFL-CIO, established the American Institute for Free Labor Development (AIFLD) to work with the government and employers to foster social and economic progress within a capitalist construct. AIFLD, part of John F. Kennedy's cold war program to thwart leftist movements in Latin America, endeavored to orient Salvadoran labor to the belief that socialism is a totalitarian threat to unions and democracy.

As industrialization expanded under the Central American Common Market, transnational monopolies built plants in El Salvador for assembling, packaging, and finishing articles imported from Japan, Western Europe, or the United States. This reduced labor costs, taxes, and transportation charges and, for no apparent reason except greed, increased the prices for some goods.[33] Under the CACM, proletarian consciousness grew, as did the economic gap between the strongest Central American states, El Salvador and Guatemala, and the weakest, Honduras. The modernization brought by the CACM worked primarily for the benefit of El Salvador's ruling sector and its U.S. partners and exacerbated class tensions in the Central American nation, as explained by Rafael Menjívar.

Thanks in part to the CACM and the Alliance for Progress, El Salvador's foreign debt swelled in the 1960s. Students and faculty at the National University blamed capitalism for ruining their country. Under leadership from the campus, in particular from Guillermo Ungo, the National Revolutionary Movement formed in 1965 and affiliated with the Socialist International.[34] The Communist party, now with 500 dedicated members heavily involved in the trade union movement and organized by leaders such as Salvador Cayetano Carpio, supported such measures as armed struggle, organizing the masses, respect for civil rights, fuller employment, higher wages, lower living costs, easier credit terms for small and medium businesses, the development of national industry, closer alliances between workers and peasants, national sovereignty, the elimination of semicolonial dependence, and solidarity with all revolutions, especially that of Cuba. No longer did the Communist party see a need to wait for maximum conditions for revolution, but it insisted that minimum conditions be created if the revolution were to triumph.[35]

Within the Communist party the *foco* concept predominated in the 1960s. It entailed the idea that liberation would emanate from one geographic zone of the nation where guerrilla actions would politicize the local people. Subsequently, the *foco* theory gave way to the idea of parallel armed mass struggles.[36] With the rejection of the *foco* theory, the ideas that the guerrillas could substitute for a revolutionary vanguard party and that the peasantry could be the new revolutionary class both failed.[37]

At the same time, new revolutionary fervor developed in a heretofore predominantly conservative sector of El Salvador. Traditionally the church worked hand in glove with the oligarchy, although a liberal social Christian tendency had existed in the church for some time. The 1891 Papal Bull *Rerum Novarum* supported the social obligations of private property, *Quadragesimo Anno* (1931) criticized laissez-faire capitalism and defended labor's right to organize. Pope John XXIII, through *Master et Magister* in 1961, and Paul VI, through *Populorum Progressio* in 1967, revived the ideas of the earlier papal messages. These measures were incorporated into the thinking of the Latin American Bishops Conference held in 1968 at Medellín, Colombia, where the more liberal and radical prelates concluded that liberation is not reserved for after death but can be achieved by struggle on earth. Christian base communities, professing liberation theology, soon appeared in El Salvador.

Although major changes took place in the church, problems involving El Salvador's surplus population, balance of trade, and border relations with Honduras converged. El Salvador's positive balance of trade in Central America grew under the CACM. Neighboring Honduras produced a favorable balance of trade outside of the region but an imbalance inside it. Honduras felt that it subsidized industrial development in El Salvador and resented the approximately 300,000 Salvadorans who resided in Honduras and vied for jobs with Hondurans. In April 1969, Honduras ordered the Salvadorans, many of whom were small farmers and second-generation residents, to leave, and in June 1969 revised its open-door policy regarding immigrants. El Salvador closed its border to immigrants. The same month a series of bitterly fought World Cup soccer matches between the two countries fueled national antagonisms. El Salvador invaded Honduras, destroyed most of its air force, and cut its roads to Guatemala and Nicaragua. The four-day "Soccer War" created great enmity between the countries, virtually eliminated Honduras's market for Salvadoran goods, and left El Salvador with many landless, unemployed peasants. The war, which Salvadoran officials thought would take people's minds off internal class conflict and build unity in a time of international crises, backfired. The landless and the unemployed became a major source of discontent in El Salvador. As their protests were met by repression, some sought new ideologies to resolve their problems.

After the Soccer War, El Salvador's oligarchy expanded its economic interests. Coffee growers invested in industry, especially in chemicals, food, paper products, petroleum, and pharmaceuticals. By 1971, six families controlled 43 percent of all cultivated land in the nation,[38] and 7.3 percent of the farms used 83 percent of the agricultural land. Conditions worsened for the workers, and the potential for revolution increased, especially among rural labor, as Menjívar, the nation's most significant academic radical, pointed out. Three major guerrilla groups emerged from mass organizations and prepared for armed struggle: the Popular Forces of Liberation, the Maoist-oriented Armed Forces of National Resistance, and the Revolutionary Army of the People, led by poet-historian Roque Dalton and supported by the disenchanted middle class, Christian Democrats, and some former Communist party members. The Communist party of El Salvador construed the 1973 overthrow of Salvador Allende's democratically elected socialist government in Chile as a failure of the idea of a peaceful road to revolution. It decided to engage in armed struggle, becoming the first Latin American Communist party to take such a stance and thus breaking a long tradition of pursuing a peaceful, generally electoral path to power. At almost the same time, just south of San Salvador, under the direction of Father José Inocencio Alas, thirty Christian base communities studied socialist and capitalist theory and agitated for agrarian reform. By 1974 Alas and his peasants organized the United Popular Action Front, the first formal revolutionary organization to come out of the Christian base communities.[39] Rural workers formed the Catholic Federation of Salvadoran Peasants, a radical peasant league, which merged with other workers' and teachers' unions and by 1978 was part of the Marxist-oriented Popular Revolutionary Bloc, which had 30,000 members. The number expanded to 80,000 by 1980.

A working class of 150,000 in the cities and over one million in rural areas existed at the peak of El Salvador's industrialization in 1975.[40] Modernization and industrialization increased the nation's external debt, as noted by Menjívar, and working-class leaders blamed El Salvador's economic dependence on U.S. entrepreneurs and their native partners. The potential strength of the workers' movement frightened the oligarchy, which backed the Armed Forces of Anticommunist Liberation, a right-wing group that promised to eradicate all Communists and their non-socialist allies. When caught between popular demands for reforms and U.S. and military pressures to retain the status quo, moderates such as Christian Democrat José Napoleón Duarte, who served as provisional president and president (1980–1989), allied with Washington and the army. The United States publicly supported the Christian Democratic party as a reformist, capitalist, and controllable alternative to right-wing dictatorship and left-wing revolution.

Antigovernment organizations multiplied rapidly and merged with one another, and the sectarian splits among Maoists, Trotskyists, Stalinists, and Guevarists that had led to violence between left-wing groups began to abate. By the 1980s El Salvador's revolutionary opposition consisted primarily of the Democratic Revolutionary Front (FDR) and the Farabundo

Martí National Liberation (FMLN) organization, which advocates of armed struggle, such as union leader Salvador Cayetano Carpio, had been building for a decade. The FMLN, the military arm of the revolutionary movement, advocated Lenin's democratic centralism, saw general insurrection as the only way to power, and endeavored to incorporate different levels of the masses into the war of national liberation, as described in the essays on Cayetano Carpio and Dalton on subsequent pages. The FMLN encompassed five organizations: the People's Revolutionary Army, the Popular Liberation Forces, the Salvadoran Communist party, the Central American Revolutionary Workers' party, and the National Resistance, all of which formerly envisioned themselves as vanguard parties and now viewed the collective as the vanguard. The FMLN controlled guerrillas, militias, and neighborhood committees. Its objectives included national independence, a popularly elected democratic revolutionary government, equitable distribution of wealth, public access to health and cultural facilities, a new popular revolutionary army to protect national sovereignty and the people, freedom of belief and religion, international peace and nonalignment, and support for private businesses that reject imperialism.[41]

The FDR, the political arm of the revolutionary movement, included progressive political groups, professionals, technicians, small business organizations, a National University component, six labor unions, and church elements. Its platform resembled that of the 1979 Nicaraguan revolution explained in Chapter 6. Although its program did not mention socialism or capitalism, it referred to a "new society," was directed toward structural reforms, and sought to eliminate imperialism, dictatorship, and the oligarchy. It stood for broad agrarian reform and expropriation of large estates.[42]

As the civil war pitted the FDR-FMLN against the oligarchy-controlled government and its U.S. allies, El Salvador's radical intellectuals considered it a Central American phenomenon that could not be understood in isolation. Radical thinkers such as Cayetano Carpio and Menjívar saw it as analogous to the Nicaraguan Revolution, as a mass move to free El Salvador from foreign domination, and as part of the international class struggle. As the civil war progressed, the various groups in the FDR-FMLN coalition moved farther to the left and continuously gained followers. By the end of the 1980s neither the FDR-FMLN nor the government had the capacity to destroy the other, but casualties increased on both sides. By 1990 the Salvadoran war had claimed more than 70,000 lives. Although U.S. military and economic aid to the government had totaled over $4 billion since 1980, the rebel combatants had footholds in twelve of fourteen provinces, and its revolutionary political education workers functioned everywhere. They followed what Rubén Zamora, one of the rebels' political leaders, described to me as Marxism with European origins and Latin American nuances.[43] The civil war that he and his colleagues pursued radicalized numerous workers and peasants who in the mid-1980s looked toward the time when the Salvadoran people would enjoy a revolutionary government.[44] But by 1990, in light of the military stalemate, El Salvador's radicals began to seek a negotiated settlement with the administration of conservative President Alfredo Cristiani elected for the 1989–1994 term. The FMLN leaders spoke about discarding the Marxist-Leninist concept of seizing power and guiding the development of socialism through a single party vanguard in favor of changing society from within by participating in the electoral process under the 1983 Constitution.

Agustín Farabundo Martí and Abel Cuenca: Revolutionary Precursors

El Salvador's contemporary revolutionaries trace their lineage to Agustín Farabundo Martí (1894–1932). Although Martí did not write books, Central American radical intellectuals have been inspired by his ideas and actions and consider them an integral part of the region's revolutionary ethos. The son of a hacienda owner in Teotepeque, Martí as a youth associated with the children of his father's laborers, from whom he developed a sensitivity to class distinctions and prejudice and disdain for social deprivation. He attended a Catholic secondary school, where he displayed an aptitude for history, mathematics, religion, literature, and athletics. In 1914 he entered the social science and law program of the National University, becoming more enamored of the thinking of Hegel, Marx, the utopian socialists, and anarchosyndicalists than of Comte, whom he regarded as an elitist and whose ideas were popular among the faculty. He called the curriculum at the university anachronistic and saw little correlation between it and El Salvador's social reality.[45] He joined a Marxist study group, where he searched for answers to his nation's perplexing economic, political, and social questions. Eventually he quarreled with, and challenged to a duel, his philosophy professor, whom he accused of defending bourgeois interests and exploitation.[46] He avoided the duel but never finished his degree. The government of José Meléndez (1918–1922) deported him to Honduras as a result of his radical activities. From Guatemala Martí denounced El Salvador's Liga Roja as a petit bourgeois organization designed to make the workers reject revolution and support the establishment.[47]

Called "El Negro" because of his dark complexion, Martí was seen by his friends as a profound thinker, an unpretentious intellectual with romantic tendencies, a calm and erudite man who had difficulty with public speaking.[48] Sometimes known as Octavio Rigueira or other pseud-onyms, Martí rarely hesitated to express his feelings. For example, he openly proclaimed his dislike for the clergy and his admiration for Leon Trotsky. In fact, on his lapel he generally wore a red star pin with Trotsky's face on it.[49] Like Trotsky, he was primarily an internationalist.

An interpreter of the ideas of others rather than a theoretician or original political philosopher, Martí eschewed reformist beliefs such as those of Alberto Masferrer. He believed that the latter's vital minimum pretended to be a remedy for the class struggle, but in fact it combated Bolshevism and imperialism.[50] He preferred Lenin's methods of dealing with imperialism by eliminating the bourgeois state based on private property and exploitation and by building a viable dictatorship of the proletariat.[51]

According to a popular but unverifiable story, Martí visited Mexico in 1923 and became acquainted with the exploits of the "Red Batallions" of workers who fought for the constitutionalists in the early days of the Mexican Revolution.[52] He saw the Mexican Revolution in an unfa-vorable light, as the workers there were subservient to the will of the middle class that directed the revolution.[53]

Martí represented El Salvador at the founding of the Central American Socialist party in Guatemala in 1925. In San Salvador he organized workers and helped establish a People's University that taught adults to read and stressed radical political economy.[54] He also worked with the Anti-Imperialist League and served as a representative of the Ca-ribbean Bureau of the International Red Aid in El Salvador.[55] In the latter capacity, Martí advocated the need for social revolution, opposed imperialism, and defended workers victimized by class warfare.

During the mid-1920s, Martí participated in a literary circle in San Salvador and worked with a secret Communist youth group. The Salvadoran government exiled him in 1925. After returning home, he was imprisoned in 1927 for his radical activities but was released after a hunger strike made him a popular hero, then was ordered into exile again. He traveled to Nicaragua in 1928, met Sandino, and received the rank of colonel in his army. For fifteen months he served as personal secretary to the Nicaraguan chieftain, whose theosophic and masonic beliefs (described in Chapter 6) he distrusted, though he felt Sandino's presence in Nicaragua was justified as an effort to oust the United States from Central America.[56] Martí claimed that Nicaragua was controlled by U.S. agents and simultaneously called Sandino a petit bourgeois *caudillo* with aspirations to govern Nicaragua in a semifeudal manner.[57] He explained that he stood with Sandino in support of the Soviet position to endorse bourgeois democratic movements of national liberation in backward states, which Lenin construed as a temporary alliance, not a permanent merger.

Martí tried, without success, to convert Sandino to his brand of ultraleft communism and to convince him to follow Comintern policies. The Nicaraguan hero considered Martí too fanatical and ultimately denounced Martí's activities on behalf of international communism. Although the two parted company, Martí never doubted Sandino's sincerity, noting, "My break with Sandino was not brought on . . . by differences on moral points, or by different standards of conduct. I refused to join him again . . . because he wanted no part of the Communist program I had been defending. His only interest was independence. . . . I solemnly maintain that General Sandino is the world's foremost patriot."[58]

Martí returned to El Salvador during the Depression, which he blamed on the machinations of global capitalism. He believed that the time was right, in the face of the prevalent hunger and despair, to move to socialism. By 1930 the Salvadoran Communist party had established, through the Regional Federation of Salvadoran Workers, the eight-hour working day, and the Popular University run by the party had become an important part of intellectual life in the nation.[59] Martí and his comrades envisioned bolder steps toward revolution.

He renewed his campaign for the release of political prisoners, and the government jailed him again. Sent into exile once more, he returned clandestinely in early 1931, whereupon he went to prison, was released, and began organizing workers and strikes on behalf of the Communist party, which he served as secretary general.[60]

The party commissioned Martí to plan an insurrection against the government of El Salvador. By this time he had organized over 10 percent of the country's work force and had built a solid constituency in the nation. Assisted by Marxist activists Abel Cuenca and Miguel Mármol, Martí planned the insurrection for January 22, 1932. By January 18, Martí and his fellow leaders had been arrested by the authorities, and they were in prison during the rebellion and the subsequent *matanza*.

Agustín Farabundo Martí told the judges at his trial, "I do not wish to defend myself because my work and that of my young comrades will be justified."[61] His words approximated those of Fidel Castro's famous "History will absolve me" speech of 1953. Contrary to the propaganda accounts of the day, Martí did not make his confession or engage in an act of contrition. It is ironic that the man who lived by the maxim "When history cannot be written with the pen, it must be written with the rifle,"[62] died at the hands of a firing squad on February 1, 1932. For the next six decades, the ideas, deeds, and example of this "rigid" Marxist revolutionary precursor would continue to unite the country's workers, peasants, and intelligentsia. The existence of today's Farabundo Martí National Liberation Movement honors his skill at putting ideas into action.

The legacy of Martí and of the 1932 insurrection has endured in part because of Abel Cuenca (1909–), who participated in it, explained it in writing, and did a masterful job of placing it into historical perspective. A survivor of the *matanza*, Cuenca serves as a major link between the revolutionaries of the 1930s and those of today.

After studying law at the University of San Carlos in Guatemala, Cuenca returned to his hometown of Tacuba, where he organized the 1932 uprising and led 1,800 men in an unsuccessful attempt to force local landowners to distribute their holdings. Following the *matanza*, he escaped to Guatemala City. He subsequently went to Honduras, where he was jailed. Upon his return to Guatemala, he served as an official in the Arbenz government until its overthrow in 1954. For the next twenty-five years, Cuenca lived in Chile; he then went to Mexico. Eventually he put his thoughts on the historical development of Salvadoran society, refined and collected over a lifetime of activism, into a book, *El Salvador: Una democracia cafetalera* (1962, El Salvador: The coffee grower's democracy).[63]

Unlike most historians, Cuenca did not dwell exclusively on the deeds of those who governed but wrote about the role of the people in the history of El Salvador. He explained brilliantly the turbulence of the 1930s, 1940s, and 1950s, when the country was beset by a succession of popular insurrections, strikes, and coups. He depicted this as a period of desperation, hope, and heroism.[64] He based his historical analysis on the conflict between the industrial bourgeoisie and the working classes.

Cuenca put partial blame for the lack of social and political progress in El Salvador on the nation's paucity of thinkers and philosophers. He has maintained that intellectual confusion has predominated in El Salvador. The country, according to him, has had few *pensadores* to counter intellectually the force of arms, or to construct democracy.[65] Generally, Salvadoran teachers, journalists, historians, political scientists, and sociologists have not analyzed society in depth. They have not looked at interrelationships historically or dialectically, nor have they examined the correlation between the horrible misery of the nation and its political and social origins.[66]

In Cuenca's opinion, Alberto Masferrer stands as the most visionary of El Salvador's thinkers. Masferrer understood the immorality of exploitation and that its primary victims were workers. But, according to Cuenca, Masferrer did not comprehend the historical laws that have kept El Salvador in a semifeudal state. He saw Masferrer's vital minimum as a "shout of desperation without resonance in the desert of the coffee democracy."[67]

Cuenca pleaded for a more systematic study of society than that made by Masferrer, who was often guided by visceral instincts. Cuenca began a semiscientific analysis by dividing Salvadoran society into eleven classes that could be studied individually and in relation to one another. These consisted of the latifundistas who owned land that produced grain, fruit, and cattle; the *terratenientes*, or masters of the huge coffee plantations; the *colonos*, or farmhands; small farmers; the urban proletariat; proprietors; the significant commercial class; shopkeepers; industrialists; white-collar workers; and artisans.[68] He found that 8 percent of the people controlled El Salvador's wealth and that the majority, the workers and peasants, have never been participants in, or beneficiaries of, the system.[69] Cuenca referred to the "Great Bourgeoisie," the antinational groups that invested in the country, including bankers, exporters, major landowners, and industrialists who allied with or depended on foreign markets or capital and had little interest in the internal market. On the other hand, he spoke about the "National Bourgeoisie," which wanted to create internal markets.[70]

Cuenca noted that traditionally El Salvador's students have been a major progressive force for change and democracy. Students have developed a valid class analysis and have provided major opposition to the coffee oligarchy.[71] They have realized that fate has nothing to do with events, which are all part of the historical process, with humans as the motor force. By empirical and historical analysis, students have figured out that when a society produces one primary product for export (coffee), it cannot provide the necessities for its citizens, and one sector of society controls the state to the detriment of the majority.[72]

When you transform the economy from a coffee export–oriented one in which all funds reside in the hands of a few reactionaries, and then begin to accentuate industrialization and use native capital for manufacturing, you can create an internal market that will inevitably conflict with the interests of the oligarchy. A struggle for control of the state will ensue between the "Great Bourgeoisie" and the "National Bourgeoisie," and progressive forces will evolve from the urban proletariat and will demand democracy.[73] Cuenca believed that this process would develop when you rid the nation of the notion that it must rely on a totally rural economy. His predictions came true in the late 1970s and in the 1980s when the struggle to eliminate the old semifeudal relations of production paralleled the quest for economic diversification.

Cuenca contended that domination by the coffee oligarchy, which opposed diversification, was consolidated after the *matanza*, when the Association of Coffee Growers became synonymous with the state. Social, economic, and intellectual progress was paralyzed, and the emerging Left was debilitated. It took about a dozen years for the Left to regenerate.[74]

Contrary to public myth, Cuenca notes that the Communist party was ideologically and politically weak in 1932. One cannot simply attribute the insurrection to Communist instigation. Communist action cohered with *campesino* unrest and the burgeoning discontent of the nascent industrial bourgeoisie. The latter two groups did not so much move against capitalism as attempt to provide a more equitable type of capitalism.[75] But since 1932, the coffee oligarchy has maintained vigilance by repeatedly ascribing blame for the violence to Soviet-inspired Communism.

To break the alliance among the landed oligarchy, its military protectors and their foreign allies, all of whom have practiced virulent anticommunism and have perpetuated a kind of continuous *matanza*, Cuenca felt that industrialization must be coupled with democratic agrarian reform.[76] This process began in 1948, as education broadened, minimum-wage legislation passed, and credit became available to small farmers. Conflict between the agrarian and the industrial capitalists heightened, and progressive forces made small gains. The coffee oligarchy worked through the Central American Common Market to resolve the internal pressures in El Salvador by delaying the redistribution of national capital for economic diversification, by diminishing workers' salaries through the elimination of competition, by weakening the popular sector's political potential by not creating more industrial jobs, and by strengthening the alliance of the Salvadoran coffee oligarchy with proimperialists from other nations.[77]

Cuenca's penetrating and pioneering "critical" Marxist analysis of the interconnections between economic and political power in El Salvador has served as a foundation for the work of two contemporary Marxist scholars, Miguel Reglado Dueñas and José Salvador Guandique. In their book *El repliegue político de la oligarquía cafetalera* (1975, The political convolutions of the coffee growers' oligarchy),[78] they add to the ideas of Cuenca the theory that the country's financially powerful propertied elite has been politically weak and therefore has ceded formal power to a military composed of mestizos of more humble origins who share common interests with, but are separated by class differences from, the oligarchy. This coalition of the military and the oligarchy currently governs El Salvador.

Salvador Cayetano Carpio:
Latin America's Ho Chi Minh

When the Salvadoran masses turned against dictator Hernández in 1944, Salvador Cayetano Carpio (1919–1983), a shoemaker's son, organized the baker's union for political action. A courtly man, "Marcial," as his comrades later called him, had spent time in a seminary and

Cayetano Carpio

according to his friends appeared impelled by a mystical force. He considered it his task to elevate the trade union movement, to promote strikes, and to raise the consciousness of the working class.[79] By the 1950s he was El Salvador's most famous union leader, one constantly in trouble with the authorities. Throughout most of the 1960s he led El Salvador's Communist party, where he gained recognition as a political strategist. Cayetano Carpio's tenacity, coupled with a bit of megalomania that caused him to think that anyone who disliked him was wrong, enabled him to maintain a straight path toward his revolutionary goals.[80] Although he spent a considerable part of his adult life in jail, exile, or underground, he never lost his fervor for struggle.

Wanting to play a more active revolutionary role, Cayetano Carpio broke from the Communist party in 1970 and went underground to build the Farabundo Martí Popular Forces of Liberation, an organization with Guevarist and Maoist tendencies that began to prepare for armed guerrilla struggle. In a critical reference to the Communist party, Cayetano Carpio stated: "Life has shown that the advance of the process of class struggle cannot be stopped with dogmatic formulas, which, at a given point, no longer correspond to objective reality and the historical need for social development."[81]

Cayetano Carpio, referred to as the Ho Chi Minh of Latin America because of his age, which was advanced for a guerrilla commander, became a symbol of hope as he initiated what he believed would be a protracted process of rebellion.[82] His reputation grew as a people's philosopher, not an original thinker with great theoretical depth but a practical, sagacious man who made people understand the necessity for revolution. For example, his book *Secuestro y capucha: En un país del "Mundo Libre"* (1979, Kidnapped and hooded in a "free world" country), written when he was in jail, vividly conveyed the horrors that befall the victims of anticommunism and documented the sadistic repression used against the democratic forces by the military in the oligarchical state.[83] Although his uncomplicated political writings generally fall into the "rigid" Marxist category and reflect a definite Leninist point of view, as a military commander he pursued pragmatic courses of action.

It is ironic that this strong critic of unnecessary violence became its victim. In April 1983 his colleagues in the Popular Forces of Liberation blamed him for the execution of his comrade Mélida Analya Montes, or Ana María. They claimed that his exaggerated sense of self-importance led him to see himself as a revolutionary purist who could not tolerate her increased leadership powers. Once the evidence was laid before him, Cayetano Carpio committed suicide.[84]

Throughout his life, Cayetano Carpio strove to understand the historical forces that caused Salvadoran conditions. He understood that the country never had mechanisms to resolve class conflicts because its oligarchy always invoked the principle of survival of the strongest, a philosophy encouraged by its economic allies. He found that in the post–World War II era North American multinational companies gained control of El Salvador's economy and structured it to fit their needs. The Salvadoran government encouraged U.S. investment, established free-trade zones with huge tax benefits, and guaranteed low wages. Entire U.S. plants relocated to El Salvador to save dollars, and the government placed no restrictions on the amount of money that could leave the country.[85] Meanwhile, unemployment never fell below 60 percent. Cayetano Carpio believed that this situation, with origins in the 1930s, built a national unity against exploitation, one that prepared the people for a popular war of liberation. He recalled that the memory of the past united the people for the future.[86]

To Cayetano Carpio, Martí's revolutionary movement failed because of limited working-class development, ignorance of the military arts, lack of arms and leadership, and a shapeless Communist party.[87] He thought that the FMLN learned from the mistakes of the 1930s. Henceforth, political parties, popular associations, and trade unions fought for genuine freedom, not the false, "free world," anticommunist freedom espoused by the United States. Since 1931, in the name of the U.S. brand of "freedom," the government had ignored the constitution and executed labor organizers as Communists and the military had employed torture (often with techniques provided by the FBI, CIA, and Interpol).[88]

Cayetano Carpio wondered how the U.S. and Salvadoran governments could associate "free-world democracy" with dictators such as Fulgencio Batista in Cuba, Rafael Trujillo in the Dominican Republic, and Marcos Pérez Jiménez in Venezuela.[89] He realized that the United States promoted aggression against the progressive forces in America but believed that imperialism or fascism could not destroy a people, citing the failure of the Nazis as an example.[90] Cayetano Carpio also discussed the types of intervention used by imperialists. "Humanitarian intervention" he equated with the belief of the Jimmy Carter administration that a deadlock existed in El Salvador's violent civil war and the U.S. need to "humanistically" stop the bloodshed by supporting intervention by the OAS Commission on Human Rights or by democratic governments. This would constitute "merciful" mediation, a dangerous and hypocritical mask of imperialism. The second level of imperialist intervention, according to Cayetano Carpio, supports the use of third governments, such as Guatemala and Honduras, to carry out direct military operations against popular forces. The third stage of intervention involves the deployment of the imperialist country's troops.[91] Cayetano Carpio believed that the U.S. interventions in the 1980s were no longer localized responses to isolated conditions but part of a more cohesive strategy designed to control Central America and the Caribbean.

Cayetano Carpio refuted the Pentagon's contention that El Salvador's was a "limited war." He called it a "special war" designed to destroy democratic organizations and exterminate population in order to deprive the revolution of resources. It approximated the war in Vietnam, where social and economic reforms neutralized the peasantry and people were terrorized into line or driven into controllable refugee camps.[92] He predicted that eventually the United States would invade El Salvador and turn it into another Vietnam—a tomb for Yankee marines[93]—a move that Washington has, so far, avoided.

Without U.S. assistance, Cayetano Carpio contended, El Salvador would fall to the popular forces rather quickly,[94] a view supported by most experts on the region. He also pointed out that U.S. policy in Central America did not correspond to U.S. public opinion or world opinion, and he stated that the U.S. people had deep humanistic values and should not be led along a militaristic path.[95]

To combat the U.S.-supported Salvadoran military, Carpio resorted to armed struggle and mass political organizing. He recruited students, Communists, and progressive Christians into his Popular Liberation Forces and incorporated them into the FMLN in 1980. In the pamphlet *La huelga general obrera de Abril 1967* (The April 1967 workers' general strike), he ruled out the *foco* theory, and recognized the need to reach out to people all over El Salvador to form support groups to help create the conditions necessary to build a Marxist, working-class party.[96] He argued against the Communist party's belief in electoral politics as the primary means to advance and rejected its policy of concluding strategic alliances with the democratic national bourgeoisie.[97] He favored a new type of Marxist-Leninist organization that had the capacity for pacific as well as military actions. He borrowed Mao's concepts of rural warfare led by student cadres[98] and considered their actions a follow-up to the revolutionary process begun by Martí. Cayetano Carpio conceived a well-organized plan to achieve change. In liberated zones under guerrilla control, a new concept of life began to be developed, new political structures devised. Popular assemblies selected leaders from among those active in public service. These leaders organized the planting and the harvests, produced household necessities, and supervised medical and sanitation projects. They inaugurated an effective educational system that explained the fundamentals of government, showed how it could be more democratic, and explored the meaning of foreign intervention versus sovereignty and independence. Cayetano Carpio's guerrillas integrated a high percentage of women into the new revolutionary society both in the rank and file and in leadership capacities.[99] They sought to eradicate over a half century of dictatorship through popular combat, which they deemed part of the bourgeois-democratic revolution that must precede socialism.[100]

Cayetano Carpio envisioned a society in which the majority would rule via democratic processes. He asserted that a need existed for a broad-based alliance guaranteeing freedom for all, including middle-size and small farmers, teachers, businesspeople, students, white-collar workers, priests, technicians, and professionals. But industrial workers and peasants would play the leading role.[101] In the new society, large landholdings, major transportation systems, electric power, refineries, foreign trade, and the coffee, cotton, sugar, and shrimp industries, would be transferred to the people. Companies owned by foreign capital would be expropriated. Public services, banking, and the economy would be centralized, and the government would provide free medical care and promote trade unionism. The revolutionary government would raise living standards, provide housing, and end illiteracy. He wanted an indigenous people's force to construct an independent economy and effect sovereign development, not Soviet Communism or a system subservient to Moscow. Cayetano Carpio also wanted El Salvador to join the Movement of Non-Aligned Countries.[102]

The new governmental policies that Cayetano Carpio projected approximated those implemented by the Sandinistas in Nicaragua in the 1980s. But he stressed the point that Nicaragua bore no responsibility for exporting revolution to El Salvador. He differentiated between the domino theory and the fact that overthrow of despotism in one place naturally inspired similar action elsewhere. He recognized that a brotherhood existed between countries based on a common historical experience but emphasized that people confronted by tyranny do not coordinate their revolutions. Each national movement springs from its own reality and has its own motor force, rhythm, and timetable.[103] He supported solidarity with like-minded Central American governments as a means to eventually halt imperialism.[104]

After the Sandinista triumph of 1979, Cayetano Carpio closed ranks with other socialists in the Americas, became more pro-Cuba, and began to cooperate more closely with the Havana regime. He claimed that the successful Cuban revolution proved that you must apply Marxism in accord with national conditions[105] and that you can achieve victory through armed insurrection.

Roque Dalton:
Seeking Justice Through Poetry and Armed Resistance

The President of my country is today called Colonel Fidel Sánchez Hernández. But General Somoza, President of Nicaragua, is also President of my country. And General Stroessner, President of Paraguay, is also a little of the President of my country although less than the President of Honduras, who is General López Arellano, and more than the President of Haiti, Monsieur Duvalier. And the President of the United States is more the President of my country than the President of my country.[106]

Roque Dalton's poem reflects the antiimperialism that pervaded his literary works and underlined his political actions. The son of a poor working woman and an absent father, Dalton (1935–1975) received his early education at Jesuit schools in San Salvador and studied law and anthropology at universities in Chile, El Salvador, and Mexico. His literary inspiration came from the works of Walt Whitman and Henry Wadsworth Longfellow, and his early political thinking was inspired by Gandhi, Neruda, his countrymen Masferrer and Martí, and especially by Guatemalan radical Otto René Castillo, who taught Dalton at El Salvador's National University.

Dalton's writings began to appear around 1956, a year before he joined the Communist party. He concluded, at an early age, that politics fell within the realm of art, that art and political commitment were life. He believed that art had to be revolutionary to be good and that revolutionary artists had to be better than those in the mainstream to succeed.[107] To him, artists who engaged in simplistic socialist realism profaned the political work that he took very seriously. As a poet, historian, and novelist, he analyzed the political problems of El Salvador, and as a humanist he represented the new socialist person described by the Cuban revolutionaries.

Dalton ran afoul of the Salvadoran government, which arrested him in 1960 and sentenced him to die before a firing squad. While he awaited execution, an earthquake destroyed the walls of his cell, and Dalton escaped, first to Mexico, then Europe. He discussed philosophy and the problems of socialism with numerous theoreticians, including French Latin American specialist Régis Debray,[108] who said that Dalton embodied the literary vanguard within the political vanguard.[109] In Prague he edited the Communist movement's *World Marxist Review*. He also traveled to North Korea and Vietnam, where he gained insights into the U.S.-sponsored destruction that would subsequently befall his Latin *compañeros* in their quest for freedom.

While living in Cuba in 1969, he, like Cayetano Carpio, broke with the Salvadoran Communist party, rejecting its "peaceful road" to socialism and intransigent Marxism. He adopted the Vietnamese concept of guerrilla insurrection as an integral part of "people's war" as espoused by No Nguyen Giap. Dalton never fully adopted the "prolonged popular war" concept of Cayetano Carpio and the Popular Liberation Forces, but he came close to it.[110]

The cosmopolitan Dalton had a talent for teaching, for conveying his political ideas, which appeared in over a dozen books of poetry and political essays. He understood his limitations and the contradictions that exist in all situations, and he realized that nothing political was black or white, that only shades of gray exist.[111] His blunt writings reveal an uncanny ability to make political distinctions and a sharp sense of humor. For instance, in a hotel in Cuba with Nicaraguan poet-priest Ernesto Cardenal, Dalton ordered a double rum on the rocks, but the drink did not come. Finally he told the waiter, "The Father asked for a drink some time ago, and he hasn't got it, and he is thirsty." When the drink arrived, Dalton noted that "there are still some remnants of clericalism in Cuba."[112] He always wrote with an eye on class relations, relations of production, exploitation, dependence, racism, and history.

After thirteen years in exile, Dalton turned from theory to praxis. He returned to El Salvador in 1973, joined the Revolutionary Army of the People (ERP), and became a second-rank leader who specialized in preparing analyses of Salvadoran society. He felt that the ERP should concentrate on building its political base rather than on military adventures. In 1975 the ERP split, and hard-liners in it, who opposed Dalton's emphasis on a political line, accused him of treason and even of being a CIA agent. They reasoned fallaciously that if he did not advocate immediate armed insurrection, he was undermining the movement on orders from the United States. Some ardent nationalists called him a Soviet or Cuban spy.[113] He was tried in absentia, found guilty, and assassinated by some of his followers who labeled him a right-wing revisionist. Although Dalton lost his life to the vicious sectarian infighting that has traditionally plagued the Left, his vision lived on through his art.

Dalton viewed El Salvador as a culturally impoverished area in which writers have generally been outsiders with no political clout, even when they have had high status in society. Writers have often been perceived as subversives and have met with violence. He claimed that one had difficulty finding a writer under forty who had not been pressured by the government or exiled from El Salvador.[114]

Despite the difficulties encountered by artists, Dalton felt that they had a great obligation to advance life, to create beauty with historic scope and social roots.[115] He concluded that the internal contradictions inherent in bourgeois art will ultimately cause it to disintegrate.[116] Thus the artist or intellectual must work to unify society, to understand its problems and find ways to overcome them, to further the antiimperialist struggle, and to clarify revolutionary ideas.

Dalton advocated using bourgeois culture against itself to change it. He supported Lenin's idea of using the valuable legacies of the past in building a new revolutionary culture.[117] He expressed considerable interest in relations between revolution and intellectuals and shared Gramsci's belief in the significant role of the intellectual in guiding societal development, in constructing a popular creative spirit and culture, and in understanding Marxism. To Dalton, intellectuals bridged the gap between the people and the bourgeois elites who shaped cultural policy and made the transition to socialism smoother by promoting understanding.[118]

Dalton sought a new Latin American intellectual revolutionary vanguard, one that would produce a vision for development. He noted that Salvadoran writers had not produced such a vision, that most twentieth-century writing in his country supported the system of U.S. dominance.[119] He believed that Salvadoran writers had to nourish themselves on the national reality, to help transform it, and to confer on the fragmented Salvadoran society the cultural characteristics and organic unity essential in good Marxist-Leninist methodology.[120] Like Gramsci, he advocated the use of literature as a guide to revolution. Dalton thought that writers must teach others how to think dialectically.[121]

Dalton followed his own advice and tried to educate his people through poetry, using five different pseudonyms in order to get his work published. In his poems, which he based on El Salvador's social history, he examined life in its complexities, not dwelling on shallow ideas or slogans, although he realized the usefulness of the latter as tools of mobilization.[122] His poems, with such wonderful titles as "On the Profit Margin, or the Boss Robs Every Worker Twice Over" and "Rhymes on National History," demonstrated Dalton's ingenuity, political irony, social conscience, Marxist ideology, revolutionary idealism, and social realism. Using rich, sensitive, yet subtle language, Dalton hoped to convey life in all of its intensity and to replace mean-spirited bourgeois thinking with socialist compassion.

As an historian, Dalton pursued the same objectives. He examined the past from a doctrinal perspective, as exemplified in his insightful monograph *El Salvador* (1963)[123] and in *Las historias prohibidas del pulgarcito* (1974, The forbidden tales of the little flea), in which he noted that since the time of the conquistadores one form or another of class-inspired guerrilla warfare has always existed in El Salvador. He also believed that a form of today's anticommunism has prevailed in El

Salvador since the eighteenth century, as those in charge, in order to attain greater power, have persecuted anybody they feared or did not like. Vast class distinctions, often based on race, have pervaded society from the colonial era to the present. From independence onward, *latifundismo* determined the relations of production. In the 1880s, when communal farms were formally dissolved, the "earth-eaters," or landowners, took over with their coffee monoculture.[124] Between 1913 and 1931, according to Dalton, El Salvador's exploited classes integrated their communitarian and revolutionary agrarian tradition with an antiimperialist vision reinforced by the Mexican and Russian revolutions and Sandino's exploits against the United States.[125] The 1920s constituted a transition era when new ideas emerged. Anarchy, trade unionism, Marxism, and the vaguely utopian thinking of Alberto Masferrer vied for adherents.[126]

Masferrer more than any Salvadoran intellectual received recognition for his opposition to social injustice and his dedication to democracy. In some ways, Dalton said, Masferrer was canonized as a national philosopher. In the prose piece "Old Shit," Dalton likens Masferrer to Argentina's nineteenth-century liberal writer President Domingo Sarmiento, who mistook the poor for savages. Masferrer preached a Christian form of turning the other cheek, chastity, anti-alcoholism, and the right to cleaner air and water and adequate housing and education. Essentially, as Martí and Cuenca noted, Masferrer advocated reform when El Salvador needed new methodology, policies, and action. Dalton saw Masferrer as sincere but also as a "holy idiot," an "exasperated great grandaddy," an accomplice of the exploiters, the harmless house critic, the acceptable voice of reform, one who naively believed he was responsible for the *matanza* and who died of melancholy, believing that he led people to their deaths.[127]

Dalton explained that "all Salvadorans who were born after 1932 were born half dead and half alive."[128] He interviewed witnesses to the *matanza* and characterized its horrors. Vivid accounts of the 1932 massacre are found in the reminiscences of Miguel Mármol, which Dalton wrote up as *Miguel Mármol: Los sucesos de 1932 en El Salvador* (1972, published in English as *Miguel Mármol*, 1987).[129] Dalton interviewed Mármol in Prague in 1966, then pieced together the latter's memoirs, a classic of the Central American Communist movement that has gone through twenty-two editions in Cuba.

According to his memoirs, Mármol (1905–), a shoemaker, helped found the Communist party in El Salvador. He helped organize and participated in the 1932 insurrection, was captured and shot, but escaped to Mexico. He returned, was recaptured by the government in 1934, spent two years in jail, then reorganized El Salvador's Communist party and was exiled to Guatemala, where he advised the Guatemalan Workers' Confederation during the Arévalo years.

Mármol examined the Central American movement for change from the early 1920s to the present, provided a history of the labor movement in El Salvador, and stressed the importance of the Communist party to it. He tended to read back into historical events ideas gained in later years. For example, Mármol often judged the 1920s by 1960s standards.[130] He admitted that he had not read *Das Kapital* or much theoretical material; he represented instead the visceral Marxist-Leninist, one with limited knowledge of world history, a word-of-mouth leftist whose ideas derive from experience.[131]

Mármol declared that in 1932 El Salvador's workers recognized the need for a bourgeois democratic revolution and for land redistribution. Because at that time foreign monopolies did not control land and property in El Salvador, the popular insurrection was purely national in character.[132]

Mármol called Dalton an intellectual and noted that such individuals, because of their theoretical training, are always more radical than workers.[133] Dalton's analyses, even of Mármol's thoughts, often appeared more radical than those of Mármol because of their greater depth and scope. Dalton knew where to probe and pursued his inquiries with Marxist methodology. His writings on the 1969 Soccer War contain solid examples of that scientific approach. He thought of the war as the culmination of the strains of capitalism in two dependent societies struggling to get ahead at the expense of each other. The war consolidated dictatorship in both nations, strengthened the power of monopolies, depleted the respective treasuries, channeled funds away from social programs and into arms purchases, and damaged the revolutionary Left in both countries.[134]

Dalton understood the complexities of U.S. intervention in Central America. He felt that the ability to hide imperialism behind the symbols of nationalism (flags, personalities, armies) while installing antinational systems accounted for U.S. successes.[135] The United States also gained control of Central America through the OAS, the CACM, and CONDECA. The United States created fascism in the region by building military and paramilitary forces to institute terror in the name of anticommunism.[136] The CIA and U.S. Agency for International Development (AID) manipulated the state and the population.[137] People disappeared; jails bulged with prisoners.

Cultural imperialism accompanied the U.S. military and political incursions. The United States strove to ensure that culture would not be contaminated by the people.[138] By controlling public culture and education, the imperialists and their allies prevented a national, and rebellious, spirit from developing. Dalton asked rhetorically why no one in the world knows Central American character. He commented that people know that Mexican culture exists, but subjugation has thwarted the emergence of Central American culture.[139]

Dalton viewed the importation of Yankee culture to Central America as part of a larger cold war strategy to divide the people, to separate the communists from the masses. Taking a page out of its Vietnam guidebook in order to control the countryside, the principal territory in dispute, the United States created strategic hamlets to subdue the population. In addition, the United States devised false democracy in El Salvador, built governmental structures around it, promulgated laws to support it, and created the fiction of legitimacy.[140]

Dalton said that the United States told its citizens that its interventions abroad protected their national interests. To gain public support the United States blamed all evil on the Soviet Union and never mentioned that all forms of socialism and all national liberation movements do not function alike ideologically or politically.[141] Dalton questioned how intelligent people could consider China's revolution as Soviet expansion, a notion derived from the idea that all Communist evil emanates from the Soviet empire.[142] Dalton inveighed against this culture of anticommunism and the violence that accompanied it in El Salvador, calling the Salvadoran conflict *la guerra especial* (the special war) in which the national government cannot control the insurgents and the United States intervenes to organize and finance the national army.

Dalton admired the way Cuba stood firm in the face of U.S. anticommunism. He identified with the Cuban Revolution, which he saw stimulating a new popular movement in El Salvador to combat the oligarchy, dictatorship, and U.S. imperialism.[143] Cuba imparted faith in progress and confidence in revolution. It demonstrated how to integrate the petit bourgeoisie into the class struggle, introduced revolutionary consciousness to the exploited classes, and helped solidify the worker-peasant alliance.[144] Dalton felt that the Cuban Revolution also purged writers of materialism and instilled in them the desire to write only for truth and beauty. He appreciated how the Cuban revolutionaries expected intellectuals to explain the revolution to others.[145] He liked the individuality that existed in the Cuban Revolution, which did not follow the patterns of collectivization and uniformity found in the Eastern European socialist states.[146] He also emphasized that Cuba's military revolution triumphed without Soviet assistance.[147]

Dalton did not construe revolution as an intellectual plaything but as a cataclysmic social, economic, and political upheaval that affects lives, and in his own life he embodied the theory and praxis vital to successful revolution.[148] He concurred with French professor Roger Garaudy that Marxism-Leninism allows one to think and live out the three great forces that move the world—humanism, scientific method, and proletarian revolution.[149]

Dalton translated his "critical" Marxist revolutionary ideas into terms Central Americans could comprehend and concluded that only through antifeudal, antiimperialist revolution could the region develop. He was committed to organizing the masses around a strategy of national resistance but contended that the struggle for Central America was regional and had to transcend national boundaries.[150] He advocated a "mass line," an antifascist front led by urban and rural workers joined by others.[151] Although he sought to learn from the errors of the past to prevent repeating them in the future, he understood that socialists, too, made mistakes and cited Stalinism as an example.[152] He believed that Vietnam presented a rich historical store from which to learn how to prepare for combat in El Salvador.[153] In his poem "Maneras de morir" (Ways of dying), he noted that the Chilean pacifists under Salvador Allende lost more than 30,000 of their comrades and asked, if the dead could speak, would they support armed struggle or electoral politics?[154]

Rafael Menjívar:
Capital Accumulation, Labor, and Land Reform

El Salvador's radical intellectual heritage primarily derives from Communist party members such as Martí, Cuenca, Cayetano Carpio, and Dalton and from the National University. No contemporary radical *pensador* better reflects academic traditions than Rafael "Lito" Menjívar (1936–), the Marxist economist and sociologist who served as dean of the faculty of economic science and as rector of the National University. From his university base, Menjívar branched out into the activist world. He became the major theoretician of El Salvador's Popular Revolutionary Bloc, founder of the Movement of Independent Professionals and Technicians, and a leader of the Democratic Revolutionary Front.

A practitioner of scientific social analysis, Menjívar's work on political economy reflects the influence of Marx, Lenin, Gramsci, and the historicism of Great Britain's Eric Hobsbawm and E. P. Thompson, who believe in large-scale laws of historical development. A vigorous empiricist and keen student of post–World War II Central America, he has, in "critical" Marxist fashion, developed new concepts and refined those of others. For example, he applied the dependency thinking of Theotonio dos Santos of Brazil and Peru's Aníbal Quijano to Central America. His books and articles are perhaps the most sophisticated on the Salvadoran left. James Dunkerley, a specialist on El Salvador, called him the heir to Roque Dalton,[155] one who surpassed his predecessor's level of analysis but lacked his poetic touch.

Class analysis pervades Menjívar's thinking. He has criticized most Salvadoran historians for not using it or for using a top-down approach in their writing. He noted that they generally write about oligarchies or bourgeoisies, and people appear in their works as amorphous masses manipulated by a *caudillo* or a populist movement. They usually interpret the actions of the dominant class and mention the contradictions between its factions. Menjívar deplored their lack of attention to the working class.[156]

In his writing, Menjívar emphasized, as did Karl Marx, the machinations of the capitalist system. He explored the concept of capital accumulation and concluded that the day that capitalists amass riches for the benefit of others, capitalism will no longer exist.[157] He found the history of capital accumulation in El Salvador to be consonant with that elsewhere in Latin America. Over the centuries, according to Menjívar, capitalist development has produced insoluble contradictions and made the Central American nations a weak link in the worldwide chain of imperialism. They constitute a point of compression, where the onerous contradictions of the past are added to the present contradictions of capitalism. Basically, a colonial or dependent situation exists and prevents the resolution of national questions.[158]

Menjívar noted that the church accumulated huge amounts of capital through bequests of land during the colonial period.[159] In the nineteenth century, these lands fell into the hands of private owners who increased capital and used force to procure inexpensive labor. As capital multiplied, its owners used it to build the infrastructure, exploit the mines, and acquire more capital.[160] Capital accumulated rapidly after 1864, when coffee expanded and the nation became an agricultural exporter. In Marxian terms, capitalism advanced with the expropriation of the lands of the small communal farms.[161] The separation of the majority of the people from the means of production (the land) initiated the modern market system in El Salvador. It also brought great social dislocation, as feudal and seigneurial ties abated.

During the second half of the nineteenth century, the rapid advance of the capitalist relations of production, the growth of the urban proletariat and the rural quasi proletariat, and a strengthened oligarchy caused class struggle.[162] At the end of the nineteenth century and during the early decades of the twentieth, European immigrants, some with money, accumulated more capital, stimulated the economy, and acquired coffee lands. Finance capital from Europe and the United States was invested in land.[163] By the 1920s and 1930s El Salvador was tied to international capital and hurt by the Depression. It had become an export-only nation, and capital fled. After World War II a new developmental model caused the production system to change. El Salvador's economy became more dependent on the outside world as coffee declined in importance and diversification occurred. A new, more sophisticated, less rural proletariat emerged, and the demand for reforms grew.[164] The CACM damaged import substitution but helped develop export industries. Modernization did not correspond to the good of society; rather, it exacerbated class tensions as the population resented being a spectator to, rather than a participant in, economic and political development.[165]

Menjívar found that modernization in El Salvador caused what economist André Gunder Frank called "the development of underdevelopment," which enabled a small sector of society to benefit at the expense of the majority, produced financial and public disequilibrium, and increased external debt. New, externally oriented technology deformed social reality and limited internal decisionmaking. The military kept the production process in line. Foreign political, social, and economic influence gained with the investment of additional capital in the nation, and external investment capital limited the development of the internal market.[166]

In addition to analyzing capital accumulation in El Salvador, Menjívar examined the role of organized labor there in the context of imperialism and the class struggle. He found that, fundamentally, organized labor had been tolerated but not permitted to flourish.[167] It has made few political advances and has not become an effective advocate of the working class, primarily because of its inability to incorporate or ally with the rural workers. Organized labor has not reached a political level commensurate with what Lenin and Gramsci referred to as the theory of syndicalism. In other words, organized labor has not transmitted protection to the working class or moved toward becoming a vanguard for the exploited classes, problems recognized by Georg Lukács in his *Geschichte und Klassenbewusstsein* (1923; *History and Class Consciousness,* 1967).[168] Workers' organizations have traditionally moved toward independence and away from state control.[169] Meanwhile, the state has not moved to educate the workers but rather to maintain their subservient position in the dependent economic system.

Menjívar's analysis of rural labor includes an examination of El Salvador's agrarian structure. Like most radicals, he has expressed considerable interest in land reform as a means to improve the human condition. He maintains that progress cannot occur without a better life for the peasants. Agrarian reform, he said, has always been a political question, as are all fundamental changes in the structure and organization of society. He rejects the idea, so often heard about in underdeveloped states, that agrarian reform is merely a matter of providing the proper technology.[170]

Ever since the liberal era of "Prussian agrarian reform," which brought the end of the communal lands, El Salvador has not produced sufficient basic foodstuffs, has not generated enough production of primary materials, and has not diversified its agricultural products.[171] Menjívar has searched for ways to rectify these weaknesses and to alter the agrarian and land tenure systems. In so doing he examined how agricultural organization in Latin America has been improved over the years. After his investigations, he challenged the standard notion of the peasantry as disinterested in revolutionary change and noted that as the rural working class has grown and as more peasants have become wage laborers, their potential for revolution has increased.

In *Reforma agraria: Guatemala—Bolivia—Cuba* (1969, Agrarian reform: Guatemala, Bolivia, Cuba), he discussed the capitalist reforms that never fully materialized in Bolivia in the 1950s and 1960s and in Guatemala in the 1950s and the socialist revolution that succeeded in Cuba. Bolivia's agrarian reform movement started to develop the economy, provided temporary social justice, and provided diversification. But Bolivia's reforms were not implemented with sufficient care and organization to ensure their institutionalization.[172] Guatemala's agrarian reforms began to undo injustice, made the people a force for change, gave the masses a taste for democracy that has endured, and touched off the U.S. fear of expropriations, which led to counterrevolution.[173] Menjívar pointed out that Cuba built cooperative organizations, maintained unity in the face of expropriations, and restructured its economic system. Cuba demonstrated the need to tailor the size of landholdings to make them efficient and to strike a balance between centralization and local operations. The problems that the Cuban Revolution experienced because of the U.S.-sponsored economic boycott showed the need for diversification and native technology and the importance of careful planning to best integrate the economy into international market systems. Menjívar stated that, most significantly, Cuba proved that agrarian revolution elevates the level of life for the masses, fosters overall economic development, and builds political support for the government.[174]

Menjívar contends that the United States has long endeavored to thwart revolution, agrarian or political, in the Americas, which it fears would undermine its power—and its profits—in the region. He is conversant with the historical evolution of the U.S. policy, beginning with the Monroe Doctrine, of establishing hegemony in Central America. He understands how the Panama Canal became a major factor, or excuse, to buttress U.S. interests in the region.[175] He supports Latin America's traditional policies of nonintervention and self-determination and realizes that the U.S. has continuously fabricated the existence of a Soviet threat in the area to justify its violation of those principles of inter-American

After decades of elite rule without strongly institutionalized political parties (except possibly the Communist party), Rafael Angel Calderón Guardia was elected president in 1940. He sought new labor laws and a social security system and openly courted Communist support. In so doing, he antagonized the major owners of the means of production and stimulated anticommunism. The nation's embryonic social democratic movement allied with the property holders to oppose Calderón and the Communists.[33]

Communist labor leadership grew on United Fruit plantations and in the cities, and the Banana Workers' Federation (formerly the Banana Workers' Union) helped establish the Confederation of Costa Rican Workers, an affiliate of the hemisphere-wide, left-wing CTAL. At the same time, Father Benjamín Nuñez founded a rival group, the non-Communist Confederation of Costa Rican Workers, "Rerum Novarum," a nonreligious union organization.[34]

During World War II, as Western democracies allied with the Soviet Union, Costa Rica's Communist party gained strength, and to make the movement more palatable to others on the Left, in 1943 it changed its name to Vanguardia Popular (Popular Vanguard) and softened its approach. The group's platform no longer mentioned class struggle or nationalization of the means of production. It called for limited agrarian reforms, economic development, and collaboration with the United States in the prosecution of the war.[35] Its leader, Manuel Mora, warned against the spread of U.S. economic influence in Costa Rica as a result of the war and simultaneously vehemently opposed fascism. During the war the Popular Vanguard was held in such high esteem that even the church did not object to Catholics' joining it.

When World War II ended, the Costa Rican government followed the lead of the United States in building antipathy for the Soviet Union. But the appeal of Communism expanded among Costa Rica's rural workers, as the war had pushed the economy further into the U.S. camp, fruit companies expanded, and small landholders found themselves dispossessed.[36] According to radical analyst Cerdas Cruz, postwar industrialization also created a new urban working class that responded favorably to leftist ideas during times of economic uncertainty. Fearing the political ascendency of the Communists, *Acción Democrática*, the organ of the Social Democratic party, in 1946 promoted the idea that the Communists were not Costa Ricans, even though they were native-born.[37]

President Calderón stood for reelection in 1948 and was defeated by Otilio Ulate. Calderón's backers, including right-wingers and Communists, revolted to prevent Ulate from taking office. Social democrat José "Pepe" Figueres raised an army to combat the *Calderonistas*. Civil war law. He finds U.S. anticommunism abhorrent and sees that it has increased since the United States lost some of its control in Latin America after the Cuban Revolution. He also notes that the Cuban model forced the United States to support capitalist reform during the early 1960s to quell some dissent and views the Alliance for Progress as a response to the Cuban Revolution, a way to place credits at the disposal of the Latin American nations and keep them linked to the U.S. economic system.[176]

According to Menjívar, between 1966 and 1968 there began a structural crisis in the world capitalist system of a magnitude unheard of since the 1930s. It reached its climax in 1978–1979, when revolutions erupted in Nicaragua and El Salvador. The United States, in the wake of the loss of the Vietnam War and the failure of the CACM, began to militarize Central America. Washington forced on the region the plan conceived by the University of Chicago School of Economics, which included the austerity programs of the International Monetary Fund that stabilize economies in favor of the wealthy, hurt the middle and lower sectors, and further exploit the workers.[177]

Menjívar concluded that the United States prefers quick solutions with little loss of life, such as it sought when it invaded the Dominican Republic in 1965 or Grenada in 1983, to a protracted Vietnam situation in which thousands die. He stated that if the United States counts El Salvador as a regional problem instead of a local one (as in the Dominican Republic), it will lead to a situation like the one in Vietnam.[178] The evaluations by this sagacious "critical" Marxist social scientist have generally been correct. To date, the United States has used what it calls "low-intensity conflict": Hesitating to embark upon a full-scale invasion of El Salvador, it has built up the Salvadoran military and attempted to defeat the revolutionaries from within, a long-term process that will probably fail.

Menjívar believes that ultimately Latin America must solve its own problems and not abide by U.S. solutions. He understands that anticommunist propaganda has made some people believe that by driving the dominant United States out of Central America, dependence on the capitalist system is replaced by dependence on the Soviet system. He and his fellow Salvadoran radicals, Agustín Farabundo Martí, Abel Cuenca, Salvador Cayetano Carpio, and Roque Dalton, have always defended the integrity of Salvadoran sovereignty and have maintained that the people of Latin America are free to deal with the Soviet Union or the United States, but they reject intervention by, or subservience to, either one. Although Salvadoran radical thought owes much to the Communist party that nurtured and sustained it from the 1920s to the 1970s, in recent decades the nation's leading leftist thinkers, including those who broke with the party, such as Roque Dalton and Salvador Cayetano Carpio, have often rejected Soviet policies in favor of a more independent Marxist approach to the country's problems.

The current generation of Salvadoran radical thinkers exhibits far more sophistication than its predecessors and much greater ability to communicate with, teach, and appeal to its fellow citizens. A quarter of a century ago, Abel Cuenca, one of the most insightful Salvadoran writers of his day, noted that his people had more confidence in human beings than in ideas. That situation no longer pertains. Thanks to the efforts of intellectuals such as Dalton and Menjívar, many more Salvadorans have come to understand liberalism and social democracy as tendencies that have co-opted the struggle for popular liberation. Marxist principles, originally articulated by Martí and Cuenca, improved upon by Cayetano Carpio, and refined by radicals such as Dalton and Menjívar, are now more influential in El Salvador than they were in Nicaragua prior to the Sandinista-led victory of 1979 or in Chile at the time of Salvador Allende's election in 1970.

4

Honduras

In Honduras a mule costs more than a congressman.
—Sam ("The Banana Man") Zemurray

Among the Central American republics, Honduras is the poorest and the least developed. Subsequent pages show a direct correlation between the nation's economic and political backwardness and its lack of intellectual development. Internal cohesion did not exist in the country until the twentieth century, and, unlike other Latin American states, Honduras had no powerful native oligarchy until the late 1950s.

Honduras is primarily a mestizo country in which 80 percent of the rural lower classes are subsistence farmers or landless squatters, and the lower class accounts for two-thirds of the population. It has no politically dominant landowning aristocracy in comparison to other Latin American nations, but 38 percent of the land is held by less than 1 percent of the people. It has a tiny urban proletariat and a low level of education.

Contemporary conditions derive from the colonial era, when the Spanish maintained a separation of classes and formed a racially based caste system. The conquerors never subjugated the regional bosses, thus each province developed its own identity, and separation rather than unity prevailed. The colony's economy, based on mining and indigo for the English textile industry, hardly flourished. Economically, socially, and culturally the nation remained a backwater throughout its history: after it opted for independence in 1812, when it was annexed to Mexico from 1821 to 1823, while it functioned as part of the Central American confederation between 1824 and 1838, and after it became a separate republic in 1838. No strong centralized state developed, peasants occupied their ancestral lands, and, unlike elsewhere in Central America, no need existed for a military to keep them in line. A strong native capitalist sector never counterbalanced the power of foreign economic interests during the nineteenth century.

Between 1821 and 1876, eighty-five presidents ruled the nation. Its most famous leader, Francisco Morazán, unified Central America during the late 1820s and the 1830s. Cultural life developed slowly in Honduras. The country's first newspaper was published in 1829, but a daily newspaper did not appear until sixty years later. In 1845 Franciscan priest and poet José Trinidad Reyes founded the Society of the Spirit of Enterprise and Good Taste along with a school in Tegucigalpa, the Academia Literaria. Two years later the government upgraded the school to university status, and it subsequently became the University of Honduras. The university followed the classic Spanish model, which concentrated on theology, with subsidiary programs in law, medicine, and the humanities. Conventional, not radical, thought pervaded the university and the country.

Liberal reforms during the 1870s and 1880s, based on the assumption that the pursuit of property by individuals, with minimum state regulation, benefits all of society, led to the investment of foreign monopoly capital,[1] which drained resources from the country. In the midst of this liberal reform era, as a result of President Marco Aurelio Soto's (1876–1883) endeavors to improve education, Honduras opened its National Library in 1880 and produced its first historical writing.

Most of Honduras's liberal educational and ecclesiastical reforms were enacted by Minister of State Ramón Rosa (1848–1893), a close friend of president Soto. In 1880 Rosa, a major nineteenth-century thinker, wrote the *Social Constitution of Honduras*, a work that exhibited traits of revolutionary liberalism and positivism. Rosa believed that societies live, grow, and perfect themselves under the influence of ideas. He understood that liberalism had failed to make social progress in Honduras but maintained his faith in progress and continued to encourage the state to intervene to foster social justice. Rosa blamed egotism for underdevelopment and felt that self-centered rulers displayed a lack of caring for others and disinterest in eliminating evil social conditions. He advocated a program of radical, government-controlled reforms. He claimed "we cannot believe that this country, so rich in resources and intelligence, could be, like Homer's Hector, condemned to the most tragic destiny."[2] To avoid that tragedy he advocated building a new progressive political party, predicated on Honduran ethics, not foreign models. The party would effect justice by fostering education, opposing the privileged classes, and favoring equal rights and benefits for all. Rosa contended that his country had no great traditions, no powerful church, no rich families, and no literary life or public spirit. But it had reactionaries and demagogues who retarded social, political, economic, and intellectual development.[3] In his own elitist and paternalistic, but nevertheless radical fashion for his day, Rosa sought to improve Honduran life.

In 1890, urban artisans and workers in light industry formed Honduras's first mutualist organization, La Democracia. By the turn of the century, Honduras had granted its first banana land concessions to the Vacarro brothers from the United States, who later turned their business into the Standard Fruit Company. Honduras's dependency increased as the country found itself in the neocolonial position described by Communist thinker Longino Becerra. At the same time, new, relatively stable political parties formed. Economic, political, and labor foundations for the twentieth century began to develop.

As the nation matured, new scholarly interest arose in the fields of history and politics. Honduras established Central America's first historical review in 1904. It lasted for five years and became the forerunner of the organ of the Honduran Society of Geography and History, formed in 1927. The realism of Leo Tolstoy and the anarchism of Peter Kropotkin, Enrico Malatesta, and Mikhail Bakunin reached the nation, and a few Honduran *pensadores* debated the contradictions between anarchy and Christianity. Native Christian thinkers tried to reconcile their religion with anarchism, whereas dedicated anarchists insisted that the incompatibilities between the two types of thinking were insurmountable.[4]

During these early years of the twentieth century, U.S. financiers assumed the servicing of Honduras's European debts. In 1907 U.S. merchant Sam Zemurray formed the Cuyamel Fruit Company. Banana plantations boomed, and by 1910 80 percent of all banana land fell under the control of U.S. proprietors. The Standard Fruit Company (Castle and Cook), the Cuyamel Company, the Tela Railroad Company (United Fruit, the largest employer in the country), and the Banco Atlantica (Chase Manhattan) ruled supreme in Honduras.[5] The banana enclave neutralized the native bourgeoisie and depleted the land and the labor force that might have been used for industrialization.

After 1912 one could barely distinguish between the politics of Honduras and those of the fruit companies. The Cuyamel firm had close ties to the Liberal party, and the Tela Railroad Company had links to the National party. The companies discouraged radical union activity, as did the political parties. The nation's literature reflected the desire of the companies and the political parties to avoid controversial ideological debates. The Ateneo de Honduras, the country's literary association, founded in 1913, also avoided discourses on radical themes.

Despite attempts by those in control of the nation's economy and politics to avoid radicalism, trade union sentiment developed. In 1916 workers struck at the Cuyamel plantations. To block the development of a left-wing trade union movement, the AF of L in 1918 advanced an anticommunist workers' program for Honduras, one that functioned within the boundaries of capitalism.[6] By the 1920s the United States had dispatched troops to Honduras six times to protect the $40 million its private corporations, primarily fruit companies, had invested there.[7] The fruit companies propagated a fear of communism, which hindered the passage of prolabor legislation until the 1950s.

Mutual benefit societies, organized around the shoemakers, railroad workers, and carpenters, enlisted about 6,000 nonmilitant workers who banded together to build working-class consciousness in the 1920s. They focused their attention on providing health and death benefits to workers' families and also promoted cultural activities. In 1921 the mutual aid societies united into the Federation of Honduran Workers, which had a strong nationalist, prochurch, and anticommunist program that emphasized class cooperation.[8] Nevertheless, for a predominantly agrarian country, Honduras had a relatively progressive labor movement, one that included some Communist sympathizers and would subsequently be the focus of attention of the country's radical writers.

As a result of the workers' movement, in 1923 leftist-oriented women, led by radical writer-activist Graciela García, established the Sociedad Cultura Feminina (Women's Culture Society), which organized a school for adults, founded a library, operated four literacy centers, and tried to prepare women to struggle for democracy. In 1927, other radicals formed the Communist party of Honduras, which operated on democratic centralist principles and lasted until dictator Tiburcio Carías Andino (1932–1949) destroyed it in 1932. Juan Pablo Wainwright, the son of an English father and Honduran mother, led the Communist party, composed in its early stages primarily of banana and railroad workers. In 1929 the Communists established their own labor organization, the Honduran Union Federation, led by Abraham Ramírez and F. Armando Anaya.[9] The same year, the United Fruit Company purchased the Cuyamel organization from Zemurray for $32 million. According to professor Víctor Meza, by the end of the 1920s owners of the fruit lands and their benefactors in the government, more fearful than ever of the spread of socialism, organized to combat leftist activity in the country.

By the 1930s, the banana enclave contained the best land in the country and controlled much of the available labor. This situation precluded the development of many other sectors of the economy. The United Fruit Company put Carías Andino in power, and during his tenure, to some extent, the institutions and infrastructure of modernity were constructed. He promoted the production of bananas and coffee while crushing the Communist party and its labor affiliates.

Carías failed to eradicate all radical intellectual opposition to his regime and to monopoly capitalism. For instance, Gustavo A. Castañeda, author of *El general Domingo Vázquez y su tiempo* (1934, General Domingo Vázquez and his times), wrote about the sovereignty of the Honduran people and their inability to shape their ideology. He saw Honduras led by special interests that opposed the collective good and maintained that liberalism would eventually lead to socialism or progressive ideas, possibly even to the abolition of private property—the last bulwark of powerful conservatism. Castañeda thought that industry should not be the property of dominant foreign powers, that economic dependence limited national sovereignty. He also worried about the exploitation of workers in a society devoid of mechanization.[10]

Castañeda and a handful of Honduran intellectuals struggled against the dictatorship of Carías, which they claimed was supported by the United States during the Good Neighbor era in order to safeguard North American interests. To prevent anticapitalist dissent and appease the United States, Carías enacted an anticommunist law in 1946 that drove the party underground and isolated it from the workers.[11] But two years later, a Communist front organization, the Honduran Democratic Revolutionary party, openly recruited members from the working class.

From the 1950s until the present, the story of the banana enclave, with its attendant themes of peasant problems, trade unionism, socialism versus capitalism, and the consequences of imperialism, would dominate the writing of an emerging generation of radical intellectuals. Thinkers like Longino Becerra, Mario Posas, and Víctor Meza would emphasize the aforementioned topics in their historically oriented books and articles.

Juan Manuel Gálvez, a lawyer for the United Fruit Company, succeeded Carías as president for the 1949–1954 term. During the new administration, a peasant cooperativist movement, composed of voluntary associations for mutual economic and social assistance, took hold in Honduras. Under the direction of Jorge St. Siegens, the movement contained 369 cooperatives and 53,000 members by 1975. The cooperativists, who recognized private property, wanted to share in governmental decisionmaking. They envisioned themselves engaged in a battle to promote public welfare, and they created a spirit of solidarity among workers who wanted to participate in national social planning.[12]

Cooperativism, with roots in Sparta, also has antecedents in ancient Asia and pre-Columbian Latin America. It developed in Europe during the Middle Ages as a result of trade guilds, and during the Renaissance cooperativists replaced medieval thought with humanism. Thanks to the commercial revolution, the European forms of cooperativism reached the New World and its supporters became participants in, but not necessarily formal advocates of, the class struggle.

The industrial revolution created new ways of life and work and introduced machines to produce consumer goods. Riches were expressed in terms of capital and capital goods, as well as land. A new bourgeoisie developed as the dominant class in Honduras and was the major possessor of money. Paternalistic obligations to workers no longer existed as they did in feudal times. The proletariat grew, as did contradictions within bourgeois capitalism, and the struggle to defend workers' rights fostered cooperativism, which became a significant element among the banana workers.[13]

Cooperativism gained ground simultaneously with the development of industry in Honduras. Over 70 percent of the country's largest firms were established between 1950 and 1968, and workers increasingly united. Multinational corporations, based in the United States, brought modernization and economic diversification to the country in the 1950s. The nation's infrastructure expanded thanks to an infusion of U.S. capital. Vigorous labor and peasant organizations emerged. The essence of socialist radicalism in Honduras evolved from the labor movement, despite U.S. efforts to keep the unions oriented to capitalist constructs.

The Organización Regional Interamericana de Trabajadores (ORIT, or the Inter-American Regional Organization of Workers), tied to the AF of L and coordinated by the State Department through labor attachés stationed in the U.S. embassy in Tegucigalpa, pushed what it called "democratic trade unionism" based on the idea that technically labor remains out of politics but that there exists a fundamental accord between labor and capital. ORIT backed U.S. businesses and operated on the premise that U.S. policy was paramount in Latin America, and certainly more important than the interests of the workers.[14] Later in this chapter, radical professor Mario Posas analyzes how ORIT worked and influenced Honduras's major labor organization.

The Communist party of Honduras, which reorganized in 1954, opposed ORIT and championed the interests of the workers, particularly those in the rural sector and on United Fruit plantations. The government immediately labeled all dissidents, including liberals, "Communists."[15]

Communist party organizers helped build the banana workers' union in 1954. The banana workers' strike of that year became the most significant event in the history of Honduras's working class. The paralyzing sixty-nine-day event radicalized many workers and led to the legalization of numerous unions and to the passage of new labor legislation.[16] As a result of the strike, the military became wary of the potential power of an organized working class, viewed neighboring Guatemala under the pro-union government of Jacobo Arbenz as a threat, and let Honduran bases be used by the counterrevolutionaries who overthrew the Guatemalan government. The U.S. government dispatched AFL-CIO mediators to Honduras. They broke the strike and eventually imposed a conservative anticommunist trade union movement on Honduras, one controlled by ORIT and later by AIFLD. (The purpose and functions of AIFLD are explained in the introduction to the preceding chapter.) Washington organized labor training courses for Hondurans at the University of Puerto Rico and in the United States. Those who attended became labor leaders under ORIT control. Eventually the United States considered the "controlled" Honduran labor situation a model for other Latin American nations.[17]

The 1954 strike constituted a conditional victory for labor and made it an interest group worthy of note. Government and private enterprises recognized the fruit company unions, which represented 160,000 workers. The right to strike and to bargain collectively became a reality, a labor code was enacted, and minimum-wage legislation was passed. The strike also led to the outlawing of the Communist party in 1955, to the formation of the National Agrarian Institute in 1961, and to the passage of agrarian reform legislation in 1962, which provided for the parceling out of land to peasants. Of greater significance, the strike caused the fruit companies to reduce their holdings and labor force in the nation and to rely more on contracted local producers for bananas. Radical writers García, Posas, and Meza contend that the 1954 strike provided important gains for the labor movement and simultaneously intensified the efforts of Honduran businesspeople and the United States to prevent trade unions from promoting socialism.

The Honduran armed forces seized power in 1956 and have maintained it ever since, except during the presidency of Liberal Ramón Villeda Morales (1957–1963), when Honduras experienced democracy for the first time. In the absence of a strong national political elite, the military was able, as a result of a 1957 constitutional provision, to eliminate civilian control over its functions.[18] By the time Fidel Castro attained power in Cuba in 1959, the Honduran military was in a strategic position to thwart all attempts to organize for social change. U.S. support for military control of Honduras increased.[19] At the same time, activists, such as Graciela García, pointed out that the Cuban experience proved that peasants, proletarians, and liberal members of the bourgeoisie, working in concert, can effect social and economic revolution.

The military and the multinational interests effectively repressed progressive political, economic, and social action but did not completely stifle intellectual dissent. A few brave radical writers called attention to the plight of Honduras. Noteworthy among them was Ramón Amaya Amador (1916–1966), whose opposition to dictator Carías, expressed in the weekly publication *Alerta* (dedicated to the defense of the banana workers), had landed him in jail and then in exile in Guatemala in the 1940s. In

Guatemala City Amaya Amador studied scientific socialism and launched his career as a novelist with *Prisión verde* (1950, Green prison), which depicted the horrors of human exploitation on U.S.-owned banana plantations in Central America. An amnesty allowed Amaya Amador to return to Honduras in 1957, whereupon he did newspaper work and wrote two more novels. He founded the leftist journal *Revista Internacional* and joined the Communist party of Honduras. An honest social historian, he wrote articles on Marxism-Leninism for the magazine *Problems of Peace and Socialism*. He stressed that Costa Rican–style social democracy could not liberate a people, and he advocated the building of a revolutionary vanguard to lead the way to national sovereignty and democracy.[20] A superb essayist, poet, and analyst of Honduras's working class, Amaya Amador publicized the nightmarish consequences of underdevelopment and of his country's repressive neocolonial state. He placed the blame on U.S. imperialism,[21] which he found curious in light of the U.S. claim of involvement in World War II to preserve democratic freedoms and defeat tyranny.[22] He demonstrated the effects of imperialism in his novel *Destacamento rojo* (1962, Red station), which examined the 1954 banana strike, the founding of the Honduran Communist party, and the struggle against ultraconservatism.

The writings of Amaya Amador became popular among disenchanted Hondurans during the 1960s. By this time, AIFLD controlled the nation's trade unions. The Central American Common Market enabled U.S. capital to obtain local businesses and dominate new areas of investment, and the banana companies began to expand in the manufacturing sector.[23] The Honduran military protected foreign investments. In 1961 the National Federation of Honduran Peasants, a quasi-radical organization, responded to inequities in society caused by foreign domination by organizing in the north, especially among the tenants on banana company lands. In 1962 the Association of Honduran Peasants formed, and its members participated in strikes and land occupations. Syndicalism grew rapidly among the peasantry, and at least six unions existed. Two groups calling themselves the Communist party of Honduras emerged during the 1960s. One favored a traditional pro-Soviet stance and sought peaceful revolution. Its ideology is explained on subsequent pages by its major theoretician, Longino Becerra. The other Communist party opted for armed struggle. At the same time, radical religious activists began to work among the peasants.

In response to the radicals' drive for modernization, the Honduran power brokers, under President (Colonel) Oswaldo López Arellano (1963–1971 and 1972–1975), tried to coopt them by enacting small-scale land reforms, a move that paid dividends. Although in other Central American countries the landowners' attempts to prevent modernization gave rise to guerrilla movements, in Honduras government sops to the people who demanded change staved off radical action.

The hundred-hour Soccer War of 1969 between Honduras and El Salvador (examined in the previous chapter) led to the withdrawal of Honduras from the CACM, about which the Honduran government complained that it did not receive a fair share of benefits. Honduras's withdrawal contributed to the organization's demise. The war also caused a split in the nation's elite, as the landholders, who did not want to compete with industry for labor, opposed the industrialists who brought new businesses to the country. The war also demonstrated the ineptitude of Honduras's corrupt military, which was saved from total defeat by the intervention of the OAS and thereafter bolstered by U.S. assistance.

Young, professional military officers agitated for and managed to implement limited agricultural and industrial reforms during the 1960s. The military hoped that such palliatives would curtail peasant militancy. New laws led to the breakup of unproductive landholdings, which were replaced by more efficient farms and labor-intensive cooperatives. These changes hurt the oligarchy but not the capitalist system.[24]

Despite the government's land reforms, peasant protests continued during the 1970s and often provoked violent reactions. Noteworthy were the events of June 25, 1975, at Juticalpa, where five peasant leaders en route to Tegucigalpa to protest delays in implementation of land distributions were massacred by the military acting in concert with cattle ranchers. The bodies of nine other protestors were subsequently found nearby. These incidents led the church, fearful of further violence, to reduce its support for radical social change.

The receptivity of the government to change during the 1970s led scholars at the National University to conduct the first serious scientific studies of Honduran society. In particular, academicians with radical proclivities began in-depth analyses of the transnational fruit companies that had been major protagonists in Honduras's economic and political life. These studies emphasized the evolution of the fruit company–military–U.S. alliance. Works such as Enrique Flores Valeriano's *La explotación bananera en Honduras: Capítulos de deshonor nacional* (1979, The development of banana production in Honduras: Chapters in national dishonor) exemplified the new trend in radical inquiry.[25]

Radical politics made some headway during the 1970s. The pro-Moscow Communist party of Honduras continued to win favor, especially among banana plantation workers. A small Maoist group calling itself the Communist Party of Honduras–Marxist-Leninist gained influence in the teachers' unions. In 1975, dissidents from the Christian Democratic party established the Socialist Party of Honduras, which promoted confrontations in rural areas. After the Sandinista victory in Nicaragua, six guerrilla-oriented revolutionary groups—the Cinchoneros (or Popular Liberation Movement), the Morazanist Front for the Liberation of Honduras, the People's Revolutionary Union, the Padre Ivan Betancourt Revolutionary Command, the American Workers' Revolutionary party, and the Lorenzo Zelaya Popular Revolutionary Front—periodically made headlines but had no mass base of support.[26]

With the rise of radicalism in Central America and mild revolutionary rumblings in Honduras, the fruit companies anticipated serious problems and continued to alter their policies. They returned land to the peasants, which fostered fruit-growing peasant cooperatives. The cooperatives provided the workers with some improved housing and social services and sold their products to the fruit companies, which were delighted to clean up their image by being free of labor disputes. Despite the fruit companies' fear of the revolutionary potential of the peasantry, Longino Becerra contends that unsophisticated peasants with their primarily local orientation cannot become the core of revolution in Honduras, and Mario Posas doubts the capacity of the peasantry to mobilize and attain political power.

The Carter administration set the agenda for Honduras's geopolitical role in Central America when it decided in 1979 that Honduras would replace Somoza's Nicaragua as a deputy in policing the Americas. Honduras's common boundaries with Guatemala, El Salvador, and Nicaragua made it a logical site for a command post for U.S. operations to destabilize Nicaragua and oppose El Salvador's revolutionaries. The United States built military and counterinsurgency bases in Honduras and began to train counterrevolutionaries (*contras*) there.

U.S. dollars flowed into the country when its popular movement was weak and its two-party political system corrupt and there existed no national industrial group capable of pushing for economic independence. By the 1980s, U.S. capital controlled 82 percent of the production of the fifty largest Honduran firms, its economy stagnated, working conditions deteriorated, the suffering of workers increased, freedom of expression eroded, and no progressive element appeared capable of leading the battle against the national security doctrine imposed by the United States.[27] The economic and ideological origins of this U.S. policy are explored and placed in a Central American context by Becerra and Meza.

Since World War II, compromise and co-optation have been the preferred mechanisms for conflict resolution in Honduras. Although class antagonisms have precipitated violent conflict in Guatemala, El Salvador, and Nicaragua, Honduras, as the result of underdevelopment, meager reforms, and military repression, has remained less socially explosive. Some liberal analysts attribute the comparative lack of institutional violence to a late-developing and more flexible ruling class, whereas others say that the nation is simply so poor that there is less to conserve or fight about. Today, under President Rafael Callejas, elected for the 1990–1994 term, the country is a de facto U.S. protectorate without social justice. Its well-organized but deeply divided labor and peasant movements still fight for their rights when they can, but their members vote for the conservative Liberal and National parties.

Honduras's weak, fragmented, and outlawed Marxist political parties cannot counter the established authorities, fail to adequately explain the country's economic and social plight to the people, and do not furnish effective platforms for labor's struggles.[28] Later in this chapter, Becerra examines various Marxist views that have not won many converts in Honduras, and Meza maintains that the answers to Honduras's problems might be found in left-wing, non-Marxist nationalism.

Since the United States moved to make Honduras a regional linchpin, the Honduran government has sought to eliminate progressive political elements and stamp out dissent. The army has cracked down on the Honduran Workers' Federation and the Christian Democratic General Workers' Confederation and has wiped out substantial segments of the country's various revolutionary movements and of the two Communist parties and the Socialist party. By the beginning of the 1990s, members of seven socialist political parties or revolutionary movements worked clandestinely in the nation, and latent potential for revolution still existed. But radical thinkers maintained low profiles in Honduras.

Graciela A. García:
Feminist Revolutionary

Machismo and fear of excessive influence by the church upon women prevented them from attaining prominent positions in Latin America's political and intellectual life until rather recently. For example, no woman qualified for inclusion among the fifty-five outstanding writers I examined in *Marxist Thought in Latin America* (1984), which excluded Central America and dealt only with established *pensadores* over the age of fifty.

Graciela García (1896–) is a rarity among Latin America's radical writers of her time: a female who gained some international prominence. By birth she was an upper-class Salvadoran, but one whose heart belonged to the working class of all of Central America and whose soul is claimed by Honduras. She spent her early years in her native land and obtained a degree in primary education from a normal school there. She then moved to Honduras, where she lived for over twenty years and had substantial political impact for over half a century.

In Honduras in 1922 she joined the first Marxist circle and displayed some advanced ideas in her numerous articles in *El trabajador Hondureño*

(The Honduran worker), the organ of the Honduran Federation of Labor, and in the newspapers *El Cronista* (The chronicler) and *El Día* (The day). She worked as a schoolteacher and as an activist-writer. Although not an original thinker, she contributed significantly to the socialist movement in Central America. The best expression of her revolutionary views, as recounted on succeeding pages, can be found in her *En las trincheras de la lucha por socialismo* (1975, In the trenches of the struggle for socialism).

García understood Central America's left wing, knew the history of the labor movement and that of the Communist party of each Central American republic, and was respected as a Communist leader of the entire region. Throughout her life she held to the romantic belief that Central America would someday fulfill the progressive dreams of Simón Bolívar and Karl Marx.

García wrote largely from memory because she had few archives to consult, and she did not use rigorous methodology. She explained the significance of women's movements in Central America in a very general way, but she made the important point that without female participation a valid workers' movement could not exist.[29] It is interesting to note that her early writings on politics and women's issues were sometimes rigid, generally militant, and Marxist-Leninist, those of her middle years fell into the "critical" Marxist category, whereas those of her later years at times displayed social democratic characteristics.

Her *Personalidades célebres de América: Ensayos biográficos* (1964, Famous American personalities: Biographical essays), which tended to be factual rather than critical, centered on people she thought contributed to independence or progress.[30] Among those from the United States, she included George Washington, Benjamin Franklin, Abraham Lincoln, Franklin Roosevelt, and Walt Whitman, whom she called a humanist "bard of democracy."[31] Among the Latin Americans in her collection were Francisco Morazán, the Honduran who worked for Central American union in the nineteenth century, and the area's outstanding liberals such as Bolívar and the Mexican Benito Juárez. She identified with Nicaragua's antiimperialist poet Rubén Darío, Cuban Marxist essayist Julio Antonio Mella, Cuba's independence leaders Carlos Manuel de Cespedes, Antonio Maceo, and José Martí, and El Salvador's Agustín Farabundo Martí. She respected the vital minimum doctrine of El Salvador's Alberto Masferrer, whom she admired for his creativity and incorrectly labeled a revolutionary.[32]

To her, Mexico's Revolution of 1910 was part of a bourgeois democratic movement that destroyed land monopolies, established democratic government, raised the cultural level of the masses, and emancipated the nation from imperialist tutelage. She had high praise for Emiliano Zapata, the Mexican peasant leader who carried out agrarian reforms.[33] She depicted Augusto Sandino as a symbol of patriotism and progressivism, an antiimperialist whose actions against the U.S. invader in Nicaragua united Latin American liberals, radicals, students, and intellectuals[34] and demonstrated that you could stand up to U.S. intervention.[35] She considered her friend Mexican philosopher and labor leader Vicente Lombardo Toledano, a man who devoted his life to turning the Mexican Revolution to the left from within, a major progressive force and revolutionary thinker, one who brought democracy and the ideology of Marx to the working classes.[36]

García enrolled in the trade union and revolutionary movements in Honduras in 1922 and began to organize the working class in the most exploited zones of the nation, the mining areas of San Juancito and the banana lands of the north coast.[37] She felt that women bore the crosses of martyrs, especially under capitalism, under which the struggle for equality with men never made much progress. García believed that proletarian women in particular were exploited in Central America, and that only when women could sell their labor did they become able to more fully participate in the struggle for change. She fought actively for these principles until she was in her eighties.[38] Linking the concept of emancipation of women to the idea of equality and respect for human rights. García insisted that women had to be accorded equality, in terms of the relations of production, to have their rights properly respected.[39] To her, feminism meant the rejection of exploitation, and because capitalism thrived on one form of exploitation or another, only socialism could bring equality of the sexes. The true feminist thus had to be a socialist.

In 1923 García helped establish, then served as secretary general of, the Women's Culture Society in Tegucigalpa, which was part of the Honduran Federation of Workers. She founded and directed the Women's Culture School for female workers, ran a seminar on women's problems,[40] and started a night school for adults that offered classes in Spanish, civics, handicrafts, mathematics, and the social sciences. She published the magazine *Women's Culture*, which stressed the social injustices befalling workers and their families in the mining and banana districts, and she opposed dictatorship.[41] García also provided inspiration for the little-known women's labor group La Mujer Hondureña (The Honduran Woman) established in 1929.

With her Communist party comrades, García encouraged women to organize and led the formation of the Honduran Trade Union Federation at a workers' and peasants' congress in 1929. The following year the Women's Culture Society chose García as a delegate to the first union congress in Honduras, which elected her its president.[42] In May 1944 she helped orchestrate women's street demonstrations in an attempt to get dictator Carías to free political prisoners, some of whom had been incarcerated for over a dozen years. In July 1944 another demonstration demanded Carías's resignation. The dictator broke up the rally with violence, imprisoned the protestors, destroyed the Women's Culture Society, and sent García into exile.[43]

In the 1960s, after a lifetime of work for feminist causes, García commented that a new kind of feminism existed, one that, without forgetting the specific problems of women, has a more multidimensional character and looks at general human problems. She concluded that modern feminists work to elevate the standard of living and cultural level of the masses (not just women) so as to raise Latin America from the feudal stage.[44]

García devoted her life to education, believing that it provided the foundation upon which to build toward the transformation of societies. By her own admission, her ideas on education were not original.[45] They derived, to some degree, from the thinking of Uruguayan antiimperialist poet José Enrique Rodó and of nineteenth-century liberal Argentine statesman-novelist Domingo Sarmiento, to whom education connoted civilization. She also borrowed from Herbert Spencer's idea that education should aspire to develop the human being completely; Rousseau's thought that education is the art of making children into adults; and Kant's belief in perfecting the human spirit.[46] García fused the concept of class struggle with educational theory. She contended that the dispossessed class could not overcome adversity without education, which was vital to the development of revolutionary consciousness.[47] To her, education represented the sum total of the process that a community or group transmits to the new generation. It contained aspirations and ideals[48] and was indispensable to democracy and modernization.

She agreed with Lenin that the state served the dominant class, which used the schools to govern. She noted that the same was true for socialist societies.[49] According to García, the state had an obligation to provide education that did not distinguish between the classes,[50] as such distinctions caused major problems. For example, where proletarian women go uneducated, their children's progress is impeded.[51]

García called pedagogy the science of education with links to psychology, philosophy, sociology, biology, economics, politics, history, and civics.[52] She felt obligated to demonstrate the realities of the world to students and to encourage them to struggle for peace and the authentic democracy that can flourish in a climate of culture.[53] She differentiated between instruction, which transmitted knowledge, methods, and facts, and education, which developed the intellect. Through education, not training, people can conceive of structural change, can free themselves from tyranny, prejudice, and error. Genuine education enables people to think, to understand science, the arts, and history.[54]

She concurred with Article 3 of the 1917 Mexican Constitution, which states that education should provide for a democratic system that corresponds to the economic, social, and cultural welfare of the majority of the people. Education should be viewed as a right, not a privilege.[55] In a socialist society, education is the patrimony of all of the people, who deserve the benefits of equal relations of production and distribution of wealth, education being part of the distribution of the wealth.[56]

García understood the value of film, radio, television, theater, and the press to education. Like Gramsci, she prized popular culture as an educational and political tool. She lamented that too often the press, radio, and television serve the interests of the industrialists and financiers who direct the people toward their interests.[57] Universities too, she believed, should be autonomous and free of the constraints of special interests.[58] In her view, the academy, especially the discipline of history, was served by two basic philosophies: One, followed by idealists, tended to support the existing unjust, oppressive regimes; the other, the preserve of the materialists, struggled for justice and fraternity.[59]

The idealist philosophy of the traditional liberal and conservative parties has, in García's estimation, not prepared them to govern. Bloodthirsty antidemocratic dictators who have not represented the people have often had the support of the traditional parties. She attributed this to the Spanish heritage of prolonged *caudillismo* and administrative corruption. She also blamed Spain for not industrializing its colonies and noted that since the colonial era the region has lagged behind economically.[60]

According to García, the independence movement in Central America was influenced by currents such as the French Revolution, which transformed France's feudal economic system into capitalism and industrial production, and British liberalism, which proclaimed commercial liberty and freedom of the seas. Whereas the French Revolution had made France's serfs into industrial workers, the Central American independence movement transformed slaves into serfs.[61] Feudalism and subservience to economic imperialism remained in Central America after independence.

Continuously gaining sophistication and ideological breadth during decades of study, García concluded that the Latin American nations have never controlled their own destinies and have always suffered under political tyrannies, first from Spain, then from the United States.[62] As she saw it, the United States emerged from the eighteenth-century bourgeois revolution with a work ethic that led to successful industrialization. The United States replaced England, France, and Germany as the primary producer and exploiter of underdeveloped lands. She characterized the United States as a market redistributor, an exporter of capital, and a nation that believed others were destined to submit to its proclamations.[63]

As García noted, Cuba, like the rest of Latin America, passed from Spanish domination to that of the United States. Eventually, Fidel Castro led a coalition of workers, *campesinos*, and progressive national bourgeois elements who liberated the nation. Cuba changed the people's relationship to the means of production and moved toward socialism. To García, this constituted proof that people can alter the course of history and transform economic and social structures. She extolled the virtues of Cuba's extensive nationalization program, its agrarian reforms, the literacy program, and its ability to survive despite counterrevolution and the U.S. economic blockade. What the Cuban Revolution wrought represented the hopes and aspirations of thousands of Latin Americans.[64]

García's analysis of the Cuban Revolution and comparison of it to the workers' movement in Central America led her to believe that the latter's proletariat had not realized its role as a vanguard of the revolution. She blamed this problem on the heterogeneity of the labor organizations, claiming that Central America's urban and rural workers, artisans, employees, and intellectuals lack the clearly defined characteristics of a working class and fail to recognize one another.[65] They must, she felt, develop class consciousness before the revolutionary process can proceed.

Longino Becerra: Adapting Communism to Honduran Reality

Communist party ideologist Longino Becerra, also known by the pseudonym Asdrúbal Ramírez, gained renown in his country as the author of wonderfully sincere books and pamphlets that clearly explain, in "rigid" Marxist fashion, the Communist position. He wrote on Leninism, Maoism, and agrarian problems in Honduras and produced a general radical history of his country.[66] His sometimes overly polemical work displays a well-rounded knowledge of Marxist ideology and a sound comprehension of the historiography of Honduras from pre-Columbian times to the present. He also exhibits disdain for Honduran historians who represent the privileged sector; write dull, nonanalytical narratives; and do not examine the role of the masses. To him, these historian's texts range from bad to worse, lack scientific rigor and method, omit class analysis, contain many distortions, convey the myths promoted by those who control society, and lack honest intellectual interest in the truth.[67]

In his works, Becerra divided the history of Honduras into four epochs. During the first epoch, 600 B.C. to A.D. 1524, "the primitive community" era, no class antagonisms existed, land was held communally, and the indigenous folk did not understand the idea of private property, nor did they have to sell their labor to survive.[68] The second historical epoch began with the arrival of the Spanish in 1524 and lasted until 1821. Under Spanish rule there existed feudal relations of production.[69] Spanish-born whites and their offspring controlled a brutal slave state in which the black and Indian workers were immiserated, and a privileged military served the dominant class and guaranteed colonial stability.[70] Toward the end of this epoch, *criollos* (American-born whites) challenged the dominant *peninsulares* (Spanish-born whites), whose privileges they envied.[71]

After more than three centuries of Spanish rule, Honduras entered a new stage of historical development determined by the advance of productive forces in the nation and in the world. New social relations emerged as capitalist production for the world market fostered a crisis that led to independence from Spain and the establishment of "democratic-state-feudalism" in Central America.[72] During this third historical epoch from 1821 to 1876, intellectuals followed scholastic philosophy and allied with the ruling elite, and life for the nonwhite masses remained unchanged.[73] In this period Francisco Morazán initiated the bourgeois democratic revolution, an idealistic and unrealizable concept in Honduras in the middle of the nineteenth century. Morazán confronted the old aristocracy and the church but could not produce change in a precapitalist society with a small bourgeois class and strong semifeudal relations of production.[74]

During the fourth epoch, from 1876 to 1982, the bourgeois elements depended on foreign capital and semifeudal landholders, and many workers still held semiservile or quasi-proletarian positions. This period was marked by unstable politics and the beginnings of the struggle against U.S. imperialism and the landed oligarchy.[75] Monopoly foreign capital became significant in 1878, when Marco Aurelio Soto joined with Washington Valentine of New York to form the Rosario Mining Company to exploit petroleum. Dependency deepened in 1899 when the Vacarro brothers established the first banana plantation in La Ceba.[76] Honduras eventually produced major profitable products for export and neglected the internal economy to the extent of having to import basic foodstuffs. A neocolonial situation developed, although a façade of sovereignty existed, and the nation was manipulated politically and economically from abroad.[77]

Becerra also noted the following important watersheds in the more recent history of Honduras: The country's first agrarian law, passed in 1888, permitted individuals to acquire national lands, and holdings continued to fall into the hands of the few until the 1960s.[78] The first significant banana-field strike took place at the Cuyamel Fruit Company in 1916. Labor-management antagonisms increased over the next four decades.

The 1954 banana strike served as a major catalyst for working-class consciousness and political action.[79] That year, the overthrow of the Arbenz government in Guatemala gave the United Fruit Company more courage to face down its Honduran workers. The strike was defeated by hunger, police repression, and duplicity. But the right to organize survived and led to a new social security law and legalized collective bargaining. Of utmost importance, the possibility of political and social change in Honduras emerged.[80]

By the 1970s, according to Becerra, Honduras had entered an advanced national democratic phase that might engender social transformations.[81] The Communist party then entrusted Becerra with the task of devising a plan to adapt general Communist concepts of social development to the Honduran reality. He tried to apply Marxist-Leninist laws flexibly,[82] proceeding on the premise that if people can agree on fundamental principles, they can progress without conflict. In other words, he believed, if people can agree on the need for socialism but differ on how to attain it, hope for reconciliation exists.[83]

Becerra based his principles for Honduras's revolution on the experiences of Russia and Cuba, combined with the unique aspects of the Honduran ethos.[84] In drawing up his plan for Honduras, he tried to demonstrate the superiority of Marxism-Leninism to Maoism,[85] which he acknowledged as one of three non-Communist-party Marxist tendencies operating in Latin America. He viewed Maoism as a post-1963 creation designed to initiate "popular war" based on China's resistance to the Japanese between 1931 and 1945 and the 1945–1949 civil war against the Kuomintang. According to Becerra, Maoism included the thinking of Lin Piao, whose seminal article "Long Live the Triumph of the People's War" stressed that power comes from the gun and that violent struggle can change the world. Lin Piao asserted that you can start a popular guerrilla war, especially against imperialism, before the idea of class struggle spreads. Out of the long and difficult popular war will grow the class struggle idea.[86] Lin Piao contended that if your major enemies are in urban areas, you should begin the fight in the countryside. Honduran Maoists believed the countryside was the best place to confront the enemy and the mountains the safest place for the revolutionaries. Becerra disagreed, claiming that advanced military technology made the countryside an unsafe place to start the struggle.[87] He considered it ridiculous to call the cities the bastions of the enemy when manual and mental workers and their middle-class allies resided there and provided cohesion to the revolution. He pointed out that in 1965 the United States needed 23,000 troops to quell dissent in Santo Domingo.[88]

Becerra referred to Trotskyism as another non-Communist road to revolution. To him, Trotskyism entailed permanent revolution and omitted vital intermediate stages, such as the liberal democratic transition phase preceding socialism. He equated Trotskyism with adventurism.[89]

According to Becerra, the third non-Communist approach to revolution, neoanarchism, is practiced by ultraleftist antiimperialist parties, which eschew parliamentary procedures. These groups, among which he counted the Uruguayan Tupamaros and Nicaragua's Sandinistas, are fundamentally guerrilla activists and not necessarily oriented to the proletariat. He called such groups the infantile Left.[90] He included among the neoanarchists thinkers such as Frantz Fanon, who postulated the concept of Third World revolution, and French theorist Régis Debray, both of whom he implied were disorganized and unscientific. He criticized them for sometimes elevating peasants to a level above the industrial proletariat in terms of their revolutionary roles. Fanon and Debray saw the peasantry as the majority and most likely to succeed in a guerrilla situation. Becerra conceded that the peasant sector was the largest in Honduras and had revolutionary potential.[91] When he condemned Fanon's partiality to peasant revolutions, he forgot that Fanon dealt with Africa, where proletarians are somewhat privileged in comparison to the average person and might have something to lose in a revolution.[92] Becerra called Debray's *foco* theory anti-Leninist adventurism, not class warfare in the traditional sense, and referred to the insurrectional *foco* as impulsive "ideological cretinism."[93] Despite the success of the *foco* theory in Cuba, Becerra believed that its proponents failed to ask, for example, how to break the power of the capitalist state. He noted that the *foco* concept runs counter to the established Communist belief in waiting for the proper revolutionary conditions.[94] He also opposed the *foco* theory because it does not stipulate that a Marxist-Leninist party is necessary for armed struggle, and *focos* can be initiated and sustained by those outside the working class.[95] He disliked the idea that some exponents of the *foco* theory thought that Central America's working class did not have the capacity to be the vanguard of the revolution. Becerra regarded Che Guevara's idea of opening many *focos* in the hemisphere as neo-Bolivarist and non-Marxist, and saw Roque Dalton's vision of a Central American *foco* as the same thing in miniature.[96]

Becerra also rejected Herbert Marcuse's concept of students as social critics and as a youth revolutionary vanguard.[97] He conceded that the key to resolving the debate over whether the vanguard should be composed of the proletariat or the peasantry might be in an alliance between the two. In Becerra's opinion, this approach, first advanced by

Marx, would of course still allow the proletariat, aided by students, to serve as the primary force.[98] Becerra and the Communists maintained that the peasantry cannot be the motor force of revolution because it has a local, not a class, identity.[99] He pointed out that in Bolivia Che Guevara did not receive peasant support for his *foco* and failed because the peasantry never adequately developed revolutionary thinking.[100] The same could be said for the Honduran peasantry, which also never unified and tended to support one or the other major political party rather than become an independent political entity.

Before the peasantry can lead a revolution, it must acquire the sophistication necessary to devise programs for agrarian reform. Becerra enunciated a comprehensive Communist platform for agrarian reform, which he hoped the Honduran peasantry would adopt as it gained political and economic awareness. The program entailed liquidating the latifundios, confiscating banana lands from the monopolies, limiting private property, nationalizing subsoil resources, and indemnifying those who lose lands. It also encompassed a vital minimum law, the elimination of tenancy contracts, peasant representation on agrarian reform boards, technical aid and financing for small farmers, agricultural diversification, establishment of agricultural cooperatives, and education for peasants.[101]

Throughout his writings, Becerra consistently cast in an international context his views on Honduras, on revolutionary theory or strategy, and on agrarian reform. His writings contain the internationalism of Bolívar, including the desire for continental security and the idea of no geographical or ideological frontiers in Latin America. Becerra believed that class struggle and revolutionary objectives transcend boundaries.[102] He advocated diplomatic relations between all nations, regardless of their ideologies,[103] as a means to initiate conflict-solving dialogues.

He urged world peace and understanding and felt that the United States constantly undermined those goals in Honduras, recalling that the United States used military force ten times in Honduras between 1906 and 1924, generally to support rulers it preferred.[104] He judged agencies such as the Inter-American Development Bank, AID, CONDECA, and the Peace Corps guilty of abetting neocolonialism in recent years.[105] He criticized the false hope created by the Alliance for Progress, under which U.S. aid came with strings attached and was designed to thwart socialism.[106] He viewed China's anti-Soviet policies as a result of a U.S. plan to turn the two major socialist nations, historical adversaries, against each other.[107] He also condemned China for allying with imperialist enemies of socialism[108] and criticized Chinese censure of Soviet "social imperialism." He relied heavily on Lenin's *Imperialism: The Highest Stage of Capitalism* (1916) to refute the Chinese allegation of Soviet imperialism on the grounds that imperialism connotes economic gain, which Soviet socialism historically negated. He justified Soviet expansion as part of international workers' solidarity.[109]

Becerra blamed many of Honduras's contemporary ills on U.S. imperialism and the militarism it supported. He dismissed as absurd the liberal notion that a military can be neutral when it enforces the will of the elite to which it is subservient or with which it shares power.[110] By the 1970s, Honduras's military filled a political vacuum caused by the failure of the governmental oligarchy to work out accommodations with diverse political parties, disorganization of the petit bourgeoisie, and no existing viable revolutionary or democratic movements.[111] He expressed concern about extensive nonproductive militarism in Honduras that emanated from military courses offered by the United States in the Panama Canal zone and the U.S. cold war mentality that compromised Honduran sovereignty. More than a decade ago, before the United States chose Honduras as the new staging area for its activities in Central America, Becerra warned about the danger to society of a military that functions as part of the superstructure and serves the class in power.[112] He predicted correctly that Honduras might subsequently suffer from a right-wing military driven by anticommunism and insensitive to human needs.[113]

Mario Posas:
Workers' Movements and Land Tenure Questions

The growth of radicalism in Honduras corresponds to that of its labor movement. Thus the nation's radical writers exhibit a preoccupation with peasant problems and the history of trade unionism. "Critical" Marxist Mario Posas is no exception. Through his efforts as author of monographs and pamphlets and as a professor of sociology at Honduras's National University, Posas has acquired a fine reputation as an analyst of Central American and Honduran worker and peasant movements and land tenure questions. He concurs with British Marxist historian Eric Hobsbawm, who challenges the dominance of political history and its practitioners who look at the Third World through elitist attitudes and Western European eyes. Posas and Hobsbawm advocate the use of social history and the need to examine questions pertaining to land tenure and the peasantry in order to understand Latin America.

In collaboration with Rafael del Cid, Posas wrote *La construcción del sector público y del estado nacional de Honduras (1876–1979)* (1981, The construction of the public sector and the national state of Honduras [1876–1979]), a critical history that reflects the global perspective he shares with fellow Honduran writers Graciela García and Longino Becerra. In the book, Posas indicated that states develop according to historical-dialectical conditions, including how capital accumulates and the level of class struggle. The state represents the dominant economic and social class, not all of the people.[114]

Prior to the 1870s, according to Posas, much of Honduras existed in precapitalist circumstances. Until that time, unlike other Central American nations, Honduras had no solid agricultural export business. Then the liberal state stimulated agricultural exports. Modern Honduras emerged between 1876 and 1948 as large landholdings developed, along with a need for an inexpensive labor force.[115] The state intervened to promote capitalist development. It organized more efficient juridical and monetary systems[116] and sponsored institutional violence to protect private investments. Local and regional control consolidated as centralization of the state took place.[117]

From 1903 to 1948, those whom Gramsci called the "traditional intellectuals," the lawyers, doctors, and engineers, exerted power and constituted the state.[118] Between 1910 and 1920, a group of worker-intellectuals emerged out of Honduras's mutual aid and artisan societies, which are described in the introduction to this chapter. The group held conferences, published newspapers, sometimes supported political candidates, and opposed *caudillismo*.[119] The activities of these embryonic radicals abated considerably during the difficult economic times and military repressions of the 1930s.

After World War II, economic diversification brought modernization, increased expansion of capital investment in agriculture, and growth in the peasant movements. The state apparatus grew in proportion to the expansion of foreign capital. During the regime of Manuel Gálvez (1949–1954) the state became especially responsive to anticommunist pressures exerted by multinational corporations.[120] Subsequently, social groups and classes organized, often under the prodding of workers, students, progressives, and Communists who learned from the Cuban Revolution that they could be a potential force for social change.

Vigorous state interventions in civil society by the López Arellano government of the early 1960s resulted in varied plans for reform. Proceeds from tax increases were used for social services to satisfy popular demands and thereby guarantee a work force for new and expanding industries.[121] Land was transferred from the national domain to private investors and peasants. Agribusiness marketed what the large and small landholders grew.[122] The state participated in a new scheme of international relations of production commanded by monopoly capital and brought about by new transfers in technology.

Posas concluded that the agrarian policies of the state during the expansion years of the 1950s, 1960s, and 1970s favored the rural exporters and their foreign partners. Improvements for the *campesinos*, whose lands were not taken over by agribusiness, were incremental.[123] At the same time, certain sectors of the bourgeoisie emerged from the expansion era with distinct political objectives. The agricultural interests linked to urban industrialists and bankers tied to foreign capital wanted to control society and limit social participation. In contrast, the industrial, financial, and agro-industrial bourgeois elements who had fewer links to imperialist capital supported reformist projects and broader social participation.[124] By the late 1970s, reformist bourgeois tendencies diminished, and the repressive state began to use the term *communist* to denominate the progressives, including those with democratic ideas.[125]

The Sandinista triumph in Nicaragua in 1979 stimulated the popular sectors in Honduras and caused some radical factions to unify. That year the Honduran National Peasant Front formed and agitated for agrarian reform, worker freedoms, and the end to governmental repression of workers, students, and clergy.[126] In 1980 the Patriotic National Front, made up of the Christian Democratic party, the Communist party, the Marxist-Leninist party, the Socialist party, the Revolutionary Movement of the People, the General Workers' Central, the United Peasants' Front, and other labor, student, and professional organizations boycotted national elections.[127] Although political conditions had not reached a stage of class-versus-class revolutionary confrontation by 1980, Posas saw a reformist movement developing that was aimed at political stability.

Posas's most valuable contributions to the radical thought of his country include historical analyses, bits of which appear above, as well as penetrating humanistic examinations of the workers' movement. He noted that the early artisan organizations did not conflict with the interests of North American entrepreneurs and thus went unhindered, but when the banana workers began to unify in the early part of the twentieth century, they encountered resistance. In *Luchas del movimiento obrero hondureño* (1981, Struggles of the Honduran workers' movement), he traced the development of the banana enclave, showed how the plantation workers determined the course of the union movement in the nation, and placed their battles in an international perspective.[128] The workers fought for their rights and political influence, denouncing the established economic system, which left them with hunger, poor salaries, and inflation. They criticized the government for depriving the unions of the legal right to function and condemned electoral frauds perpetrated by the ruling oligarchy.[129]

Labor-management conflict occurs, as Marx and Engels stated, when workers perceive that their work exceeds the value of their compensation. Struggles for salaries are common in capitalism, and, as Lenin noted, strikes occur when the great mass of workers are salaried. Posas agreed with Lenin that strikes lead workers to unite and recognize the importance of unions to contain capitalists and that they help the masses understand how the social order works and what causes exploitation. In other words, strikes develop class consciousness.[130]

In contrast to Marxist-Leninist unionization, Posas indicated there exists "free democratic unionism," unions organized to elevate the standard of living, reenforce liberty and representative democracy, and combat and destroy communist movements. According to Posas, this union system, favored by the United States, advocated abandoning the concept of class struggle and substituting constructive relations between workers and investors.[131] Using the ideas of Gramsci, Posas demonstrated how "free democratic unionism" used diverse mechanisms of co-optation against Honduras's union leaders to impede the working masses' desires for managerial autonomy and to prevent proletarian unity from evolving into left-wing political parties.[132]

From the first significant banana workers' strike in 1916 until the Depression, strikes were generally short-lived, spontaneous reactions to deteriorating conditions and were met by state-directed repression.[133] The first Honduran peasant organizations originated in the 1920s and were based on Leninist concepts of alliances between workers and peasants.[134] Posas gives Graciela García credit for setting the foundations for union progress during the 1920s. By 1930, the Honduran Workers' Federation had organized fifteen peasant leagues and stirred *campesino* interest in politics, even at the national level.[135] Peasants demanded access to the land, credits, machinery, and technical and organizational assistance.[136] During the 1930s, the banana companies, especially United Fruit, consolidated their monopoly by absorbing their competition.[137] Dictator Carías employed state-of-siege tactics against the workers from the early 1930s to 1948, and their movements suffered serious setbacks.

After the departure of Carías, the union movement changed as a result of industrialization and economic diversification, especially the rise of the urban textile industry.[138] Vital unions (such as the Workers' Coordinating Committee, composed of matchstick makers, graphic artists, construction workers, shirtmakers, butchers, and shoemakers) appeared and were led by the Honduran Revolutionary Democratic party, ideologically tied to the leftist Confederation of Latin American Workers.[139] Renewed labor activism culminated in the banana strike of 1954. The strike established precedent for negotiations between classes, brought improved conditions for modernization, increased state paternalism,[140] democratized politics somewhat, and organized the proletariat.[141]

In *Lucha ideológica y organización sindical en Honduras (1954–65)* (1980, Ideological struggle and union organization in Honduras [1954–65]), Posas examined the ideological contradictions that existed when unions were legal in Honduras, a period in which class struggle intensified and the state-aided bourgeoisie, in collaboration with imperialists, strove to maintain control over the proletariat in the wake of the Cuban Revolution.[142] He pointed out how, immediately after the 1954 strike, the anticommunist ORIT, guided by the U.S. embassy in Tegucigalpa, tried to fix unionism into a non-class-oriented, AFL-CIO mold.[143] Honduran workers were told that conflicts between workers and capitalists should not exist, unions should organize workers to obtain better working conditions and create harmony with owners, rights of workers are always inferior to those of capitalists, and workers who do not accept the above premises should be denounced to the police. ORIT circulated many books, pamphlets, and newspapers to propagate these attitudes and called its efforts "*sindicalismo libre y democrático*" (free democratic unionism).[144] The ORIT-oriented National Association of Honduran Peasants became the most important workers' organization in the country.[145] At the same time, the National Federation of Peasants emerged as the first organization to transcend group boundaries and to view the struggle of the peasants as part of the fight against imperialism and domestic repression.[146] Posas also stressed that radical university students played a key role in organizing the peasantry during the 1960s.[147]

By the 1970s, the efforts of the AF of L, ORIT, and AIFLD had succeeded, and the radical presence in the labor movement was greatly overshadowed by capitalist-oriented unions such as the Honduran Confederation of Workers. This organization of rural and urban workers, and the Honduran Private Enterprise Council, which controlled modernization in the country, concluded a "national unity" pact that provided for minimal reforms.[148] Numerous examples exist of how the peasants lost control to the multinational companies. For instance, in 1975 the Peasant Associative Enterprise of Isletas, with 900 members, formed to take over land damaged by Hurricane Fifi in 1974. Supported by Honduras's National Agrarian Institute, the Union of Standard Fruit Company Workers persuaded the government to expropriate the land and proclaimed, "We have managed to create a little bit of socialism in the jaws of Standard Fruit Company." The Isletas cooperative agreed to let Standard Fruit market its produce. On February 12, 1977, the Honduran military, supported by Standard Fruit, invaded the cooperative's offices and arrested its board of directors. The army named a new board, expelled most of the cooperative's members, and began to operate for the benefit of those in control. By 1981 the National Agrarian Institute controlled the cooperative. It then ceased to function as a cooperative and became a state-run business for the profit of Standard Fruit.[149] Under the theories of state capitalism espoused by many social democrats, state intervention in the economic realm is designed to regulate businesses and protect the interests of the workers. As it has existed in Honduras, Posas indicates, the converse has been true.

The workers' movement has been on the defensive during the 1970s and 1980s, caught between electoral frauds and repressive police-state regimes urged on by monopoly capitalism.[150] By the 1980s, Posas saw a limited capacity for peasant mobilization, mostly in the northern littoral of the country. He felt that a national peasant class consciousness was growing, which translated into a desire for political power. He noted that historically the peasant class has been weak, and reactionary forces have been able to keep it down. But in the struggle for the land, an anticapitalist mentality, or dynamic, has arisen. When capital controls the state, it also creates an experimental antistate or revolutionary proletarian dynamic.[151]

Víctor Meza:
From 1870s Liberal Reform State to 1980s Pentagon Republic

Víctor Meza (1945–), social critic, labor analyst, political journalist, and professor of political science at the National Autonomous University of Honduras, has served time in prison for his antiestablishment views. At this writing, he was reputed to be on a hit list drawn up by the Honduran military. His friends speculate that only his international reputation has saved him from assassination. Driven by the desire to alter Honduras's status as Central America's least-developed and least-known state, Meza has, through his books and articles, tried to encourage development and acquaint outsiders with his country. *Política y sociedad en Honduras* (1981, Politics and society in Honduras), a collection of his commentaries that, for the most part, appeared in the newspapers *El Día* (The Day) and *Tiempo* (Time), emphasize the incredible corruption that has retarded Honduras's government, the enormous U.S. presence there, and that, in what he called the "ideological monolith," minorities have no right to dissent.[152]

In his role as social critic, he asserted that Hondurans mistake reform for revolution. For example, they see capitalist agrarian reform as socialism. In his estimation, Honduras's national bourgeoisie has the psychological makeup of the businessperson, not the captain of industry. In Meza's view, the national bourgeoisie is not oriented to production, building, or work. He criticized the national bourgeoisie for rarely putting at the disposal of the citizens its intellectual capital, and for succumbing to "banana bribes" or working for the transnational companies rather than the country. To him, the national bourgeoisie represents individualistic capitalists who do not care for the people.[153]

Meza also condemned Bonapartism, or neomilitarism, by which politically biased armed forces make false claims of impartiality.[154] This he saw as part of Honduras's right-wing, do-nothing nationalism, which manifests itself in absurd patriotism and chauvinism. He pointed out that, in contrast, left-wing, not necessarily Marxist nationalism transforms societal economic structures, develops the nation, benefits the people, and defends political and economic sovereignty and the principle of self-determination.[155]

He contended that foreign investment made Honduras into a right-wing economic enclave, but that capitalist relations of production gave rise to working-class movements.[156] Such insights demonstrate that Meza, like any sound Marxist, has a thorough understanding of capitalism and how it fosters inequality and conflict. However, in his estimation, he differs from the majority of professors in Honduran universities, who he says are not Marxists. They use Marxist terminology but practice traditional, often imprecise, Aristotelian logic. To Meza, Marxism is a scientific doctrine, not a superficial method to be invoked carelessly by professors who are ignorant of it and its enormous bibliography. According to him, this occurs because Hondurans with a neocolonial mentality cannot tolerate critical thinking that illuminates underdevelopment and dependence.[157] Conversely, though most Honduran professors are capitalists, students, who come from various strata of the middle class, often have a revolutionary and more enthusiastic outlook. Students can afford to question the status quo. But like the petit bourgeoisie, they are prisoners of reality and desire who cannot do much to foster change, even if they want to alter the possibilities for the future.[158]

Meza, like Posas, looks to the past to try to understand the origins of and possible solutions to current problems. He attributes many ills in contemporary society to the 1876 liberal reforms, based upon positivist philosophy, that encouraged alliances between local oligarchs and foreign investors who built the coffee enclave economy.[159] Although the 1876 reforms brought structure and cohesion to a previously factionalized body politic,[160] they also oriented Honduras to the world market. During the last decades of the nineteenth century and the first two of the twentieth, Honduras became a U.S.-dominated banana company enclave. The banana economy established a new economic form based on immense production and modern marketing techniques, one necessitating an enormous labor force. It led to monopoly capital, denationalization, new relations of production for plantation workers, and the development of the workers' movement.[161] Corruption became a major component of the banana concessionaire system described and analyzed previously in this chapter. Unlimited concessions to the banana companies were followed by the belief that stronger internal security enhanced institutional stability.[162] The state defended the banana companies, even when not in the best interests of Hondurans to do so.[163] The enclave economy, although intended to concentrate on the external market, controlled vital sectors of the internal economy. For example, a system of company stores enabled the banana monopolies to regain funds paid out in salaries.[164]

As a result of the banana economy, workers developed higher levels of combativeness and political awareness. This led to increased government repression, as detailed in Meza's critical Marxist study *Historia del movimiento obrero hondureño* (1981, History of the Honduran workers' movement).[165] This perspicacious analysis of the labor movement provides unique observations on the social conditions of workers. Meza depicts the history of the organized proletariat as one of clandestine operations, sacrifices, conspiracies, and a process of struggle through strikes. He notes that immediately after 1916, newspapers disseminated information about the workers' movement in descriptive, not analytical, terms.[166] Nevertheless, this aroused radical awareness. Gradually radical sentiments about the plight of labor began to surface in print, especially after the 1921 Workers' Congress, which was pervaded by a socialist aura. In contrast to those who date the founding of the Honduran Communist party to 1927, Meza contends that it formed in 1922 after the Workers' Congress.[167] He believed that communism gave the workers a new analytical approach to their problems and provided their struggle with an ideological dimension.[168] Meza maintains that fear of communism existed by the late 1920s, when Honduras's Socialist Revolutionary party, an anticommunist organization, was established and worked for class harmony and social reform.[169]

During the 1930s, according to Meza, workers' movements gained momentum all over Central America. This led to the implantation of dictators by those who opposed worker control and left-wing politics. The government of El Salvador proposed an anticommunist pact to control immigration to prohibit the entry of Communists into Central America, to watch frontiers, to censor the social content of motion pictures, and to cooperate on the diplomatic level to counter Communist doctrines. The Honduran government of Carías supported this early (1935) attempt to unify anticommunist action.[170]

A decade later, the left-wing Honduran Revolutionary Front announced its declaration of principles, which included the overthrow of Carías by armed force, the resolution of economic problems, and the establishment of constitutional rights to strike, fix salaries, set minimum working hours, and set up social security insurance. Honduran radicals moved to destroy fascism at home after it had been eradicated in Europe.[171] Following the ouster of dictator Carías in 1948, more direct moves to the political left became feasible. The Communist party of Honduras then proclaimed its Marxist-Leninist-Stalinist principles. It vowed to fight imperialism, democratize the nation, expropriate latifundios, distribute land to peasants, establish domestic peace, and terminate dependency.[172] This served as a prelude to the 1954 strike.

During the 1954 strike, Honduran workers invoked the Universal Declaration of the Rights of Man, including the right to satisfactory working conditions and the right to participate in the country's political and cultural life. Organized labor began to consolidate its position, an occurrence that lasted until 1963. The Central American Common Market then built a climate favorable to foreign investment in the agro-extractive industries,[173] and there arose what Meza called the "new Inquisition" dedicated to anticommunism and practicing political intolerance.[174] The U.S. Alliance for Progress buttressed the Honduran domestic policy of preventing socialism. The country forged a foreign policy that operated subject to the dictates of the United States in the international sphere and to those of the Honduran military in the domestic realm. In other words, Honduras's national interests were deformed by the repressive concept of national security, interpreted by the military and distorted by global and regional U.S. interests. Honduras was forced into the East-West conflict.[175] Its foreign policy was no longer based on the tenets of nonintervention or self-determination, principles that fell victim to anticommunism.

The Sandinista-led victory in Nicaragua in 1979 constituted a threat to the regional power structure of Central America. According to Meza, in the U.S. view Honduras then assumed an important geopolitical position that required the establishment of a civilian regime to satisfy appearances and a military one to maintain control. The United States learned from the Vietnam War that its citizens would not tolerate the deaths of their loved ones in distant military engagements. With the imperial benediction of Reagan, Honduras accepted the role of U.S. military surrogate in Central America.[176] The Honduran government made false claims about being democratic and protecting human rights. It proclaimed neutrality with regard to revolutionary Nicaragua, an assertion Meza referred to as duplicity or "duality."[177]

Currently, Honduras faces numerous crises. The government is almost bankrupt. Social conditions deteriorate, unemployment grows, and real wages drop in a nation that already has the lowest per capita income in North, Central, or South America. The monetary policies of Milton Friedman and the conservative University of Chicago school of economics, implemented by the U.S. embassy, impose an austerity program that severely damages the workers and increases the profits of the multinational corporations.[178] The socialist-realism reflected in the radical literature of

Graciela García and Longino Becerra, with emphasis on the long-term struggles of the workers' movements and the Communist party, has been eclipsed by the "critical" Marxist studies of Mario Posas and Víctor Meza who utilize the latest social science techniques and methodology to analyze society. Their investigations emphasize the development of organized labor, and they demonstrate how it has contributed to the façade of political pluralism in Honduras but has not produced a significant voice for the workers in politics nor eased the plight of the peasants. Posas and Meza, in light of the United States' hemispheric and Central American policies, further explain how Honduras, historically for sale to the highest bidder, evolved from the quintessential banana republic to the Pentagon's republic. Although they do not work on the theoretical level of Guatemala's Edelberto Torres Rivas or El Salvador's Rafael Menjívar, Posas and Meza represent the highest caliber of radical thought found in Honduras, where anticommunism has inhibited the development of progressive intellectuals since the 1920s.

5

Costa Rica

America is more than a geographic nation: it is a way of life, and to understand it you have to adjust to the highest values of justice and liberty, it is a state of the heart for millions of people. For them, any limitation or interference is exasperating: the spiritual evolution of America, has made it incompatible as a colony.
—Vicente Sáenz

Foreigners often view Costa Rica as a microcosm of the United States. To them, it represents an enigma, a primarily Caucasian, democratic, highly literate, welfare-minded, politically stable, anticommunist Latin American state. Costa Rica's people, or *Ticos*, give the impression that they prefer moderate to radical solutions and are basically conformists.

Despite, or perhaps because of, a primarily literate work force, a relatively large intelligentsia, political cohesion, and liberal democracy, Costa Rica has not produced a plethora of radical thought. Nevertheless, radical intellectuals exist in Costa Rica, and they believe that the dynasty of the conquistadores has survived in their country, where power has always been in the hands of one class. In the view of Costa Rica's radicals, hidalgos (noblemen) have controlled political and economic life since the inception of the colony, and the plebeians have lived in relative misery. Over the years, groups within the ruling class have fostered modernization but have not substantially restructured relations of production.[1]

The Spanish established the first permanent settlement in the region at Cartago in 1563. By the beginning of the seventeenth century, Costa Rica had only 600 Spanish inhabitants. Because of its unique colonization pattern, it developed a distinct economic and social structure, one based on independent small properties. The colonial economy did not provide the large landowners, the corrupt bureaucracy, or the church with the power that they had elsewhere in Spanish America. Without mineral production (despite the name Costa Rica, or rich coast), Indian labor, imported slaves, and a mainstay cash crop, its elites did not become an extraordinarily wealthy class and needed no military to keep the oppressed in line.

The absence of feudal structures in colonial Costa Rica helped determine its development. The elites concentrated on administering the territory and used their power modestly. A middle class developed, along with a sense of civic responsibility among the elites. Ties to Great Britain enabled the agrocommercial oligarchy to establish strength based on exports. Foreign capitalists joined with nationals and extended the process of dependency.

The introduction of coffee in 1808 changed the position of many peasants, who lost their lands and became wage laborers on coffee *fincas.*[2] Three classes existed in Costa Rica by the nineteenth century: the coffee-growing elites, made up of a tiny group of families who controlled politics; the small coffee growers, who depended on the elites to sell their coffee; and the peons, who depended on both of the other groups.[3] By 1821 the national bourgeoisie held political power and began to solidify its position as the dominant class, as analyzed by Rodolfo Cerdas Cruz later in this chapter.

Two years after independence, in 1823, when its population numbered less than 60,000, Costa Rica joined the Central American Federation of states, from which it withdrew in 1838 because of provincial quarrels. Juan Mora Fernández became the first head of state in 1824, and from then until 1889 Costa Rica had twenty-five chief executives who held office for over three months, only one of whom was elected. Over half of the time the presidents were generals, most of whom came from the coffee aristocracy.

For almost four centuries Costa Rica produced no prominent writers. The region had no printing press until 1830[4] and no newspaper until 1833. The University of St. Thomas was established in San José in 1843 and operated until 1888 but turned out no prominent radical thinkers. The 1856–1857 war with Nicaragua united the Costa Rican people and stimulated nationalist and noninterventionist thought. Embryonic workers' and popular movements developed during the last third of the nineteenth century. In 1874 Francisco Calvo, a priest interested in meeting human needs, organized the Artisan Mutual Aid Society, which published a newspaper, *El Artesano* (The artisan), that referred to itself as an organ for working-class interests.[5] Simultaneously, liberal political thought spread in the nation, as exemplified by the work of José María Castro Madriz (1818–1892), who promoted John Stuart Mill's ideas of liberty and separation of church and state and advocated the use of scientific positivism in education.[6]

An autonomous Costa Rican workers' movement evolved in the late nineteenth century while the nation expanded its commitment to coffee production for export. Since that time, class struggle has been a significant determinant in the economic, political, and ideological life of Costa Rica, and the level of social struggle in the country has determined the course of societal ·development,[7] factors that bourgeois scholars who idealize Costa Rican liberalism have been loathe to admit.

By the 1880s, Costa Rica was known as the "liberal republic," a term used to differentiate it from the previous rule of the more conservative *cafetaleros* (coffee growers) and from the "liberal democracy" that began in 1948. Under the administration of President Próspero Fernández (1882–1885), Costa Rica moved to separate church and state. An 1884 law established free compulsory secular education, which led to a high literacy rate. The government placed restrictions on the church and closed all but the law faculty of the Jesuit-dominated University of St. Thomas.[8] At this time intellectuals known as El Groupo Olimpo (The Eminent Group, or Olympians) or as the Generation of 1888 ushered in an era of positivist thought. Under its guidance investigative and polemical journalism developed, along with democratic liberal ideals.[9] Universal education and democratic practices led to growth in the middle class, which had its own identity and, unlike elsewhere in Latin America, did not always try to emulate the upper class. The Generation of 1888 championed the free enterprise system and encouraged foreign investment, especially in the railroad and banana industries. Its thinking dominated Costa Rican politics for almost half a century. It advocated electoral democracy, consequently preparing the way for the establishment of both the personalist Democratic Constitutional party and the Progressive Liberal party, thus initiating Costa Rica's two-party system in 1889.

Socialist ideas arrived from Europe in the 1880s and influenced the program of the Independent Democratic party led by Félix Arcado Montero a decade later.[10] The papal encyclical *Rerum Novarum* of Leo XIII in 1891 attacked feudalism and monarchy for causing the exploitation of workers and supported Catholic social democracy as an alternative to socialism. As a result of the encyclical, Costa Rica's Catholic Action party worked to obtain fair salaries for workers and gained considerable influence in the Artisan Society.[11]

While liberalism affected the nation's political life, foreign economic penetration increased. In 1890 U.S. entrepreneur Minor Keith completed construction of a railroad from San José to Limón to facilitate the exportation of coffee. While building the line he developed banana plantations along the route to provide additional freight revenue. He garnered considerable wealth and in 1899 helped organize the United Fruit Company, which eventually owned over 800,000 acres in the country. The banana industry, unlike the coffee industry, constituted an enclave economy controlled from abroad. Foreign investment and political and social control were consonant with the "order and progress" objectives of positivism espoused by U.S. entrepreneurs and Costa Rican leaders.

By the turn of the century, Costa Rica, with 300,000 inhabitants, had developed a civic conscience, liberal tendencies, and a few families with strong political influence. Positivism had a firm grip on the country, and Krausism, a form of rationalism with religious overtones, made some converts among intellectuals. The latter followed the teachings of Karl Christian Krause (1781–1832), who believed in pantheism, that the universe was a divine organism. To him, man constituted the highest component in the universe and progress occurred by extending internal unity in society. Costa Rican proponents of Krausism visualized spreading their beliefs to all fellow citizens.

Anarchist thought, which reached the nation during the last decades of the nineteenth century, according to Cerdas Cruz, gained adherents by the beginning of the twentieth century. Novelist Joaquín García Monge (1881–1958) founder of the Workers, Peasants and Intellectuals Alliance; journalist Mario Sancho Jiménez (1889–1948); essayist Elías Jiménez Rojas (1869–1945); and political thinker and politician Omar Dengo (1888–1928) were prominent among Costa Rica's peculiarly pacifistic anarchists. Led by Dengo, an antimilitarist and teacher at Costa Rica's Normal School, these optimistic intellectuals, known as the Grupo Germinal, in 1913 established a social studies–oriented center to educate workers. The center subsequently helped foster the General Confederation of Workers and the Reformist political party.[12]

An outstanding radical-activist in the group was Jiménez Rojas, a Paris-educated pharmacist whose thought encompassed positivism and anarchism. A universal man who wrote essays and the three-volume *Renovación* (1911–1913, Renovation), edited numerous journals, and practiced philanthropy, Jiménez used observation and analysis to understand and improve the human condition. His work lacked methodological rigor but had an impact upon the political thought of the day.[13] He defended individual rights, believed in social solidarity, and regarded bourgeois liberalism as inimical to socialism. To him, Costa Rican politics emanated from a system of republican bondage. It represented a heartless parliamentary system in which the upper class chose the candidates and the people voted, hardly a genuine democracy.[14] Jiménez also rejected a rigid socialism that transforms the state into the total master. He believed that Costa Rica had the potential to form an ideal balanced state in which justice and peace prevail[15] and government is run by a small group of humanists who are not power-hungry.

Costa Rica's anarchists protested against increased U.S. involvement in Latin American affairs after the opening of the Panama Canal in 1914. Within a few years, antiimperialist convictions, together with the example of the Russian Revolution, inspired Aniceto Montero to start a socialist party. In 1919 he formed Costa Rica's first viable Marxist-Leninist political organization, which attracted members of the dissatisfied intelligentsia.[16] Labor supported the basically reformist, nonrevolutionary Socialist Center Montero created and worked through it to attain political and economic leverage.[17] The center held conferences, circulated literature with antiimperialist and socialist themes, and encouraged students and workers to study Marxism and understand the Russian Revolution.[18]

Political activity and ideological diversity grew during the 1920s. The 1921 general labor strike, the nation's first, raised political consciousness, established the eight-hour working day, and forced wage increases. In 1923 the defrocked priest Jorge Volio, influenced by the *Rerum Novarum*, founded the Reformist party, which opposed imperialism, especially that of the United Fruit Company.[19] Two years later the Civic League, a political organization hostile to foreign, particularly U.S., capital, was organized. The Civic League would ultimately unite with the Communist movement.[20]

A Costa Rican section of the Anti-Imperialist League was established in 1927. It expressed solidarity with Augusto Sandino's campaign against the United States in Nicaragua and criticized the execution in the United States of anarchists Nicola Sacco and Bartolomeo Vanzetti.[21] The following year a Costa Rican section of the antiimperialist Popular American Revolutionary Alliance (APRA) was established.[22] The Workers' Revolutionary Culture Association, which functioned as a popular university and a Marxist study group, took shape in 1928 and began operations in 1929,[23] the same year that the Communist party formed. Directed by Manuel Mora, Jaime Cerdas, Ricardo Soto, and Gonzalo Montero, the association opposed government repression of workers and pursued goals parallel to those of the Communist party, with which it merged in 1931.

The Depression hurt the agro-export sector of society, which managed to transfer most of the effects of the economic crisis to the lower classes. Workers' salaries dropped throughout the nation as the government initiated a reformist "new deal" with social democratic implications.[24] The world demand for coffee and bananas dropped and the shock waves of dependency reverberated throughout Costa Rica. Socialists such as Sáenz attributed the poor economic conditions to a disintegrating capitalist system, which engendered a moral crisis that gave rise to fascism in

Germany, Italy, and Spain. The Communist party found this a propitious time to organize. Unlike most other Latin American Communist parties with ties to Moscow, it developed *comunismo criollo*, a native brand of Marxism with strong democratic and progressive currents,[25] which eventually caused militant leftists to refer to it as the traditional Left. Manuel Mora, supported by students and intellectuals, led the Communist party, which championed the rights of urban workers and peasants. In 1930 Mora and his associates founded the short-lived General Union of Workers, the first central labor organization in Costa Rica. Henceforth, the Communists constituted a vital part of the country's trade union movement.

Meanwhile, the omnipresent United Fruit Company used its economic, social, and political power in arbitrary and coercive fashion. It discriminated against nonwhites and mistreated some of its employees. A Costa Rican cooperativist movement, with origins in the nineteenth-century mutual aid societies, rose to oppose United Fruit politics. The reformist cooperativists advocated democratic changes, wanted to limit personal ambitions that damaged the collective good, and promoted the spirit of solidarity.

Mora and his Workers' and Peasants' Bloc, which the Communist party called itself after the fearful legislature outlawed it, also backed reforms, and did so in a manner that frightened the upper class but was accepted by the other classes as in the best interests of the people. The Communists agitated for a social security program, workers' compensation, wage parity, maternity leaves, minimum wages, better sanitation, legalization of unions, the right to strike, the end of *latifundismo*, government control of public services,[26] the abolition of private property, the nationalization of subsoil resources, state control over industrial monopolies,[27] and free education at all levels. The Communists became the major representatives of the working class and strove to wrest political control from the bourgeoisie. Between 1931 and 1935 the party advocated the creation of worker and peasant councils to implement the measures noted above and managed to win a few offices in congressional and municipal elections.

During the 1930s, Carlos Luis Fallas (1909–) played a major role in Communist activities in Costa Rica. A man of humble origins with two years of schooling beyond the primary grades, he went to work on a banana plantation at sixteen then labored as a stevedore. At twenty-two he became a shoemaker and got involved in union organizing and Communist party politics.[28] In 1933 Costa Rica celebrated May Day for the first time. Fallas delivered an inflammatory speech in San José and was arrested and sentenced to a year in exile in the banana region of Limón. He began to organize plantation workers and educate them politically. He united black and white laborers by focusing their discontent on the fruit companies, and he petitioned United Fruit for salary increases, a six-hour day, better working and living conditions, medical care, and union recognition.[29] As secretary general of the Banana Workers' Union, he, along with Manuel Mora, directed the partially successful strike of 1934, provoking violence that touched off upper-class pressure to discredit the Communists as deceptive participants in an international conspiracy that threatened Costa Rica's religious, family, and political institutions.[30] Fallas subsequently served as a deputy in congress and wrote about Costa Rica's workers. Revealing the soul of a revolutionary who identified with the tragedy of the working class, his novels traced the history of *latifundismo* and examined peasant life. In *Mamita Yunai* (1941), for example, he explained vividly the injustices that befell banana workers living in subhuman conditions. This novel and others, such as his somewhat autobiographical *Marcos Ramírez* (1952), are to Costa Rica what the work of Maxim Gorky was to Russia. They represent the enormous spirit and heart of the patriot for whom criticism is equated with love of country. The title of his *Reseña de la intervención y penetración Yanki en Centro América* (1954, Outline of Yankee intervention and penetration in Central America) indicates whom he primarily blamed for the plight of Costa Ricans.[31] His novels still have a readership, but he is perhaps best remembered as the radical activist-writer who promulgated Costa Rica's 1943 Work Code.

The strike by Fallas's banana workers, with Communist party support, as well as the latter's few electoral successes, triggered an anticommunist backlash by 1934. Liberal president Ricardo Jiménez (1932–1936) believed it possible to combat communism with ideas, not violence, a philosophy that enabled the Costa Rican Communist party to avoid the degree of bloodshed experienced by Communist parties elsewhere in Central America. Anticommunism emanated from a mirage of progress under the hegemony of Creole capitalism. Costa Rica's middle class believed that society could only advance under the political guidance of the landowners and their bankers.[32] Despite strong opposition, the Communist party continued to function, and its influence spread. In 1935 the erudite Vicente Sáenz, whose dialectical worldview and independent socialist program are detailed later in this chapter, founded the Socialist party.

By then, Costa Rica's Communists, Socialists, and ruling class all viewed education as the key to societal development. They were ecstatic in 1940 when the government formally established the University of Costa Rica in the suburbs of San José. Politics soon became the preoccupation of those involved in university life, and within a generation the campus would be a main center for the discussion of radical ideas.

ensued for two months, whereupon the victor, Figueres, installed a junta that governed for eighteen months and then turned the presidency over to Ulate, who remained in office until 1953.

Figueres and his cohorts vehemently pursued anticommunism. They asserted that the Communists had totalitarian tendencies and constituted a danger to democracy. Although stressing consensus, class harmony, and political pluralism, the government outlawed the Popular Vanguard and the Communist labor federation.[38] From 1948 until the 1970s, the Communists had to operate under front organizations. Their leader, Manuel Mora, worked tirelessly to counteract Figueres's anticommunist campaign and made a strong case for international coexistence between the socialist and capitalist worlds. Meanwhile, Figueres abolished the army to encourage peace and to ensure that he would not be overthrown by the military when he became president.

In the wake of the 1948 upheaval, the social democrats created a consensus atmosphere that caused a fear or distrust of other political orientations. Figueres's dominant National Liberation party repressed the Left and rejected revolution. According to Figueres, only like-minded reformists who wanted to spread some benefits of economic expansion, but not totally redistribute the wealth, could be called democrats.

The cold war forced Costa Rican radicals to alter their tactics. Rather than attack the lack of genuine democracy in a society in which Marxists were precluded from participating in the electoral process, the Left stressed antiimperialism and pushed for nationalization of foreign-owned lands. The radicals believed that it was easier to demonstrate foreign penetration than to convince bourgeois democrats that they did not have participatory democracy. The Left hoped to illustrate by example that sovereignty and independence were illusory under Costa Rican capitalism.

While socialists struggled to gain followers, a new political ideology, *solidarismo*, emerged in Costa Rica. The brainchild of anticommunist lawyer and professor of political economy Alberto Martén, *solidarismo* stipulated that labor-management problems could be solved by following a state-enforced labor code, along with agrarian, fiscal, and monetary reforms. The author of *El movimiento solidarista* (1947, The solidarity movement), Martén believed that a natural function of money was to serve the community. By placing money under the control of the salaried citizens of Costa Rica, not the banks of the rich, and sharing it with the masses, he hoped to build a popular movement. Martén suggested that 5 to 15 percent of all profits be put at the disposition of the workers and used for their well-being. By making assistance for the workers mandatory, not gratuitous, he expected to curtail antagonism between management and labor.[39] In many ways, *solidarismo* buttressed the state-capitalist-reformist prejudices of the social democrats and thereby undermined socialism.

Although ostracized from the legal political arena, communism and socialism stayed alive in the intellectual realm. Books representing all ideological persuasions were published, even during the height of the cold war in the 1950s. Liberals and radicals at the University of Costa Rica debated the merits of the reformist system, and the latter pressed for working-class involvement in political decisions. They made the point that the nation's educational system should not primarily serve the interests of the ruling national bourgeoisie. Nevertheless, neither educational policies nor access to political power changed while Figueres's moderate to liberal National Liberation party (PLN) or its more conservative opponents controlled the nation during the 1950s and 1960s.

Throughout the 1950s, the United States pointed to Costa Rica as a model anticommunist Latin American democracy. Since the inception of the cold war, U.S. aid, coupled with effective propaganda, has led many Costa Rican citizens to admire uncritically the hemisphere's most powerful state. By the early 1960s, the Kennedy administration tried to involve Costa Rica, which had no army, in a Central American defense alliance. By middecade, Costa Rica's internal police forces were guided by the U.S. Southern Command and the CIA under orders to stem the tide of Cuban and Soviet aggression in the hemisphere. Students protested, asserting that the Costa Rican constitution prohibited foreign military control in the nation. By this time, radical thinkers such as Sáenz and Mora had proclaimed their support for the Cuban Revolution, which they viewed as a significant step toward attaining socialism in the Americas. The United States countered by supporting the right-wing Free Costa Rica Movement, and it pushed the government further into an anticommunist counterinsurgency position.[40]

Despite U.S. pressures and government restraints, a new Communist-led General Confederation of Workers formed in the 1960s. In 1962 a new Socialist party, which supported the Cuban Revolution, emerged and was quickly declared illegal. Costa Rican scholars, many of them trained abroad in the social sciences, obtained university positions from which they articulated radical positions. A tiny left-wing faction espousing the ideas of Castro, Debray, Guevara, Ho Chi Minh, and Mao developed within the PLN. But for most PLN followers the concept of socialism simply implied the good life, honest elections, and economic sufficiency.[41] In essence, Figueres and the social democrats partially co-opted socialism by misrepresenting its meaning and telling the people that their government followed socialist practices, and by implementing a brand of state capitalism that organized and encouraged agricultural production, diversified the economy, and improved education and living conditions for a number of citizens.

The successful reforms of the social democrats, together with growing U.S. influence and massive doses of cultural imperialism, could not extinguish radicalism in Costa Rica. By the 1970s, when the coffee aristocracy took a backseat to an emerging middle class in terms of political leadership, the Communist party went from a position in which it could exist as an organization but not run candidates for office, to a position of full political participation. The Communists, now called the Socialist Action party and still led by Mora, ran candidates for national offices in 1970. Three years later, the PLN restored full diplomatic relations with the Soviet Union. Also during the 1970s, Alejandra Calderón, daughter of the former president, helped organize the Trotskyist-oriented Socialist Workers' Organization, and the Costa Rican Youth Vanguard, a Marxist-Leninist organization, became active among students. At the same time, Communist-led peasant leagues, designed to obtain land for *campesinos*, formed and took part in land seizures. Even non-Communist United Fruit Company workers saw the Communists as close allies whose leadership had won them salary increases and benefits.[42] As government policies toward left-wing radicalism relented, so did its tolerance for right-wing reactionaries, and the Free Costa Rica Movement conducted witch-hunts with its private army.

Since the 1970s, radical thinkers have frequently lambasted the PLN for not painting a valid picture of national reality, for promoting a false consciousness among its followers and for the outside world.[43] Radical critics such as José Luis Vega Carballo have pointed out that liberal democracy has been a good instrument for exercising subtle, nonviolent dominion and for creating an illusion of class harmony. Others, like Cerdas Cruz, have illustrated that dependency and imperialism have combined to weaken democracy in Costa Rica and have created social and economic problems that capitalism cannot solve.

Left-wing thought has become a permanent part of the Costa Rican landscape. Students at the University of Costa Rica and at the new (1976) private National Autonomous University have affiliated with campus branches of radical political parties. Socialists have often won student government elections, and a disproportionate number of professionals have expressed Marxist beliefs. Radical ideas are more widely disseminated as reading grows in popularity. Scholarly books, including those written by Marxist professors such as Cerdas Cruz and Vega Carballo, have been made available through the Central American University Press, a regional publishing system housed at the University of Costa Rica, and through Editorial Costa Rica and the nation's Ministry of Culture and Education. But as Cerdas Cruz is quick to mention, Costa

Rica's universities, which are designed to prepare people for industrial management positions and to promote capitalism, are hardly hotbeds of radicalism.

The Costa Rican Left has grown in size and political sophistication and has gained cohesion. In 1978 the Communists joined with the Socialist party and the Revolutionary Movement of the People, a small organization allied with Nicaragua's Sandinista guerrillas, to form the United People's party. The Sandinista proletarian philosophy appealed to some Costa Ricans as their form of capitalism entered a crisis. The General Confederation of Workers and other Communist-led unions united in 1980 to form the Unitary Confederation of Workers, composed primarily of public employees and banana workers. As the Costa Rican economy sagged at the beginning of the 1980s, radicals criticized the government for holding norms that were democratic in tone but elitist in practice and for keeping the working class submissive. Cerdas Cruz indicated that whereas the welfare state helped society in general, it fostered production that primarily benefited the bourgeoisie. Radicals predicted the downfall of a society in which the common good played second fiddle to individual satisfaction.

For their part, backers of the system maintained that Costa Rica's liberal democracy perpetuated the Iberian tradition of centralized authority, and subordination of individual interests to the common good. Historian Charles Ameringer made the valid point that although class and racial prejudice exist, Costa Rica has been more egalitarian than other countries, and cultural homogeneity has made it less likely to use repression, even as the gap between the rich and poor widens.[44]

Historically, radicals have found it difficult to attract a substantial audience for their critiques of Costa Rican society when the lower sectors, even though exploited, are fairly well-off in comparison to their counterparts in other Central American states. Only when capitalism falters, as it did during the Depression, has the Left been listened to closely. Currently, Costa Rica's population more than doubles every twenty years, its unchanged economic system cannot keep pace with the needs of society, and the middle-class model of development has reached an impasse. A century of enormous banana company profits has not helped capital accumulate in the country, and agrarian capitalism has led to the downward mobility of the workers. Foreign monopolies have extracted funds from the nation and have not left enough money for those other than the elites to prosper.[45]

When Third World welfare states run out of cash and credit, they generally either seek revolutionary (socialist) solutions or turn to the right. When a significant portion of the intelligentsia of another small liberal Latin American state, Uruguay, talked about a socialist restructuring of the country's failing socioeconomic system in the early 1970s, and a left-wing urban guerrilla movement formed there, the owners of the means of production and their allies eliminated electoral democracy and implanted a vicious dictatorship. Costa Rican radicals maintain that a similar fate could befall their country.

The nation's fragmented Left still believes that it has a future because the political consensus based on reformism cannot endure the pressure of economic hardships and its effects on daily life. However, it is doubtful that the United States would permit revolution to occur in Costa Rica. U.S.-induced militarism is on the rise in Costa Rica as pressure from the marginal population swells and the fragile truce among the land-owners, the middle class, and the workers deteriorates. Costa Rican President Oscar Arias Sánchez hoped that the Esquipulas II peace plan that he designed to terminate regional hostilities and that was accepted by the Central American republics in August 1987 would prevent the extreme Right or Left from altering the balance of political and social control in his country and preserve its liberal state. Arias appeared to have achieved that goal by the time Rafael Calderón Fournier, a close friend of the United States, succeeded him in the presidency for the 1990–1994 term.

Vicente Sáenz:
Socialist Man of Letters

Between 1917 and 1960 Costa Rican socialist Vicente Sáenz (1896–1963) wrote twenty-four major books and became an intellectual force in Central America and Mexico. This son of a middle-class San José family displayed an early interest in the classics, history, and literature and received a bachelor's degree in science and letters in 1915. He explored the United States the following year and returned to Costa Rica to found and write editorials for the journal *La Prensa* in 1919.

The cultured, well-traveled, widely read Sáenz identified with three U.S. writers, radicals Waldo Frank and Carleton Beals and liberal scholar Samuel Guy Inman. He shared their optimism for the development of Latin America and hope for the realization of dignity for its people. In a clear, objective, sometimes dynamic style, he wrote about liberty, justice, culture, and the nation-state.[46] His moral outrage against imperialism and despotism so affected the climate of opinion that some opponents referred to him as an intellectual *caudillo*. He wrote forceful narratives, did not abstract thought, and used little of the methodology or jargon generally associated with dialectical materialists.

His works displayed historical perspective and a broad humanistic-democratic vision. He considered intellectuals underpaid laborers who had a better social position than manual workers.[47] Like Gramsci, he contended that intellectuals should play a key role in building popular culture and in developing the people's political sensibilities. He felt that many proletarians could not defend themselves and needed the assistance of intellectuals.[48] In "critical" Marxist fashion, he championed workers' causes.

Numerous Latin American thinkers influenced Sáenz. He referred positively to Masferrer's vital minimum concept,[49] acknowledged intellectual debts to Darío, Rodó, and Argentine positivist José Ingenieros, who stressed that ideals are not necessarily truths but beliefs. He admired and wrote about Latin American liberators Bolívar, Morazán, and José Martí and looked to past liberation movements to inspire future ones. He emulated the way the Cuban Martí transmitted energy to others in the quest to eliminate tyranny. He saw Martí, Sandino, and Arévalo as the conscience of their people, brave kindred spirits who opposed foreign imposition. He drew an analogy between Martí and Venezuelan novelist Rómulo Gallegos as Latin American cultural giants who opposed barbarity. He shared Martí's emphasis on the need to have faith in the culture of "our America" (Latin America) in order to progress, as opposed to believing in the tenets of "their America" (the United States), and he strove to keep the Cuban's spirit alive.[50]

Throughout his life, Sáenz moved from one venture to another with ease, grace, and skill. His accomplishments over just one decade provide a good example of his talents. In 1935 he founded the political-literary magazine *Liberación* (Liberation) in Costa Rica, worked for the Popular Front to unite political forces against fascism, and founded the Socialist party of Costa Rica.[51] The next year he organized the Popular Culture Center to propagate socialist ideas and spread general culture. He traveled to Spain to support the republic in 1937, and he assisted the Arévalo government of Guatemala at the United Nations in 1945.

Sáenz's actions were always guided by his dialectical view of the world and his desire for economic liberation for the majority. His economic plan would negate the supremacy of private property, nationalize natural resources and public services, expropriate enormous landholdings, preserve church property as part of the national domain, institute fiscal equality between nationals and foreigners, impose progressive taxes and rents, modernize industry, increase production, and reduce the power of the monopolies and private banks. He sought legislation to effect equality before the law for men and women, minimum wages, social security, a forty-hour work week, collective bargaining, agricultural cooperatives, and children's and women's work laws.[52]

The crash of 1929 confirmed his belief in the necessity of implementing the above programs through socialism. He equated the Depression with a deterioration in the capitalist value system, as a material and moral crisis that precipitated fascism. In his view, Europe was erupting as part of the agony of international capitalism, while Latin America still struggled to get out of the feudal stage[53] that he blamed on its Spanish heritage. He noted, "There appears the fusion of the autochthonous elements with the two Spains that we carry in ourselves, whose cosmic sense of life, whose mysticism and introspection, passions and intolerance, merits and virtues are reflected and collide in the new world and in our souls."[54] He meant that there was a liberal and generous Spain and an absolutist Spain rooted in scholasticism and feudal ways. Spanish American independence never overcame the latter, from which its most retrograde and privileged classes have learned how to profit.[55]

Sáenz severely criticized members of those avaricious classes who attributed the area's underdevelopment to the Malthusian belief that population grows according to geometric progression and food production according to arithmetic progression. He argued that the world produced plenty for all to eat but that the capitalist system allocates the most to a few, thus leaving many hungry. He believed a conflict existed between the prevailing mode of production and the concept of private property because the end result is the unequal distribution of wealth. Like Marx, he condemned Malthusian thought as antirevolutionary, as a policy that justifies working-class misery, and as a means of depriving humanity of hope for social and economic progress.[56]

Sáenz believed that socialism could alleviate many of Latin America's ills, and he wanted to implement it and social change in a constitutional manner. He called suppression of private property a Communist characteristic and believed that private property could be regulated through the constitutional process.[57] He founded the Socialist party in 1935 with a platform that approximated that of Britain's state capitalist Labour party. The Socialists opted for legalism and gradualism as defined by bourgeois society rather than the class struggle advocated by the Communists.

According to Sáenz, what he called *Morismo* (the thought of Manuel Mora) contradicted Marx in that Mora wanted to move to communism by skipping the socialist stage of development.[58] Sáenz called the Communists unrealistic and maintained that the communist stage was unattainable immediately in Costa Rica, where feudal and semifeudal relations of production still existed. He believed that the most his Socialist party could do was to transform the existing system to capitalism and then socialism.[59] Sáenz and Mora engaged in a running battle over strategy and ideology. Sáenz, who wrote about the frauds of anticommunism, unwittingly played into the hands of the anticommunists by stating incorrectly that the endeavors of Costa Rica's Communists were always directed toward promoting Soviet vanguardism.[60]

The Socialist party and Sáenz stressed educational improvements. They wanted to create a new Popular Autonomous University with courses about the origins of the capitalist crisis and social and economic studies taught from international and social-transformation perspectives. The party also campaigned against the Monroe Doctrine, under which the United States granted itself the right to intervene in the affairs of the Latin American states. The Socialists favored the Drago Doctrine, which prohibits armed intervention resulting from public debt, and the Calvo Clause, which recognized the right of states to apply their laws to foreign nationals doing business in their territory. The party also supported Mexico's Estrada Doctrine, which treats diplomatic recognition not as approval of a government but as acceptance of its de facto status.[61] Overall, the Socialist programs and Sáenz's ideas for political, social, and economic change gained considerable respect in liberal circles and contributed significantly to the reforms (discussed in the introduction to this chapter) enacted by Calderón and by the social democrats in the last four decades.

While working through the Socialist party to reform society, Sáenz, through his writings, focused on the effects of the U.S. presence in the Americas. He criticized U.S. intervention and warned that it had rendered Latin America politically and economically dependent. He viewed foreign monopolies as modern equivalents of colonial *encomiendas*, which gave Spaniards control over native communities,[62] and averred that Costa Rica would never have liberty while it remained a colony. He complained about the North Americanization of Central America but conveyed the impression that the imperialists could be reasoned with, that through protests they could be persuaded to change their modus operandi.

Sáenz wondered why foreign interventions were always conducted in the name of peace, progress, and civilization,[63] and he questioned the willingness of Latin American governments to cooperate in giveaways to U.S. companies. Using the word *succionadores* (suckers) to describe the activities of U.S. corporations in the area, he drew analogies between the firms and sixteenth-and seventeenth-century pirates. These enterprises, he said, did not contribute to Latin American civilization, they took away from it.[64] He believed that major economic forces, such as the United Fruit Company, had an obligation to return a high percentage of their profits to the communities where they operated profitably, that corporations should provide the communities with schools, hospitals, roads, and so on.

Paradoxically, Sáenz did not express hostility to the U.S. government but was grateful to it for granting huge amounts of assistance, much of which was, ironically, given to combat socialism. He had a fond spot for Abraham Lincoln and Franklin Roosevelt, who he believed opposed "manifest destiny," racial discrimination, and imperialism.[65] But he lamented that U.S. citizens, before the 1950s, studied Latin America superficially or with contempt[66] and supported a dangerous foreign policy determined by material interests.[67]

Sáenz also criticized the British presence in Belize, Guyana, the Malvinas (Falkland Islands), and Antarctica, and he supported all Latin territorial claims in these areas.[68] In his book *Rompiendo cadenas: Las del imperialismo en Centroamérica y en otras repúblicas del continente* (1961, Breaking the chains of imperialism in Central America and in other republics of the continent), he inveighed against capitalist corruption and abuses of minorities. He claimed that stronger adherence to inter-American law and the concept of equality of nations before the law would curtail U.S. domination in Central America.[69]

In *Nuestras vías interoceánicas* (1957, Our interoceanic routes) Sáenz stated that waterways such as the Suez and Panama canals should always be open to all traffic and that dominion over them by one nation impaired that accessibility.[70] He opposed all unilateral control and actions in the Americas and suggested replacing the Monroe Doctrine and U.S. "dollar diplomacy" with a multilateral hemispheric alliance.[71]

On the international level Sáenz believed in Central American unity as a deterrent to U.S. expansion. On the diplomatic level he strove to control the power of the major international capitalists and their partner, the church. He agreed with Henry George that religion allies with injustice to work against the national aspirations of the masses.[72] He supported Arévalo's concept of a democratic Central American union to cooperate with the United Nations and oppose tyranny. When the OAS was established in 1948, he saw it as a means of attaining equality, sovereignty, and economic justice and as a counterbalance to U.S. power. He did not foresee the danger of U.S. control of the organization[73] but predicted incorrectly that the OAS would provide the democratic unity necessary to isolate and drive out the hemisphere's dictators, who preserved the dependency aspects of imperialism.

By the early 1950s, Sáenz claimed that the battle for liberation had begun as a result of Costa Rica's social reform programs and Arévalo's advances in Guatemala. To him, patriotism and nationalism, not communism, were bringing about independence.[74] At that time his views appeared to be more those of a social democrat than a socialist. But in the early 1960s he took a firsthand look at the Cuban Revolution, liked what he saw, and believed that through idealism, international law, and various types of socialism, his dreams for Latin America were being fulfilled.

Manuel Mora:
The "Red Pope"

For more than half a century, Manuel Mora (1910–) and communism have been synonymous in Costa Rica. A descendant of Spanish conquistadores, Mora was born in San José. His father held various governmental posts and then fell upon hard times. At an early age Mora rebelled against social injustice and his family's suffering. He noted how the Russian Revolution dealt with social problems and examined what he considered to be the revolutionary message of his countryman Jorge Volio, the Reformist party founder who spoke against the wealthy and social inequities. Mora studied law and immersed himself in the writings of Kropotkin, Marx, Engels, and Lenin. In 1928 he founded the Revolutionary Culture Association, the Marxist discussion circle mentioned in the introduction to this chapter,[75] and the following year he started the Communist party of Costa Rica. He prepared for political battles by becoming familiar with the thinking of noteworthy liberals and radicals. His ideas reflect the influence of Bolívar on independence, the antiimperialism of Haya de la Torre, and the thought of British economist John Hobson, who made the first systematic analysis of imperialism and gave it a basically economic interpretation. Mora particularly liked *Dollar Diplomacy* (1925), the classic study of U.S. imperialism by North American radicals Scott Nearing and Joseph Freeman. He also believed that English socialist thinker Harold Laski's depiction of the typical Englishman as a merchant who wants more applied to Costa Ricans as well.[76]

Mora's compatriots regard him as "our Red Pope," a man for all seasons who has served the nation as ideological mentor, polemicist, and congressional deputy. He has devoted his life to politics and to the transformation of the social order while defending Costa Rican sovereignty vociferously.[77] The author of numerous articles and pamphlets, Mora is respected by his most ardent opponents as a vigorous idealist. Although not an original thinker, he is held in high regard by most sectors of society as a tireless champion of the people, an effective politician, and an honest spokesman for the Communist party.

He served as a deputy in the Legislative Assembly from 1934 to 1948 and again from 1970 to 1974, helped lead the semisuccessful banana workers' strike against the United Fruit Company in 1934, and ran for the presidency in 1940 and 1974. During the 1948 civil war, he led the Communists in an alliance with Calderón's forces against Figueres. When the opposition won, the Communist party was outlawed and Mora went into exile. He returned in 1949 and by 1953 had built the General Confederation of Workers.

Mora began communicating his ideas in 1930 through the newspaper *Revolución*, run by his law school colleagues and antiimperialist groups. He asked why in Costa Rica, with plentiful food, water, minerals, and good climate, children died of malnutrition. He concluded that the problem could only be solved by building a government of the people, and not by electoral democracy alone.[78]

With the assistance of Carlos Luis Fallas, Mora began to proselytize for the Communist party among the banana workers in 1931.[79] He ran the party collectively, according to notions of democratic centralism that encouraged members to express their opinions and to educate the masses for socialism. Mora emphasized that the party functioned as a restraining organization, not an electoral one. It provided vital opposition and kept other groups in check.[80]

He assumed the post of secretary general of the Communist party in 1931. Under his guidance it struggled to abolish Costa Rica's semicolonial status. It hoped to do so by eliminating private property, socializing the means of production, and reorganizing the economy. It sought to empower the working class and create a council of workers and peasants to help govern, abolish child labor, initiate the eight-hour workday, suppress the national liquor factory, emancipate women, revise unfair foreign contracts, eliminate latifundios, nationalize transportation and public services and mineral resources, reduce the bureaucracy, and enact a civil service law.[81]

As early as 1934, Mora realized that the party had to establish objectives through national realities, that Costa Rica was not the USSR.[82] No one doubted the loyalty or patriotism of the party, as Mora wanted no intransigence or mystery in *Tico* communism,[83] the native form of the ideology that is scrutinized in the introduction to this chapter. The party supported non-Communist-run progressive juntas all over the country, which spearheaded mass actions for local demands such as electricity or potable water. The progressive juntas mobilized people against oppressive businesses and government.[84] The Communists claimed responsibility for the institutionalization of Costa Rica's social guarantees, the right to organize and strike, the yearly minimum wage, paid holidays, labor courts, rent controls, profit and property taxes, the work code, the social security system, and the electoral code that protects small parties, helps preserve democracy, and acts as a national conscience.[85]

Since before World War II the party has constituted a major force against fascism. Mora described fascism as a form of imperialism that tends to curtail social revolution. Fascist imperialism occurs in expansionist capitalist nations, such as Germany, Italy, and Japan, which lack primary materials and markets for their finished products. It results from capitalism that builds vicious economic cycles of expansion and bellicosity, which leads to militarism, war, and repression.[86]

Mora worked to end fascism and to consolidate democratic regimes in Latin America. Costa Ricans praised his stands until cold war propaganda gave *comunismo criollo* a foreign connotation and cast doubt on the integrity of the Popular Vanguard. But by the 1970s, Mora managed to rebuild the image of the party as more democratic and nationalist than revolutionary. Mora worked for social revolution through legal means and political compromise. His efforts went a long way toward relaxing tensions and permitting Costa Rica to restore full diplomatic relations with the Soviet Union in 1973.[87] His national stature remained high, but his place in the party eventually slipped. In 1983 some militant comrades denounced Mora as a hopelessly out-of-date bourgeois revisionist, and the party replaced him as secretary general with Humberto Vargas Carbonell, giving Mora the ceremonial post of party president.[88] The frustrated Mora then founded a rival organization, the Costa Rican People's party, which stressed the preservation of popular participation in economic and governmental affairs and downplayed working toward the development of a Marxist state.

One can see why Mora's "critical" Marxism has gained more acceptance in Costa Rica than the "rigid" Marxism practiced by some of his fellow Communist leaders elsewhere in Latin America. Unlike them, he has at times advocated class cooperation instead of class warfare.[89] He never violated national traditions, preferring the word *Costaricanism* to *communism*, though recognizing the international character of Marxism. He tried to foster a national revolution rather than an imported one or one for export.[90]

In his numerous speeches in the legislature, Mora tried to inform his fellow deputies about the value of Marxist analysis and the strengths of socialism.[91] He told them that society is an organism that lives in a natural state that evolves in conformity with the laws of dialectical materialism. He also stressed that to transform a social order and attain independence, his people had to sacrifice some of the comforts of life.[92] He pointed out to his colleagues that liberalism emerged in the Middle Ages and constituted a middle-class struggle against the upper class and despotism, and that liberty, equality, and fraternity cannot exist in a liberal society in which the economy is controlled by one class.[93] In Costa Rica, where private property prevails, he noted that the majority of the people have nothing—and you cannot have liberty if you have nothing. Thus the system, which does not work for most people, must be changed.[94] He maintained that if European-style liberalism, which supports the concept of private property, is not exotic in Costa Rica, neither should be European-style Marxism, which opposes private property.[95]

Mora also insisted that the socialist and capitalist worlds must coexist and even cooperate, that only two paths are open to them, armed conflict or commercial relations.[96] He rejected the premise that peaceful coexistence is social pacifism that repudiates class struggle for all times and places. He constantly searched for areas of agreement between the two ideologies. For example, he stressed that *Tico* communism did not oppose small property holders whose actions did not harm the majority. He eschewed violence, and in the face of great pressure over the years, he exercised and urged remarkable restraint, a characteristic emulated by many Costa Rican radicals. Unlike other frustrated leftists in Latin America, he did not become more confrontational or turn toward armed insurrection.

While building *comunismo criollo*, Mora maintained contacts with, and expressed opinions about, other left-wing movements in Latin America. For instance, he claimed that Guatemala's Arévalo, who called himself a socialist, did not understand socialism. To Mora, Arévalo was an emotional egalitarian who looked for marginal solutions to problems but did not know how to use scientific thought to overcome them.[97] Mora pointed to Chile's president Salvador Allende, in contrast, as a fine example of a socialist ascending to power through the ballot box, without a revolution.[98] In fact, though Allende did reach office in 1970 without a revolution, he had little power.

Before Fidel Castro announced his Marxism-Leninism, Mora defended the Cuban Revolution as fulfilling the dreams of liberation of José Martí. He later depicted the Cuban Revolution as a manifestation of 1917 and as part of world revolution. He claimed that Costa Rican Communists and Castro shared common objectives, yet have approached revolution differently. Mora and his Popular Vanguard cohorts realize that Cuba's bourgeois democratic stage, or period of democratic antiimperialism, was almost nonexistent, but they believe that conditions differ in Costa Rica, where the country must go through a long bourgeois democratic period before proceeding to socialism.[99] Meanwhile, the *Fidelistas* wonder if their *Tico* comrades will ever find the time ripe for revolution.

Mora does not view Cuba as a Soviet colony or as a security risk in the hemisphere, and he accused the United States and its allies of economic aggression against the Caribbean island. He pointed out how liberal Venezuelan President Rómulo Betancourt plotted with Nicaragua's Anastasio Somoza to invade Cuba,[100] and how José Figueres has always portrayed Castro as a malevolent dictator because "Don Pepe" feared that if the truth about life in Cuba were made public, *Fidelismo* might become more popular in Costa Rica. Mora understands that Costa Rica's policies concerning Cuba have largely been molded in Washington. Despite his disagreement with the U.S. approach to Castro, he stresses that the Costa Rican Communists are not the enemy of the United States, but of imperialism. He has sought good relations with the United States[101] but has understood its objectives and policies more clearly than did his somewhat naive countryman Vicente Sáenz.

According to Mora, the United States has long desired to control economic relations in the Americas. It promulgated the Monroe Doctrine in 1823 to defend its expansion in the hemisphere and created the Pan American Union, the commercial predecessor of the OAS, in 1889 to facilitate economic dominion in the region and to combat British competition.[102] The United States also made Puerto Rico into a colony and does not hesitate to use violence to get its way there. Moreover, the United States sanctioned the assassination of Sandino in Nicaragua in 1934 and subsequently supported Somoza to further its imperialist objectives.[103]

Mora has long believed that imperialism will destroy Costa Rican sovereignty, and he has demonstrated that the latter has eroded in proportion to the growth of U.S. investment in the nation. He noted that, in its ever-present quest for new markets, the United States has put the machinery of the State Department at the disposal of Wall Street.[104] He called the U.S. invasion of Mexico in 1916 obedience to Standard Oil, which feared that the Mexican Revolution would compel the nationalization of foreign-owned petroleum. He believed that the U.S. occupation also resulted from Woodrow Wilson's moral imperialism. In Mora's opinion, Roosevelt's Good Neighbor Policy was a public relations ploy to obscure U.S. designs on Latin America.[105] Mora interpreted Lázaro Cárdenas's expropriation of foreign oil in Mexico in 1938 as a monumental antiimperialist move on the part of the Mexican president.[106]

At the beginning of World War II, Mora expressed skepticism when the United States demanded that the Central American nations relinquish some national sovereignty for the sake of collective protection against the Axis. He suspected that the United States built wartime alliances to further its economic ambitions, pointing to Calvin Coolidge's statement that "behind each American dollar there is a Yankee bayonet."[107] Mora later recalled that in 1945 the U.S. government used the pretext of the war to enter into treaties with the Central American republics that extracted concessions that helped convert the area into a base of U.S. military operations.[108] He even regarded the construction of the Pan American Highway as a military maneuver, a road to protect the Panama Canal and expedite troop movements.[109]

Mora alluded to the hypocrisy in U.S. anticommunism. For example, after World War II, the United States aided Communist Marshal Tito in Yugoslavia in the hope of building economic ties to Europe, while simultaneously overthrowing the non-Communist Arbenz in Guatemala, who nationalized United Fruit properties.[110] Mora realized that anticommunism, such as that practiced in Guatemala, could harm capitalist social reform. He understood that the United States considered Central America its sphere of influence and would manipulate the area's politics and economy to its advantage.

Mora viewed the Central American Common Market as a prime example of U.S. avarice and as a program that also enabled the United States to further its anticommunist activities. The CACM provided a major market for U.S. products and a place for its investment. By integrating the economies of the Central American nations, the CACM raised industrial production under the direction of the major multinational corporations such as Nabisco, Grace, and Procter and Gamble. Their investments intensified U.S. military and political influence in Costa Rica.[111] Mora and his cohorts argued that the CACM would kill native industry. They believed that the CACM, based on the U.S. model in which the initial phase of economic development is foreign-financed industrialization, would in the long run turn Central America into another Puerto Rico. Instead, they contended, agrarian structures in the region had to be modified so that excess profits natives made from agriculture could be used to build the infrastructure.[112]

Although the United States shaped and buttressed the CACM during the 1960s, Costa Rica began to encounter a balance-of-payments problem because of limited markets for coffee and bananas, which constituted 96 percent of its exports.[113] Mora predicted correctly that by the 1980s a major financial crisis would occur, then the United States, through its control of the International Monetary Fund and the World Bank, would penetrate even further into the economic, social, and political life of the nation, which would have to agree to adopt restrictive austerity measures and possibly even remilitarize in order to obtain loans to help offset its deficits and prop up its faltering economy.[114]

Rodolfo Cerdas Cruz:
Diagnostician of Institutionalized Democracy

In contrast to the legendary "Red Pope," Manuel Mora, stands academician Rodolfo Cerdas Cruz (1939–), an outstanding member of the newer generation of radical thinkers. After obtaining a law degree in Costa Rica, Cerdas did postgraduate study at the Institute of Philosophy of the Academy of Science in the USSR, followed by doctoral work in political sociology at the Sorbonne in Paris, completing his studies with a 1973 dissertation, "Stratégie et tactique de l'Internationale Communiste en Amérique Latine" (Strategy and tactics of the Communist International in Latin America). He specializes in problems of economic development, movements for social change, and in diagnosing Costa Rican society. Cerdas has served as professor and director of the School of Political Science at the University of Costa Rica, as secretary general of Costa Rica's small Popular Front party, and as a Deputy in the Legislative Assembly.

His prolific writing reflects familiarity with the major modern radical thinkers of Latin America and the English-speaking world. He borrowed freely from Paul Sweezy and Maurice Dobb to explain the capitalist system (or, more precisely, the transition from feudalism to capitalism) and like them believed that you can tell from the mode of production, not from distribution, when the social relations of production change from feudal to capitalist.[115] He has relied on the analysis of Argentine socialist Aníbal Ponce to understand the colonial capitalist origins of Latin America and on the thinking of Brazilian Ruy Mauro Marini to explain dependency. Arévalo's *The Shark and the Sardines* confirmed his view that imperialism is the capstone of the pauperization Marx spoke about and that U.S. imperialism often encourages and maintains dictatorship in the Americas.[116] Unquestionably, Cerdas's heroes have been Marx, José Martí, Lenin, Chilean poet Pablo Neruda, and Nicaragua's Augusto Sandino. In *Sandino, El Apra y la Internacional Comunista: Antecedentes históricos de la Nicaragua de hoy* (1983, Sandino, APRA, and the Communist International: Historical antecedents of today's Nicaragua), he had high praise for the Indo-Hispanic internationalism of Sandino and the *Apristas* and for their shared belief in Indian sovereignty and workers' solidarity.[117]

Cerdas's work reflects a historical perspective, as is evident in his analysis of the development of Costa Rica's nation-state and its rulers. He explained that in Costa Rica a contradiction between native economic power and foreign political power led to conflict during the colonial period that helped precipitate the movement for independence. After independence, Costa Rica created a state with fundamental political power held by the national bourgeoisie.[118] By 1821, the bourgeoisie began to consolidate its position as the dominant class. An open economic system contributed to the power of this class, which still controls the nation and the degree of progress and liberty available to most of its citizens.[119]

Cerdas cited President Braulio Carrillo (1835–1837 and 1838–1842) as the architect of the Costa Rican nation-state. An authoritarian type inspired by Rousseau, Carrillo consolidated power, issued a constitution that provided stability, established precedents for state intervention in the economy, and gave the country the basis for its liberal democracy. Under him, coffee began to be a major export commodity and the United

States the primary purchaser, as the nation's economy turned away from Europe.[120]

Cerdas noted that Costa Rica's nineteenth-century drive for Central American integration became a social force or development tool, a mechanism to increase production, expand markets, attract investment, and thereby increase the power of the national bourgeoisie.[121] He also showed that while the liberal state's power increased during the 1880s and 1890s, anarchism and the concept of the general strike were imported from Spain.

Then it took the labor movement almost four decades to learn how to use strikes effectively.[122] By 1919 considerable working-class opposition to liberal domination existed, a Socialist Center was established, and an organized Left began to work toward changing the capitalist system of social relations. The Left did not succeed in restructuring the system but did, by 1920, foster reforms such as the eight-hour day and labor legislation.

Unlike South American countries such as Chile, which tended, via import substitution, to develop a bit during World War I, Costa Rica did not industrialize until World War II, at a time when transnational companies proliferated. Without a Costa Rican industrial class, foreign corporations took charge of the economy and allied with, and undermined, the national bourgeoisie.[123] Industrialization, according to Cerdas, gave rise to a new working class that, because of the unstable economic climate, was responsive to the ideas of the Left. The ruling elite quickly made some concessions to the working class to prevent it from developing a degree of solidarity that would constitute a serious challenge. A U.S.-style labor movement evolved in which the workers were satisfied with a few consumer goods and did not ask to participate in social and political decisions. Cerdas called this, at best, a reformist society, run by a pseudoaristocracy, with labor leaders who replicated the AFL-CIO mentality. He pointed out that the old banana worker unionists from the 1930s knew better and were not taken in by this bourgeois form of trade unionism.[124]

Cerdas asserted that in subsequent decades the CACM and the Alliance for Progress tied Costa Rica closer to the United States, strengthened a U.S. brand of unionization, fortified the multinationals, and enhanced dependency.[125] He contended that under these circumstances the national bourgeoisie was not guided by U.S. economic policies per se, but by the characteristics of foreign capital.[126]

Having looked at the development of the Costa Rican nation-state from Cerdas's historical perspective, we turn to his idealized version of what it could be. Going on the premise, as did Engels, that man's natural state is emancipated,[127] Cerdas advocated a nation-state that provides individual and group liberty. His ideal state would organize and direct the abolition of exploitation.[128] He wanted a new democracy, a nation-state with a new bloc of social forces and genuine mass participation, a state that would revive native cultural values and lead within the bounds of national reality.

Cerdas viewed the crises in Costa Rica as emanating not just from leadership, values, or the constitutional political system, but from the economic and social structures and the role of the state.[129] He found Costa Rica's fundamental problems to be ideological and tied to world capitalism. He debunked the myth of free enterprise, maintaining that capitalist Costa Rica is dependent, not free.[130] Under the prevailing ideology, he believed, there could be no genuine development in the future because of dependency, and he predicted that democratic liberties in Costa Rica would diminish.[131]

Cerdas wanted the state to turn away from Keynesian solutions designed to assist the capitalists rather than the working-class majority. He granted that Costa Rica's welfare state distributed goods and services to the community but said that it also promoted production that heavily favored the dominant bourgeoisie.[132] Cerdas identified two major and conflicting components of the bourgeoisie currently vying with each other for political power. The newer, U.S.-oriented entrepreneurial elite is dedicated to the secondary and tertiary economic sectors of society, or business and industry. The traditional agro-export oligarchy is dedicated to primary production and is especially dissatisfied with the government. Cerdas called this an institutional crisis.[133] Costa Rica's major traditional political parties have been unable to settle the conflict, its old Marxist parties are petrified,[134] and the liberal democracy cannot cope with the economic and social problems of the modern state. Thus what Cerdas called Costa Rica's "institutionalized democracy" is failing.[135]

Despite the existing crises, organized labor and the radical intellectual elements find it difficult to penetrate the power bloc to the extent necessary to obtain some political control. Cerdas concluded that Costa Rica's revolution is a long way off.[136] Some of the country's problems might be solved by a move to the neofascist right as has taken place elsewhere in Latin America, but they are not likely to be resolved by reformism—the path that led to the crises.

He noted that Costa Rica's universities exist to train professionals and technicians for industry and to enhance capitalist development, and cannot cope with problems such as those noted above, whose resolution requires thinking that exceeds Costa Rican intellectuals' prescribed bounds.[137] As Cerdas stated, before the universities can solve crises, they must realize that Costa Rica's liberal democracy is not the product of logical historical development. The idyllic liberal Costa Rica found in textbooks represents the conquest of the Costa Rican people by a retrograde democratic system. The university communities must learn that whereas they construe the term *democratic* as positive, it is in fact relative.[138]

Costa Rica can solve its social and economic problems, said Cerdas, if it builds a social base anchored by rural and urban workers, assisted by the petit bourgeoisie. These groups, well organized and unified, can effect a process of national liberty if simultaneously the industrial and agrarian components of the national bourgeoisie ally to free Costa Rica from imperialist domination. Together, the working class and bourgeois elements could build on the existing democratic tradition and increase popular participation. This new power bloc, in order to forge independent development, would have to be profoundly nationalist, antiimperialist, against hegemony, for socialism, and led by an authentic, independent Marxist-Leninist organization.[139]

Cerdas worked to create such an organization, the Popular Front party that functioned in a "critical" Marxist manner. He devoted a great deal of time to explaining its ideology and functions to its potential members, the students and intellectuals of Costa Rica. To him, as to Marx, socialism expressed the most vital interests of the working class. It is not a doctrine for sects but one for the proletariat to use to illuminate its path to revolution. It fulfills the workers' historical mission to liberate humanity from oppression and to foster a new type of social thought.[140] Marxism is not a mechanistic way to solve all problems; rather, it is a method, a basic ideology that permits you to solve problems not by being dogmatic, but through study that allows you to see the verities of social interaction and what causes or prevents change. It directs the majority class to seek truth and does not organize for repression.[141]

Cerdas warned, as did Lenin, that during the transition from capitalism to communism repression is always necessary to remove the former exploiters of society. But he noted that the repression is only transitory, and once the new machinery is in place the repression begins to disappear.[142] He negated the idea that you have to curtail personal and political liberty to have socialism.[143] He agreed with Laski that the Soviet Union has had to remain ever-vigilant against external aggression, that in so doing it has maintained a state without popular participation, but that this does not mean that all Communist states will be oppressive dictatorships.[144] Cerdas claimed that the dictatorship of the proletariat in the USSR is not something monstrous that retards the advancement of humanity and added that progress has been made in the Soviet Union, despite negative portrayals in U.S. newspapers and magazines.[145] According to Cerdas, dictatorship of the proletariat refers not to a utopia, but to a society without exploitation, a classless society with a Communist party as the vanguard of the working class it defends until the workers can control their own interests.[146]

Cerdas credited the Costa Rican Communist party for understanding and operating within the country's reality, for not being hidebound and doing things the Moscow way. Although he praised Communist leader Mora's accomplishments on behalf of the workers, Cerdas complained that the Communists have often confused workers who cannot comprehend how the party defends their interests and why it believes that it can effect the transition to socialism through the bourgeois parliamentary process.[147]

In spite of Cerdas's eloquent justifications for Marxism, the ideology has met vociferous opponents in the Costa Rican academy. In 1959 university rector Rodrigo Facio held a conference during which he denounced Marxism. Cerdas responded with "La conferencia del rector Facio sobre marxismo. Una respuesta." (1960, Rector Facio's conference on marxism: An answer), which became quite well known in academic circles. Cerdas opposed the anticommunism of Facio, who painted a distorted picture of Marxism as synonymous with Soviet totalitarianism. Cerdas deplored the narrow-mindedness of the anticommunists and emphasized that Marxism is humanism in practice, not humanism in the abstract.[148] Besides trying to erase preconceived, erroneous notions about Marxism, Cerdas has also tried to educate Costa Ricans about the accomplishments of the Marxist movement in Latin America. His monograph *Farabundo Martí, la internacional comunista y la insurrección salvadoreña de 1932* (1982, Farabundo Martí, the Communist international and the Salvadoran insurrection of 1932) explained how the embryonic Communist party, the 1919 railroad workers' strike, the 1921 shoemakers' strike, and the establishment of the Regional Federation of Workers in 1924, combined with the international capitalist crisis had precipitated the 1932 uprising in El Salvador.[149] Coffee then accounted for 95.5 percent of El Salvador's exports. With no industrial base to sustain the country through the Depression, coffee prices dropped, the economy fell, the people suffered, and violence erupted.

Cerdas called the Communist-led upheaval in El Salvador an inappropriate attempt to convert a nonexistent bourgeois democratic revolution into a socialist one.[150] He recognized the insurrection as a working-class endeavor to gain the right to participate in decisions affecting its fate, as the beginning of the rejection of dependency, and as an effort to build a viable revolution by directing the peasants' enormous energies against the bourgeoisie.[151] The 1932 uprising revealed the disposition of the workers and peasants to try to effect change. They wrote a glorious chapter in the history of the international revolutionary movement, one unfortunately overshadowed by the reprisals of the *matanza.*

Cerdas pointed out that five months later the abortive Salvadoran move toward socialism inspired a short-lived Chilean socialist republic. For years to come, the dream of radical change remained alive, as evidenced by the Farabundo Martí National Liberation Movement of the 1980s.[152] Contemporary Central American revolutionaries find Cerdas's critical analyses, including the piece on the Salvadoran conflict, most useful as they develop their ideologies and plan strategies for the future.

José Luis Vega Carballo:
The Liberal State and Indirect Domination

Cerdas's colleague in political sociology at the University of Costa Rica, José Luis Vega Carballo (1943–), studied in his native San José, then received a B.A. at Brandeis and an M.A. at Princeton. A superior synthesizer of political history, his books reflect the thinking of Marx; the Latin American *dependentistas;* Talcott Parsons, who studied relationships between ideology and the state; Max Weber, who searched for essences within history; and Immanuel Wallerstein and the world systems analysis school.

Like Cerdas, Vega built his studies on historical foundations, but he has filtered his observations through a slightly different but nevertheless still "critical" Marxist lens. He demonstrated that Costa Rica's colonial heritage differed from that of most of Latin America. Other colonies were established for exploitation; Costa Rica was a place for private farmers to live. After the Spanish destroyed most of the Indian population, ethnic homogenization took place. Once the Spanish were expelled, political power corresponded to the social structure.[153] A class system based on inexpensive agricultural labor and foreign dependence developed, without the extremes of coercion and violence found in other Central American states.[154]

From 1821 to 1842, a period Vega called the "patriarchal state," a small oligarchy ruled.[155] Liberal ideas and white supremacy grew, as did the principle—unique within Latin America—of subordination of the military to civilian political power.[156] Since the presidency of Juan Mora Fernández (1824–1833), a system of patrimonial oligarchy has existed under which the state has appeared little different from civil society but has been controlled by the owners of the means of production. When Morazán took over in 1842, the dominant white class and foreign capital controlled the state.[157] By the time the transition to liberalism was complete in 1890, the state had been consolidated as part of the world market.[158] The country built a legal system around the concepts of private property and capital accumulation to serve the bourgeoisie. Vega called this "indirect domination."

A popular insurrection in 1889 fostered electoral reforms that led to this indirect domination, which paved the way for a more open political system. State and civil service employees had more say, state capitalism grew, and a new class of quasi-intellectual bureaucrats emerged. The owners of the means of production ruled indirectly through the government.[159] Indirect domination combined liberalism, paternalism, and legality with a tradition of municipal government and public education. Under indirect domination the liberal teachers became Costa Rica's army.[160]

According to Vega, during World War I and over the next forty years, the oligarchic liberal state changed. The state intervened in the economy more frequently, as did the middle class. The country's technobureaucracy functioned as a sociopolitical vanguard of the middle class and maintained a Uruguayan-style welfare state.[161] New political-intellectual minorities and labor unions arose after the beginning of the Depression as the demand for social mobility increased. At the same time, the small independent planters entered the political process and competed for political power. According to Vega, between 1930 and 1950 Costa Rica experienced a reaction against its oligarchy and mobilized for popular reforms. By then new political-ideological elements had broken from the prevailing system,[162] including various types of radicals.

Vega designated the era from 1949 on, the Second Republic,[163] which closely corresponds to the "liberal democracy" period examined in the introduction to this chapter. He noted that during this epoch, Figueres started reforms, the cold war introduced major tensions, economic crises began, and national sovereignty eroded as a result of regional economic integration and pressures from the United States. For a while, the reforms absorbed popular demands. But increased dependency subsequently created internal colonialism, which benefited the cities at the expense of the countryside. Misery and underdevelopment expanded as the peasantry paid the high cost of industrialization. Only in the early 1970s did a significant number of Costa Rican intellectuals begin to see the country as an international satellite and start to discuss the problems resulting from the new dependency.[164]

Vega does not expect the nation's social and economic problems to be rectified by the traditional political parties, which suffer from personalism and immorality.[165] The parties, to use Gramsci's terms, have inorganic relationships to various groups of clients. They distribute favors to win what Vega called the "election carnival."[166] Nor do the traditional parties represent the aspirations and interests of the majority. They are manipulative and pander to the masses but protect the interests of the owners of the means of production. They do not scientifically examine society or plan its development. Rather, they are reactive, handling problems as they arise. Although they are sclerotic, the parties perpetuate the myth of flexibility without providing channels of genuine participation for the new working classes. Under the traditional parties, with their ties to multinationals, Costa Rican dependency deepens. Vega concurred with Cerdas on the need to develop a new independent socialist mentality in Costa Rica to supplant that of the archaic political establishment, if the nation is to avert a national catastrophe.[167]

Vega realizes that the country's early education program prepared the people well for their elite-run positivist system. Since the nineteenth century, Costa Rica has built a strata of teachers, jurists, writers, and thinkers who have subscribed to the notion of the liberal, upwardly mobile society, directed its cultural apparatus, and sustained the belief in the state as the social benefactor.[168] Most Costa Ricans covet middle-class status and have been trained to ascend the ladder into it in order to reap the benefits of a system designed to bolster that sector.[169] They want their slice of the liberalism that Gramsci said is always introduced by legislation, regimented by the state, and maintained by coercion.[170]

Vega proved that historically the liberal Costa Rican nation-state has always operated according to the requisites of capitalism, with its predominantly paternalistic relations of production.[171] He showed that the state did not form spontaneously, nor has it been the exclusive product of the acts of great people. The expressions of the interrelationships of social forces, not constitutional provisions, have determined real political power.[172] Somehow the state managed to acquire an aura of legitimacy that has enabled it to exercise social control through education and by inculcating the myth of equality rather than by the use of force.[173] It has built, and maintained, great respect for its law and authority. This respect is often greater than the morality of those who supposedly uphold the law. The state, according to Vega, became synonymous with lawyers who contribute to the system of indirect domination and influence most facets of Costa Rican life.[174]

A subservient, dominated working class exists in this lawyer-run society that is not as bad off as its counterparts in other Central American nations. Vega maintains that in Costa Rica's industrial society, this subordinate majority can effect social change and societal development. He believes that in today's modern world greater opportunities exist for the working classes to unify to gain political power and to build a qualitatively different form of life.[175]

Although Costa Rica has attained higher living standards than the other Central American states, and its government and native and foreign capitalist scholars have frequently depicted its socioeconomic system as a miniature version of that of the United States, its radical thinkers maintain that the majority of their fellow citizens would be better served by socialism. Following this line of thought, Vega and his contemporary Cerdas Cruz have built upon the belief of their predecessors Sáenz and Mora that humanity can be liberated and social change implemented if the competitive and destructive individual ego, rampant in capitalist society, can be diminished in favor of the socialist notion of working for the collective good. For decades these and like-minded Costa Rican socialist activists have maintained that a materialist conception of the world would vitiate the traditional paternalistic views that have predominated and retarded social development in their country.

The four "critical" Marxist thinker-writers examined in this chapter reflect on the defects in Costa Rica's long tradition of institutionalized democracy and acknowledge that it has produced greater sophistication in the art of peaceful politics than exists elsewhere in Central America. Nevertheless, they seek to replace existing capitalist ideas with more humanistic socialist ones in order to precipitate a revolution. Before this ideological transformation can be made, they agree that you must first eliminate the elite monopoly on the transmission of knowledge and reshape the country's value system.[176] They admit that this is a difficult task to accomplish in light of a century of liberalism that most Costa Ricans equate with reforms, democracy, and stability and that they fear might be lost in the course of a failed revolution.

By the 1990s, the credibility of Costa Rica's radical social and political commentators rose as the nation became more militarized, its economy deteriorated, 25 percent of the Costa Ricans lived below the poverty level, drug scandals and governmental corruption increased, urban and rural unions lost power, workers faced repression, the CIA and the U.S. Information Agency purchased friends in the media, and freedom of expression diminished.

6

Nicaragua

Tyrants do not represent nations, and liberty is not won with flowers.
—Augusto César Sandino

Central America's largest nation, Nicaragua, named after the powerful Indian chief Nicarao, currently has the region's lowest population density. In the early sixteenth century the native population was approximately 1 million. Within a quarter century after the arrival of Spanish conqueror Gil González in 1522, the Indian population was reduced to tens of thousands by disease brought by the Spaniards, deaths in battle, and Spain's export slave trade. Antiimperialist struggle and class conflict in Nicaragua began with Indian resistance to Spanish rule, according to Marxist theoretician Jaime Wheelock Román. Over the long colonial period, Nicaragua became a predominantly mestizo nation in which a small elite dominated the economy through the exportation of beef, hides, and lumber.

Nicaragua attained independence in 1822 as part of the newly formed Mexican empire; the following year it joined the Central American Federation. Elites still maintained economic and political control, and foreigners exercised a disproportionate amount of power in the country. Internal power struggles ensued, and for most of the nineteenth century political stability proved elusive.

Despite prolonged political and social turmoil, a segment of Nicaragua's population has always been devoted to learning and ideas. A college authorized by Charles II of Spain was founded in León in 1670 and became the National University during the second decade of the nineteenth century. Politics became a major interest of university students. In 1835 the government established the country's first newspaper as a vehicle for political expression.

159

After separation from the Central American Federation in 1838, Nicaragua fell victim to a struggle between the Liberal and Conservative political parties, both dominated by the landed aristocracy. Political rivalries grew between the Liberal city of León and Granada, the Conservative stronghold. To further complicate matters, the British occupied Greytown (San Juan del Norte) on the Caribbean coast, where British and U.S. businesses vied for transportation rights, as Nicaragua had the potential for the fastest land and water route across the Central American isthmus.

In 1848, after the discovery of gold in California, Nicaragua was a logical shortcut for those who wanted to go from the Atlantic coast to the Pacific. New Yorker Cornelius Vanderbilt, supported by Nicaragua's Conservative party, started a transit company to convey passengers across Nicaragua. Commercial interest in Nicaragua grew, and in 1850 the United States and Great Britain entered into the Clayton-Bulwer Treaty, which stipulated that if a canal were constructed across the isthmus, neither nation would maintain exclusive control over it or colonize Central American territory.

Soldier of fortune William Walker of Tennessee, who believed in the United States' Manifest Destiny and represented financier J. P. Morgan's interests in a Nicaraguan transit route, was invited into the country by Liberals from León. In 1855 Walker and his band of mercenaries entered Nicaragua, and the next year he declared himself president, proclaimed slavery legal, and made English the official language. This set in motion a war pitting most of Central America against the invader, who initially had the implied support of the U.S. government. Walker was forced out of Nicaragua in 1856. He attempted another Central American filibustering expedition in 1860, whereupon he was captured by the British and handed over to the Hondurans, who tried and executed him. Years later, poet Rubén Darío depicted Walker's adventures as the first in a series of U.S. incursions attributable to the desire for additional territory.

After the Walker fiasco, Nicaraguans began to denounce the U.S. presence on the isthmus. For example, José de Marcoleta (1802–1881), a writer known as the father of Nicaraguan diplomacy, protested against the U.S. colony on the Atlantic coast that went by the name of the Central American Land and Mining Company, and he questioned the actions of Walker. A famous letter, "Un cien nicaragüenses al pueblo de los Estados Unidos" (1858, A hundred Nicaraguans to the people of the United States), referred to Walker and his followers and complained about U.S. citizens' breaching the nonintervention precepts of the Monroe Doctrine.[1]

As coffee production began in the 1860s, Nicaragua's infrastructure improved, as did its transportation, education, legal, and educational systems. The export economy expanded, along with liberal philosophy. Granada established a school for college preparation in 1874, and a literary group formed in that city two years later. By the 1880s, Nicaraguan students and the nation's small intelligentsia paid attention to critical ideas, especially those pertaining to the odious aspects of intervention. The country's first analytical literary society formed in León in 1881 and organized courses and conferences. That year the National Library opened in Managua. The nation's first general circulation newspaper, *El Diario de Nicaragua*, appeared in 1884.[2] The intelligentsia read pieces by Juan Donoso Cortés on socialism, liberalism, and Catholicism.[3] Newspapers became more popular in Nicaragua than in El Salvador, Honduras, or Guatemala and whetted the reading public's appetite for politics, both national and international. As poetry became part of the national ethos, poets were respected, and those whose work encompassed political themes were revered. For example, poet Rubén Darío, who lived most of his life in the nineteenth century, became the most quoted man in Nicaraguan history. His twentieth-century counterpart, Ernesto Cardenal, is currently one of the most venerated individuals in the country. Foreign interest increased in Nicaragua as a potential site for an interoceanic waterway, and antiimperialist ideas assumed a prominent place in the type of Nicaraguan political prose and poetry made famous by Darío and continued by Cardenal.

After the expulsion of Walker, the Conservatives ruled Nicaragua until the presidency of Liberal José Santos Zelaya (1893–1909). He ushered in modern liberalism and inaugurated Nicaragua's first genuine, somewhat cohesive, government. When Zelaya, who wanted to build a transisthmian canal with Japanese or German financing, canceled some U.S. concessions in the country, Washington threw its support behind his Conservative opponents.

Reactionaries, who did not hesitate to sell their country's sources of wealth to foreigners for a profit, struggled for political and economic control with the less avaricious Liberals. Both groups, which constituted the ruling class, were guided by European positivism, with its tenets of "order and progress" and "survival of the fittest." By the turn of the century, positivist thought dominated in intellectual circles, where radical ideas were rarely espoused. At this time, the closest the country came to a working-class movement were tiny mutual aid societies that were hardly bastions of radicalism.

The Liberal yet authoritarian Zelaya, a positivist, tried to modernize Nicaragua, promoted Central American unity, got the British to depart from the Atlantic coast, and refused to grant the United States canal-building rights that would have relinquished Nicaraguan territorial sovereignty. Conflict between the United States and Nicaragua mounted.

Washington's persistent meddling in Latin American affairs was well known in Nicaragua, thanks in part to the writing of Darío, especially his ode *To Roosevelt* (1904), which warned about the Anglo menace.

The United States supported the Nicaraguan Conservatives, and when Zelaya executed two U.S. mercenaries in 1909, Washington dispatched troops to the area. The United States forced Zelaya into exile, and its intervention offended the Nicaraguans and elicited a strong antiimperialist reaction. The erudite Benjamín Zeledón, a newspaper editor and lawyer and a Liberal follower of Zelaya, led an uprising against the U.S. puppet, President Adolfo Díaz, in 1912. U.S. marines went into Nicaragua, where they remained until 1925. Conservative troops captured Zeledón and dragged his dead body through the village of Niquinohomo, where the teenage Augusto Sandino witnessed, and was outraged by, the spectacle.

By the second decade of the twentieth century, the victimization of Nicaragua by the United States was well known throughout Latin America. Salvadoran physician-writer Hildebrando Castellon H. organized the Central American Patriotic League to arouse public opinion against U.S. intervention in Nicaragua.[4] At the same time, the U.S. government asked New York banks to extend loans to Nicaragua to prop up the Díaz government. In return, the United States was permitted to manage Nicaragua's customs collections until 1924. Under the Bryan-Chamorro Treaty of 1914, Nicaragua granted the United States the right to build a canal across Nicaragua. This prevented another nation from constructing a waterway to compete with the U.S.-controlled canal in Panama and further antagonized Nicaraguan nationalists.

After the Russian Revolution, Nicaragua's antiimperialist and nationalist intellectuals began to build bridges to the nation's working classes. In the early 1920s, an embryonic labor movement became active in politics. The Free Federation of Workers, a socialist-oriented union, was established in León and lasted until the 1930s. The Nicaraguan Federation of Workers, with a capitalist social-reform orientation and loose ties to the AF of L, formed in 1923.[5] By this time, coffee accounted for most of Nicaragua's export earnings, and its banana, gold, and rubber industries were U.S.-dominated.[6] Workers started to make the connections between their impoverishment and foreign investment in their country. Even Simeón Pereira y Castellon, bishop of the diocese of Nicaragua, complained about the negative influence of U.S. capital.[7]

The Central American Communist party started in 1925, and its ideas rapidly spilled over into Nicaragua, where there existed considerable hostility toward the U.S. troops who had been there since 1912 and who helped maintain the Conservative party in power. A Liberal rebellion broke out in 1926. Coolidge claimed that the Soviet Union incited the insurrection to threaten the Panama Canal and the security of the United

States, and that anti-U.S. actions by Nicaraguans would embolden Mexico to nationalize U.S.-controlled petroleum holdings. To prevent a loss of prestige, Coolidge sent U.S. troops back into Nicaragua, where they remained until 1933. To obtain appropriations for arms for the U.S. puppet, Díaz, Coolidge assured Congress that he had evidence of Mexican Bolsheviks' involvement in the Nicaraguan uprising.

A seven-year antiimperialist war of liberation led by Augusto Sandino against the United States began in 1926. Sandino's exploits against U.S. ground and air forces attracted attention throughout the Americas, establishing a precedent for armed insurrection designed to curtail social injustice and foreign intervention. Vanguardia, a nationalist Nicaraguan literary group, formed in 1927 and supported Sandino, whose ideas on defending Nicaraguan sovereignty, reconciling nationalism with hemispheric unity, populism, and the role of God in revolution became familiar to its members. Nicaragua's Communist party did everything in its power to encourage and win over Sandino's movement but failed because its sectarian approach conflicted with Sandino's endeavors to unite a broad range of forces. The Communists did succeed in having their ideas discussed in Nicaragua by rebels, workers, and intellectuals. Nicaraguan poet Salomón de la Selva (1893–1959) organized a Pan American Workers' Conference in Washington in 1927, and in U.S. journals like *The Nation*, he defended Sandino and condemned imperialism.[8] Maximo Soto Hall, influenced by Nearing and Freeman's *Dollar Diplomacy* (1925), wrote *Nicaragua y el imperialismo norteamericano* (1928, Nicaragua and North American imperialism), which traced the history of U.S. intervention in the Central American republic.

While Sandino's guerrilla offensive was under way, the Nicaraguan Patriotic Union, a staunch opponent of the U.S. occupation, published the newspaper *Patria* (Fatherland), which defended national sovereignty and tried to induce Nicaraguan youth to support the insurgents. The organization also engaged in mass actions to get its message across to the public, and in 1930 mounted a demonstration of over 10,000 people in Managua. U.S. marines retaliated by persecuting Patriotic Union members.[9]

Nicaraguan novelist Hernán Robleto wrote *Sangre en el trópico: La novela de la intervención Yanqui en Nicaragua* (1930, Blood in the tropics: The novel of Yankee intervention in Nicaragua) in which he chronicled the 1926 civil war between the Liberals and Conservatives and blamed U.S. support of the Conservatives on Wall Street. His novel *Los estranguladores: El imperialismo Yanqui en Nicaragua* (1933, The stranglers: Yankee imperialism in Nicaragua) reiterated the themes of his previous work.[10] Both of his books had to be published outside of Nicaragua.

Nicaraguan miners and workers, along with Salvadoran Agustín Farabundo Martí, organized the Nicaraguan Workers' party in 1931. A few middle-class students and petit bourgeois elements also backed the group, which had some Leninist tendencies but professed no political ideology. The government persecuted the organization and branded it "Communist."[11]

Liberal Juan Bautista Sacasa won the presidency in 1932 in a U.S.-supervised election, and he immediately appointed his nephew Anastasio "Tacho" Somoza García head of the U.S.-trained Guardia Nacional (National Guard). In 1933 the U.S. marines went home. Government forces assassinated Sandino, who was still advocating collectivist programs, and Somoza tried to obliterate the memory of the guerrilla leader. Henceforth, mere mention of Sandino resulted in a prison sentence. The government persecuted socialists and neutralized the small, basically artisan labor movement for the next two decades. A "blueshirt" organization, patterned after Italy's fascists, worked to keep the Left in line.

Although the government and Somoza equated unionism with Bolshevism, in 1934 the Nicaraguan Workers' party attempted to start a union movement. For five years, through its newspaper *El Proletario* (The Proletariat), the party campaigned for state control of industry and agriculture, state ownership of land, cancellation of debts owed to other nations, socialist education, and an end to the idea of Central American union under imperialism.[12] A Communist faction in the Nicaraguan Workers' party broke away and formed the pro-Moscow Socialist party and published the newspaper *Senderos* (Pathways). In 1939 Somoza disbanded the party and sent its leaders into exile.[13]

Somoza assumed the presidency in January 1937 and changed the constitution to permit himself to rule through puppets until 1956. Communists at times worked informally with the dictator to allow their movement time to gain a foothold in organized labor. Using Popular Front tactics, the Communists allied themselves with progressive capitalist groups that opposed fascism. They strove to win Somoza's confidence, and Mexican labor leader Vicente Lombardo Toledano convinced the Nicaraguan strongman that it would be beneficial to have a Nicaraguan labor organization under Communist control. In 1944, in response to the belief in Nicaragua that if the war for democracy in Europe was worth supporting, more democratic practices should be instituted at home, Tacho permitted the formation of the Nicaraguan Confederation of Workers, led by the reconstituted Socialist (Communist) party.[14] According to radical thinker Carlos Fonseca, the Communists displayed little theoretical sophistication, primarily because Nicaragua's Marxist movement, unlike others in Latin America, had no nineteenth-century roots.

An air of guarded cordiality existed between the Left and the government. In 1944 a group of young liberal dissidents formed the Democratic Youth Front, out of which came the intellectuals who in the late 1950s founded the guerrilla movement of El Chaparral, a precursor to the Sandinista National Liberation Front (FSLN). A prominent member of the Youth front was Rigoberto López Pérez, the poet who subsequently assassinated Anastasio Somoza.[15]

An informal group known as the Generation of 1944 worked among students to draw analogies between European fascism and the Somoza dictatorship.[16] Antifascists, who opposed another term in office for Somoza, broke from his Liberal party and formed the Independent Liberal party (PLI). Some PLI members believed it legitimate to engage in armed insurrection of the Sandino variety to eliminate dictatorship. Remnants of the Generation of 1944 and the PLI eventually joined the FSLN.[17]

By 1947 Somoza feared that he had unleashed a monster by allowing the Left to develop. He moved to crush his radical critics by abolishing the Communist-led Nicaraguan Confederation of Labor. With the cold war under way, all opposition to the government was labeled "red." Some Communist leaders went to jail, and the union movement was severely weakened, but not dead. In late 1948 the Communists managed to found the short-lived General Confederation of Workers. That year the modern University of Nicaragua opened, and students and professors there kept alive interest in radical political activities and trade unionism.

Nicaragua's bourgeoisie modernized through the expansion of the cotton industry in the 1950s. Coffee became less important, dependency deepened, and the gap between the ruling class and the peasantry widened.[18] Dependency and the pauperization it caused fueled the fires of antiimperialism, and organizations such as the National Union for Popular Action agitated for democratic nationalist reforms. Anti-Somoza and anti-U.S. sentiment grew among workers and the intelligentsia, especially after the CIA used Nicaraguan territory as a staging area for the overthrow of the Guatemalan government in 1954.

López Pérez avenged the death of Sandino by shooting Somoza in 1956, calling his act the beginning of the end of tyranny.[19] Luis Somoza succeeded his father as president. Nicaraguan intellectuals increasingly began to look to their past to understand the present and to Sandino for inspiration to rectify society's ills. By 1958 a new Sandinista-type war, led by General Ramón Raudeles, had begun in the north. Raudeles endeavored to revive the insurrection that had ended in 1934, and during the next five years twenty armed uprisings against the Somozas occurred. Radical university students joined the rebellion and called themselves the "Autonomy Generation." Prominent among the young anti-Somoza radicals was Sergio Ramírez, who founded and edited the left-wing literary journal *Ventana* (Window). Ramírez later exposed the violence of the Somozas in *¿Te dió miedio la sangre?* (1977), translated in 1984 as *To Bury Our Fathers*, the first novel by a Nicaraguan published in English.

Young Nicaraguan radicals were influenced by Edelberto Torres, biographer of Sandino and father of social scientist Edelberto Torres Rivas. The elder Torres, a distinguished man of letters, conveyed the antiimperialism of Sandino and Darío to 1950s students eager for heroes. Those exposed to Torres, such as Fonseca, received critical analyses, an appreciation of Nicaragua's historical tradition, and a radical-humanist approach to the future. Torres negated the views of the dictator, who propagated the myth that Nicaraguan identity proceeded exclusively from the Spanish and that Indian civilization was superfluous.[20]

Revolutionary consciousness, especially among university students, reached new heights. The Chinese and Cuban revolutions provided models for members of the Generation of 1959, who promoted awareness of the horrors of the Somoza dictatorship. After the fall of Cuba's Batista, autocrats all over Latin America felt a bit less secure. According to Marxist thinker Tomás Borge, "The Cuban revolution certainly sent a shower of terror through the ruling classes of Latin America. . . . Fidel was for us the resurrection of Sandino, the answer to our reservations, the justification of the dreams and heresies of some hours before."[21] Looking to Cuba as an example, Borge and other Nicaraguan intellectuals saw a need to pursue military victory in the countryside, for the time being to deviate from the traditional Communist road to revolution, which entailed organizing the urban proletariat. Luis Somoza became aware of the *Fidelista* influence in his country and in June 1959 accused Cuba of supporting efforts to topple his government. The United States then ordered its navy to stop any "Communist-led" invasion of Central America.[22]

Somoza encouraged industrialization and agricultural diversification during the 1960s. State intervention in the economic sphere increased, with profits primarily accruing to the Somoza family. The Central American Common Market formed in 1961 and opened the nation to more U.S. investment, increased proletarian poverty, and unemployment. As explained by Jaime Wheelock, the CACM also emphasized the type of industrialization that benefited the wealthy, increased the flow of capital abroad, and detracted from the development of the nation's abundant natural resources. Native entrepreneurs desired a bigger cut of the new profits, and workers wanted jobs and better wages; together with the intellectuals they talked about a more equitable and democratic government.

Discontented young radicals expressed a desire to know the truth about Nicaragua's past. Three who believed that they found it, Fonseca, whose concept of *Sandinismo* is discussed later in this chapter, Silvio Mayorga, and Borge, left the Nicaraguan Socialist party in 1960 and established the Nicaraguan Revolutionary Youth Group, an organization inspired by Che Guevara and the *foco* theory. From Honduras, the next year, they organized the FSLN patterned after Cuba's 26th of July movement and dedicated to building a revolution based on Sandino's belief that the nation's liberal and conservative politicians were traitors who had to be replaced by worker and peasant leaders.

The Sandinistas wanted to abolish the old order and its economic power base, rebuild the economy with a mixture of private and state enterprises, reduce class inequities, improve living standards, form a popular democracy, protect human rights, eliminate corruption, and design a nonaligned, antiimperialist, internationalist foreign policy. They strove to get people to interpret society through a new political consciousness and to understand the historical past and analyze it critically.[23]

While the Sandinistas built a revolutionary cadre, the Communists developed a relatively cohesive program for Nicaragua. In 1964 they published the "Plan of Basic Reforms," predicated on the idea that political and organizational success depended on raising the theoretical level of the nation's small urban work force and of the peasantry.[24]

Luis Somoza died of natural causes in 1967, and his brother Anastasio "Tachito" Somoza replaced him as president as a result of a rigged election. Within three years the greedy Tachito acquired a fortune conservatively estimated at $3 to $4 million. In addition, his family owned most of the best land in the country, the textile and shoe industries, the national airline, a major shipping company, an auto dealership, banks, hotels, real estate, newspapers, and radio and television stations. The Somozas controlled everything from parking meters to prostitution. Bourgeois rivals for political and economic power began to think about a Somoza-less Nicaragua that would allow them, under the façade of democracy, to realize a greater share of the spoils.

From the mountains of Matagalpa the FSLN stepped up its assaults in 1966–1967 but received little popular support. At first even the Communists refused to assist them, claiming that they acted prematurely. Gradually, a number of Communists decided that guerrilla action was not precipitous. Most of the old Communists who opposed armed insurrection were expelled from the party and in 1976 they established the new Communist Party of Nicaragua, professing to be pro-Moscow and anti-Sandinista.[25]

Various types of dissent against the Somoza regime emerged during the 1970s. Liberation theologists, led by, among others, Father Ernesto

Cardenal, acknowledged the right to fight for social justice. A small Maoist group, the Popular Action Movement, organized the Workers' Front in 1974. The same year, dissidents from the Conservative, Liberal, Communist, and Social Christian parties formed the Democratic Liberation Union, a petit bourgeois opposition organization. Four labor federations criticized the government, and the Sandinistas worked to unify anti-Somoza forces.

Within the FSLN, three tendencies emerged. Followers of the "prolonged popular war" tendency operated out of the mountains, developed guerrilla strategy, and tried to build mass support for armed insurrection. They believed that a lengthy struggle would nurture socialist consciousness. "Proletarian" tendency supporters saw a contradiction between emphasis on the guerrilla war that depended on peasant backing and the role of the urban workers in the revolution. The Proletarians, organized by theoretician-writer Jaime Wheelock, wanted a Marxist-Leninist workers' party as the vanguard of the revolution and emphasized political education among urban dwellers. The "insurrectional" tendency followers, or *terceristas* (third force), advocated broad class alliances and the rapid overthrow of the Somoza government.[26] The *terceristas* felt that by maintaining a pluralistic image the FSLN would get the support of governments hostile to Somoza.[27] The three tendencies learned how to function collectively, to ameliorate their differences, and to prevent internal tensions from tearing the fabric of their movement.

The FSLN understood the value of the written record in raising the consciousness of the oppressed. In the best tradition of the Left, FSLN leaders wrote political tracts and gave numerous interviews. Leaders like Cardenal, Fonseca, Wheelock, Borge, and Ricardo Morales Avilés put their revolutionary thoughts on paper and built intellectual bridges to the masses as part of the movement's education process.

To better understand the modern version of *Sandinismo*, let us look briefly at the ideas of one of the important FSLN intellectuals who is not examined subsequently in this book. Ricardo Morales Avilés (1939–1973) organized Nicaraguan exiles during the 1960s, helped build the FSLN, and in 1971 became a member of its directorate. He explained Marxist ideas in terms of Nicaragua's reality and wrote with clarity and firmness. To conquer people through ideas, he bathed his subversive works in dignity, justice, and love. His essays, even his poetry, defended the concept of progress through revolution[28] and showed how Gramsci's idea of class hegemony and Mao's theory of class contradictions pertained to Nicaragua. He demonstrated how the Marxist approach to revolution could lead to liberation from middle-class and imperialist domination and to democratic worker and peasant power.[29] He advocated ideological diversity and stressed building alliances with non-Marxists upon points of concurrence.[30] He proved that the revolutionary intellectual served as a force in the historical process, in the struggle to organize the revolution, to create a new anticapitalist mentality, and to combat distortion of the culture.[31]

Morales implored Nicaraguans to put revolutionary theory into practice, to accept the historical destiny of the worker to abolish exploitation,[32] and to understand the Nicaraguan revolution as part of an international process.[33] He taught that individual conscience does not determine existence but rather that existence determines conscience. He maintained that the horrors of humanity emanated from learned behavior that could be unlearned, just as social relations of production could be changed.[34] Although he was captured and executed in 1973, many cohorts adopted his belief that a Marxist approach to politics was essential to *Sandinismo* but a Marxist worldview was not.[35]

The history of the Sandinistas' monumental struggle against the Somoza regime has been told repeatedly and need not be recreated here. Suffice to say that under Sandinista leadership, Nicaraguan popular forces drove out Somoza in July 1979. Nicaragua suffered greatly during the insurrection. Between January 1978 and July 1979, 50,000 people died and 150,000 were wounded. In all, 2 percent of Nicaragua's population perished.[36]

By 1979 the Sandinistas had gained political maturity from almost two decades of organizing and struggle. A Sandinista-led junta then governed Nicaragua and had an opportunity to implement some of its radical ideas. The Sandinistas regarded themselves as a vanguard of Nicaragua's popular classes. Their brand of *Sandinismo*, which replaced *Somocismo*, followed theoretical guidelines explained in the essays in this study, in some ways approximated Trotsky's theory of permanent revolution,[37] and contained a bit of political mythology.

The Sandinista leadership, as evident in the sections on Fonseca, Cardenal, and Wheelock, confirmed the principle that theory is not dogma but rather a guide to action. By blending Sandino's thinking, social democracy, Marxism, Castroism, Christian communitarianism, and liberation theology, the Nicaraguan revolutionaries attempted to prevent their movement from becoming monolithic. The Sandinistas advocated socialism, believed that it would take a long time to create, and pursued a revolution of national liberation. They supported a mixed economy, as Wheelock explained, accords with the middle class, and political pluralism. The more radical Sandinistas wanted a quicker transition to socialism, doubted the value of political pluralism, and wanted to replicate the ideological aspects of the Cuban Revolution.

Sandinista leader Daniel Ortega won the presidency in 1984 in a fair election. Ortega and his cohorts began to create an antiimperialist state.

They understood that they lived in an interdependent world and that dependency cannot be terminated, though it can be diversified. Revolutionary Nicaragua sought new sources of imports and new markets for exports and strove to break its overreliance on trade with the United States but not to sever trade relations with that nation. Washington moved to overthrow the Sandinista-led regime by cutting off trade with it and by creating a counterrevolutionary army, the *contras*. The United States drove the Nicaraguans into commercial relations with the Soviet Union, which Washington labeled a "red threat." Wheelock claims that an anticapitalist current has grown in the hemisphere since the appearance of socialism in Cuba, and that U.S. actions against Nicaragua were attempts to curtail this trend and to retain economic hegemony in the Americas. Despite the conduct of the United States, the Soviet Union continued to trade with the Nicaraguans but stressed that it would not provide troops if the United States directly attacked the Central American state.

The United States portrayed Nicaragua as a Soviet satellite, and the Moscow-oriented Nicaraguan Communist party called the Sandinistas ideological deviants. Nicaragua's Communists opposed the Sandinistas, whom they chided for not towing the Leninist line. At the same time, Cuba, which the United States accused of being the primary Soviet surrogate in the Americas, recognized the Sandinistas but not the Nicaraguan Communists.

To the Sandinistas, democracy has meant more than just elections; it has connoted popular participation in political, social, and economic affairs. It also has signified equal access for everyone to all types of cultural activities and freedom to pursue and express creativity, unique characteristics of revolution defined by radical poet-priest Cardenal. Democracy, in the minds of the Sandinistas, would begin only when social inequalities and the vestiges of foreign control disappeared.

Radical thinkers held positions of state responsibility throughout Nicaragua during the Ortega administration (1984–1990). For example, writer Sergio Ramírez served as vice-president, Cardenal as minister of culture, Wheelock as minister of agriculture, and Borge as minister of interior and head of state security. Although I have not selected Borge as a major subject, his views have commanded a large audience and merit mention. A systematic thinker and practitioner of self-criticism, his articles, speeches, and books reflect the resolve of Sandino and provide additional insight into how the Sandinistas think and operate. Especially profound are his analyses of the life and work of Fonseca.

After the overthrow of Somoza, Borge served as a member of the nine-person junta that governed the nation between 1979 and 1985. He worked to foster a mixed economy and emphasized that although private enterprise existed, Nicaragua's economy was not at the service of the business sector.[38] He insisted instead that "the Sandinista Front needs to draw its sustenance from the working class."[39]

Borge pointed out that courses in history tell about Athenian democracy and philosophical and political dialogue but rarely show how all of that was the exclusive property of the nobles. He claimed that the bourgeois ideologies of Locke and Montesquieu, with their concept of separate executive, judicial, and legislative powers were out of fashion. Thus capitalist states ignored the three powers, and Ronald Reagan conducted terrorism without congressional approval. Borge rejected the "sterile rigor of the positivists," whose bourgeois states have made people equal before the law but have not offered them equal social relations.[40] Without the latter, the former is meaningless.

He stated that the revolution must educate and work for the common not individual good, and that the popular church embodied these attributes, whereas the conservative church, which supported the Somozas, did not follow Christ's teachings of brotherhood.[41] His ideas on the need to ally Christians and Marxists are supported by the thinking of Father Cardenal. To Borge, the revolution stood for true equality, the freedom to accept or reject God and religion. It also meant liberation for women, freedom from housework, equal job opportunities and equal pay,[42] and improved social relations between the sexes.

Borge explained the FSLN's mission in terms of two phases. The first, or national liberation, phase of the revolution included the war against Somoza's National Guard and the bourgeoisie. During this period the Sandinistas represented the historical interests of the working class and unified society. After the military victory, during the second phase, the Sandinistas struggled to consolidate large segments of society to confront the common enemy—U.S. imperialism. The revolutionaries encountered serious contradictions as they tried to effect cohesion. According to Borge, they wanted to give priority to the majority, and simultaneously maintain the support of the industrial and agricultural capitalists. They failed to convince the owners of the means of production to cut ties to imperialism, to relinquish their political expectations, and to use their abilities and experience to benefit the country as a whole.[43] The Sandinistas could not make the United States accept that Nicaragua was no longer a client and understand that there can exist a non-Stalinized workers' and peasants' state. In February 1990 the Sandinista movement suffered a severe setback. Ortega, its presidential candidate, lost a democratic election to a fourteen-party coalition headed by Violeta Barrios de Chamorro, and the FSLN lost control of Nicaragua's National Assembly. The essays on the following pages demonstrate how radical ideas have evolved in Nicaragua from the nineteenth century thought of Darío to that of the late-twentieth-century Sandinistas.

Rubén Darío:
Nicaragua's National Treasure

More has been written about Nicaraguan poet Rubén Darío (1867–1916) than any other Spanish American writer, with emphasis on his poetry, not his politics. Although many people familiar with Latin America immediately think of him in relation to antiimperialism, to categorize him as a radical would be misleading. He is included here because he was one of the first very well-known Latin Americans to condemn U.S. expansionism and because he is Nicaragua's national treasure. His symbolic but unphilosophical and generally nonanalytical ideas constitute a part of the emotional foundation upon which Nicaraguan radicals have built.

Born Félix Rubén García Sarmiento in Metapa (now Darío City), Darío was raised by a quasi foster family, a situation that might have contributed to the sense of inner turmoil that led to his creativity. He published his first volume of poetry at thirteen. While a teenager he read all of the liberal French writers in addition to Darwin, Galileo, Luther, Milton, Shakespeare, and Spinoza. He developed an interest in U.S. and Russian culture and in Gorky's and Victor Hugo's concern for the downtrodden.

Darío had a combative, perhaps rebellious, spirit and eventually died from a lifetime of drinking. Receiving wide acclaim as he moved about the world, he spent his early years in Nicaragua and El Salvador, moved to Chile in 1886 to work as a journalist, and in 1889 went to Europe, where he remained until 1914. In Europe Darío had little contact with the Left. He made a living as a newspaper correspondent and diplomat, served as Nicaragua's minister to Spain in 1908, but gained a reputation as a modernist poet. True to the modernist tradition, he defied norms, had a critical attitude, and was sensitive to change. He abhorred crass materialism but appreciated the beauty and comforts of life.

While in Spain as a correspondent for Argentina's *La Nación*, he witnessed the anarchist movement in action and realized that workers were becoming aware of their rights.[44] In Madrid he befriended existentialist philosopher Miguel de Unamuno. Darío enjoyed the company of thinkers and believed that they had an obligation to uplift humanity, to replace evil with good, although he often believed himself foolish for thinking that way.[45]

Politically, Darío was sometimes progressive, generally liberal. His essays and articles were often a bit disjointed and definitely more descriptive than critical. In his heart he was an internationalist and a

Nicaraguan nationalist. Sandinista poet-priest Cardenal referred to him as "the greatest geographical event in Nicaragua," meaning that Darío's modernism put the nation on the map in the nineteenth century. Anthologies of his works have been published in many languages. Nicaragua celebrates his birthday as cultural independence day. His compatriots cherish him and bestow upon him the title *poeta* (poet).

Traditionally, poetry has been Nicaragua's most powerful tool of communication. Darío found poetry in Nicaragua's Indian past and in the nation's perpetual struggle for liberation.[46] He understood the value of poetry and how it preserves tradition in a country where illiteracy is rampant. He believed that poets should work unencumbered by ideology or politics, which existed on a lower plane than art.[47] As a modernist he felt obligated to reflect on the human predicament, to discover a sense of belonging.[48] He wanted to preserve the arts and literature from the social and historical forces that threatened them.

He made an antielitist plea for ideological pluralism, the acceptance of other modes of thought, and the rejection of barbarism. He admired those traits in the work of José Martí, whom he called *maestro* (teacher).[49] Darío's *Refutación al presidente Taft* (1911, Refutation of President Taft), a protest against the U.S. invasion of Nicaragua, reflected Martí's antiimperialism.[50] Darío also wrote a beautiful eulogy for Martí in which he said the Cuban was "possessed with the secret of excellence in communion with God and Nature"[51] (the atheist Martí might have objected). Darío greatly contributed to the cult of Martí.

Literary critics, who preferred the nineteenth-century Americanist tendency to integrate politics and literature, judged Darío somewhat negatively. For example, Uruguayan antiimperialist poet Rodó admired Darío's work but stated that "Rubén Darío is not the American poet"[52] because he did not reflect the American literary tradition. Cuban Marxist analysts José Portuondo and Juan Marinello thought that Darío evaded social and political issues. Angel Rama, in *Rubén Darío y el modernismo* (1970, Rubén Darío and modernism), found a close relationship between Darío's modernism and capitalism. To Rama, Darío's subjectivism, individualism, and quest for novelty were manifestations of liberalism.[53] A whole body of scholarly criticism examines the relationship of Darío's poetry to society and contends that for the most part his work displayed a detachment from social issues.[54]

By his own admission, Darío was a timid man who found it difficult to involve himself in political matters. He had numerous opportunities to write about, or engage in, politics but generally chose not to do so. His autobiography reveals much more interest in world travel and literature than in politics.[55] His twenty-four short pieces on political themes[56] generally exhibit no great perspicacity but demonstrate a love for justice. One senses that he looked upon most politicians with skepticism. However, he viewed Nicaraguan President José Zelaya (1893–1909) as an exception who curtailed clericalism; improved education, transportation, and commerce; modernized society; professionalized the military; and enabled the lower class to advance a bit.[57]

Darío thought that aggrieved people with diverse philosophies should form coalitions to fight for their common needs. He did not understand how profound philosophical differences prevented people from allying.[58] He was an unreliable assessor of the political character of societies, which he looked at superficially. He believed himself to be a much better judge of political life in Latin America than he was.

Most of his observations tended to be visceral and not based on serious study. His superficiality can be seen in his attitudes toward women. He claimed that they needed education and that where they competed in the marketplace, such as in the United States, they contributed to progress. His article "The American Woman" typifies his work. It included a few observations on women in the workplace and some shallow conclusions but lacked evidence and a developed analytical structure.[59] Further illustrating his shortage of intellectual rigor is his glib contention that the transition from the nineteenth to the twentieth century included movement toward human liberty, though he also claimed that humanity tended toward Darwinism. He criticized "the madness of war,"[60] talked about peace and freedom, but advanced no ideas about how to attain these objectives.

In "¿Por que?" (1892, Why?), he attacked social injustice, mentioned workers' misery, and equated democracy with social justice,[61] saying that the bandits owned the stores and that tyranny comes in three forms, economic, religious, and political.[62] He believed man's lust for property contributed to inhumanity but felt no need for class struggle. He did not always see how capitalism's emphasis on material wealth hurt certain elements of society,[63] yet he complained in *La Nación* in 1901 that art and literature had become slaves to an industrialism whose main goal was financial.[64]

In the realm of formal ideas, Darío recognized the influence of Krause's panentheism, Comte's positivism, and Nietzsche's belief in man's quest for power in Latin America and believed that Latins preferred the thought of the French, with whom they shared a kindred spirit, to that of Germans.[65] He saw the explosion of anarchism in Spain and attributed it to the thought of Bakunin and Pierre-Joseph Proudhon, but he was more interested in the actions of the anarchists than their theories and had difficulty understanding their willingness to engage in violent acts.[66] He was aware of socialism but understood it only superficially.

His work reflects the pain of Latin America's historical reality. He defended the region's Hispanic traditions and had an interest in relations between its countries. In particular, he looked to the independence era and the efforts of its leaders Hidalgo, Morazán, San Martín, and Bolívar for inspiration. He did not comprehend Latin America's working-class mentality, preferring to take his clues from middle-class intellectuals. He wrote about the conflicts between the Miskito Indians and the British on the Atlantic coast and claimed that the territory they occupied belonged to Nicaragua.[67] In *La Nación* in Buenos Aires in 1895 he wrote about the insurrection in Cuba, which he viewed as a racial conflict in part.[68]

In 1906 Darío served as secretary to the Nicaraguan delegation to the Pan American Conference in Rio, where he tried to further inter-American cooperation. He even wrote a poem, "Greetings to the Eagle," welcoming the influence of the Yankees, whom he did not hate and some of whose traits, such as vigor, he even admired.[69]

Becoming a passionate advocate of Central American union, he envisioned all Spanish America banding together to campaign for peace and to condemn tyranny and foreign aggression. He wanted closer commercial, industrial, and scientific relations between the states of the isthmus.[70] He wrote an ode to the archetypal Liberal, Justo Rufino Barrios, who reconstructed the Union of Central America.[71] In 1884 Darío worked for Nicaraguan president Adán Cárdenas on matters pertaining to a plan for Central American union. His poem "La Unión Centro Americana" (1886, Central American Union) pointed out the national ego factors precluding unity, noted distrust between the states and regional differences, and expressed pessimism about attaining cohesion.[72]

Darío understood nationalism and patriotism but did not like when they led to war to obtain glory or to prove superiority.[73] He feared that the United States had a need to dominate the Americas, and he dubbed it the "Colossus of the North." He noted that Bolívar showed similar fear and hesitated to invite the United States to the first Pan American Congress in Panama in 1826.[74] Darío understood how U.S. hunger for land led it to acquire almost half of Mexico during the 1830s and 1840s, and he was aware that by the end of the nineteenth century U.S. Secretary of State Blaine cultivated new Latin American markets by trying to settle disputes through arbitration.[75] In his article "El triunfo de Calibán" (1898, The triumph of Caliban), he cited the Monroe Doctrine as a grand design for continental control; referred to the "infamous Yankee appetite"; noted U.S. incursions into Brazil, Colombia, Mexico, Nicaragua, Peru, and Venezuela; and asserted that he did not want to join the Yankees and prostitute his Latin heart to Caliban.[76] He predicted that ultimately millions of people in Latin America would speak English as a result of U.S. aggression.[77] He also wrote about imperialism's spreading slavery in areas such as Latin America.[78]

Darío castigated the "blue-eyed" William Walker for his forays into Nicaragua to establish a slave state. He tied Walker's endeavors to the Vanderbilt transportation enterprise, to U.S. land hunger, to the coming of the United Fruit Company, and to U.S. occupation troops.[79] As Darío saw it, Walker brought terror to Nicaragua, and his ouster brought the second independence.[80] Darío's opposition to avarice or imperialism was not based on radical political theory. He did not regard the United States as the embodiment of capitalism or think in terms of a conflict between social and economic interests. Instead, Darío criticized the United States because he refused to accept the notion of Anglo-American cultural superiority.[81]

Darío was infuriated by U.S. Secretary of State Richard Olney's arrogant assertion in 1895 that the "U.S. is practically sovereign on this continent."[82] Early in 1904, Darío wrote "To Roosevelt" in biblical, Walt Whitman–style verse. This work, more than any other, has been seized upon by those who want to furnish Darío with radical credentials. Darío viewed Roosevelt as a prime example of the imperialist mentality, saying of him, "You think that life is fine, that progress is an eruption, that the future is wherever your bullet strikes."[83] He questioned the optimistic doctrine of material progress that pervaded the United States[84] and criticized Roosevelt's dedication to the acquisition of national and personal wealth.[85] In 1910 he said that Roosevelt lived like a bourgeois, was received like a sovereign and spoke like an apostle, but that he found him banal.[86] Darío disliked Roosevelt's "Big Stick" diplomacy in Panama[87] and saw the U.S. effort to secure a canal route as a contradiction to the Monroe Doctrine.[88] In 1895 he correctly prophesied that a canal under U.S. aegis would make the United States the hemisphere's protector. He maintained that a canal should be for all Americans.[89] "To Roosevelt" warned of U.S. designs on "our America." Darío's apprehensions were not those of a primarily political person but of one who had humane instincts.

Augusto César Sandino: "The Freeman's General"

Augusto Sandino (1895–1934) is as synonymous with Nicaragua's populist desire for liberation as Darío is with poetry. Born illegitimately in Niquinohomo, near Granada, Sandino at age nine accompanied his peasant mother into debtor's prison. Later his prosperous father took him in and had him educated through secondary school. While running the family farm, the teenage Sandino realized how merchants took advantage of peasants, and he organized a cooperative marketing association to help the latter. He understood why those of his father's class fared well whereas his peasant mother became a streetwalker.

Sandino always referred with pride to his Indian heritage, and he especially revered "El Indio," Benjamín Zeledón, who fought against Díaz, as noted in the introduction to this chapter. Recognizing that race helped determine one's class in Nicaragua, Sandino dedicated himself to assist the second-class mestizos who made up three-quarters of the country's population.[90] He also discerned a relationship between Spanish imperialism and racism.

The audacious, somewhat straightlaced, uncompromising Sandino regarded himself as a city worker and a man of action, not a theoretician. But he kept extensive records and liked to write, particularly about social justice. He was a good correspondent, and his declarations and letters were collected by the Sandinista-led Nicaraguan government of the 1980s, which diligently preserved the records of its thinkers.[91] He wrote with a poetic style, sensitively, yet pierced straight to the heart of matters. Sandino once signed a note to a military adversary, "Your most obedient servant who adamantly desires to put you in a handsome tomb with beautiful bouquets of flowers."[92] He also spoke eloquently, viewed erudition as a tool of liberation, and promoted culture and reading among the peasants.

Sandino's ideas emanated from his experiences. He claimed to be a clairvoyant who received extrasensory messages,[93] believed he had a messianic mission to defend Nicaraguan sovereignty, and fancied himself a Nicaraguan Quixote ready to die defending his people against injustice. He was a disciplinarian who demanded obedience from his troops but a humanitarian who cared deeply for them. Nicaraguans regard him as a *pensador* as well as a guerrilla fighter, one who elaborated the possibilities of the future.

At age twenty-five Sandino injured a local politician in a quarrel and had to leave his hometown. He worked briefly in Nicaragua, went to work on a United Fruit Company plantation in Guatemala, and then entered Mexico, where he labored for a U.S. oil firm. While in Mexico during the 1920s, he was ridiculed by native workers who were inflated by the achievements of their revolution and condemned Nicaraguans for their subservience to the United States.[94] Sandino fell under the influence of Mexican anarchists led by Ricardo Flores Magón. According to philosopher Donald Hodges, Sandino combined anarchism with spiritism to form anarchospiritism.[95] He was also impressed by the exploits of the Mexican peasant revolutionary Zapata, who sought land for his people.[96] While living in Tampico, Sandino went to meetings of theosophical groups and at times relied more on intuition than logic. For example, he preferred an *abrazo* (embrace) to a handshake, claiming "that way the fluids are transmitted much better."[97] He became a follower of the Magnetic-Spiritual School of the Universal Commune, a Buenos Aires-based group that added to spiritualism the belief that not just the human body, but all things are full of spirits. It also rejected religious faith and worship and did not try to reconcile religion with modern science.[98]

While in Mexico, Sandino spent most of his spare time in political discussions or reading and studying. He recognized and wrote about the forces of U.S. imperialism at work.[99] In May 1926 he left his job as a gasoline sales supervisor at the Huasteca Petroleum Company in Veracruz, and returned to Nicaragua to pursue his goal of terminating his nation's perpetual domination by foreigners.[100]

While working for a U.S. gold mining company at San Albino, he found that he could arouse the political consciousness of his fellow workers. In October 1926, perceiving himself as the successor to Zeledón, Sandino took up the constitutionalists' cause and with twenty-five followers led an unsuccessful attack on the government fortress at nearby Jícaro.[101] He learned guerrilla tactics and how to befriend the local folk and win their support. By January 1927 Sandino and about 800 guerrillas entered the northwestern mountains, proclaiming "liberty or death." Throughout that year the U.S. marines sought to penetrate Sandino's secret fortress, El Chipote, and were regularly ambushed and repulsed.[102] He continued his opposition to the U.S.-supported Guardia Nacional until 1933.

Washington and the church branded Sandino an outlaw and an atheist Communist. But he was far from a simple bandit. To most Nicaraguans, Sandino was a noble patriot, an egalitarian who did not hesitate to regard women as equals in combat. Latin American intellectuals applauded his antiimperialist actions. Socialist men of letters such as Peru's José Carlos Mariátegui and Argentina's Alfredo Palacios and Manuel Ugarte praised Sandino's struggle, which resembled a class war. Similar praise came from the all-American Anti-Imperialist League, which used Sandino's half-brother Sócrates to speak at rallies on his behalf. In Mexico, Venezuelan Marxist Gustavo Machado organized the Hands Off Nicaragua Association, composed of intellectuals from various nations, which raised money for Sandino.[103] Peruvian liberal antiimperialist Haya de la Torre lauded him, as did the Comintern. The First Antiimperialist Congress of 1928 took a stand in his behalf. But overall, he received little financial backing from anywhere and not much support, proportionately, from the capitalist world.

After the cessation of hostilities in 1933, Sandino continued to call his movement nationalist and antiimperialist and stated that capitalism could be carried out with dignity, that liberalism was alive.[104] Seeing the connection between the social and the political, he understood the major Nicaraguan problems and observed how politics influenced people's lives. He pointed out that the nation's two-party oligarchical rule did not work and categorized Nicaraguans as "honorable" or "coward" Liberals and "sell out" Conservatives.[105]

Close examination of his writings and practices reveals the existence of a philosophy far more radical in orientation than he has generally been credited with in the past. In *Intellectual Foundations of the Nicaraguan Revolution* (1986), Donald Hodges concluded that Sandino was quite deep philosophically and ideologically, not a crackpot who dabbled in simplistic ideas. Sandino understood the relationship between capitalism and imperialism and between national and class self-determination, and saw how the working class suffered at the hands of oligarchies. He sought a revolutionary social transformation, not merely a humane utopian movement, and endeavored to unite the workers and peasants as the backbone of a new society.[106] In a famous manifesto of July 1, 1927, Sandino declared himself an idealistic artisan, an internationalist, and a liberal revolutionary,[107] though by that he did not mean that he gave precedence to individual liberty over collective liberty. Hodges demonstrated that Sandino advocated a populist program,[108] that he was an anarchocommunist with a theosophy of liberation who couched his ideology in a patriotic and liberal fashion to attract followers.[109] To Sandino, patriotism meant nationalism, nationalism contained elements of populism, and populism could lead people to communism. He backed people's nationalism based on protective legislation for peasants and workers and foresaw an international workers' revolution.[110] He also viewed antiimperialism as an inherent element in Central American nationalism.

Sandino reflected the antiimperialist influence of the Left in Latin America, as espoused by Darío, José Martí, Rodó, Palacios, Ugarte, and Mariátegui. He agreed with their belief in the need to acknowledge and extoll Latin American values.[111] He agreed with French socialist Pierre-Joseph Proudhon that "property is theft."[112] He pointed out the class base needed for resistance and stressed his plebeian origins, considering it an honor to come from the oppressed masses. He hoped somehow to overcome class conflict and to see the working-class majority attain the control it should have in a democracy.[113]

Sandino had faith in the ability of the workers and peasants to organize and persist until they gained victory. He agreed with Mexican anarchist Flores Magón that the workers' struggle against capital is a matter of human justice and class interest.[114] He realized that freedom and workers' control would have to be won through the use of armed force.[115] The guerrilla leader acknowledged that he preached a determinist social doctrine and that stimuli for his thought came from the extreme left.[116] On the other hand, left-wing intellectuals called him everything from a utopian pacifist to a Jacobin, and conservatives presented him as a Soviet-oriented Communist. Somewhere in between lies the truth. Sandino preferred the Bolsheviks to social democrats or Western European socialists, whom he viewed as compromisers.[117] But he would probably have chosen a universal commune over Bolshevism, for whereas Bolshevism relied on laws and institutions to give people equality, the natural commune discovers the law in each person and makes society dependent on individuals.[118]

Sandino recognized the Communist party as part of the antiimperialist movement but not as the vanguard.[119] Hodges asserts that he successfully challenged the Comintern's claim to a monopoly on Communist revolution in the hemisphere.[120] At the same time, he generally maintained good relations with the Communists and occupied a prominent place in the international movement's propaganda. The Mexican Communists, frustrated by their inability to place him under their influence, eventually broke with him and accused him of dishonesty.[121] The Comintern and his former guerrilla comrade Agustín Farabundo Martí called him a petit bourgeois liberal *caudillo*. Sandino used the attacks to discredit the U.S. State Department's charges that he was a Communist.[122] After Martí broke with Sandino over ideology, he still referred to him as the greatest patriot in the world. Currently, the Communist party of Nicaragua regards him as someone who fought against the U.S. occupation, not imperialism, and unfairly criticizes him for having no specific social revolutionary programs.

Sandino put forth a rather comprehensive program. It entailed establishing a popular independent government, organizing workers' land cooperatives, using the national wealth for the benefit of the masses, and building intercontinental integration without U.S. intervention.[123] He also advocated laws limiting workday length, regulation of imports to provide more jobs, equal pay for women for equal work, regulation of child labor, and recognition of the right to organize labor.[124] Sandino believed that because Nicaragua was largely unoccupied, progress could be achieved by creating voluntary, state-owned agricultural cooperatives in the hinterlands, which would form a type of utopian socialism.[125] The inspiration for these cooperatives came from the Spanish anarchists, from whom he also adopted the red and black colors of the Sandinista banner that symbolize liberty or death.

Sandino saw the problems of Central America as regional and believed that the other countries of the area were morally obligated to assist in the struggle against the United States.[126] Once the U.S. forces withdrew from Nicaragua, he moved in 1933 to create a Central American union[127] by reviving the 1821 agreement promoted by Morazán.[128] He claimed his army of free people of conscience to be the Autonomous Army of Central America.[129]

In some ways, he believed that he carried on the work of his hero, Bolívar, "the Liberator." In a forty-five-point plan, he spoke about fighting for a frontierless Latin America. He wrote about creating a Latin American court of justice with a rotating presidency supported by an army of citizen-student soldiers.[130] He hoped that the court would adjudicate disputes, supervise the Panama Canal, preside over the breakup of U.S. military bases in the hemisphere, regulate foreign capital, promote tourism, maintain the peace, establish a mechanism to cancel objectionable contracts between American states, create a unified tariff scale, and curtail U.S. expansion.

Sandino referred to the United States as "the eagle with larcenous claws."[131] He resented and moved to abrogate the Monroe Doctrine, which implied that only those from the United States were American. He suggested that the nation cease referring to itself as "America" and use the name"United States of North America,"[132] still a somewhat inaccurate title as Mexico and Canada are in North America. He also opposed Manifest Destiny and the aspects of white superiority in U.S. imperialism.

Sandino believed that inevitably a new interoceanic canal would be built in Nicaragua[133] and feared that U.S. banks would control it.[134] He said that the United States manipulated the Pan American Union and encouraged the area's dictators for its own benefit.[135] He pleaded with the Latin American states to finance a united front against the United States and against bloodthirsty dictators such as Cuba's Gerardo Machado and Venezuela's Juan Vicente Gómez.[136] He believed that Nicaragua's struggle would become international "as the colonial and semi-colonial people unite with the people of the imperialist nations."[137] He saw U.S. capitalism as the last stage of imperialist development and noted the role played by the AF of L in the imperialist stage of the Americas.[138] He also cited the exploitation of Nicaragua's Atlantic coast as a manifestation of British imperialism[139] and sought to free that area's natives from foreign control.

Nicaragua's National Guard, according to Sandino, was an extension of the United States and the enemy of the republic.[140] The Guard, trained by the United States to maintain the established order, symbolized a shift in U.S. policy. No longer did Washington have to dispatch troops to Latin America; instead, it trained and subordinated native militaries.[141]

Sandino initially claimed that U.S. citizens would not condone their country's actions in Latin America but later revised his thinking and asserted that they simply did not care what their government did abroad. Yet he harbored no malice toward U.S. citizens, saying "I have nothing against North Americans. Let them come to Nicaragua as workers, not as bosses."[142] He did, however, despise the U.S. government, which he saw as a tool of Wall Street. Washington considered him a dangerous model, and when Cecil B. de Mille requested State Department permission to make a film about him, it was denied.[143]

Nicaraguan social democrats, socialists, liberals, and Marxist-Leninists have invoked Sandino's ideas and emulated his actions. In their eyes he continued the resistance of Zeledón, fought for the rights of Indians and the weak, and placed the wretched social and political situation in their country under international scrutiny. The fame of the "freeman's general," as French socialist writer Henri Barbusse called him,[144] reached as far as China, where the Kuomintang named one of its divisions after him. He inspired Alberto Bayo, the Cuban-born former Spanish officer who advised Fidel Castro on guerrilla warfare. Cuba's revolutionaries, like Nicaragua's Sandinistas, learned from Sandino's shortcomings about the necessity of destroying opponents' militaries completely. The Nicaraguan chieftain failed to do so, and it led to his demise.

Sandino's actions created a new sensibility known as *Sandinismo,* which encompassed the active nationalism adopted by the FSLN in its bid to turn Nicaraguan patriotism against the bourgeoisie. Sandino believed in God, and the FSLN borrowed his position on religion. To him, God represented the basis of love and social justice, the need to struggle, as did Jesus, for freedom. For Sandino and the latter-day Sandinistas, the final judgment would come in the form of the destruction of injustice and the breaking of the chains of imperialism. Sandino's thoughts and actions led to the FSLN's fight to recover Nicaragua's national resources, to create new political forces, and to defend workers' and peasants' revolution on an international plane.

Sandino forced the withdrawal of U.S. troops from Nicaragua in January 1933, and his guerrillas entered into peace accords with the Nicaraguan government. Conflict between the Sandinistas and the National Guard continued for a year. In an alleged attempt to resolve differences, Sandino was invited to attend a dinner at the presidential palace on February 21, 1934. Upon leaving, he was arrested by the National Guard and machine-gunned to death. Despite his death, Sandino's ideas and spirit helped topple the same Somoza-led National Guard forty-five years later.

Carlos Fonseca Amador:
Sandinista Theorist and Revolutionary Martyr

No one has done more to extend the Sandino legacy than Carlos Fonseca Amador (1936–1976), whom many Nicaraguans view as their contemporary revolutionary father. Fonseca, the ideological strategist of the 1960s and 1970s, wrote essays clarifying what had to be done and served as an organizer of thought leaving a comprehensive written history of the Sandinista movement. He believed that only an educated populace could sustain a revolution, and he fostered the drive for education, reflected in the remarkable jump in books published in Nicaragua. Under the Somozas the figure was about a half-dozen books a year; by the 1980s under the Sandinistas, approximately seventy titles were published annually.

The illegitimate son of a domestic mother and a laborer father, Fonseca sold newspapers in the streets of Matagalpa as a child and read everything he could find. He developed an antipathy for dictators and institutional terrorism and began to work actively against them while in secondary school. In 1953 Fonseca and his classmate Tomás Borge were introduced to the works of Marx and Engels and began their revolutionary activities. Fonseca was also guided by the writings of Darío, Gorky, Mao, and Neruda. By 1954 he was selling *Unidad*, the Communist party newspaper, and had founded the magazine *Segovia*. He wrote his high school thesis on the themes of capital and work, graduated first in his class in 1955, began to collect the writings of Sandino, and departed for Managua and the National University. At the university he edited the student newspaper, was elected head of student government, and formed the institution's first Marxist study group. A member of the Communist party, he was arrested after the assassination of Anastasio Somoza in 1956 and spent a month in prison, where he was tortured.

When a student strike closed the university in 1957, Fonseca traveled to Moscow. He then wrote *Un nicaragüense en Moscú* (1957, A Nicaraguan in Moscow) praising the Soviet economic and social welfare achievements. Although he considered the Soviet Union a useful model, he did not want Nicaragua to become a subservient clone of that state.

After he returned from the USSR, he promoted Sandino's ideas through speeches and articles. He was arrested in 1958 for leading protests against the visit to Nicaragua by Milton Eisenhower, brother of the U.S. president. He then organized the Democratic Nicaraguan Youth, a group that opposed the dictatorship, and he was deported to Guatemala in 1959. In early 1959 Fonseca made his way to Honduras and joined the antigovernment Rigoberto López Pérez column, which then infiltrated the mountains of Nicaragua's El Chaparral. There Fonseca was seriously wounded by the National Guard.[145] He recovered in Cuba, became familiar with the mechanics of Cuba's guerrilla war, and struck up a friendship with Che Guevara, from whom he learned about the feasibility of revolutionary theory emanating from revolutionary action. In Cuba Fonseca wrote a serious analysis of the history of *Sandinismo* entitled *Viva Sandino* (Long live Sandino).[146] He decided that the early *Sandinismo* had developed antiimperialist and revolutionary positions but had not built sufficient class consciousness to effect a revolution.

By 1961 Fonseca was displeased with the dogmatic orthodox Communist party in Nicaragua, whose program he felt was not adequately revolutionary. In Tegucigalpa, Honduras, in July of that year he, Borge, and Mayorga founded the Sandinista National Liberation Front. To them, the time appeared ripe for a revolution as the economy deteriorated and peasants' political consciousness grew.[147] The FSLN, inspired by Algeria's revolt against French colonial rule and the revolutions in China, Cuba, and Vietnam, embarked on a program of guerrilla warfare to overthrow the Somoza administration.

The government arrested Fonseca in 1964 and deported him to Guatemala in early 1965. He reentered Nicaragua, was recaptured in Managua, and spent six more months in jail. When the FSLN shifted its base of operations to Costa Rica in 1969, Fonseca was imprisoned there. The following year he was released as part of a hostage exchange. He again landed in Cuba, where he wrote, organized, and studied revolutionary theory and tactics. In 1975 he returned to Nicaragua to engage in battle. The following year Fonseca was killed in combat by the Guardia Nacional. The FSLN's "supreme commander" was dead, but his revolutionary thought lived.

Fonseca instilled in his followers an appreciation of historical analysis. He demonstrated how violence by political forces within the exploiting class has been used in the nation since independence in 1821. He showed that the country lacked a tradition of peaceful transferal of political power or electoral honesty and that a precedent of armed rebellion against oppression existed. He noted that "ideological obscurantism" carried over from the colonial era prevented Nicaraguans from attaining the full awareness necessary to struggle for social change. He saw battles in the past guided by instinct rather than consciousness and felt that Marx's views on Spain were applicable to Nicaragua, that the people were traditionally rebellious but not revolutionaries.[148]

Fonseca exhorted Nicaraguans to fight against U.S. aggression, which he charted. He noted that in 1850, under the Clayton-Bulwer Treaty, the United States arrogated to itself rights to build a canal across Nicaragua. In 1854 a U.S. warship reduced the port of San Juan del Norte to ashes. The next year William Walker arrived. In 1870 the United States meddled in Nicaraguan internal affairs. In 1907 a U.S. vessel occupied the Gulf of Fonseca, and two years later the United States was involved in armed action against Nicaragua. The United States took sides in Nicaragua's civil war in 1910, intervened militarily between 1927 and 1934, and from then on protected the Somozas.[149]

Nicaraguans suffered as much from internal oppression as from external aggression. When 10,000 Indians in Matagalpa rebelled in 1881, according to Fonseca, that signified the decomposition of feudalism and established a precedent for Sandino's actions against domestic despotism and foreign imperialism.[150] After Sandino's death, Somoza pretended that his own Liberal party represented the national bourgeoisie, and his National Guard protected neocolonial exploitation by U.S. monopolies and their native capitalist allies.[151] Fonseca pointed out that Nicaragua had no industrial proletariat and that the peasants constituted the resistance but could not sustain it after the assassination of Sandino.[152] With Somoza at the helm, Nicaragua remained at a Neanderthal level ideologically.

Marxists from neighboring nations could not penetrate Nicaragua or build on Sandino's spirit of revolution.[153] The Nicaraguan Socialist (Communist) party formed in 1944 and followed the line of Earl Browder of the U.S. Communist party, which advocated conciliation with capitalists. Nicaragua's Communists were mostly artisans. They suffered from a low ideological level, many of them feeling it a matter of survival to proclaim their support for Somoza. Radical intellectuals were rare in Nicaragua. Intellectuals in general identified with the church, some with fascism.[154]

Until the late 1950s, Fonseca agreed with the Communists that Nicaragua was not ready for revolution.[155] Between 1958 and 1960 over sixty armed actions against Nicaragua's dictatorship took place, and Venezuelan despot Marcos Pérez Jiménez was ousted. Fonseca then concluded that those events revived the spirit of Sandino.[156] A revolutionary gestation period began. Analysis led to action. Fonseca and his radical cohorts realized that they could not change the pacifist line of the Communists, and they established the FSLN. Conditions were right for change in the 1960s, when approximately 1 percent of Nicaraguans finished primary school, 10 percent of the people died in childhood, and 60 percent of the deaths were caused by curable diseases.

Although Fonseca would have preferred to achieve social revolution via the ballot box, he saw little chance of that in Central America, where, except for Costa Rica, violence was a fundamental part of social change.[157] He believed that radicals must be guided by revolutionary methods. He perceived Ho Chi Minh as a model revolutionary, an advanced thinker who advocated an end to oppression and a union of all people, one who understood the vagaries of protracted warfare.[158] He concluded that pacifism did not alleviate misery in India and that only armed struggle would free the Nicaraguans.[159] He realized that Marxist revolutionary ideas arrived late in Nicaragua, primarily because the nation had no early socialist inspiration from Europe,[160] and that the nation's young radicals had little political or theoretical sophistication.

He was a "critical" Marxist who understood the diversities in Marxist thinking and chose his theory carefully. For instance, Fonseca favored the ideas of the young Marx, the activist-critic who made theory subordinate to action, and he had less faith in the more mature Marx, for whom revolution was a natural outgrowth of the contradictions in capitalism and who advocated patience before embarking on a revolutionary course.

Using Marxism as a tool to analyze the national situation, Fonseca believed that national conditions would shape the revolution. He proved that Cuban conditions were not Nicaragua's and that updated versions of Sandino's, not Che's, concepts of military strategy and political organization were best suited to Nicaragua.[161] To mobilize the masses for revolution, he contended, both scientifically oriented theory as well as nonrational beliefs that relate to human emotions are needed, an idea he picked up from the writings of Mariátegui.

Fonseca claimed that the revolution in Nicaragua should embrace Marxism and liberalism, as well as Christian socialism.[162] To him, sectarianism was the major enemy of unity.[163] He urged his comrades to understand that liberalism opposed dictatorship and that social Christianity did not have to side with the forces of reaction.[164] He believed that ultimately the working class would lead the victorious revolution and realized the dangers of a revolution in a society devoid of proletarian leadership. Because the country had limited industrialization, he placed his faith in the peasants, with their tradition of struggle, and counted on the student sector to lead the popular fight.[165] The working class, he maintained, does not spontaneously assume a vanguard position but has to do it as industry develops, as the political level of the workers rises.[166]

Fonseca believed it essential not to hide revolutionary goals, a weakness of the Cuban Revolution, whose abrupt turn to the left jarred and disappointed liberals and social democrats. He openly opted for armed force over electoral farce and decided that a viable political organization had to lead, but remain close to, the masses.[167] He warned that armed uprising does not necessarily lead to revolution and cited the example of Indonesia, where the insurrection converted the nation from a colony to a neocolonial capitalist state,[168] precisely what the liberal Somoza opponents of the 1970s, turned *contra* leaders of the 1980s, wanted to do.

Initially, Fonseca and the FSLN borrowed Guevara's *foco* theory based on the belief that irregular forces can defeat a professional military, that you can engage the enemy without waiting for the proper conditions Marx suggested were necessary, and that rural guerrilla tactics are preferable because urban guerrillas are vulnerable to government repression. After its rural force created objective conditions for revolution, the FSLN moved to a broader, Vietnam-style guerrilla war and later added the urban component to the conflict.[169] Fonseca and the FSLN also taught that the revolution had to go beyond eliminating Somoza, it had to strip power from the entire exploiting class.[170] Once in political control of Nicaragua, the FSLN never accomplished that goal.

Fonseca and his corevolutionaries learned from Sandino how to garner support among the local peasants by teaching them to read and sow better crops and by giving them eyeglasses and medicine. He found that social backwardness and the absence of a socialist tradition precluded factional debates among the peasants over such issues as the relative merits of Leninism as opposed to social democracy.[171] The peasants, not bogged down by political sectarianism, were receptive to Sandino's ideas of antiimperialism, national sovereignty, opposition to existing political parties, the need for armed struggle, the existence of a people's army in peacetime, working-class political leadership, a cooperativist economy, the end of exploitation, and internationalism.[172] Fonseca successfully conveyed to the peasantry that he saw in Sandino and his ideas not an ethereal symbol, not an abstraction, but guides for understanding Nicaraguan reality and transforming it in a revolutionary way.

Both Fonseca and Sandino viewed the class struggle as the motor of history.[173] Fonseca referred to Sandino as the Nicaraguan expression of the values of international communism.[174] But he did not hesitate to criticize Sandino for not institutionalizing the revolutionary process in Nicaragua, or to castigate the Communists for incorrectly categorizing the guerrilla chieftain as a petit bourgeois populist.[175]

Fonseca decided that a conventional Socialist or Communist party could not succeed in Nicaragua, so he conceived of *Sandinismo* as a political and ideological force to take advantage of the existing trends or strengths in Nicaragua, namely, nationalism, Marxism, and Catholicism.[176] Fonseca, who insisted that the movement use Sandino's name, represented the watershed between the old, orally transmitted, folkloric *Sandinismo* and the new Marxist form that combined theory with love, tenacity, and mysticism. Fonseca forged a belief in a quasi-universal, progressive, ever-changing truth. He created a sense of opposition to hierarchy and supported the idea of equality among leaders.[177] He implored his comrades to practice revolutionary modesty to combat bourgeois vanity, which causes personal rivalries and weakens collective endeavors. He advanced the concept of massive class struggle, under the laws of historical process, to generate popular power that leads to socialism and communism. Fonseca infected his cohorts with the optimism necessary to succeed and the determination to organize and reorganize—the key to revolutionary victory. Utilizing the method Gramsci suggested, he explained the validity of revolutionary praxis by using familiar terms understandable to people on diverse intellectual and cultural levels.

Rather than building a political party, Fonseca organized a front to carry out tasks commonly associated with a party, while elevating the workers to a prominent political place in society. He helped spawn an enduring ethos. Borge explained that ethos by noting that when he was in prison an officer informed him of Fonseca's death, and he replied, "No colonel, you're wrong. Carlos Fonseca is one of the dead who never die."[178]

Commander Víctor Tirado depicted Fonseca as the FSLN's most important creator.[179] Commander Wheelock asserted that Fonseca's authority was transmitted to the organization with profundity, and from the outset that authority was received as an organic substance, something not linked to individuals.[180] Fonseca made a commitment to collectivism guided by the FSLN, instituted procedures for self-criticism in the FSLN, and insisted that one could criticize the course of the revolution without being a counterrevolutionary. Without continuous constructive criticism, he believed, the revolution would become sterile and dogmatic.

Above all, Fonseca taught the Sandinistas that concrete action is insufficient without revolutionary ideology and programs. The FSLN's 1969 program embodies the thought of Fonseca as extrapolated from the ideas of Sandino and from Nicaragua's historical reality. This brand of *Sandinismo* became synonymous with popular guerrilla war, popular power, land for the peasants, the end of exploitation and misery, women's emancipation, a popular patriot army, revolutionary culture and teaching, respect for religious beliefs, an independent foreign policy, popular unity in Central America, and veneration of national martyrs such as Sandino.[181] Carlos Fonseca too became one of the venerated.

Ernesto Cardenal:
God's Revolutionary Minister of Culture

The early lives of Sandino and and Fonseca differed greatly from that of poet-priest Ernesto Cardenal (1925–). When he was five, Cardenal moved with his well-to-do conservative family to León, where Darío had lived. At seven he wrote a poem paying homage to Darío. He claimed that "Rubén . . . was a very devout boy who went to confession every Saturday at the church of St. Frances. Likewise, I went to confession every Saturday at the same church."[182] After attending Jesuit primary and secondary schools, Cardenal went to the National University of Mexico in 1942 to study literature. Between 1947 and 1949 he pursued graduate work at Columbia University in New York. After a year of travel in Europe, he returned to Nicaragua in 1950 and began to write historical poems and to translate Anglo-American poetry. He joined the illegal National Union of Popular Action and wrote an anti-Somoza article for *La Prensa*.[183] In 1954 he participated in the "Conspiracy of April," an abortive assault on Nicaragua's presidential palace.

Cardenal decided to become a Trappist monk and entered Our Lady of Gethsemani monastery in Kentucky, where his novice master and friend was the well-known writer-poet Thomas Merton. Finding his health too frail for the monk's existence and that he was not emotionally suited for a life of isolation, Cardenal left Gethsemani to study theology in Mexico. From 1961 to 1965 he studied for the priesthood in Colombia. He gained respect for the thinking of Colombian priest and guerrilla fighter Camilo Torres, who had been inspired by the European worker-priest movement and French philosopher Jacques Maritain, who encouraged Catholics to enter secular politics and work actively for social justice. Camilo Torres also adopted a spiritual Marxism and opposed foreign and native exploitation.[184]

Cardenal returned to Nicaragua in 1966 and, on the poverty-stricken islands of Solentiname in the southern part of Lake Nicaragua, he founded a contemplative lay community. In Solentiname Cardenal analyzed radical literature and wrote many poems and epigrams. The Somoza regime threatened him with a charge of treason for criticizing the government. In a cartoon in Somoza's newspaper, *Novedades*, the bearded, beret-wearing priest was depicted as a dirty hippie.[185]

During the 1960s, Cardenal was turned toward radicalism by Father Uriel Molina. Molina, a well-educated parish priest, started a Christian community, which analyzed Nicaraguan society using Marxist methodology and opposed Somoza. Molina and Cardenal agreed that Christians and Marxists had to ally to defeat the dictator.[186] In 1972 Molina founded the Christian Revolutionary Movement to mobilize radical Catholics, and in 1973 it affiliated with the FSLN, which Cardenal subsequently joined.

In late 1976, Cardenal represented the Sandinistas before the Bertrand Russell Human Rights Tribunal in Rome. He was tried in absentia for treason and was convicted by the Somoza regime, which resented the splendid job he did of explaining the goals of the FSLN to other nations. After the triumph of the revolution, Cardenal joined the revolutionary government. When ordered by the Vatican to relinquish his position as minister of culture, he refused, and he occupied that office until it was abolished in early 1988. He wondered why, if the church wanted a more moral regime in Nicaragua, it would oust priests in favor of a totally secular government. Never before had the church rejected an opportunity to hold some political power. But anticommunist Pope John Paul II feared the left-leaning government of Nicaragua. To illustrate his disapproval of the Sandinistas, in March 1983 in Managua the pope delivered a homily devoid of compassion and did not even suggest reconciliation between Nicaragua's conservative church hierarchy and the Sandinista-led government. When Cardenal kneeled to kiss his ring, the pope withheld his hand and waved a finger of admonition in the priest's face, an act Nicaraguans construed as an insult.

The approach Cardenal has used in his writing and his pastoral work, which displeased the pope, reflects the influence of Merton. Merton encouraged Cardenal to found a politically centered community and suggested that the first rule for it be that there be no rule. He advised Cardenal that in Latin America contemplation could not be divorced from the political struggle.

For twelve years Cardenal worked among the 1,000 poor peasants and fisherman who inhabited the thirty-eight islands on the archipelago of Solentiname. They examined the Bible in light of their personal experiences and together developed an austere life-style based on the ideological conceptions of the early Christians and the utopian ideas of pre-Marxist socialists. They admired what they thought were the classless ancient Maya societies where everyone got his or her due and no one profited at the expense of a neighbor. They also adhered to Merton's concept of nonviolent opposition to those militating against the realization of the kingdom of heaven on earth.[187] The Solentiname commune prepared the peasants for revolution, teaching them that it does not conflict with the Catholic faith. The commune's notions were based on the premise that the major function of Christianity was to shape a fair society, and it sought to do that by interpreting the Scriptures in revolutionary fashion.[188]

Solentiname was the antithesis of the crass bourgeois world of the Somozas. Each Sunday the community, including Cardenal, engaged in a dialogue based on a gospel reading, from which there emanated simple yet profound ideas.[189] Members also read some of the writings of Marx, Mao, and Castro. Cardenal recorded the dialogues in the four volumes *El evangelio en Solentiname* (1975; *The Gospel in Solentiname*, 1976) an unsophisticated but poignant contribution to liberation theology, which contains numerous parallels between Nicaragua's political reality and the gospels. For example, it noted the parallel between the death of Sandino and that of Jesus, both of whom were betrayed and killed, one by Roman soldiers and the other by the National Guard. Both believed that their deaths would lead to liberation.[190]

When the volumes were published in Spain, the Nicaraguan government prohibited their importation on the grounds that they used the gospels to preach communism.[191] By the mid-1970s Solentiname had gained recognition for its accomplishments in the arts, its opposition to

Somoza, and its dedication to social change. Its members came to believe that church social doctrine empowered them to join the Sandinista National Liberation Front. When the National Guard destroyed the community in 1978 as revenge for the military actions of some of its members, Cardenal informed the government:

> The government of Nicaragua has accused me of illicit association with the National Liberation Front of Sandino [FSLN]. . . . I declare publicly that I do belong to the FSLN and this is an honor.
>
> I consider it my duty as a poet and as a priest to belong to this movement. In these Latin American countries which are fighting for their liberation, the poet cannot be alien to the struggle of the people and much less can a priest.
>
> I belong to the FSLN above all because of my fidelity to the gospel. It is because I want a radical and profound change, a new fraternal society in accord with the teachings of the gospels. It is because I consider this a priestly struggle.[192]

The survivors of Solentiname sought refuge in Costa Rica, from where Cardenal publicized his FSLN connections. The actions of Cardenal and the Solentiname community drew more of the faithful, laypeople and clergy, into the guerrilla forces.[193]

From the Solentiname experience came Cardenal's message that people, not God, made unequal social classes and organized the world poorly.[194] According to Cardenal, the early Christians sought a perfect communist society in which Marx's dictum "from each according to his abilities, to each according to his needs" prevailed.[195] To the poet-priest, *Sandinismo* and radical Catholicism shared honesty, dedication, love of neighbor, concern for the poor and the oppressed, and subordination of materialism to fulfillment of the spirit.[196]

Cardenal declared, "You can't be with God and be neutral."[197] He came to believe that the gospel has to be heard and then put into practice.[198] Blending Christian communalism with socialism changed Cardenal's life. At one time he would have accepted or have been resigned to the will of God, even if it entailed an arrest by police agents of a totalitarian state. By the 1970s he espoused the need to alter that state and prevent the arrest.

Cardenal viewed private property as synonymous with robbery, which contradicts the gospel.[199] According to him, "In paradise everything is owned in common, and with sin private property was introduced."[200] Christ believed that wealth was unjust because it was stolen. It should be divided because it belongs to others.[201] Those who put up capital and do not work are parasites who live at the expense of others, and those who consume the most do not work.[202] The wealthy think that their prosperity comes from money working for them, but the labor of the poor brings riches.[203] Without the profit seekers, for example, medicine prices would be lower and Nicaragua could eliminate diseases.[204]

Cardenal stated that you cannot serve two masters, God and money,[205] that there cannot be true peace while capitalism and imperialism exist.[206] He interpreted the earthquake that destroyed Managua in 1972 as an act of God designed to eliminate the unequal distribution of wealth. It occurred symbolically at Christmas to point out that the rich have more than they could want, and the poor have nothing.[207] If you eliminate disparities in wealth you get rid of the oppressor class and create equality, and that leads to peace.[208]

Cardenal's views changed dramatically in 1970 when he went to Cuba for two weeks to judge a poetry contest and stayed for three months. He commented on the shortcomings of the Cuban Revolution in *En Cuba* (1972; *In Cuba*, 1974) and praised its accomplishments. He referred to his 1970 trip to Cuba as a second conversion: "Before then, I saw myself as a revolutionary, but I had confused ideas. I was trying to find a third way, which was the Revolution of the Gospel, but then I saw that Cuba was the Gospel put into practice. And only when I converted to Marxism could I write religious poetry."[209] The Cuban Revolution connoted love of neighbor as gospel in action, or "efficacious charity," to use the phrase of Camilo Torres.[210] Cuba exemplified society working toward the perfection desired by God, wherein all people came together.[211]

Upon encountering Havana without commercialism, without contrasts between opulence and poverty, Cardenal realized that his Solentiname retreat had not withdrawn from the world, only the capitalist world.[212] He read Christian values into the Cuban Revolution. In subsequent years he became aware that there was a fundamental difference between the Cuban and Nicaraguan revolutions. Cuba was oblivious to the church whereas Nicaragua incorporated the popular church into the Sandinista ethos.[213] Cardenal concluded that God selects people to liberate their societies and that the liberation of Cuba led to the liberation of Nicaragua. He read the values of the early Christians into Guevara's concept of the "new person," in particular the idea that humanity is a single body with eternal life, a body that people must share.[214] The Cuba experience taught him that individuals can die, but the people endure, a philosophy embodied in the revolutionary slogan "homeland or death."[215] After visiting Cuba, Cardenal equated the development of revolutionary consciousness with the second coming of Christ, to be followed by communism, which represented the kingdom of God on earth.[216]

In Cardenal's ideal socialist revolution, leaders are not made into gods. Leaders will eventually disappear, and the people will rule. No one aspires to command; leadership is a responsibility imposed by the community.[217] Each revolutionary step forward unites the community more. Humanity forms a superorganism composed of conscious organisms. A person does not lose his or her individuality in the superorganism but forms part of a greater whole.[218]

Cardenal noted that freedom of artistic creativity and individuality are fundamental principles of revolution.[219] As minister of culture, Cardenal endeavored to promote freedom of expression and excellence in music, poetry, painting, crafts, theater, folklore, scholarly research on the national heritage, museums, films, libraries, and recreation. To him, culture exists to transform reality, to create the new revolutionary person and the equitable society envisioned by Jesus.

Cardenal's writings stress the areas of congruence between Christian and Marxist revolutionaries, and he calls himself a Christian Marxist. He sees the monk's ideal of transforming *cupiditus* (cupidity) into *caritas* (love) as analogous to Marx's passing from capitalism to communism. The monk seeks change by altering consciousness, the Marxist by revamping the economic substructure.[220] To Cardenal, Marxist atheists share Jesus' faith in the struggle for liberation.[221] Marxism is a scientific method for studying society and effecting social change. Christ too sought social change and did not prescribe what method to use to attain it. Science, or knowledge derived from study, tells us how to proceed.[222] Marx found that God always appeared on the side of the dominant power, and Cardenal concurred that is true of the God of most religions but not true of the God of the Bible.[223]

Cardenal takes the Marxist concept of dialectical materialism, in which matter is eternal, one step farther, and says "if material is eternal, there is an eternal life, and an eternal consciousness."[224] Although Marx did not know what would come after communism, Christ knew where he was going, and Cardenal likes the certainty of Christianity.[225]

Cardenal's communist interpretation of Christian morality and tradition represents one tendency in the FSLN. On the other side, the FSLN's atheist Marxists generally contend that inequality is overcome by raising the cultural and material level of workers to that of professionals, an upward move. Cardenal's approach to equality, according to Donald Hodges, levels downward and alienates potential supporters among those with higher education as it disregards differences based on merit.[226] Hodges contends that attempts to establish the consistency of Marxism and Christianity are not very convincing. He says that the evidence used by those who reconcile Marxism with Christianity is selective, but they have succeeded in building a broad Christian-Marxist alliance for revolution, one not hindered by fundamental ideological differences.[227]

Many Marxist purists do not accept Cardenal's rationale for reconciling his brand of "critical" Marxism with Christianity, yet they generally respect the goals of his theology of liberation. He goes on the premise that all are equal before God and that God works through us to achieve liberation. Cardenal realizes that historically the church has not always accepted this position. Since the fourth century and the days of Roman Emperor Constantine, the church has often coexisted with repressive governments while directing the faithful to remember their sins and to accept their lot in life, including misery, in exchange for the promise of a better existence in the hereafter. Cardenal rejects that approach, preferring to view Christianity as an extension of Christ's mission to free people from oppression. To him, freedom from human oppression connotes liberation from other's sins.[228]

Cardenal knows that in the encyclical *Rerum Novarum* (1891) Pope Leo XIII recognized that society was divided into classes, and Pope Pius XI in *Quadragesimo Anno* (1931) referred to class struggle.[229] Cardenal reasoned that armed struggle is effective charity, designed to feed the hungry, clothe the naked, and teach the ignorant.[230] He concurred with the Vatican II (1962–1964) declaration that laypeople should take an active role in church activities, and with Pope Paul VI's *Populorum Progressio* (1967), which criticized imperialism, neocolonialism, and capitalism that dehumanizes. He supported the declaration of the 1968 Medellín Latin American Bishops Conference that people have a right to alter institutions that violate their lives and to struggle for freedom from economic dependency.

After the articulation of liberation theology at the Medellín conference, Christian base communities appeared in Central America and engaged in social action. Members of the communities deplored bourgeois society's use of Christianity to legitimize domination and the church's imparting a sacred quality to capitalist democracy because it incorrectly perceived charity as incompatible with revolutions. They criticized the church for often seeing human rights as synonymous with the rights of the ruling class.[231] They combined the Christian idea that humans are alienated from God and their fellow beings with the Marxist notion that the system contributes to human alienation. Liberation theology, by no means a homogeneous school of thought, generally refers to the elimination of alienation by taking the means of production away from individuals and giving them to institutions primarily concerned with the common good.[232]

The 1979 Puebla Latin American Bishops Conference examined the theories and practices of the national security state, liberal capitalism, and Marxism. Although the conference did not accept Marxism, it condemned exploitative capitalism and police states.[233] By this time

Cardenal was intrigued by liberation theology. He liked its devotion to the poor and the common good and its refusal to glorify nationalism at the expense of humanity. He accepted it as a reaction to the institutionalized violence of dependent capitalism. To him, liberation theology did not represent a Christian ideology of revolution but rather a process of reflection based on understanding the faith and Christianity's historical commitment to liberation. That conservative Pope John Paul II attended the Puebla conference and spoke against the progressive measures adopted at Medellín and then in 1980 ordered Cardenal and other Nicaraguan clergymen to drop out of secular politics attests to the effectiveness of liberation theology and its influence on Nicaragua's popular church.

Cardenal points out that Sandinista support for the popular church, or church of the poor, is not an attempt to divide the Catholic church but to demand from it a positive position on social change, ideas congruent with those of Borge stated at the beginning of this chapter. Nicaragua's popular church reaches out to the poor, supports freedom of religion and expression, and believes that one can be a Christian and a revolutionary. It eschews the use of religion for political purposes and therefore views priests' roles in government as secular, acknowledging that religion has a different purpose from the state, which represents believers and nonbelievers.[234]

Most Nicaraguans respect Cardenal as a priest, love him as a poet, and think of him as the heir to Rubén Darío and as one who has combined the romantic tradition with service to the revolution. Since the late 1950s, his realistic revolutionary poetry has been extremely popular in Latin America, possibly as a reaction to the excessive literary tradition of poetry in the region.[235] His free-verse style reflects that of Pablo Neruda, Ezra Pound, William Carlos Williams, and Walt Whitman. From Pound he learned that capitalism oppressed culture and used it for profit, concepts that led him to explore the meaning of imperialism.[236]

He calls his work *exteriorismo* (exteriorism), poetry created from images of the world around us, although some of it has a personal dimension. It is designed to forge a new humanity and change society. It contains elements of the original *Sandinismo,* Catholic prayer, Marxist thought, and nationalist fervor. It analyzes the past with an eye to shaping the future.[237] Cardenal's poetry repudiates the world of avarice that precipitates institutionalized terror, which he attributes to private property.[238] He directs his revolutionary poems at the masses and attempts to bridge the gap between art and life. He combines political themes with biblical love. Cardenal is fascinated by flying and soaring objects such as birds and planes and by the heavens. His work represents a flight into Nicaraguan history and life. His goal is liberation not only for people but for the rivers, lakes, trees, and animals.

Cardenal integrates popular and high culture and international and native culture.[239] He does not use the term *cultural imperialism,* naively contending that imperialism is only economic and military. He works to democratize culture, to remove from it the connotation of elegance reserved for the privileged. As did Marx, Cardenal believes that it is criminal to give the people anything materially inferior. He has become famous for promoting poetry workshops, even among illiterates, and for affirming the idea that anyone who uses the mind can engage in intellectual pursuits. He noted with pride that "Nicaragua is the only country in the world where poetry produced by the police is published."[240] He quotes Gramsci, who called culture "the critic of exploitation,"[241] and in Gramscian fashion he uses culture to mobilize people for politics.

Jaime Wheelock Román:
The Marxist Component of *Sandinismo*

A number of Nicaragua's Sandinista leaders, such as Cardenal and Wheelock (1946–), do not come from proletarian origins, but their sentiments lie with the workers. Wheelock, the son of landed gentry, obtained his early education at Catholic schools, which left him with a sense of Christian humanism. While a university student during the late 1960s, he joined the FSLN opposition to Somoza. In 1970 he went to Chile, where he studied and worked for a year with the agrarian reform program of Salvador Allende's Popular Unity government. He subsequently learned how the United States destabilized Chile and fostered the disintegration of its economic and political system by exacerbating class conflict and separating the middle sectors of society from Allende. He understood that to prevent a repetition of the Chilean experience in Nicaragua, it would be necessary to install an armed people's government that could not easily be overthrown.[242]

Wheelock returned from Chile in 1971 to help organize the FSLN for armed resistance, and he led its proletarian wing, whose program is described in the introduction to this chapter and on subsequent pages. He attained the FSLN's highest rank (commander), wrote four books, and became known for his insightful historical analyses of Nicaraguan dependence. He traveled to East Germany and resided there long enough to sharpen his grasp of Marxist theory. In 1979 he became a member of the nine-person Sandinista National Directorate and minister of agricultural development and agrarian reform. He immediately established a reputation as an erudite and sophisticated Marxist economist. A popular and exceptionally articulate speaker, he is a "critical" Marxist and highly regarded as an FSLN political theorist who reconciles the ideology set forth by Sandino and Fonseca with contemporary conditions.

Wheelock traced the history of the indigenous anticolonialist struggle in Nicaragua. Beginning in 1527, under the first Spanish governor, the area's Indians were repressed and used as slaves. Ideological dissenters were subject to the death penalty, as religion, class, and cultural ideology was imposed upon the natives.[243] For three centuries, according to Wheelock, Indian resistance to Hispanic rule was a form of class conflict over control of the means of production and the land.[244] He debunked the idea of a Spanish American melting pot, for Spain's colonizers displayed an attitude of superiority as they carried out their civilizing mission.[245] Native resentment to Hispanic occupation never subsided, as evidenced by the current desire of the Miskito Indians to remain outside of the Spanish culture.

After independence, Nicaragua's quasi-feudal economic and social systems did not change much until the 1830s. Then a class reaction occurred as Indians who were deprived of their lands became wage laborers on large plantations and began to express their discontent. This dispossessed labor force became the foundation for Sandino's struggle.[246]

In his book *Nicaragua: Imperialismo y dictadura* (1975, Nicaragua: Imperialism and dictatorship), Wheelock noted that with the elimination of self-sufficient peasant farms in the late nineteenth century, Nicaragua became part of the international capitalist marketplace. Simultaneously, liberals representing a rising agricultural bourgeoisie began to clash with the old conservative feudal oligarchy. In 1893 the liberal bourgeois revolution, mentioned at the outset of this chapter, temporarily resolved the conflict. But middle-class control of the nation was upset in 1909 when the United States intervened, the conservative oligarchy resumed control, and Nicaragua relinquished its financial assets to Wall Street.[247] The Depression then prevented the accumulation of national capital and enabled the United States to control the bourgeoisie and put dictator Somoza in charge.[248]

Wheelock contended that World War II strengthened U.S. domination as Somoza consolidated his position and acquired enormous wealth. During the war Nicaragua became a source of basic materials for the United States. After the war the economy rebounded slowly, the infrastructure developed, cotton production was accentuated, and dependency deepened.[249] By the 1950s, after half a century of conservative oligarchic control, some power was conceded to local politicians. Then, to impede the replication of the Cuban Revolution, Nicaragua was incorporated into the global imperialist strategy in the 1960s. Investment capital flowed in under the Alliance for Progress and the CACM, a façade of reform was constructed, and Peace Corps volunteers arrived, all as part of a U.S. counterinsurgency policy.[250] Somoza protected capitalism and its imperialist component, but a rivalry developed between his supporters and bourgeois elements who wanted a larger share of the economic pie. The latter, conservatives who did not advocate genuine democracy or basic reforms, had constituted the majority of the anti-Somoza forces since World War II. By the 1970s, Somoza's economic rivals, together with the FSLN-led proletariat, began to clamor for the end of the dictatorship.

Wheelock emphasized that dependent capitalism began under Spain, was taken over by Great Britain, and then expanded by the United States.[251] To him, early nineteenth-century U.S. interest in Nicaragua stemmed from the desire to facilitate commerce by building an interoceanic canal. Later the United States justified its military presence in Nicaragua as insurance for the nearby Panama Canal, a rationale it reinforced by promoting a nonexistent cold war threat to the waterway.

Wheelock noted that the United States has been in a state of hysteria since the appearance of revolutionary Cuba, which it tried to make disappear legally and politically.[252] U.S. efforts to undermine Cuba have failed, but Washington has stiffened its resolve to prevent radical social change elsewhere in the Americas. Wheelock stressed that the United States has employed anticommunist Cuban exiles, some with ties to the Mafia and drug-runners, to try to thwart revolution in Nicaragua. He also told observers not to misconstrue the Sandinista-led government's admiration for Cuba's revolutionary accomplishments as synonymous with Nicaragua's joining the Soviet bloc.[253]

He claimed that imperialism is in crisis, as evidenced by severe economic problems in countries such as Brazil and Costa Rica, and its proponents fear radical change and move to halt it by the use of violence. The imperialists refused to stand by and see nations with dissimilar ideologies, such as Nicaragua under the Sandinistas, do well. For example, Washington disliked that in 1983, before the *contra* war devastated the Nicaraguan economy by depriving it of 50 to 60 percent of its funds, Nicaragua was faring better, in terms of food production, than under Somoza.[254] To prevent independent economic or political successes, the United States has created strong dictatorial governments in Latin America, which operate within the framework of imperialist economic relations.[255] But Wheelock contended that the Nicaraguan Revolution shattered the classic model of U.S. domination in the Americas with client governments supported by oligarchies, the church, the military, and draped in pseudodemocratic ideology. He noted that the United States pushed for new elections in Nicaragua in 1984, not believing that they would be more democratic than earlier ones, but as a means to oust the revolutionary government,[256] a tactic that eventually proved effective in 1990.

Wheelock maintained that Reagan was guided by Richard Nixon's book *The Real War* (1980), which stipulated that World War III began with the rise of socialism before World War II. Nixon and Reagan shared a "Manichean mentality" that saw Soviet evil everywhere. Although they claimed to seek peace, they really unleashed war against falsely perceived villains.[257] Wheelock pointed out that Reagan's policies forced Nicaragua, under the Sandinistas, to seek arms from everyone, thus affecting its nonalignment position. But Nicaragua basically viewed itself as part of a Western European–Latin American alliance.[258] He stated that Washington denied a Sandinista request for military assistance in 1979 but insisted that the revolutionary government pay for U.S. weapons supplied to Somoza, weapons that killed 50,000 Nicaraguans.[259]

Wheelock understood that the United States could have obliterated Nicaragua with nuclear devices but felt that ultimately it would have learned that there are no winners in an atomic war.[260] A U.S. invasion of Nicaragua, however, would only have prolonged the war. He felt that by 1986 the *contras* were strategically defeated and could only execute acts of desperation, and he correctly predicted that if peace accords were agreed upon, the United States would continue to support the *contras*. Although the Central American nations wanted peace, the United States did not.[261] It continued to pursue a military policy toward Nicaragua that neither represented the sentiments or the best interests of the people of both countries.[262] The U.S. government did not believe that it was in its best economic interest to have Nicaragua stop following the agro-export model and industrialize to provide for the material needs of its people. Washington was determined to topple the Sandinistas from power.

Wheelock maintained that, in the past, Nicaragua's dependence has weakened its bourgeoisie, that its business class lacked independence, political power, or a government of its own. What he called Nicaragua's "consular bourgeoisie" before the revolution served U.S. interests to serve itself.[263] When the Sandinistas took power, they wanted to create a state in which the poor were treated like human beings and had the opportunity to enjoy the benefits of modern civilization.[264] They wanted to change the system under which the major agricultural growers produced for the external market, and the internal market was served by those operating under precapitalist conditions. They favored altering the relations of production created by the CACM, which developed import substitution that enabled U.S. companies to invest in drugs, cabarets, hotels, machinery, and technology[265] when Nicaragua should have been developing its plentiful national resources such as fish, lumber, minerals, and agriculture. Wheelock pointed out that during the last two decades of Somoza rule, foreign debts grew,[266] as 1 percent of Nicaragua's producers accounted for 85 percent of its exports (cotton, coffee, beef, and sugar) and cultivated 48 percent of its land. Under Somoza, U.S.

companies such as American Cyanamide, Pennsalt-Hercules, Monsanto, Standard Fruit, Nabisco, Esso, Standard Steel, Grace, and Mennen dominated the economy.[267]

After the revolution, Wheelock believed, the Sandinista-led government had to form a sector of state production that united the most developed and vital areas of the economy. It had to transform family farms into more productive cooperatives. At the same time, the state accepted coexistence with private producers.[268] As minister of agriculture, Wheelock sought to modify Nicaragua's land tenure system to confer stability, to distribute land in a rational manner, and to enhance production. He wanted to save the best croplands for internal use, not export, and advocated the use of modern technology to increase production for both export and internal consumption.[269]

To initiate the land reform process, Wheelock began to place the Somoza lands into the hands of the people.[270] By 1989 he had supervised the redistribution of about 50 percent of the nation's cultivable farmland (5 million acres) to more than 112,000 peasant families. He started to build strong economic ties to socialist nations, where Nicaragua could sell goods for a fair price. In other words, he diverged from reliance on a capitalist system of manipulated competition and unreasonable profit.[271]

The government controlled more of the means of production in order to distribute the nation's economic surplus equitably.[272] In cases where the flight of foreign exchange and decapitalization endangered the economy, Wheelock advocated closing unpatriotic private enterprises that operated in their own, not Nicaragua's, best interests.[273] He supported nationalization of foreign businesses, natural resources, strategic industries, and the banks. He worked to build an economic system that would coexist with capitalism but would be geared to the reduction of alienation and the improvement of the living standards of all the people, not just of individual capitalists. In private, Wheelock expressed doubts about the long-term efficacy of the mixed economy, but while the Sandinistas were in power he saw it as a viable solution to Nicaragua's economic problems.

Many of Wheelock's solutions for Nicaragua's problems emanated from his belief that capitalism created a working class that developed a revolutionary consciousness and the desire to emancipate itself. He and the members of the proletarian tendency identified with the workers' struggles and sought to make the FSLN the vanguard party of the laboring class. Wheelock and his proletarian-tendency colleagues originally envisioned making the FSLN into a Marxist-Leninist party, which did not occur because some elements in the organization feared that Marxist-Leninist vanguards were potentially dangerous. Wheelock felt that such vanguards could indeed be dangerous but believed that they were often necessary to push history forward.[274]

To him, the Sandinista vanguard represented the interests of all exploited people and consolidated the revolution against the powerful capitalist bourgeoisie. He warned that revolutionary power could not live side by side with bourgeois power because the latter could not accustom itself to not controlling culture and society.[275] He pointed out that under the Sandinistas the role of the bourgeoisie was limited to production, to be used only to live, not as an instrument of power.[276] The Sandinistas strove to prevent the bourgeoisie from rupturing the revolution by keeping its profits in the country, restricting its ability to purchase foreign currency, and limiting its properties.[277] These regulatory measures went against tradition in Nicaragua and were never accepted by the business sector. At the same time, the Sandinistas respected the patriotic bourgeoisie, which helped guarantee the revolution's unity. He viewed the ruling Sandinista party of the late 1980s as capable of working with all segments of society. Like Gramsci, he conceived of the party not as a closed group that sought to rule from above but as a vehicle to mobilize consensus for social change.

Wheelock used his own brand of flexible Marxism to analyze and organize the revolution. He believed that scientific planning would change society. When asked if Nicaragua followed the Soviet Marxist model, he stated that diversity was the key to the Sandinistas, who represented many more viewpoints than found in the two identical political parties in the United States. He maintained that class struggle did not have to follow a traditional pattern.[278]

In trying to resolve the contradictions between nationalism and internationalism and those inherent in the concept of a mixed economy, he explained that you must extract what will work from various Marxisms, then apply it, along with other useful theories, to the Nicaraguan reality. He pleaded for the use of Marxist theory as a heuristic device rather than a bible.[279]

Wheelock stated that the Sandinistas had no desire to make Nicaragua a power in the world, that they simply opposed despotism and intervention. He contended that revolutions are not exported but made by the people and that the Sandinistas did not want to arm their neighbors.[280] He pointed out that Nicaragua had a formidable army to defend itself but no air force or navy to use in external forays.[281]

Wheelock carefully noted that the revolution was not antireligion but antibourgeois politics.[282] Rejecting the criticism that the Sandinistas were atheists and opposed Christianity, he said that the Sandinistas carried out the Commandments and adhered to the dictum that blessed are the humble and the poor.[283]

On the question of the periodic press censorship imposed by the Sandinistas, Wheelock stressed that only the capacity of counterrevolutionaries to destabilize was curtailed,[284] that you cannot permit your institutions to be undermined by a newspaper such as *La Prensa*, which was supported by a U.S. government bent on overthrowing the revolution.[285] Wheelock's last point especially impressed me in early 1986 when I heard Jaime Chamorro Cardenal, codirector of *La Prensa*, admit that his newspaper had just received a $240,000 subsidy from the U.S. Congress–financed National Endowment for Democracy.[286] I wondered if the United States would have permitted Hitler to underwrite a pro-Nazi newspaper in Washington, D.C., during World War II. To what extent *La Prensa's* anti-Sandinista diatribes damaged the FSLN-led regime will never be fully ascertained. But we can be sure that the U.S.-financed *contra* war, the U.S. economic embargo against Nicaragua, and the millions of dollars the United States spent to support the Sandinista's opposition contributed significantly to the destabilization of the country, which was to a great degree responsible for the February 1990 election defeat of Ortega and his revolutionary program. The Sandinista leadership also admitted that their errors in governmental management to some extent prevented the reelection of Ortega and led to their loss of a majority in the National Assembly. In particular they realized that they failed to forge a solid alliance with the peasantry, which often turned against them.

Wheelock and his Sandinista *compañeros* will always point with pride to what the Nicaraguan Revolution accomplished, even with a U.S. gun pointed at its head. For years to come they will ascribe considerable blame for their political downfall to the *contra* war and other dastardly acts by the United States. Some of the FSLN's hard-line Marxist intellectuals will also attribute the movement's failure to retain political power to its inability to rapidly turn Nicaragua into a socialist state. As they see it, ideological pluralism and the mixed economy enabled bourgeois elements to remain in place and to ally with the United States' counterrevolution. What occurred in Nicaragua, they will tell you, is precisely what the Cuban Revolution prevented by removing counterrevolutionaries from positions of power and moving directly to socialism. The Sandinistas point out, however, that had they emulated the Cuban experience, they would have risked an invasion by the United States.

The radical thought and praxis of Sandino, Fonseca, Cardenal, and Wheelock helped forge a progressive movement that won control of the state and maintained it for over a decade. Between 1979 and 1990, radical intellectuals played a major role in shaping Nicaragua's political and social thought and converting theory into governmental praxis.

Cardenal and Wheelock, from positions in the state power structure, contributed to a movement that increased literacy, improved health conditions, redistributed income, initiated agrarian reform, nationalized the industrial structure (if not industry itself), and eliminated a corrupt and tyrannical system, dominated by oligarchs and foreigners, that caused excessive poverty and social instability. Fonseca, Cardenal, Wheelock, and their colleagues took aspects of Darío's liberal antiimperialism, added to it the ideological pluralism, patriotism, and radical concepts of Sandino, then blended in diverse attributes of Third World, Cuban, Christian, and "critical" Marxism to create a uniquely Nicaraguan Revolution.

Sandinista activist-intellectuals endeavored to create and institutionalize mechanisms that militated against economic dependency that erodes national sovereignty. They sought to educate the people to prepare them for a better life, to help them understand the origins of their impoverished past and the importance of resisting a resurgence of the forces that have historically precluded progress for Nicaragua's majority. Radicals such as Cardenal and Wheelock emphasized that *Sandinismo* was not democratic simply because it eliminated the Somoza dynasty and because the country held periodic elections, but by reason of mobilizing the heretofore ignored working classes and poor, empowering them for the first time to participate in the nation's political, economic, social, and cultural processes. Although the Sandinistas lost control of Nicaragua's government, the movement's radical intellectuals believe that the spirit of *Sandinismo* still pervades the parliamentary democracy they established, which guarantees political parties representing all sectors of society the right to participate equally in elections and to occupy seats in the legislature in proportion to their popular support. They also express satisfaction in the belief that their revolutionary political and social base is entrenched as a result of their vital grassroots organization, which exists throughout the country.

7

Conclusions

The urgency of the present movement requires of the intellectual a triple militancy: first, taking part in progressive political organizations; second, maintaining a committed stance in professional work; and third, injecting one's work into the real world of the mainstream media. . . . While the political liberation may not guarantee the cultural liberation of our America, culture might lead the way to political victory.
—Luis Britto García

This chapter contains observations and conclusions not found else-where in this book. It provides additional insights into the problems and themes that have preoccupied Central America's radical thinkers and that they have endeavored to comprehend, explain, and resolve.

Before I go on, let me note that the task of theoretically oriented intellectuals has historically been difficult in Central America, where leaders have not traditionally followed flexible political and social theory. The colonial era produced a legacy of absolute authority, and during the postindependence period a tendency toward military leadership developed that rejected political and social theory as a guide to action. The intellectual heritage of the nineteenth century generally does not include democratic, participant political values, and in fact it gave rise to pessimism about them in the future. After positivism caught on in the late nineteenth century, political and social theory became more widely recognized in Central America. Positivism, which has remained the philosophy of the region's ruling class, also provided an elitist authoritarian doctrine to which radicals could react.[1]

The Central American radical intellectuals we have examined have generally concurred with Gramsci that the dominant class controls through the state and that the intellectuals who direct communications prevail upon the people to accept the ideology and the legitimacy of the established order. Gramsci called this phenomenon hegemony and noted that it existed in despotic societies as well as in liberal democracies. We have seen it in every Central American state.

One reason that hegemony has been so unrestrained in Central America is the absence of early radical opposition. Unlike in South America, Mexico, or Cuba, in Central America little European radical intellectual influence appeared in the nineteenth century. During the early twentieth century, anarchosyndicalist thought had much less of an impact in Central America than in the major countries of Latin America. When radical ideologies gained some popularity in Central America in the 1920s, their proponents were by no means unified in thought or praxis. For example, from the late 1920s to the mid-1930s the international Communist movement regarded middle-class, antiimperialist, radical nationalists as counterrevolutionaries because they were tied to foreign financing and unable to complete the bourgeois democratic revolution. Within a given nation in the region, radical unity did not occur until the recent emergence of the FSLN in Nicaragua and the FDR-FMLN in El Salvador.

In comparison to South America, Mexico, or Cuba, Central America has not produced much original radical thought. But the majority of the area's radical thinkers, albeit not extremely innovative, have tried to adapt to the realities of their respective societies and have worked in a flexible, nondogmatic fashion. Sixteen of the twenty-one who received primary attention on the preceding pages—Galich, Toriello, Torres Rivas, Cuenca, Dalton, Menjívar, García, Posas, Meza, Sáenz, Mora, Cerdas, Vega Carballo, Fonseca, Cardenal, and Wheelock—fall into the "critical" Marxist category. One person from this group (Cardenal) also deserves the designation Christian Marxist. Three major writers (Martí, Cayetano Carpio, and Becerra) are best classified as "rigid" Marxists because of tendencies toward dogmatism and uncritical polemicizing. One rather bourgeois liberal (Darío) and one populist revolutionary liberal (Sandino) contributed significantly to the radical tradition, as did one social democrat (Arévalo). All of these thinkers have helped elevate the historical consciousness necessary to understand the political, economic, and social origins of the area's problems and thereby, especially in recent years, have contributed to the improvement of the social sciences. They have also fostered greater sensitivity to the human condition and have imparted to the masses the spirit essential to attain political and social power.

Central America's radical thinkers constitute a small and sometimes cohesive fraternity. They tend to read one another's works, travel extensively, attend the same conferences, exchange ideas, share overall objectives, and sometimes collaborate on political or scholarly projects. All of the radicals discussed at length in this book have considered

Darío's prescient warnings about the dangers of foreign intervention and have analyzed thoroughly the causes and effects of the legendary exploits of Sandino and Agustín Farabundo Martí. Thinkers who reached intellectual maturity after 1930 learned from Peruvian José Carlos Mariátegui's *Siete ensayos de interpretación de la realidad peruana* (1928; *Seven Interpretative Essays on Peruvian Reality*, 1971). Mariátegui combined Marxist analysis of the material base of society with his own ideas on its superstructure and concluded that, given existing conditions, it was best to omit the classical Marxist bourgeois democratic revolution and proceed directly to an indigenous national liberation movement.

Since the 1940s and 1950s, Central American radicals have been familiar with Sáenz's views on inter-American cooperation and law, and Arévalo's perspectives on anticommunism and how it negates social reform. In recent decades, the humanistic poetry of Dalton and Cardenal and their views on blending art with revolutionary work have enriched and enlightened radicals throughout the Americas. Cardenal's explications of liberation theology and Christian Marxism have created more receptivity to the revolutionary church by the area's heretofore "rigid" Marxists and skeptical non-Marxist radicals. At the same time, Mora has persuaded Communist party members in Latin America to apply Marxist analysis to national historical conditions and to eschew European-oriented formulas for socialist development, thus breaking down, to some degree, the stereotype of Communist party intransigence. Galich and Toriello, among others, have convinced radical colleagues of the fallibility of bourgeois reforms. Torres Rivas has enhanced the credibility of "critical" Marxist thought by proving to a generation of Central American students and professors that Marxist analysis clarifies conundrums but posits no general theory that pertains to all countries equally. Despite Marx's wishful thinking, the nation-state endures. Torres Rivas's sagacious studies of its various formations are consulted and respected throughout the western hemisphere.

From Chapter 3 we can ascertain that Menjívar employed Torres Rivas's scholarship on the nation-state to illustrate the myriad contradictions of capitalism and the important role of rural labor in Central America's class struggle. From the facts gathered for this book, we can also speculate with some assurance that García's views were tempered by those of Sáenz, with whom she conferred. It is clear from these, and the dozens of other connections noted throughout this book, that the ideas of Central America's radicals have transcended national boundaries and the area's writer-thinkers have learned from one another. But it is essential to point out that the primary influences on them have come from abroad. Bookstores in Central America stock very few works by radicals from neighboring nations. Most Central American radical thinkers who reached adulthood after the middle of the twentieth century have been relatively wordly, multilingual people born into the middle class. They have relied primarily on the ideas of major political, social, and economic theorists from Europe and the English-speaking world. No contemporary thinker from another Central American country, or even from another Latin American state, has had as profound an impact upon any Central American *pensador* examined between these covers as has, for example, the Italian Antonio Gramsci, who stressed adapting Marxism to predominantly rural societies, an important concept in an area where peasants outnumber proletarians.

In contrast to the writers examined in my books *Marxist Thought in Latin America* (1984) and *Roots of Revolution: Radical Thought in Cuba* (1987), Central America's radical thinkers have generally used fewer philosophical and classical references but have drawn to the same degree upon a broad range of European intellectual traditions that give shape and texture to thought. The Central Americans also have worked within a continental Latin American cultural milieu. Those who produced most of their work before 1960 used less scientific methodology than their younger colleagues. Like their counterparts elsewhere in Latin America, Central American radicals have sought beauty and contributed to it through prose, fiction, plays, and poetry. They have promoted culture and, following the suggestion of Gramsci, have used it as a device for political mobilization.

Like other Latin American radicals, the Central Americans have had their dream of a perfect future marred by their region's imperfect past, which has included racism and sexism. For instance, just as in South America, Central America's intellectual circles have been dominated by white men. Central American women have suffered from dual exploitation, by capital and by males. I note sadly that only one female appears among the major writers examined in preceding chapters. Engels saw a division of labor between the sexes in the capitalist world, with man master of the forest and woman master of the home. Perhaps, as Engels suggested, only by introducing women into public industry can the barriers to greater equality be toppled in Central America.

It is encouraging that as Central America's radical thinkers gain more political and social influence, sexist impediments break down. To use Gramsci's phrase, a "war of position" is waged by Central American radical intellectuals against those exercising hegemony. Within that war, women battle the ruling class and machismo for a place in the intellectual community and for a leadership role in restructuring society's institutions. Thanks to movements such as the FSLN and FDR-FMLN, feminism and female representation in Central America's intelligentsia is increasing substantially.

In Central America, where social, economic, and political problems are more severe and there is less wealth to conserve than in the United States, a high percentage of contemporary intellectuals have adopted radical philosophies. Unlike their bourgeois counterparts, who, in their endeavors to refrain from value judgments, endorse the status quo, Central America's radicals tend to confront it. They passionately oppose the exploitative aspects of society such as racism and sexism, which bourgeois thinkers often support. Although in the United States a strong belief exists that intellectuals, especially radicals, have a negligible influence upon politics, in Central America intellectuals and radicals receive more respect and have more political clout. Radical intellectuals in both Central America and the United States function as social critics, but the Latinos are much more apt to attract a following for their policy alternatives. Consequently, they are often considered dangerous by the ruling elites who silence them or drive them into exile. Nevertheless, because the area's problems demand immediate solutions, Central Americans place a great deal of faith in these individuals who combine thought with praxis and who test ideas and values against reality and attempt to stimulate new conditions for societal advancement.

The activities of most of the writers examined in this book help debunk the myth that radical thought is associated with the obscurantism of armchair academics and rarely guides revolutionary action. This study has shown that by blending thought and praxis, Central American radicals (such as Dalton, Menjívar, Cerdas Cruz, and Wheelock), have strengthened their scholarship. On the other hand, political activism has sometimes forced individuals (such as Cayetano Carpio and Becerra) to adhere to party discipline or to support oversimplified dogma or theory that offended their own intellectual sensibilities or diminished their credibility as critical analysts. Some radicals have accomplished rare intellectual feats, their ideas moving others to action. The efforts of radicals have resulted in higher wages, better working conditions, land reform, improved housing, finer education, social welfare and security systems, more efficient central planning, and the overthrow of dictators. Many of the social, economic, and political improvements implemented by liberal capitalist or social democratic governments originated in the platforms of radical parties. At times, the radicals have succeeded in making the reform-minded parties understand, and even accept, economic determinism. Radical ideas have also contributed enormously to the development and legalization of trade and peasant unions and have caused schisms in the Roman Catholic church and fostered new, progressive wings of that institution.

The preceding pages demonstrate that Central America's radicals represent a number of diverse opinions with various nuances. Their ideologies are rarely static and usually in a state of constant flux. They generally do not see "truths" but only interpretations subject to change. They conclude that people are persuaded to believe in absolute truths, that such persuasion is a characteristic of power that enables the state to force compliance.

Central American radical writers believe that dissension, disagreement, and struggle are vital to the development of humanity. They pursue different theories, strategies, and tactics. Although not always patient with one another, they share a desire to interpret what exists and to find out what is possible.

Central American radicals do not tend to exaggerate the significance or the difficulty of their work in order to inflate their importance. They do not attribute too much credence to academic credentials or consider their roles as mental laborers more prestigious or valuable than those of manual workers. They believe in creating worker-intellectuals, maintaining that when mental workers constitute a privileged elite and control society's thinking and planning, manual laborers remain exploited. They contend that genuine education includes critical evaluation of questions, not just the dissemination of information, and that it will ultimately negate the "truths" of the prevailing system.

The radical authors in this book have generally perceived of conservatism as a striving for compassionless power; they have been contemptuous of liberalism, which has failed to solve the problems of their respective societies. They seek to reconcile the conflicts that result from the struggle between the theoretical state, which they believe has an obligation to express the public's interest, and the established state, which is usually governed by ruling-class concerns. They realize that to rectify this dichotomy they must join immediate social needs to popular political struggles. To help do this they feel compelled to propagate their ideas in print, which often puts their lives in jeopardy.

Beginning in the second decade of the twentieth century, Central American radical thinkers have looked to, in succession, the Mexican, Russian, Chinese, and Cuban revolutions as models for the elimination of U.S. domination and for ways to stimulate interest in radical nationalism, government planning, and social change. The preponderance of today's radicals hold socialist visions and understand that social change will be far more complicated to achieve than Marx and his nineteenth-century successors imagined. Perhaps Marx erred when he predicted that capitalism carried the seeds of its own destruction, that because of class struggle it would deteriorate into barbarism or progress to socialism. The United States, the dominant capitalist state in the Americas, remains strong. However, the impetus for socialism in Central America comes partially from the failure of the United States, which has forged dependent capitalism in the region, to provide for the basic needs of the people in its client states.

Modern Central American revolutionaries have learned that first an insurrection must overthrow the unjust state, then social power must be taken over by the new state, which has to restructure society if the revolution is to endure. Most Central American radicals now agree that a primary motor force for revolution is the working class but that socialism is not necessarily an inherent characteristic of that class. They believe that one way to instill socialism is to raise the consciousness of the proletariat and the peasantry.

The majority of the area's radicals contend that fundamental human needs—food, shelter, employment, education, and health care—are being met best in the Third World in socialist states such as China and Cuba. They know that historically socialism has a spotty record in the world, and they realize that, contrary to Marx's prediction, the majority of successful revolutions have occurred in backward states without strong industrial proletariats. Their evidence also negates the idea of building socialism from above. Nevertheless, for socialism to be institutionalized in Central America, there must exist an organization within the national revolution or reform movement to eventually lead the transformation of society.

Central American Marxist thinkers have studied and illuminated their societies' ills by the use of existing modes of radical analysis. They believe that history recounts class struggle. They have followed Marx's contention that human beings make their own history, but not under circumstances of their own choosing, and philosopher Georg Lukács's notion that each crisis signifies a deadlock in the evolution of the capitalist order. They have regarded Marxism as a philosophy about structures and relationships that enables them to comprehend the roots of the problems in their countries. They also have learned from Marx to analyze the past, not to venerate it. To Marx's social and economic theories they have added political dimensions articulated by Lenin, who shaped a social revolutionary force. From Gramsci they have drawn methods designed to unify thought and praxis to destroy bourgeois society and build socialism. Naturally, they have adapted their thinking to contemporary conditions. After all, when Lenin advocated violent revolution, he never envisioned the possibility of nuclear retaliation.

Central American radicals diagnose societal ills in terms of economic dysfunction. They are aware that the world has become increasingly interdependent, that it has moved closer to a single economy, but that for almost five centuries their countries have been in colonial or neo-colonial positions, their decisionmaking autonomy limited by extraordinary economic dependence on dominant foreign nations and businesses unconcerned with Central America's best interests. They worry about their economies, which rely on a few export crops and minerals. These exports prevent the development of overall economic health as they depend on an international market controlled by major industrial states. Export agribusiness hinders agricultural diversification, causes shortages of foodstuffs, raises prices beyond the workers' ability to pay, and retards national and social integration. The radicals also understand that economic developmentalism in the area has increased the disparity between the rich and the poor. They feel that where a substantial proletariat does not exist to act as an agent to change the economic situation, intellectuals and others must do so.

Central American radical intellectuals believe that to foster political, economic, and social change, the five nations must alter their relationship to the United States. The United States has traditionally been guided by the philosophy of Locke, who emphasized individual initiative and rights, and has theoretically always championed these beliefs and those who supported them in Central America. The region's radicals have been more concerned with equitable distribution of wealth in society than with individual initiative and rights, which can translate into a person's right to acquire great wealth at the expense of others. Inherent in the radicals' struggle to rid the region of U.S. imperialism is the need to abolish certain individual rights in favor of collective ones.

As Central America's antiimperialist movement has grown over the past seven decades, it has convinced more citizens of the region that imperialism is an integral part of the ideological conflict pitting greedy capitalist values against fairer socialist ones. Most radicals maintain that imperialism cannot be reformed or moderated, only eliminated through socialist revolution. Their antiimperialist movement has fostered socialist consciousness, which in turn has increased U.S. and native anticommunism.

Central American radical writers categorize the United States not as an agent of democracy, but as an extractor of surplus value, as a colonial ruler that controls local elites. To these intellectuals, U.S.-style democracy is a right-wing authoritarian concept. They maintain that the United States cannot even tolerate nationalist capitalism because it threatens U.S. interests. The United States calls nationalist reform "Communism," labels groups determined to protect their own interests "terrorists," and refers to national class conflict as "East-West" struggles. Although the cold war now appears to have ended in Europe, most radical *pensadores* see the United States as determined to continue it in Central America until all leftist revolutionary movements in the area are eliminated.

The region's radicals point out that people in the United States, where almost everybody claims to be middle class and the middle class aspires to upper-class prerogatives, have difficulty understanding class conflict. When class clashes occur, the United States does not hesitate to support unpopular governments that protect upper- and middle-class interests against those of the dissatisfied working-class majority. Radicals conclude that the United States desires a Central America unified under its economic, political, and military aegis and uses force against nations that dare to move to the left. Radicals wonder when the U.S. government will learn that such behavior is unproductive, that it creates the conditions that make socialism more attractive.

Historically, when a socialist alternative appeared possible, the United States equated it with Soviet expansion. If a Central American country increased trade or diplomacy with the USSR, as Nicaragua did during the 1980s, it made itself vulnerable to U.S. reprisals. Central American radicals understand that when Washington considers a nation important, Moscow does not necessarily concur. They know that the Soviet Union did not want, nor could it afford, economically draining dependencies in Central America but hoped to see independent socialist states there. When questioned about the domino effect of revolution in Central America, the area's radicals quickly assert that conditions of capitalist development, or underdevelopment, rather than Soviet subversion cause revolutionary situations. They regret that negative factors about the Soviet Union, such as Stalinism, have enhanced the growth of anticommunism in the region. But they credit Central America's Communist parties for their early and continued leadership against imperialism and note that many Communists and former Communists have been prime movers behind national liberation movements such as El Salvador's FMLN and Nicaragua's FSLN.

Antiimperialism, antidictatorship, and crises in capitalism have been the driving forces of national liberation movements in Central America throughout the twentieth century. Currently, the region's radical *pensadores* who support such movements do not believe that their countries are locked into a traditional political model or that Asian or European theories of revolution can be used, without modifications, to fit local conditions. They feel that national considerations will always preclude plans for Central American confederation, that even the solidarity of socialism could probably never overcome national differences. From studying the past, they have also learned that national liberation movements have always had an existential component and have never been completely the result of revolutionary class consciousness. In every revolutionary situation in Central America, interclass-related factors have been merged with other elements, including intraclass struggles.

We have found that radical intellectuals have historically maintained a presence in Central America's revolutionary situations. Unlike bourgeois thinkers, they have not seen themselves as manipulating other classes to attain power, but rather have viewed themselves as unselfish agents of change and social justice. They believe, as did Lenin, that they have an obligation to provide the masses with an ideology. In recent years they have tended to relate their efforts to popular movements, which include peasants, white-and blue-collar workers, small business people, and pertain to legal and illegal, armed and purely political struggles on all levels. Today's radicals refer less and less to strictly "working-class movements."

Currently, the area's radical thinkers, Marxists and non-Marxists, are more likely to support multigroup coalitions and alliances with other progressives than did their predecessors. Contemporary Central American radicals often regard narrow-based left-wing political parties, or van-guards, as passé or perhaps merely as catalysts to change incapable of fostering revolution on their own. The recent histories of El Salvador, Guatemala, and Nicaragua show that broad-based social movements, perhaps encompassing some political parties, have made the genuine strides toward revolution. Vanguard party formation, based on the Cuban experience, might occur not as a precondition to revolution, but after the overthrow of the oppressive regime, during the period of consolidation of revolutionary power. As in the Sandinista case, it might occur during the military phase of the revolution.

Prior to the establishment of socialism in Cuba, which has greatly improved the living standards of that nation's people, most Central American intellectuals accepted historian Miles Wortman's assessment of their area's nineteenth-and twentieth-century history as a "struggle between the Hapsburg heritage of economic and political traditional society, regional autonomy, and Christian ideals and the Bourbon legacy of liberal economics, centralized authority, and enlightened thought."[2] Today most of the area's intellectuals agree that liberal economics, centralized authority, and enlightened thought have not solved the region's problems. To Wortman's list of factors traditionally important in the region, a growing number of them now add class struggle and historical materialism. Cuba's successes have compelled intellectuals to view Central American history in a new light and to reassess the worth of scientific socialism. The Cuban Revolution illustrated the connections between imperialism and declining economic and social conditions, and it showed that the overall quality of life improved for most people when native working-class interests took control of institutions formerly dominated by the upper and middle classes and foreigners.[3] Most Central American intellectuals now conclude that in El Salvador, Guatemala, Honduras, and Nicaragua, the plantation tradition has precluded the development of a political tradition of democratic representative government responsive to the needs of the people. In these countries, unlike in Costa Rica, political moderates historically have not been able to acquire and retain power.

Central America's social scientists agree that the area suffers from a culture of violence. The liberals believe that it emanates from authoritarian traditions whereas the radicals attribute it to class struggle and the vagaries of imperialism. Most radicals also contend that the region's problems will only be solved by the abolition of precapitalist and capitalist modes of production and exploitation, freedom from foreign economic control, and the establishment of national cohesion.

Central America's radical thinkers point out that history is on their side, that humanity has continuously progressed in the past, and that the tide is slowly turning toward their idealized versions of society. They believe that currently antidictatorship and antiimperialist movements are coalescing. In Nicaragua the dictatorship was overthrown and the battle against imperialism continues. The struggle in El Salvador proceeds, and Hondurans and Guatemalans are engaged in the fight against the forces of reaction. Even Costa Rica is not immune from radical movements, as its welfare-state economy deteriorates rapidly.

Optimistic radicals of the 1990s discern an erosion in the level of public approval of those who control Central America's national security states. No longer can the rulers diffuse class antagonism, placate the masses, and perpetuate themselves in power by instituting a few reforms that do not resolve social conflicts. As a result of the Cuban and Nicaraguan revolutions, the civil war in El Salvador, the protracted guerrilla campaign against the brutal Guatemalan military, and the use of Honduras as a U.S. base for regional counterinsurgency, political consciousness has been raised in Central America. Increasingly, Central Americans distinguish between U.S.-style electoral democracy, in which citizens have the right to vote for candidates carefully selected by the ruling class, and participatory democracy, which affords people a genuine say in the direction of society. More Central Americans opt for what social critic Noam Chomsky calls meaningful democracy, which presupposes "the ability of ordinary people to pool their limited resources, to form and develop ideas and programs, put then on the political agenda, and act to support them."[4]

Central America's radical thinkers maintain that it is ludicrous to believe that a society is democratic when the rights of popular and individual choice do not extend to the social relations through which preferences are expressed. They prefer genuine democracy, with its concern for social justice, to formal democracy, with its trappings of elections and freedom to do what you cannot afford. Central America's dominated classes are awakening and calling upon their respective states to protect their interests. Similar demands in developed nations have led to the expansion of welfare-state capitalism or social democracy. In neocolonial possessions akin to those in Central America, such demands have often led to socialism, which can better protect national interests against foreign incursions.[5]

Radical writers who combine thought and praxis have, for the most part, existed in Central America for less than a century. They have frequently served as a voice for those unable to speak for themselves. They are a vital breed that has increased in number, theoretical scope, and commitment since the Cuban Revolution. Because of the intellectual efforts and practical activism of the thinkers examined in this book, Central America's peasant leagues, trade unions, universities, and popular movements now abound with individuals who view the region's problems from diverse radical perspectives and who struggle for emancipation and social justice with dedication and appreciation of their potential. Central America's radical thinkers have added to the area's traditions of instinctual antiimperialism and antidictatorship the belief that without revolutionary theory there can be no revolution.

Notes

Chapter 1

1. Aleksander Gella, *The Intelligentsia and the Intellectuals: Theory, Method, and Case Study* (Beverly Hills: Sage Publications, 1976), pp. 48–50.

2. Sheldon B. Liss, *Roots of Revolution: Radical Thought in Cuba* (Lincoln: University of Nebraska Press, 1987), p. xvii.

3. Marvin Harris, *Cultural Materialism: The Struggle for a Science of Culture* (New York: Vintage, 1980), p. ix.

4. Richard J. Bernstein, *Praxis and Action: Contemporary Philosophies of Human Activity* (Philadelphia: University of Pennsylvania Press, 1971), p. ix.

5. Ibid., p. 76.

6. Adolfo Sánchez Vázquez, *The Philosophy of Praxis* (London: Merlin Press, 1977), pp. 149–156.

7. Bernstein, *Praxis and Action*, pp. 307–309.

8. Carl Boggs, *Gramsci's Marxism* (London: Pluto Press, 1976), p. 17.

9. Ibid., p. 35.

10. The material in this section is, for the most part, distilled from Sheldon B. Liss, *Marxist Thought in Latin America* (Berkeley: University of California Press, 1984), pp. 13–30.

11. M. M. Bober, *Karl Marx's Interpretation of History* (New York: W. W. Norton, 1965), p. 128.

12. Ibid., pp. 206–207.

13. C. Wright Mills, *The Marxists* (New York: Delta, 1962), pp. 96–104.

14. Immanuel Wallerstein, *The Capitalist World-Economy* (London: Cambridge University Press, and Paris: Editions de la Maison des Sciences de l'Homme, 1979), p. ix.

15. Ibid., p. x.

16. Louis Hartz, *The Founding of New Societies: Studies in the History of the United States, Latin America, South Africa, Canada, and Australia* (New York: Harcourt Brace and World, 1964), pp. 3–7.

17. Rafael Heliodoro Valle, *Historia de las ideas contemporáneas en Centro-América* (Mexico City: Fondo de Cultura Económica, 1960), p. 7.

18. Terence K. Hopkins and Immanuel Wallerstein, *World-Systems Analysis: Theory and Methodology* (Beverly Hills: Sage Publications, 1982), p. 58.

19. Steve C. Ropp and James A. Morris, eds., *Central America: Crisis and Adaptation* (Albuquerque: University of New Mexico Press, 1984), pp. 16–18.

20. Ronaldo Munck, *Politics and Dependency in the Third World: The Case of Latin America* (London: Zed, 1984), p. 234.

21. Liss, *Marxist Thought*, p. 37.

22. See Salvador Mendieta, *Alrededor del problema unionista de Centro-América*. Vol. 1. *El unionismo en la política transaccionista de Nicaragua*. Vol. 2. *Mundialidad del problema* (Barcelona: Tip. Maucci, 1934). These volumes serve as a kind of history of the Partido Unionista Centroamericano during the 1920s. The author could not get them published in Central America.

23. Liss, *Marxist Thought*, p. 35.

24. Ropp and Morris, *Central America*, pp. 20–21.

25. Munck, *Politics and Dependency*, p. 252.

Chapter 2

1. Carlos Guzmán-Böckler and Jean-Loup Herbert, *Guatemala: una interpretación histórico-social* (Mexico City: Siglo XXI, 1975), pp. 101–121.

2. Mario Monteforte Toledo, *Guatemala: Monografía sociológica* (Mexico City: Instituto de Investigaciones Sociales, Universidad Nacional Autónoma de México, 1965), p. 404.

3. Ronaldo Munck, *Politics and Dependency in the Third World: The Case of Latin America* (London: Zed, 1984), p. 236.

4. Franklin D. Parker, *The Central American Republics* (London: Oxford University Press, 1964), p. 131.

5. Ibid., p. 133.

6. Manuel Galich, *Del pánico al ataque* (Guatemala City: Editorial Universitaria, 1977), p. 337. The 1893 census showed an illiteracy rate of 88.6 percent.

7. Tom Barry, Beth Wood, and Deb Preusch, *Dollars and Dictators: A Guide to Central America* (Albuquerque: Resource Center, 1982), p. 118.

8. Graciela A. García, *Páginas de lucha revolucionaria en Centroamérica* (Mexico: Ediciones Linterna, 1971), p. 200.

9. Roger Plant, *Guatemala: Unnatural Disaster* (London: Latin American Bureau, 1978), p. 39.

10. Archer C. Bush, *Organized Labor in Guatemala, 1944–1949: A Case Study of an Adolescent Labor Movement in an Underdeveloped Country* (Hamilton, N.Y.: Colgate University, 1950), Part 3, pp. 1–2.

11. Monteforte Toledo, *Guatemala*, pp. 314–316.

12. Ibid., pp. 387–388.

13. Jim Handy, *Gift of the Devil: A History of Guatemala* (Boston: South End Press, 1984), p. 119.

14. Monteforte Toledo, *Guatemala*, p. 389.

15. Daniel James, *Red Design for the Americas: Guatemalan Prelude* (New York: John Day, 1954), p. 48. Cuenca then went to work for the Guatemalan government, first in El Salvador, then in Costa Rica.

16. Bush, *Organized Labor in Guatemala*, pp. iv, 6.

17. Luisa Frank and Philip Wheaton, *Indian Guatemala: Path to Liberation* (Washington, D.C.: EPICA, 1984), p. 26.

18. Handy, *Gift of the Devil*, p. 115.

19. Rarihokwats, ed., *Guatemala! The Horror and the Hope* (York, Pa.: Four Arrows, 1982), p. 11.

20. Susanne Jonas, "Guatemala: Land of Eternal Struggle," in *Latin America: The Struggle with Dependency and Beyond*, eds. Ronald H. Chilcote and Joel C. Edelstein (New York: Schenkman, 1974), p. 169.

21. See Jaime Díaz Rozzotto, *El carácter de la revolución guatemalteca: Ocaso de la revolución democrático-burguesa corriente* (Mexico City: Ediciones Revista Horizonte, 1958).

22. Gabriel Aguilera Peralta, "Terror and Violence as Weapons of Counterinsurgency in Guatemala," *Latin American Perspectives* 7 (2–3) (Spring–Summer 1980):94–96.

23. Ibid., p. 100.

24. Ibid., p. 92.

25. Luis Augusto Turcios Lima, "Carta abierta del Movimiento Revolucionario 13 de noviembre," in *Turcios Lima* (Havana: Instituto del Libro, 1969), p. 95.

26. Richard Gott, *Guerrilla Movements in Latin America* (Garden City, N.Y.: Anchor Books, 1972), pp. 85–86.

27. Ibid., p. 73.

28. Ibid., p. 74.

29. Ibid., pp. 63–64.

30. Ibid., pp. 77–79.

31. Jonathan Fried et al., eds., *Guatemala in Rebellion: Unfinished History* (New York: Grove Press, 1983), p. 186.

32. José Fortuny, "Under the Banner of Proletarian Internationalism," *World Marxist Review* 7 (12) (December 1964):45–46.

33. Phillip Berryman, *The Religious Roots of Rebellion: Christians in Central American Revolutions* (Maryknoll, N.Y.: Orbis Books, 1984), p. 171.

34. Aguilera Peralta, "Terror and Violence," p. 101.

35. Eduardo Galeano, *Guatemala: Occupied Country* (New York: Monthly Review Press, 1969), p. 136.

36. Fried, *Guatemala in Rebellion*, p. 158.

37. Frank and Wheaton, *Indian Guatemala*, pp. 70–76.

38. Barry, Wood, and Preusch, *Dollars and Dictators*, p. 126.

39. Center for the Study of the Americas, *Listen Compañero: Conversations with Central American Revolutionary Leaders* (San Francisco: Solidarity Publications, 1983), p. 79.

40. Juan José Arévalo, *La inquietud normalista. Estampas de adolescencia y juventud 1921-1927* (San Salvador: Editorial Universitaria de El Salvador, 1970), p. 33.

41. Ibid., p. 145.

42. Juan José Arévalo, *Istmania, o la unidad revolucionaria de Centroamérica* (Buenos Aires: Editorial Indoamérica, 1954), pp. 39–42.

43. Juan José Arévalo, *Escritos políticos y discursos* (Havana: Cultural, 1953), p. 165.

44. Pedro Alvarez Elizondo, *El presidente Arévalo y el retorno a Bolívar* (Mexico City: Ediciones Rex, 1947), pp. 60–61.

45. Arévalo, *Istmania*, pp. 28–29.

46. Juan José Arévalo, *Guatemala: La democracia y el imperio* (Buenos Aires: Editorial Palestra, 1964), p. 216.

47. Angela Delli Sante Arrocha, *Juan José Arévalo: Pensador contemporáneo* (Mexico City: Costa-Amic, 1962), p. 60.

48. Ibid., p. 56.

49. Ibid., p. 52.

50. Samuel Guy Inman, *A New Day in Guatemala: A Study of the Present Social Revolution* (Wilton, Conn.: Worldover Press, 1951), p. 15.

51. Robert J. Alexander, *Organized Labor in Latin America* (New York: Free Press, 1965), pp. 203–205.

52. Peter Calvert, *Guatemala: A Nation in Turmoil* (Boulder: Westview Press, 1985), p. 47. Harold E. Davis, ed., *Latin American Social Thought* (Washington, D.C.: University Press of Washington, 1961), p. 483.

53. Juan José Arévalo, *Escritos pedagógicos y filosóficos* (Guatemala City: Tipografía Nacional, 1945), pp. 239–264, 280.

54. Fernando Berrocal Soto, "Juan José Arévalo: El hombre y el político," *Revista de filosofía de la Universidad de Costa Rica* 5 (9) (January–June 1966):194.

55. Inman, *A New Day*, p. 15.

56. Arévalo, *Escritos políticos*, p. 144.

57. José M. Aybar de Soto, *Dependency and Intervention: The Case of Guatemala in 1954* (Boulder: Westview Press, 1978), p. 116.

58. Constantino Láscaris, "Algunos pensadores centroamericanos," *Revista de filosofía de la Universidad de Costa Rica* 15 (41) (July–December 1977):282–284.

59. Arévalo, *Guatemala: La democracia*, p. 152.

60. Arévalo, *Escritos políticos*, p. 219.

61. Arévalo, *Escritos pedagógicos*, pp. 94–95.

62. Juan José Arévalo, *Anti-Kommunism in Latin America* (New York: Lyle Stuart, 1963), pp. 23–24.

63. Davis, *Latin American Social Thought*, p. 491.

64. Ibid., p. 487.

65. Alvarez Elizondo, *El presidente Arévalo*, p. 65.

66. Arévalo, *Anti-Kommunism*, pp. 66–70.

67. Berrocal Soto, "Juan José Arévalo," pp. 195–199.

68. Arévalo, *Anti-Kommunism*, p. 164.

69. Ibid., p. 132.

70. Ibid., pp. 127–129.

71. Arrocha, *Juan José Arévalo*, pp. 44–46.

72. Díaz Rozzotto, *El carácter*, pp. 67–131.

73. Davis, *Latin American Social Thought*, pp. 485–486.

74. Heliodoro Valle, *Historia de las ideas*, pp. 111–113.

75. Marie-Berthe Dion, *Las ideas sociales y políticas de Arévalo* (Santiago de Chile: Prensa Latinoamericana, 1958), pp. 56–60.

76. Arévalo, *Escritos pedagógicos*, p. 96.

77. Arévalo, *Guatemala: La democracia*, p. 205.

78. Alvarez Elizondo, *El presidente Arévalo*, pp. 209–227.

79. Ibid., pp. 61–64.

80. Arévalo, *Anti-Kommunism*, p. 47.

81. Arrocha, *Juan José Arévalo*, pp. 97–100. Juan José Arévalo, *The Shark and the Sardines* (New York: Lyle Stuart, 1961), pp. 113–114.

82. Richard H. Immerman, *The CIA in Guatemala: The Foreign Policy of Intervention* (Austin: University of Texas Press, 1982), p. 49. Charles D. Ameringer, *The Democratic Left in Exile: The Antidictatorial Struggle in the Caribbean, 1945–1959* (Miami: University of Miami Press, 1974), p. 60.

83. Diego Córdoba, "Personalidad, obra y paradigma de Juan José Arévalo," *Cuadernos Americanos* 114 (1) (January–February, 1961):121.

84. Arévalo, *Shark and the Sardines*, pp. 149–156.

85. Arévalo, *La inquietud normalista*, p. 286.

86. Arrocha, *Juan José Arévalo*, pp. 74–77.

87. Arévalo, *Shark and the Sardines*, p. 149.

88. Ibid., pp. 50–51.

89. Ibid., pp. 10–11.

90. Ibid., pp. 105–106.

91. Ibid., p. 197.

92. Ibid., pp. 75–88.

93. Ibid., p. 13.

94. Arévalo, *Guatemala: La democracia*, pp. 51–52.

95. Ibid., pp. 102–105.

96. Arévalo, *Shark and the Sardines*, p. 10.

97. Dion, *Las ideas sociales*, p. 169.

98. Arévalo, *Shark and the Sardines*, p. 152.

99. Arévalo, *Anti-Kommunism*, p. 11.

100. Ibid., pp. 166–167.

101. Ibid., pp. 168–174.

102. Ibid., p. 183.

103. Ibid., pp. 193–213.

104. Ibid., pp. 157–160.

105. Rarihokwats, *Guatemala*, p. 9.

106. Manuel Galich, "A ciento cincuenta años del congreso de Panamá: Bolivarismo y panamericanismo," *Casa de las Américas* 16 (96) (May–June 1976):417. See Sheldon B. Liss, *Roots of Revolution: Radical Thought in Cuba* (Lincoln: University of Nebraska Press, 1987), for additional analyses of the works of these authors.

107. Manuel Galich, "La guerra antiimperialista de 1855 en Centro América," *Historia y sociedad* (7) (Fall 1966):37–44.

108. Galich, "A ciento cincuenta años," pp. 16–17.

109. Ibid., pp. 4–17.

110. Manuel Galich, "Internal Reasons for the Defeat," *Tricontinental* (2) (1967):66–67.

111. Ibid., pp. 67–68.

112. Galich, *Del pánico*, pp. 11–12.

113. Galich, "Internal Reasons," p. 70.

114. Immerman, *CIA in Guatemala*, p. 37.

115. Galich, *Del pánico*, p. 157.

116. Ibid., p. 112. Galich, "Internal Reasons," p. 70.

117. Galich, "Internal Reasons," p. 80.

118. Galich, *Del pánico*, pp. 368–370.

119. Galich, "Internal Reasons," pp. 68–69.

120. Ibid., pp. 73–75.

121. Ibid., p. 79.

122. Galich, *Del pánico*, pp. 373–374.

123. Galich, "Internal Reasons," p. 123.

124. Manuel Galich, "The Dangers of Practicing Democracy," *United Nations World* 5 (1) (September 1951):43.

125. Galich, "Internal Reasons," p. 75.

126. Galich, "Dangers of Practicing Democracy," p. 43.

127. Galich, "Internal Reasons," p. 77.

128. Julio Adolfo Rey, "Revolution and Liberation: A Review of Recent Literature on the Guatemalan Situation," *Hispanic American Historical Review* 38 (May 1958):248–249.

129. Galich, *Del pánico*, pp. 381–382.

130. Galich, "Internal Reasons," pp. 78–79.

131. Galich, *Del pánico*, p. 383.

132. Galich, "Internal Reasons," p. 80.

133. Galich, "Dangers of Practicing Democracy," p. 43.

134. See Manuel Galich, *Por que lucha Guatemala, Arévalo y Arbenz: Dos hombres contra un imperio* (Buenos Aires: Elmer Editor, 1956).

135. Rey, "Revolution and Liberation," pp. 248–249.

136. Galich, *Del pánico*, p. 384.

137. Guillermo Toriello Garrido, "Introduction," in *Guatemala in Rebellion: Unfinished History,* eds. Jonathan L. Fried et al. (New York: Grove Press, 1983), p. xiii.

138. Guillermo Toriello Garrido, "On the Role of the United States and Israel," in *Guatemala: Tyranny on Trial,* eds. Susanne Jonas, Ed McCaughan, Elizabeth Sutherland Martínez (San Francisco: Synthesis Publications, 1984), p. 28.

139. Guillermo Toriello Garrido, *Tras la cortina de banano* (Havana: Editorial de Ciencias Sociales, 1981).

140. Guillermo Toriello Garrido, *Guatemala, mas de 20 años de traición* (Caracas: Editorial Ateneo de Caracas, 1980).

141. Ibid., pp. 126, 131.

142. Guillermo Toriello Garrido, *La batalla de Guatemala* (Mexico City: Ediciones Cuadernos Americanos, 1955), pp. 47–51.

143. Guillermo Toriello Garrido, *A Popular History of Two Revolutions: Guatemala and Nicaragua* (San Francisco: Synthesis Publications, 1985), p. 11.

144. Toriello Garrido, *Tras la cortina*, p. 27.

145. Ibid., p. 84.

146. Ibid., pp. 319, 373.

147. Toriello Garrido, *Popular History*, p. 29.

148. Toriello Garrido, *Batalla de Guatemala*, p. 59. In 1953 and 1954 the government expropriated 392,950 acres of uncultivated land for which it paid $1,185,116 in compensation.

149. Ibid., p. 261.

150. Galeano, *Guatemala*, p. 53.

151. Jonas, McCaughan, and Sutherland Martínez, *Guatemala*, p. 168.

152. Toriello Garrido, "Introduction," p. xv.

153. Toriello Garrido, *Popular History*, pp. 31–32.

154. Stephen Schlesinger and Stephen Kinzer, *Bitter Fruit: The Untold Story of the American Coup in Guatemala* (Garden City, N.Y.: Anchor Books, 1982), p. 179.

155. John D. Martz, *Central America: The Crisis and the Challenge* (Chapel Hill: University of North Carolina Press, 1959), p. 53.

156. Immerman, *CIA in Guatemala*, p. 148.

157. Aybar de Soto, *Dependency and Intervention*, p. 239.

158. Toriello Garrido, *Batalla de Guatemala*, pp. 126–134.

159. Toriello Garrido, "On the Role," p. 27.

160. Toriello Garrido, *Popular History*, p. 19.

161. Toriello Garrido, *Guatemala, mas de 20 años*, p. 211.

162. Ibid., pp. 42–43.

163. Guillermo Toriello Garrido, *¿A donde va Guatemala?* (Mexico City: Editorial Nueva, 1956), p. 60.

164. Ibid., pp. 21–26.

165. Toriello Garrido, *Guatemala, mas de 20 años*, p. 48.

166. Ibid., p. 80.

167. See Ibid.

168. Ibid., pp. 70–72.

169. Ibid., p. 146.

170. Ibid., p. 132.

171. Ibid., p. 152.

172. Ibid., pp. 214–215.

173. Ibid., pp. 153–154.

174. Toriello Garrido, *Tras la cortina*, pp. 42–43.

175. Toriello Garrido, *Guatemala, mas de 20 años*, p. 216. Toriello Garrido, "On the Role," p. 29.

176. Toriello Garrido, "On the Role," p. 28.

177. Toriello Garrido, *Popular History*, pp. 3–4.

178. Fried, *Guatemala in Rebellion*, p. xvii.

179. Guillermo Toriello Garrido, "Message from the Central American and Caribbean Anti-Imperialist Tribunal," St. George's, Grenada, March 13, 1982, pp. 1–2.

180. Toriello Garrido, *Popular History,* pp. 4–7.

181. Edelberto Torres Rivas and Julio César Pinto S., *Problemas en la formación del estado nacional en Centroamericana* (San José: ICAP, 1983), p. 144.

182. Edelberto Torres Rivas, *Las clases sociales en Guatemala* (Guatemala City: Universidad de San Carlos, 1962), p. 114.

183. Torres Rivas and Pinto S., *Problemas en la formación,* p. 169.

184. Edelberto Torres Rivas, *Procesos y estructuras de una sociedad dependiente (Centroamérica)* (Santiago: Ediciones Prensa Latinoamerica, 1969), p. 45.

185. Edelberto Torres Rivas, *Interpretación del desarrollo social centroamericano* (San José: Editorial Universitaria Centroamericana, 1981), pp. 65–66.

186. Edelberto Torres Rivas, "The Central American Model of Growth: Crisis for Whom?" *Latin American Perspectives* 7 (2–3) (Spring–Summer 1980):26.

187. Torres Rivas, *Interpretación del desarrollo,* pp. 32–34.

188. Torres Rivas and Pinto S., *Problemas en la formación,* pp. 33–34.

189. Edelberto Torres Rivas, "The Nature of the Central American Crisis," in *Towards an Alternative for Central America and the Caribbean,* eds. George Irvin and Xabier Gorostiaga (London: George Allen and Unwin, 1985), pp. 40–41.

190. Torres Rivas, *Procesos y estructuras,* pp. 143–145.

191. Torres Rivas, *Interpretación del desarrollo,* pp. 15–19.

192. Torres Rivas, "Central American Model," p. 34.

193. Torres Rivas, *Interpretación del desarrollo,* p. 20.

194. Ibid., p. 38.

195. Torres Rivas, "Central American Model," p. 43.

196. Torres Rivas, *Procesos y estructuras,* p. 201.

197. Edelberto Torres Rivas, "Presentation by the Prosecutor," in Jonas, McCaughan, and Sutherland Martínez, *Guatemala,* pp. 16–17.

198. Edelberto Torres Rivas, "Central America Today: A Study in Regional Dependency," in *Trouble in Our Backyard: Central America and the United States in the Eighties,* ed. Martin Diskin (New York: Pantheon Books, 1983), pp. 20–23.

199. Ibid., pp. 10–11.

200. Edelberto Torres Rivas, "Problemas de la contrarevolución y la democracia en Guatemala," *Nueva sociedad* 53 (March–April 1981):110.

201. Edelberto Torres Rivas, "Notas para comprender la crisis política centroamericana," in *Centroamérica: Crisis y política internacional,* ed. Jaime Labastida et al. (Mexico City: Siglo XXI, 1982), p. 48.

202. Torres Rivas, "Nature of the Central American Crisis," p. 39.

203. Torres Rivas and Pinto S., *Problemas en la formación,* pp. 142–143.

204. Ibid., pp. 137–138.

205. Edelberto Torres Rivas, *Crisis del poder en Centroamérica* (San José: EDUCA, 1981), p. 24.

206. Torres Rivas and Pinto S., *Problemas en la formación,* p. 160.

207. Ibid., p. 155.

208. Ibid., pp. 35–36.

209. Torres Rivas, "Nature of the Central American Crisis," p. 47.

210. Edelberto Torres Rivas, "The Origins of Crisis and Instability in Central America," *Contemporary Marxism* 14 (Fall 1986):50, 56.

211. Toriello Garrido, *Guatemala, mas de 20 años*, pp. 212–213.

212. Torres Rivas, "Presentation by the Prosecutor," p. 21.

213. Torres Rivas, *Crisis del poder*, pp. 145–147.

214. Ibid., p. 236.

215. Torres Rivas, "Presentation by the Prosecutor," p. 20.

216. Edelberto Torres Rivas, "Guatemala: Medio siglo de historia política," in *América Latina: Historia de medio siglo*, Vol. 2, ed. Pablo González Casanova (Mexico City: Siglo XXI, 1981), pp. 151–159.

217. Torres Rivas, "Problemas de la contrarevolución," p. 103. In 1944 there were 120 priests and 18 monks in Guatemala; by 1965–1966, 531 priests, 739 monks, and 96 brothers operated there, and 434 of the priests were foreigners, mostly from North America and Spain.

218. Torres Rivas, "Presentation by the Prosecutor," pp. 7–8.

219. Munck, *Politics and Dependency*, p. 242.

220. Torres Rivas, "Nature of the Central American Crisis," pp. 45–46.

221. Torres Rivas, "Central America Today," p. 29.

222. Torres Rivas, "Origins of Crisis and Instability," pp. 55–56.

223. Torres Rivas, "Nature of the Central American Crisis," p. 51.

224. Torres Rivas, "Problemas de la contrarevolución," p. 109.

225. Edelberto Torres Rivas, "Seven Keys to Understanding the Central American Crisis," *Contemporary Marxism* 3 (Summer 1981):50–61. Torres Rivas, "Notas para comprender," pp. 52–60.

226. Edelberto Torres Rivas, *Repression and Resistance: The Struggle for Democracy in Central America* (Boulder: Westview Press, 1989), pp. 70–71.

Chapter 3

1. James Dunkerley, "Class Structure and Socialist Strategy in El Salvador," in *Crisis in the Caribbean*, eds. Fitzroy Ambursley and Robin Cohen (New York: Monthly Review Press, 1983), p. 130.

2. Roque Dalton, *Miguel Mármol* (Willimantic, Conn.: Curbstone Press, 1987), p. xiii.

3. Rafael Menjívar, "El Salvador: The Smallest Link," *Contemporary Marxism* 1 (Spring 1980):20–21.

4. Alastair White, *El Salvador* (New York: Praeger, 1973), p. 87.

5. Rafael Menjívar, *Formación y lucha del proletariado industrial salvadoreño* (San Salvador: UCA Editores, 1979), p. 25.

6. Ibid., p. 26.

7. Thomas P. Anderson, *Matanza: El Salvador's Communist Revolt of 1932* (Lincoln: University of Nebraska Press, 1971), p. 22.

8. Liliam Jiménez, *El Salvador: Sus problemas socio-economicos* (Havana: Casa de las Américas, 1980), p. 170.

9. White, *El Salvador*, p. 93.

10. Thomas P. Anderson, *The War of the Dispossessed: Honduras and El Salvador 1969* (Lincoln: University of Nebraska Press, 1981), pp. 15–16.

11. Anderson, *Matanza*, p. 23. White, *El Salvador*, p. 94.

12. Rafael Helidoro Valle, *Historia de las ideas contemporáneas en Centro-América*. (Mexico City: Fondo de Cultura Económica, 1960), p. 295.

13. Robert J. Alexander, *Communism in Latin America* (New Brunswick, N.J.: Rutgers University Press, 1957), p. 366.

14. Jorge Arias Gómez, *Farabundo Martí: Esbozo biográfico* (San José: Editoral Universitaria Centroamericana, 1972), pp. 39–48.

15. Alexander, *Communism in Latin America*, p. 237.

16. Anderson, *Matanza*, pp. 24–25.

17. Lisa North, *Bitter Grounds: Roots of Revolt in El Salvador* (Toronto: Between the Lines, 1982), pp. 33–34.

18. Anderson, *Matanza*, p. 45.

19. Alberto Masferrer, *Obras escogidas*, Vol. 1 (San Salvador: Editorial Universitaria, 1971), p. 237.

20. Ibid.

21. Masferrer, *Obras*, Vol. 2, pp. 53–79.

22. Ibid., pp. 77–79.

23. Ibid., pp. 77–78.

24. Jorge Arias Gómez, "Agustín Farabundo Martí: Esbozo biográfico," *La Universidad* (San Salvador) 4 (July/August 1971):215.

25. Mario Menéndez Rodríguez, *Voices from El Salvador* (San Francisco: Solidarity Publications, 1983), p. 116.

26. James Dunkerley, *The Long War: Dictatorship and Revolution in El Salvador* (London: Verso, 1983), p. 23.

27. Alexander, *Communism in Latin America*, p. 368.

28. Menjívar, "El Salvador: The Smallest Link," p. 22.

29. A. Petrujin and E. Churílov, *Farabundo Martí* (Moscow: Editorial Progreso, 1985), p. 88.

30. Alberto Gualan, "Years of Valiant Struggle (35 Years of the Communist Party of El Salvador)," *World Marxist Review* 8 (6) (June 1965):65.

31. White, *El Salvador*, p. 169.

32. Gualan, "Years of Valiant Struggle," p. 66.

33. José Sánchez, "Social Developments in El Salvador and the Policy of the Communist Party," *World Marxist Review* 8 (8) (August 1965):13.

34. Ronald H. McDonald, "El Salvador," in *Political Parties of the Americas*, ed. Robert J. Alexander (Westport, Conn.: Greenwood Press, 1982), p. 392.

35. Sánchez, "Social Developments," p. 16.

36. Menjívar, "El Salvador: The Smallest Link," p. 23.

37. Dunkerley, *The Long War*, pp. 89–90.

38. Dunkerley, "Class Structure," p. 131.

39. Tommie Sue Montgomery, "Liberation and Revolution: Christianity as a Subversive Activity in Central America," in *Trouble in Our Backyard: Central America and the United States in the Eighties,* ed. Martin Diskin (New York: Pantheon Books, 1983), pp. 85–86.

40. Dunkerley, "Class Structures," pp. 136–137.

41. Tommie Sue Montgomery, *Revolution in El Salvador* (Boulder: Westview Press, 1982), p. 147.

42. Dunkerley, "Class Structures," pp. 141–142.

43. Personal interview with Rubén Zamora, Managua, Nicaragua, January 9, 1986.

44. See José Ventura, *El poder popular en El Salvador* (Mexico City: Mex Sur, N.D.)

45. Arias Gómez, *Farabundo Martí,* pp. 16–19.

46. Jiménez, *El Salvador,* p. 123.

47. Richard Gillespie, "Agustín Farabundo Martí," in *Biographical Dictionary of Marxism,* ed. Robert A. Gorman (Westport, Conn.: Greenwood Press, 1986), p. 220. Anderson, *Matanza,* pp. 34–35.

48. Anderson, *Matanza,* p. 33.

49. Dunkerley, *Long War,* p. 26. Gillespie, "Agustín Farbabundo Martí," p. 221.

50. Arias Gómez, *Farabundo Martí,* p. 94.

51. Petrujin and Churílov, *Farabundo Martí,* pp. 15–16.

52. Jiménez, *El Salvador,* p. 122.

53. Arias Gómez, *Farabundo Martí,* p. 22.

54. Robert Armstrong and Janet Shenk, *El Salvador: The Face of Revolution* (Boston: South End Press, 1982), p. 21.

55. Gillespie, "Agustín Farabundo Martí," p. 220.

56. Arias Gómez, *Farabundo Martí,* p. 50.

57. Ibid., pp. 52–53.

58. Víctor Alba, *Politics and the Labor Movement in Latin America* (Stanford: Stanford University Press, 1968), p. 281.

59. Petrujin and Churílov, *Farabundo Martí,* p. 49.

60. See Petrujin and Churílov, *Farabundo Martí,* p. 65. A few records of the Central Committee were preserved and were later consulted by Petrujin and Churílov. They differ with Miguel Mármol, who claimed that Martí did not serve as secretary general of the Communist party's Central Committee.

61. Anderson, *Matanza,* p. 66

62. Gillespie, "Agustín Farabundo Martí," p. 221.

63. See Abel Cuenca, *El Salvador: Una democracia cafetalera* (Mexico City: ARR–Centro Editorial, 1962).

64. Ibid., p. 15.

65. Ibid., pp. 41–42.

66. Ibid., pp. 25–27.

67. Ibid., pp. 39–40.

68. Anderson, *Matanza,* p. 11.

69. Cuenca, *El Salvador,* pp. 29–30.

70. Ibid., p. 174.

71. Ibid., p. 71.

72. Ibid., p. 76.

73. Ibid., pp. 78–80.

74. Ibid., pp. 106–107.

75. Ibid., pp. 105–106.

76. Ibid., p. 171.

77. Ibid., pp. 144–145.

78. Miguel Reglado Dueñas and José Salvador Guandique, *El repliegue político de la oligarquía cafetalera* (San Salvador: Tipografía Santa Anita, 1975).

79. Salvador Cayetano Carpio, "Violencia popular, un preocupación central," in *Pueblos en armas*, ed. Marta Harnecker (Managua: Editorial Nueva Nicaragua, 1985), p. 128.

80. Schafik Jorge Handal, "Interview by Mark Fried," *NACLA Report on the Americas* 20 (5) (September–December 1986):40.

81. Menéndez Rodríguez, *Voices from El Salvador*, pp. 16–17.

82. Mario Menéndez Rodríguez, *El Salvador: Una auténtica guerra civil* (San José Editorial Universitaria Centroamericana, 1980), p. 27.

83. Salvador Cayetano Carpio, *Secuestro y capucha: En un país del "Mundo Libre"* (San José: Editorial Universitaria Centroamericana, 1979).

84. Philip L. Russell, *El Salvador in Crisis* (Austin: Colorado River Press, 1984), p. 137.

85. Center for the Study of the Americas, *Listen Compañero: Conversations with Central American Revolutionary Leaders* (San Francisco: Solidarity Publications, 1983), pp. 15–16.

86. Salvador Cayetano Carpio and Mélida Anaya Montes, *La guerra popular en El Salvador* (Mexico: Ediciones de la Paz, 1982), pp. 78–80.

87. Menéndez Rodríguez, *Voices from El Salvador*, p. 23.

88. Cayetano Carpio, *Secuestro*, pp. 7–8.

89. Ibid., p. 144.

90. Cayetano Carpio and Anaya Montes, *La guerra*, p. 77.

91. Adolfo Gilly, "An Interview with Salvador Cayetano Carpio ("Marcial")," *Contemporary Marxism* (3) (Summer 1981):13–14.

92. Center for the Study of the Americas, *Listen Compañero*, pp. 19–22.

93. Menéndez Rodríguez, *El Salvador*, p. 47.

94. Gilly, "An Interview," p. 13.

95. Center for the Study of the Americas, *Listen Compañero*, pp. 38–39.

96. Menéndez Rodríguez, *Voices from El Salvador*, pp. 37–38.

97. James Dunkerley, "Salvador Cayetano Carpio," in *Biographical Dictionary of Marxism*, ed. Robert A. Gorman (Westport, Conn.: Greenwood Press, 1986), p. 68.

98. Cayetano Carpio, "Violencia popular," pp. 136–137.

99. Center for the Study of the Americas, *Listen Compañero*, pp. 25–26.

100. Salvador Cayetano Carpio, "The Final Offensive," in *El Salvador: Central America in the New Cold War*, eds. Marvin Gettleman et al. (New York: Grove Press, 1981), pp. 119–120.

101. Menéndez Rodríguez, *Voices from El Salvador*, pp. 40–41.

102. Ibid., pp. 42–44.

103. Center for the Study of the Americas, *Listen Compañero*, pp. 36–37.

104. Menéndez Rodríguez, *Voices from El Salvador*, p. 30.

105. Cayetano Carpio, "Violencia popular," p. 126.

106. Roque Dalton, *Taberna y otros lugares* (San Salvador: UCA/Editores, 1983), p. 31.

107. Roque Dalton, *Poemas clandestinos* (San Francisco: Solidarity Publications, 1984), p. ii.

108. Roque Dalton and Eduardo Bähr, *Guerra a la guerra* (Tegucigalpa: Editorial Universitaria, 1981), pp. 106–107.

109. Ibid., p. 110.

110. James Dunkerley, "Roque Dalton García," in *Biographical Dictionary of Marxism*, ed. Robert A. Gorman (Westport, Conn.: Greenwood Press, 1986), p. 85.

111. Roque Dalton et al., *El intelectual y la sociedad* (Mexico City: Siglo XXI, 1969), p. 11.

112. Ernesto Cardenal, *In Cuba* (New York: New Directions Books, 1974), p. 271.

113. Russell, *El Salvador*, p. 132.

114. Dalton et al., *El intelectual*, pp. 25–26.

115. Roque Dalton, *Poetry and Militancy in Latin America* (Willimantic, Conn.: Curbstone Press, 1981), pp. 19–20.

116. Ibid., p. 12.

117. Ibid., pp. 51–52.

118. Dalton et al., *El intelectual*, p. 20.

119. Dalton, *Poetry and Militancy*, p. 13.

120. Ibid., pp. 14–15.

121. Dalton et al., *El intelectual*, pp. 94–95.

122. Dalton, *Poetry and Militancy*, pp. 23, 47.

123. See Roque Dalton, *El Salvador* (Havana: Casa de las Américas, 1963).

124. Ibid., p. 40. Ventura, *El poder popular*, p. 20.

125. Menjívar, "El Salvador: The Smallest Link," p. 21.

126. Dalton, *El Salvador*, pp. 45–46.

127. Dalton, *Poetry and Militancy*, pp. 131–133.

128. Menjívar, "El Salvador: The Smallest Link," p. 22.

129. Dalton, *Miguel Mármol* (Curbstone Press).

130. See Roque Dalton, *Miguel Mármol: Los sucesos de 1932 en El Salvador* (San José: Editorial Universitaria Centroamericana, 1972).

131. Ibid., p. 539.

132. Jiménez, *El Salvador*, p. 212.

133. Dalton, *Miguel Mármol* (Curbstone Press), p. 492.

134. Roque Dalton, *Las historias prohibidas del pulgarcito* (Mexico City: Siglo XXI, 1974), pp. 7–8.

135. Roque Dalton, "Notas sobre el sistema imperialista de dominación y explotación en Centroamérica," *Organización Continental Latinoamericana de Estudiantes* (Havana) (66) (June 1972):2.

136. Ibid., p. 19.

137. Ibid., pp. 10–13.

138. Roque Dalton, "Culture and Revolution in Central America," *World Student News* 28 (11–12) (1965):30.

139. Ibid., p. 31.

140. Roque Dalton, *Las enseñanzas de Viet-Nam* (California: Comités de Solidaridad "Cmdte. Ernesto Jovel Funes" y "Roque Dalton," 1981), pp. 15–17.

141. Ibid., p. 10.

142. Ibid., p. 11.

143. Dalton, *El Salvador*, p. 46.

144. Dalton et al., *El intelectual*, pp. 97–98.

145. Ibid., pp. 12–14.

146. Cardenal, *In Cuba*, p. 37.

147. Dalton, *Las enseñanzas*, p. 11.

148. Dalton et al., *El intelectual*, p. 93.

149. Dalton, *Poetry and Militancy*, pp. 24–25.

150. Dalton, "Notas sobre el sistema," p. 16.

151. Dunkerley, "Roque Dalton García," p. 85.

152. Dalton et al., *El intelectual*, p. 133.

153. See Dalton, *Las enseñanzas*.

154. Dalton, *Poemas clandestinos*, p. 71.

155. James Dunkerley, "Rafael Menjívar," in *Biographical Dictionary of Marxism*, ed. Robert A. Gorman (Westport, Conn.: Greenwood Press, 1986), p. 235.

156. Rafael Menjívar, *Formación y lucha*, pp. 9–10.

157. Rafael Menjívar, *Acumulación ordinaria y desarrollo del capitalismo en El Salvador* (San José: Editorial Universitaria Centroamericana, 1980), p. 11.

158. Menjívar, "El Salvador: The Smallest Link," p. 19.

159. Menjívar, *Acumulación ordinaria*, pp. 112–124.

160. Ibid., p. 36.

161. Ibid., pp. 85–90.

162. Menjívar, "El Salvador: The Smallest Link," p. 20.

163. Menjívar, *Acumulación ordinaria*, pp. 127–129.

164. Rafael Menjívar, *Crisis del desarrollismo: Caso El Salvador* (San José: Editorial Universitaria Centroamericana, 1977), pp. 18, 62.

165. Ibid., pp. 134–135.

166. Ibid., p. 136.

167. See Menjívar, *Formación y lucha*.

168. Ibid., p. 122.

169. Ibid., p. 121.

170. Rafael Menjívar, *Reforma agraria: Guatemala—Bolivia—Cuba* (San Salvador: Editorial Universitaria de El Salvador, 1969), p. 9.

171. Menjívar, *Crisis del desarrollismo*, p. 95.

172. Menjívar, *Reforma agraria*, pp. 281–282.

173. Ibid., pp. 123–124.

174. Ibid., pp. 143–145.

175. Menjívar, *Acumulación ordinaria*, p. 60.

176. Menjívar, *Crisis del desarrollismo*, pp. 9–11, 14.

177. Menjívar, *Formación y lucha*, pp. 105–108.

178. Rafael Menjívar, "The First Phase of the General Offensive," *Contemporary Marxism* (3) (Summer 1981):21.

Chapter 4

1. Sheldon B. Liss, "On Honduras: Exploring a Key Colonial Backwater," *Guardian* (November 26, 1986), p. 17.

2. Harold E. Davis, ed., *Latin American Social Thought* (Washington, D.C.: University Press of Washington, 1961), pp. 336–350.

3. Ibid., p. 348.

4. Víctor Meza, *Historia del movimiento obrero hondureño* (Tegucigalpa: Editorial Guaymuras, 1981), pp. 12–13.

5. Philip E. Wheaton, *Inside Honduras: Regional Counterinsurgency Base* (Washington, D.C.: EPICA, 1982), p. 4.

6. Meza, *Historia del movimiento*, p. 32.

7. James A. Morris and Steve C. Ropp, "Corporatism and Dependent Development: A Honduran Case Study," *Latin American Research Review* 12 (2) (1977):31–32.

8. Richard Swedberg, *The Honduran Trade Union Movement, 1920–1982* (Cambridge, Mass.: Central American Information Office, 1983), p. 2.

9. Robert J. Alexander, *Communism in Latin America* (New Brunswick, N.J.: Rutgers University Press, 1957), p. 323.

10. Rafael Heliodoro Valle, *Historia de las ideas contemporáneas en Centro-América* (Mexico City: Fondo de Cultura Económica, 1960), pp. 3–4, 227.

11. Swedberg, *Honduran Trade Union*, p. 8.

12. See Juan Ramón Martínez B. *Historia del movimiento cooperativo* (Tegucigalpa: Instituto de Formación e Investigación Cooperativista, 1975 or 1976).

13. Ibid., p. 28.

14. Swedberg, *Honduran Trade Union*, p. 17.

15. James A. Morris, *Honduras: Caudillo Politics and Military Rulers* (Boulder: Westview Press, 1984), p. 11.

16. Swedberg, *Honduran Trade Union*, pp. 11–12.

17. Serafino Romualdi, *Presidents and Peons: Recollections of a Labor Ambassador in Latin America* (New York: Funk and Wagnalls, 1967), pp. 254–56.

18. Richard Lapper and James Painter, *Honduras: State for Sale* (London: Latin American Bureau, 1985), pp. 42–44.

19. Liss, "On Honduras," p. 17.

20. Carlos Aldana, "Biografía de Ramón Amaya Amador: Apostal de la liberación," *Pensamiento Económico* (Honduras) 1 (3) (July–September 1975):24–28.

21. Longino Becerra, "Prólogo" of *Prisión Verde* by Ramón Amaya Amador (Tegucigalpa: Editorial Ramón Amaya Amador, 1974), pp. 15–16.

22. Ramón Amaya Amador, *El "Indio Sánchez." Síntesis biográfica de un revolucionario centroamericano* (San José: Editorial Borrasé, 1948), pp. 12–21.

23. Lapper and Painter, *Honduras,* p. 55.

24. Ibid., pp. 63–64.

25. See Enrique Flores Valeriano, *La explotación bananera en Honduras: Capítulos de deshonor nacional* (Tegucigalpa: Editorial Universitaria, 1979).

26. Nancy Peckenham and Annie Street, eds., *Honduras: Portrait of a Captive Nation* (New York: Praeger, 1985), p. 219.

27. Liss, "On Honduras," p. 17.

28. Ibid.

29. Graciela A. García, *Páginas de lucha* (Tegucigalpa: Editorial Guaymuras, 1981), pp. 67–70.

30. See Graciela A. García, *Personalidades célebres de América: Ensayos biográficos* (Mexico City: Costa-Amic, 1964).

31. Ibid., p. 169.

32. Ibid., pp. 163–167.

33. Ibid., pp. 81–88.

34. Ibid., pp. 173–179.

35. Graciela A. García, *Páginas de lucha revolucionaria en Centroamérica* (Mexico: Ediciones Linterna, 1971), pp. 221–226.

36. García, *Personalidades,* pp. 109–110.

37. Mario Posas, *Las sociedades artesanales y los orígines del movimiento obrero hondureño* (Tegucigalpa: ESP Editorial, 1978), p. 1.

38. García, *Páginas de lucha,* p. 67.

39. García, *Personalidades,* p. 33.

40. Posas, *Las sociedades,* p. 1.

41. Peckenham and Street, *Honduras,* p. 237.

42. Posas, *Las sociedades,* p. 1.

43. Peckenham and Street, *Honduras,* p. 237.

44. García, *Personalidades,* p. 33.

45. Graciela A. García, *Por la superación de la educación en México* (Mexico City: Costa-Amic, 1971), p. 133.

46. Ibid., pp. 6–7.

47. Ibid., p. 5.

48. Ibid., p. 7.

49. Ibid., pp. 11–12.

50. Ibid., p. 81.

51. Ibid., p. 22.

52. Ibid., p. 79.

53. Ibid., p. 24.

54. Ibid., pp. 28–30.

55. Ibid., p. 61.

56. Ibid., p. 67.

57. Ibid., pp. 69–71.

58. Ibid., p. 77.

59. Ibid., p. 134.

60. García, *Páginas de lucha revolucionaria,* pp. 13–14.

61. García, *Personalidades,* p. 563.

62. Ibid., pp. 173–174.
63. Ibid., p. 127.
64. Ibid., pp. 193–195.
65. García, *Páginas de lucha revolucionaria*, p. 31.
66. See Longino Becerra, *Evolución histórica de Honduras* (Tegucigalpa: Baktún Editorial, 1982).
67. Longino Becerra, *Síntesis de la historia de Honduras* (Tegucigalpa: Editorial Ramón Amaya Amador, 1979), p. 2.
68. Longino Becerra, *El problema agrario en Honduras* (Havana: Centro de documentación sobre América Latina, Juan F. Noyla, 1964), p. 2. Becerra, *Evolución histórica*, p. 12.
69. Becerra, *Evolución histórica*, p. 59.
70. Ibid., p. 53.
71. Becerra, *Síntesis*, pp. 14–15.
72. Ibid., p. 14.
73. Becerra, *Evolución histórica*, pp. 76–77.
74. Ibid., pp. 107–112.
75. Longino Becerra (Asdrúbal Ramírez), *Línea general política del P.G.H.* (Tegucigalpa: Ediciones El Militante, 1975), p. 13.
76. Ibid., p. 11.
77. Ibid., pp. 11–12.
78. Becerra, *El problema agraria*, p. 13.
79. Longino Becerra (Asdrúbal Ramírez), *El maoismo en Honduras* (Tegucigalpa: Ediciones Compol, 1974), p. 83.
80. Longino Becerra, "The Early History of the Labor Movement," in *Honduras: Portrait of a Captive Nation*, eds. Nancy Peckenham and Annie Street (New York: Praeger, 1985), p. 101.
81. Longino Becerra (Asdrúbal Ramírez), *Los militares patriotas y la revolución hondureña* (Tegucigalpa: Ediciones Compol, 1972), pp. 51–52.
82. Becerra, *Línea general*, p. 6.
83. Ibid., pp. 47–48.
84. Ibid., p. 7.
85. See Becerra, *El maoismo*.
86. Longino Becerra (Asdrúbal Ramírez), *Leninismo y antileninismo en América latina* (Tegucigalpa: Ediciones Compol, 197?), pp. 7, 9.
87. Becerra, *El maoismo*, p. 106.
88. Ibid., p. 108.
89. Becerra, *Leninismo*, pp. 13–15.
90. Ibid., pp. 15–20.
91. Becerra, *El maoismo*, p. 87.
92. Ibid., p. 79.
93. Ibid., pp. 67–73.
94. Ibid., p. 73.
95. Ibid., p. 80.
96. Ibid., pp. 77–78.
97. Becerra, *Línea general*, p. 27.

98. Becerra, *El maoismo*, p. 91.

99. Becerra, *Línea general*, pp. 23–24.

100. Becerra, *El maoismo*, p. 108.

101. Becerra, *El problema agraria*, pp. 88–102.

102. Becerra, *El maoismo*, pp. 62–63.

103. Becerra, *Línea general*, pp. 32–34.

104. Becerra, *Síntesis*, p. 23.

105. Becerra, *Línea general*, p. 13.

106. Becerra, *El problema agraria*, p. 58.

107. Becerra, *El maoismo*, pp. 135–140.

108. Becerra, *Línea general*, p. 59.

109. Becerra, *El maoismo*, pp. 120–129.

110. Becerra, *Línea general*, pp. 51–52.

111. Becerra, *Los militares*, p. 28.

112. Ibid., pp. 14–15.

113. Ibid., p. 31.

114. Mario Posas and Rafael del Cid, *La construcción del sector público y del estado nacional de Honduras 1876-1979* (San José: Editorial Universitaria Centroamericana (EDUCA), 1981), p. 2.

115. Mario Posas, *El movimiento campesino hondureño: Una perspectiva general* (Tegucigalpa: Editorial Guaymuras, 1981), p. 3.

116. Posas and del Cid, *La construcción*, pp. 9–22.

117. Ibid., p. 236.

118. Ibid., p. 75.

119. Posas, *Las sociedades*, p. 5.

120. Posas and del Cid, *La construcción*, pp. 236–237.

121. Ibid., p. 238.

122. Mario Posas, "Política estatal y estructura agraria en Honduras (1950–1978)," *Estudios Sociales Centroamericanos* (24) (September–December 1979):58, 115.

123. Ibid., pp. 111–114.

124. Ronaldo Munck, *Politics and Dependency in the Third World: The Case of Latin America* (London: Zed, 1984), pp. 246–247.

125. Mario Posas, "Tendencias ideológicas actuales en el movimiento obrero hondureño," *Anuario de Estudios Centroamericanos* (6) (1980):43.

126. Posas, *El movimiento campesino*, pp. 37–38.

127. Ibid., p. 222.

128. Mario Posas, *Luchas del movimiento obrero hondureño* (San José: Editorial Universitaria Centroamericana, 1981), p. 217.

129. Posas, "Tendencias ideológicas," p. 53.

130. Posas, *Luchas del movimiento*, pp. 13–15.

131. Mario Posas, *Lucha ideológica y organización sindical en Honduras (1954-65)* (Tegucigalpa: Editorial Guaymuras, 1980), pp. 17–18.

132. See ibid.

133. Posas, *Luchas del movimiento*, p. 217.

134. Mario Posas, *Conflictos agrarios y organización campesino: Sobre los orígenes de las primeras organizaciones campesinas en Honduras* (Tegucigalpa: Editorial Universitaria, 1981), p. 10.

135. Posas, *El movimiento campesino*, p. 9.

136. Ibid., p. 19.

137. Posas, *Luchas del movimiento*, p. 215.

138. Posas, *Las sociedades*, p. 50.

139. Posas, "Tendencias ideológicas," p. 26.

140. Posas, *Luchas del movimiento*, pp. 219–220.

141. Posas, *Lucha ideológica*, p. 89.

142. See ibid.

143. Ibid., pp. 11–16.

144. Ibid., p. 16.

145. Ibid., p. 41.

146. Posas, *Conflictos agrarios*, p. 89.

147. Ibid., p. 23.

148. Posas, *El movimiento campesino*, p. 29.

149. Mario Posas, "In the Jaws of the Standard Fruit Company," in *Honduras: Portrait of a Captive Nation*, eds. Nancy Peckenham and Annie Street (New York: Praeger, 1985), pp. 152–156.

150. Posas, "Tendencias ideológicas," p. 54.

151. Posas, *El movimiento campesino*, pp. 47–48.

152. Víctor Meza, *Política y sociedad en Honduras* (Tegucigalpa: Editorial Guaymuras, 1981), p. 144.

153. Ibid., p. 47.

154. Ibid., pp. 105–106.

155. Ibid., pp. 103–104.

156. Meza, *Historia del movimiento obrero hondureño*, p. ix.

157. Meza, *Política y sociedad*, p. 108.

158. Ibid., p. 52.

159. Víctor Meza, ed., *Antología de documentos sobre la situación y evolución del movimiento obrero en Honduras (1970–1979)* (Tegucigalpa: Editorial Universitaria, 1981), pp. 12–13.

160. Víctor Meza, *Honduras: La evolución de la crisis* (Tegucigalpa: Editorial Universitaria, 1982), p. 11.

161. Meza, *Historia del movimiento*, pp. xii–xiii.

162. Vilma Laínez and Víctor Meza, "The Banana Enclave," in *Honduras: Portrait of a Captive Nation*, eds. Nancy Peckenham and Annie Street, (New York: Praeger, 1985), pp. 35–36.

163. Meza, *Política y sociedad*, pp. 57–58, 64–65.

164. Laínez and Meza, "Banana Enclave," p. 37.

165. See Meza, *Historia del movimiento*.

166. Ibid., p. 21.

167. Ibid., pp. 15–16.

168. Ibid., p. 35.

169. Ibid., pp. 38–39.

170. Ibid., pp. 56–57.
171. Ibid., p. 63.
172. Ibid., pp. 63, 65.
173. Meza, *Antología*, pp. 14–15.
174. Meza, *Política y sociedad*, pp. 48–49.
175. Víctor Meza, "Recent Developments in Honduran Foreign Policy and National Security," in *Honduras Confronts Its Future*, ed. Mark B. Rosenberg and Philip L. Shepherd, (Boulder: Lynne Rienner Publishers, 1986), pp. 220–224.
176. Meza, *Honduras: La evolución*, pp. 31–32.
177. Ibid., p. 37.
178. Ibid., pp. 38–41.

Chapter 5

1. Samuel Stone, *La dinastía de los conquistadores: La crisis del poder en la Costa Rica contemporánea* (San José: Editorial Universitaria Centroamericana, 1975), pp. 46–47.
2. Mitchell. A. Seligson, *Peasants of Costa Rica and the Development of Agrarian Capitalism* (Madison: University of Wisconsin Press, 1980), p. xxxi.
3. Stone, *La dinastía*, p. 96.
4. Enrique Anderson-Imbert, *Spanish-American Literature—A History*. Vol. 1 (Detroit: Wayne State University Press, 1969), p. 326.
5. Vladimir de la Cruz, *Las luchas sociales en Costa Rica 1870–1930* (San José: Editorial Universidad de Costa Rica and Editorial Costa Rica, 1980), pp. 25–26.
6. Luis Barahona Jiménez, *El pensamiento político en Costa Rica* (San José: Editorial Fernández-Arce, 1972), pp. 68–69.
7. De la Cruz, *Las luchas sociales*, p. 19.
8. Charles D. Ameringer, *Democracy in Costa Rica* (New York: Praeger, 1982), pp. 18–19.
9. Stone, *La dinastía*, p. 268.
10. De la Cruz, *Las luchas sociales*, p. 47.
11. Edwin Chacón León, *El sindicalismo en Costa Rica: Ensayo histórico* (San José: Centro de Estudios Laborales CA, 1980), pp. 6, 9.
12. De la Cruz, *Las luchas sociales*, pp. 79–84.
13. Constantino Láscaris, *Desarrollo de las ideas filosóficas en Costa Rica* (San José: Editorial Costa Rica, 1965), pp. 253–256.
14. Barahona Jiménez, *El pensamiento político*, pp. 106–107.
15. Láscaris, *Desarrollo de las ideas*, pp. 256–258.
16. De la Cruz, *Las luchas sociales*, p. 99.
17. Jorge Mario Salazar Mora, *Política y reforma en Costa Rica 1914–1959* (San José: Editorial Porvenir, 1981), pp. 56–57.
18. De la Cruz, *Las luchas sociales*, p. 215.
19. Ameringer, *Democracy*, pp. 23–24.
20. Stone, *La dinastía*, p. 289.
21. De la Cruz, *Las luchas sociales*, pp. 198–199.
22. Ibid., p. 152.

23. Ibid., p. 213.

24. Chester Zelaya et al., *¿Democracia en Costa Rica? Cinco opiniones polémicas* (San José: Editorial Universidad Estatal a Distancia, 1978), pp. 103–104.

25. Richard Biesanz, Karen Zubris Biesanz, and Mavis Hiltunen Biesanz, *The Costa Ricans* (Englewood Cliffs, N.J.: Prentice-Hall, 1982), p. 182.

26. Thomas M. Leonard, *The United States and Central America, 1944–1949: Perceptions of Political Dynamics* (University: University of Alabama Press, 1984), p. 17.

27. Salazar Mora, *Política y reforma*, p. 59.

28. Seligson, *Peasants of Costa Rica*, p. 70.

29. Ibid., pp. 70–71.

30. John Patrick Bell, *Crisis in Costa Rica: The 1948 Revolution* (Austin: University of Texas Press, 1971), p. 12.

31. See Carlos Luis Fallas, *Reseña de la intervención y penetración Yanki en Centro América* (Mexico City: Fondo de Cultura Popular, 1954).

32. Rafael Heliodoro Valle, *Historia de las ideas contemporáneas en Centro-América* (Mexico City: Fondo de Cultura Económica, 1960), pp. 288–289.

33. John A. Peeler, *Latin American Democracies: Colombia, Costa Rica, Venezuela* (Chapel Hill: University of North Carolina Press, 1985), p. 30.

34. Robert J. Alexander, *Organized Labor in Latin America* (New York: Free Press, 1965), pp. 214–217.

35. Robert J. Alexander, *Communism in Latin America* (New Brunswick, N.J.: Rutgers University Press, 1957), pp. 385–388.

36. Bell, *Crisis in Costa Rica*, p. 46.

37. Ibid., pp. 52–53.

38. Susanne Bodenheimer, "The Social Democratic Ideology in Latin America: The Case of Costa Rica's Partido Liberación Nacional," *Caribbean Studies* 10 (3) (October 1970):52.

39. Láscaris, *Desarrollo de las ideas*, p. 9.

40. John Sax-Fernández, "The Militarization of Costa Rica," *Monthly Review* (May 1972):61–63.

41. Burt H. English, *Liberación Nacional in Costa Rica: The Development of a Political Party in a Transitional Society* (Gainesville: University of Florida Press, 1961), p. 132.

42. Seligson, *Peasants of Costa Rica*, p. 76.

43. Bodenheimer, "Social Democratic Ideology," p. 50.

44. Ameringer, *Democracy in Costa Rica*, pp. 3–4.

45. Seligson, *Peasants of Costa Rica*, pp. 48–49, 56, 86.

46. Barahona, *El pensamiento político*, pp. 141–142.

47. Vicente Sáenz, *América hoy como ayer* (Mexico City: Editorial América Nueva, 1955), p. 22.

48. Vicente Sáenz, *Ensayos escogidos* (San José: Editorial Costa Rica, 1983), p. 69.

49. Ibid., p. 344.

50. Vicente Sáenz, *Martí. Raíz y ala del libertador de Cuba* (Mexico City: Editorial América Nueva, 1955), pp. 7, 116–117, 123.

51. Sáenz, *Ensayos escogidos*, pp. 421–422.

52. Salazar Mora, *Política y reform*, pp. 51–53.

53. Sáenz, *América hoy*, pp. 10–11.

54. Vicente Sáenz, *Latin America Against the Colonial System* (Mexico City: Unión Democrática Centroamericana, 1949), pp. 187, 189.

55. Ibid.

56. Sáenz, *América hoy*, pp. 19–24.

57. Barahona, *El pensamiento político*, p. 145.

58. Sáenz, *Ensayos escogidos*, p. 60.

59. Ibid., pp. 51–52.

60. Ibid., p. 66.

61. Ibid., p. 33.

62. Sáenz, *Latin America*, p. 226.

63. Sáenz, *América hoy*, p. 38.

64. William S. Stokes, "The Pensadores of Latin America," in *The Intellectuals: A Controversial Portrait*, ed. George B. de Huszar (Glencoe, Ill.: Free Press, 1960), p. 424.

65. Barahona, *El pensamiento político*, pp. 145–146.

66. Sáenz, *Latin America*, p. 189.

67. Ibid., p. 129.

68. Ibid., p. 83.

69. Vicente Sáenz, *Rompiendo cadenas: Las del imperialismo en Centroamérica y en otras repúblicas del continente* (Buenos Aires: Editorial Palestra, 1961), pp. 181–182.

70. See Vicente Sáenz, *Nuestras vías interoceánicas* (Mexico City: Editorial América Nueva, 1957).

71. Salazar Mora, *Política y reforma*, p. 53.

72. Sáenz, *América hoy*, p. 50.

73. Vicente Sáenz, *Paralelismo de la paz y de la democracia* (Mexico City: Unión Democrática Centroamericana, 1946), p. 20.

74. Sáenz, *Rompiendo cadenas*, pp. 343–345.

75. Miguel Salguero, *Tres meses con la vida en hilo: crónicas y entrevistas (Manuel Mora—José Figueres)* (San José: Editorial Universidad Estatal a Distancia, 1981), pp. 130, 135–136.

76. Manuel Mora Valverde, *Discursos 1934–1979* (San José: Editorial Presbere, 1980), p. 51.

77. Salguero, *Tres meses*, pp. 5–7.

78. Mora Valverde, *Discursos*, pp. 625–630.

79. Salguero, *Tres meses*, p. 137.

80. Oscar Aguilar Bulgarelli, *Democracia y partidos políticos en Costa Rica (1950–1962)* (San José: N.P., 1977), p. 88.

81. De la Cruz, *Las luchas sociales*, pp. 249–253.

82. Mora Valverde, *Discursos*, p. 21.

83. Ibid., pp. 95–98.

84. Jorge Jiménez, "Progressive Juntas in Costa Rica," *World Marxist Review* 2 (5) (May 1959):69.

85. Mora Valverde, *Discursos*, pp. 20, 700–707. Francisco Espinoza, "Experience of the Communists of Costa Rica," *World Marxist Review* 6 (7) (July 1963):37.

86. Manuel Mora Valverde, *Imperialismo: Nuestra soberanía frente al Departamento de Estado* (San José: Partido Comunista de Costa Rica, 1940), pp. 87–94.

87. Biesanz, *The Costa Ricans*, p. 182.

88. Harold D. Nelson, ed., *Costa Rica: A Country Study* (Washington, D.C.: Foreign Area Studies, American University, 1984), p. 216.

89. Leonard, *The United States and Central America*, p. 23.

90. Barahona, *El pensamiento político*, pp. 147–148.

91. See Mora Valverde, *Discursos*.

92. Barahona, *El pensamiento político*, p. 149.

93. Mora Valverde, *Discursos*, pp. 38–39.

94. Ibid., p. 23.

95. Láscaris, *Desarrollo de las ideas*, pp. 342–343.

96. Mora Valverde, *Discursos*, p. 352.

97. Salguero, *Tres meses*, p. 159.

98. Ibid., p. 132.

99. Eduardo Mora Valverde, *4 artículos en respuesta al revolucionarismo pequeño burgués* (San José: Editorial Rumbo, 1975), p. 5.

100. Mora Valverde, *Discursos*, pp. 478–498.

101. Ibid., pp. 247–248.

102. Ibid., p. 342.

103. Mora Valverde, *Imperialismo*, pp. 40–41.

104. Ibid., pp. 25–26.

105. Ibid., pp. 62–63.

106. Ibid., p. 118.

107. Ibid., p. 8.

108. Mora Valverde, *Discursos*, p. 522.

109. Mora Valverde, *Imperialismo*, pp. 73–74.

110. Mora Valverde, *Discursos*, pp. 245–289.

111. Eduardo Mora Valverde, *Centro América en la integración económica latinoamericana* (San José: Ediciones Revolución, 1969), pp. 29, 36, 40.

112. Ibid., pp. 71–73.

113. Mora Valverde, *Discursos*, p. 446.

114. Ibid., p. 434.

115. Rodolfo Cerdas Cruz, *La crisis de la democracia liberal en Costa Rica. Interpretación y perspectiva* (San José: Editorial Universitaria Centroamericana, 1978), pp. 107–108.

116. Rodolfo Cerdas Cruz, "La conferencia del rector Facio sobre marxismo. Una respuesta," *Revista de la Universidad de Costa Rica* (20) (March 1960):95–102.

117. Rodolfo Cerdas Cruz, *Sandino, El Apra y la Internacional Comunista: Antecedentes históricos de la Nicaragua de hoy* (Lima: Comisión Nacional de Ideología y Doctrina del Partido Aprista Peruano, 1983), pp. 61–62.

118. Rodolfo Cerdas Cruz, *Formación del estado en Costa Rica* (San José: Editorial Universidad de Costa Rica, 1978), p. 63.

119. Ibid., p. 193.

120. Cerdas Cruz, *La crisis de la democracia*, pp. 31–39.

121. Ibid., p. 89.

122. Ibid., p. 65.

123. Ibid., p. 170.

124. Ibid., pp. 152–154.

125. Ibid., pp. 112–122.

126. Ibid., pp. 129–131.

127. Cerdas Cruz, "La conferencia," p. 58.

128. Cerdas Cruz, *Formación del estado*, pp. 45–58.

129. Cerdas Cruz, *La crisis de la democracia*, p. 167.

130. Rodolfo Cerdas Cruz, "Costa Rica: Problemas actuales de una revolución democrática," in *¿Democracia en Costa Rica? Cinco opiniones polémicas* (San José: Editorial Universidad Estatal a Distancia, 1978), p. 167.

131. Cerdas Cruz, *La crisis de la democracia*, p. 178.

132. Cerdas Cruz, "Costa Rica," pp. 150–152.

133. Cerdas Cruz, *La crisis de la democracia*, pp. 150–152.

134. Ibid., pp. 181–183.

135. Ibid., p. 178.

136. Ibid., p. 158.

137. Ibid., p. 160.

138. Cerdas Cruz, "Costa Rica: Problemas," pp. 129–130.

139. See Cerdas Cruz, "Costa Rica: Problemas."

140. Cerdas Cruz, "La conferencia," pp. 122–123.

141. Ibid., pp. 121–122.

142. Ibid., p. 69.

143. Ibid., pp. 60–61.

144. Ibid., p. 71.

145. Ibid., pp. 73–76.

146. Ibid., p. 26.

147. Ibid., pp. 61–64.

148. Ibid., p. 25.

149. Rodolfo Cerdas Cruz, *Farabundo Martí, la internacional comunista y la insurrección salvadoreña de 1932* (San José: El Centro de Investigación y Adiestramiento Político Administrativo [CIAPA], No. 7, September, 1982), pp. 8, 22.

150. Ibid., p. 33.

151. Ibid., pp. 31–32.

152. Ibid., pp. 68, 70–72.

153. José Luis Vega Carballo, *Estado y dominación social en Costa Rica: Antecedentes coloniales y formación del estado nacional* (San José: Instituto de Investigaciones Sociales, Facultad de Ciencias Sociales, Universidad de Costa Rica, 1980), p. 1.

154. José Luis Vega Carballo, "Estapas y procesos de la evolución sociopolítica de Costa Rica," *Estudios Sociales Centroamericanos* 1 (1) (January–April 1972):68.

155. José Luis Vega Carballo, *Orden y progreso. La formación del estado nacional en Costa Rica* (San José: Instituto Centroamericano de Administración Pública, 1981), p. 318.

156. Vega Carballo, *Estado y dominación,* pp. 10, 25.

157. José Luis Vega Carballo, *Democracia y dominación en Costa Rica* (San José: Instituto de Investigaciones Sociales, Facultad de Ciencias Sociales, Universidad de Costa Rica, 1981), pp. 15–16.

158. Vega Carballo, *Orden y progreso,* p. 263.

159. Vega Carballo, *Democracia y dominación,* pp. 28–31.

160. Ibid., p. 27.

161. Ibid., p. 26.

162. Vega Carballo, "Estapas y procesos," p. 57.

163. Ibid., p. 68.

164. Ibid., pp. 69–70.

165. José Luis Vega Carballo, *La crisis de los partidos políticos tradicionales de Costa Rica* (Costa Rica: Ediciones Academia Costarricense de Bibliografía, 1978), p. 6.

166. Ibid., pp. 8–13.

167. Ibid., pp. 16–21.

168. Vega Carballo, *Democracia y dominación,* pp. 35–37.

169. Ibid., p. 40.

170. Vega Carballo, *Estado y dominación,* pp. 48–49.

171. Vega Carballo, *Orden y progreso,* pp. 217–218.

172. Vega Carballo, *Estado y dominación,* p. 2.

173. Vega Carballo, *Orden y progreso,* p. 155.

174. Ibid., p. 133.

175. José Luis Vega Carballo, Elena Gil, and Walter V. Costanza, *Tres temas en la América Latina hoy: Consideraciones en torno al cambio social, la mujer en el mundo del trabajo, el militarismo en América Latina* (San José: Centro de Estudios Democráticos de América Latina, 1970), p. 18.

176. Ibid., pp. 17–18.

Chapter 6

1. Instituto de Estudio del Sandinismo, *Pensamiento antimperialista en Nicaragua. Antología* (Managua: Editorial Nueva Nicaragua, 1982), pp. 47–53, 346–348.

2. Jorge Eduardo Arellano, *Panorama de la literatura nicaragüense* (Managua: Ediciones Nacionales, 1977), pp. 22–24.

3. Ibid., p. 26.

4. Instituto de Estudio, *Pensamiento,* p. 344.

5. Carlos Pérez Bermúdez and Onofre Guevara, *El movimiento obrero en Nicaragua* (Managua: Editorial El Amanecer, S.A., 1985), Part 1, pp. 25–29.

6. George Black, *Triumph of the People: The Sandinista Revolution in Nicaragua* (London: Zed, 1981), p. 10.

7. Instituto de Estudio, *Pensamiento,* pp. 153–168.

8. Ibid., pp. 351–352.

9. Pérez Bermúdez, *El movimiento obrero*, Part 1, pp. 32–33.

10. Enrique Anderson-Imbert, *Spanish American Literature: A History*. Vol. 2. (Detroit: Wayne State University Press, 1969), pp. 515–516.

11. Pérez Bermúdez, *El movimiento obrero*, Part 1, pp. 34–43.

12. Ibid., Part 1, pp. 56–60, 69, 101–102.

13. Robert J. Alexander, *Communism in Latin America* (New Brunswick, N.J.: Rutgers University Press, 1957), pp. 379–380.

14. Ibid., pp. 380–381.

15. Black, *Triumph of the People*, p. 30.

16. Jesús M. Blandón, *Entre Sandino y Fonseca* (Managua: Departamento de Propaganda y Educación Política del FSLN, 1982), p. 15.

17. Black, *Triumph of the People*, pp. 29–30.

18. Ibid., p. 37.

19. Guillermo Toriello Garrido, *A Popular History of Two Revolutions: Guatemala and Nicaragua* (San Francisco: Synthesis Publications, 1985), p. 48.

20. Mike Wallace, "Interview with Nicaraguan Historians," *Radical History Review* 33 (September 1985):15.

21. Bruce Marcus, ed., *Nicaragua: The Sandinista People's Revolution. Speeches by Sandinista Leaders* (New York: Pathfinder Press, 1985), p. 109. Speech of May 20, 1983.

22. Richard Millett, *Guardians of the Dynasty: A History of the U.S.-created Guardia Nacional de Nicaragua and the Somoza Family* (Maryknoll, N.Y.: Orbis Books, 1977), p. 225.

23. See Wallace, "Interview with Nicaraguan Historians."

24. Luis Sánchez, "Nicaraguan Communists in Van of the Liberation Movement?" *World Marxist Review* 11 (2) (February 1968):32–34.

25. Black, *Triumph of the People*, p. 72.

26. Ibid., pp. 92–99.

27. EPICA Task Force, *Nicaragua: A People's Revolution* (Washington, D.C.: EPICA, 1980), p. 11.

28. Ricardo Morales Avilés, *Obras: No pararemos de andar jamás* (Managua: Editorial Nueva Nicaragua, 1983), pp. 114–123.

29. Ibid., p. 88.

30. Ibid., p. 161.

31. Ibid., pp. 102–104.

32. Ibid., p. 24.

33. Ricardo Morales Avilés, *La dominación imperialista en Nicaragua* (Managua: Secretaría Nacional de Propaganda y Educación Política del FSLN, 1980), p. 37.

34. Morales Avilés, *Obras*, pp. 89–90.

35. Donald C. Hodges, *Intellectual Foundations of the Nicaraguan Revolution* (Austin: University of Texas Press, 1986), p. 190.

36. A similar percentage in the United States would equal 4.5 million dead.

37. See Paul Le Blanc, *Permanent Revolution in Nicaragua* (New York: Fourth Internationalist Tendency, 1984).

38. Marcus, *Nicaragua*, pp. 66, 177–178.

39. Ibid., p. 28.

40. Marcus, *Nicaragua*, p. 265.

41. Tomás Borge, *La revolución combate contra la teología de la muerte. Discursos (cristianos) de un comandante Sandinista* (Managua: N.P., 1982), pp. 14–26.

42. Tomás Borge, "Women and the Nicaraguan Revolution," in *The Nicaragua Reader: Documents of a Revolution Under Fire,* eds. Peter Rosset and John Vandermeer (New York: Grove Press, 1983), pp. 329–331.

43. Marcus, *Nicaragua*, pp. 25–26.

44. Charles D. Watland, *Poet-Errant: A Biography of Rubén Darío* (New York: Philosophical Library, 1965), p. 175.

45. Ibid., pp. 84, 161.

46. Harry E. Vanden, "The Ideology of the Insurrection," in *Nicaragua in Revolution,* ed. Thomas W. Walker (New York: Praeger, 1982), p. 42.

47. Keith Ellis, *Critical Approaches to Rubén Darío* (Toronto: University of Toronto Press, 1974), p. 112.

48. Cathy Login Jrade, *Rubén Darío and the Romantic Search for Unity: The Modernist Recourse to Esoteric Tradition* (Austin: University of Texas Press, 1983), p. 4.

49. Sheldon B. Liss, *Roots of Revolution: Radical Thought in Cuba* (Lincoln: University of Nebraska Press, 1987), p. 47.

50. See Angel Augier, "Poet to Poet: Rubén Darío's Cult of José Martí," *Granma Weekly Review* (May, 19, 1985).

51. See Rubén Darío, "Jose Martí," *Granma Weekly Review* (May 19, 1985).

52. Ellis, *Critical Approaches,* pp. 29–30.

53. Ibid., p. 53.

54. Ibid., p. 25.

55. See Rubén Darío, *Autobiografía* (Madrid: Editorial Mundo Latino, 1920).

56. See Rubén Darío, *Prosas políticas* (Managua: Ministerio de Cultura, 1983). Rubén Darío, *Textos socio-políticos* (Managua: Ediciones de la Biblioteca Nacional, 1980).

57. Darío, *Prosas políticas,* pp. 137–144.

58. Rubén Darío, *Crónica política,* Vol. 11, *Obras completas* (Madrid: Biblioteca Rubén Darío, 1924), pp. 122–128.

59. Ibid., pp. 249–250.

60. Ibid., p. 137.

61. Ellis, *Critical Approaches,* p. 40.

62. Darío, *Textos socio-políticos,* pp. 9–10.

63. Darío, *Crónica política,* pp. 206–210.

64. Darío, *Textos socio-políticos,* pp. 39–40.

65. Darío, *Crónica política,* pp. 103–104.

66. Darío, *Textos socio-políticos,* pp. 41–44.

67. Darío, *Prosas políticas,* pp. 67–70.

68. Dario, *Textos socio-políticos,* pp. 22–24.

69. Watland, *Poet-Errant,* p. 201.

70. Jaime Wheelock Román, *Diciembre victorioso* (Managua: Editorial Nueva Nicaragua, 1982), pp. 33–34.

71. Edelberto Torres, *La dramática vida de Rubén Darío* (Havana: Editorial Arte y Literatura, 1982), pp. 62–63.

72. Jaime Wheelock Román, *Nicaragua: The Great Challenge* (Managua: Alternative Views, 1984), pp. 32–37.

73. Darío, *Crónica política*, p. 143.

74. Darío, *Prosas políticas*, p. 124.

75. Instituto de Estudio, *Pensamiento*, pp. 57–60.

76. See Darío, *Textos socio-políticos*, originally published in "El triunfo de Calibán," *El Tiempo* (Buenos Aires) May 20, 1898.

77. Darío, *Prosas políticas*, p. xix.

78. Darío, *Textos socio-políticos*, pp. 49–54.

79. Ibid., pp. 55–58.

80. Ibid., pp. 59–67.

81. Sheldon B. Liss and Peggy K. Liss, eds., *Man, State, and Society in Latin American History* (New York: Praeger, 1972), p. 293.

82. Darío, *Prosas políticas*, pp. 127–128.

83. Liss and Liss, *Man, State, and Society*, p. 294.

84. Ibid.

85. Watland, *Poet-Errant*, p. 224.

86. Darío, *Textos socio-políticos*, pp. 45–47.

87. Darío, *Prosas políticas*, p. xix.

88. Instituto de Estudio, *Pensamiento*, pp. 55–56.

89. Darío, *Prosas políticas*, pp. 73–81.

90. Black, *Triumph of the People*, p. 15.

91. See Augusto C. Sandino, *El pensamiento vivo*, 2 vols. (Managua: Editorial Nueva Nicaragua, 1981).

92. Millett, *Guardians of the Dynasty*, p. 66.

93. Hodges, *Intellectual Foundations*, p. 15.

94. Neil Macauley, *The Sandino Affair* (Chicago: Quadrangle Books, 1967), p. 53.

95. Hodges, *Intellectual Foundations*, p. 14.

96. Edelberto Torres, *Sandino y sus pares* (Managua: Editorial Nueva Nicaragua, 1983), p. 32.

97. Gregorio Selser, *Sandino* (New York: Monthly Review Press, 1981), pp. 117–118.

98. Hodges, *Intellectual Foundations*, pp. 13–15.

99. Sandino, *El pensamiento vivo*, Vol. 1, p. 79.

100. Karl Bermann, *Under the Big Stick: Nicaragua and the United States Since 1848* (Boston: South End Press, 1986), p. 193.

101. Ibid.

102. Ibid., pp. 192–202.

103. Torres, *Sandino*, p. 128.

104. Sandino, *El pensamiento vivo*, Vol. 2, pp. 294, 299, 301–302.

105. Ibid, Vol 1, p. 137.

106. Wallace, "Interview with Nicaraguan Historians," p. 12.

107. Sandino, *El pensamiento vivo*, Vol. 1, pp. 117–118.

108. Hodges, *Intellectual Foundations*, p. 12.

109. Ibid., p. 19.

110. Ibid., pp. 79–80.

111. Jorge Eduardo Arellano, *Lecciones de Sandino* (Managua: Ediciones Distribudora Cultural, 1983), p. 42.

112. Hodges, *Intellectual Foundations*, p. 10.

113. Sandino, *El pensamiento vivo*, Vol. 1, p. 389.

114. Hodges, *Intellectual Foundations*, p. 38.

115. Marcus, *Nicaragua*, p. 110.

116. Macauley, *Sandino Affair*, p. 157.

117. Hodges, *Intellectual Foundations*, p. 53.

118. Ibid., p. 54.

119. Sandino, *El pensamiento vivo*, Vol. 2, pp. 25–39.

120. Hodges, *Intellectual Foundations*, p. 71.

121. Macauley, *Sandino Affair*, p. 160.

122. Joseph O. Baylen, "Sandino: Patriot or Bandit?" *Hispanic American Historical Review* 31 (3) (August 1951):412.

123. Augusto C. Sandino, Carlos Fonseca Amador, FSLN, *Nicaragua: la estrategia de la victoria* (Mexico City: Editorial Nuestro Tiempo, 1980), p. 74.

124. Sandino, *El pensamiento vivo*, Vol. 1, pp. 299–300.

125. Henri Weber, *Nicaragua: The Sandinist Revolution* (London: Verso, 1981), p. 14.

126. Sandino, *El pensamiento vivo*, Vol. 1, p. 243.

127. Arellano, *Lecciones*, pp. 65–68.

128. Sandino, *El pensamiento vivo*, Vol. 2, pp. 347–350.

129. Ibid., pp. 351–354.

130. Arellano, *Lecciones*, p. 58.

131. Selser, *Sandino*, p. 98.

132. Arellano, *Lecciones*, p. 45. Sandino, *El pensamiento vivo*, Vol. 1, pp. 271–272.

133. Sandino, *El pensamiento vivo*, Vol. 2, p. 435.

134. Ibid., Vol. 1, pp. 246–247.

135. Ibid., Vol. 2, pp. 70–71.

136. Instituto de Estudio, *Pensamiento*, p. 318.

137. Macauley, *Sandino Affair*, pp. 113–114.

138. Sandino, *El pensamiento vivo*, Vol. 2, p. 90.

139. Arellano, *Lecciones*, pp. 102–104.

140. Sandino, *El pensamiento vivo*, Vol. 2, p. 336.

141. John Weeks, "An Interpretation of the Central American Crisis," *Latin American Research Review* 21 (3) (1986):45–46.

142. Baylen, "Sandino," p. 419.

143. Black, *Triumph of the People*, p. 19.

144. Weber, *Nicaragua*, p. 13.

145. Black, *Triumph of the People*, p. 76. Tomás Borge, *Carlos, the Dawn Is No Longer Beyond Our Reach* (Vancouver: New Star Books, 1984), p. 88.

146. See Carlos Fonseca Amador, *Obras*, Vol. 2. *Viva Sandino* (Managua: Editorial Nueva Nicaragua, 1985), pp. 21–85.

147. Black, *Triumph of the People*, p. 75.

148. Carlos Fonseca Amador, "Nicaragua: Zero Hour," in *The Nicaragua Reader: Documents of a Revolution Under Fire*, ed. Peter Rosset and John Vandermeer (New York: Grove Press, 1983), p. 128.

149. Carlos Fonseca Amador, "Nicaragua: Zero Hour," in *Sandinistas Speak*, ed. Bruce Marcus (New York: Pathfinder Press, 1982), pp. 26–28.

150. Fonseca Amador, *Obras*, Vol. 2, p. 34.

151. Fonseca Amador, "Nicaragua: Zero Hour," in *The Nicaragua Reader*, p. 126.

152. Ibid., p. 129.

153. Fonseca Amador, *Obras*, Vol. 2, p. 85.

154. Fonseca Amador, "Nicaragua: Zero Hour," in *The Nicaragua Reader*, p. 130.

155. Carlos Fonseca Amador, *Obras*, Vol. 2. *Bajo la bandera del sandinismo* (Managua: Editorial Nueva Nicaragua, 1985), p. 243.

156. Black, *Triumph of the People*, p. 76.

157. Fonseca Amador, *Obras*, Vol. 1, p. 284.

158. Ibid., pp. 331–332.

159. Margaret Randall, *Risking a Somersault in the Air: Conversations with Nicaraguan Writers* (San Francisco: Solidarity Publications, 1984), pp. 106–107.

160. Fonseca Amador, *Obras*, Vol. 2, p. 35.

161. Harry E. Vanden, "Carlos Fonseca Amador," in *Biographical Dictionary of Marxism*, ed. Robert A. Gorman, (Westport, Conn.: Greenwood Press, 1986), p. 110.

162. Black, *Triumph of the People*, p. 90.

163. Fonseca Amador, *Obras*, Vol. 1, pp. 124–125.

164. David Nolan, *The Ideology of the Sandinistas and the Nicaraguan Revolution* (Coral Gables: Institute of Interamerican Studies, University of Miami, 1984), p. 26.

165. Carlos M. Vilas, *The Sandinista Revolution: National Liberation and Social Transformation in Central America* (New York: Monthly Review Press, 1986), pp. 115–116.

166. Borge, *Carlos, the Dawn*, pp. 62–63.

167. Vanden, "Carlos Fonseca," p. 111.

168. Fonseca Amador, *Obras*, Vol. 1, p. 142.

169. Nolan, *Ideology of the Sandinistas*, p. 24.

170. Black, *Triumph of the People*, p. 90.

171. Fonseca Amador, *Obras*, Vol. 1, pp. 196–215.

172. Fonseca Amador, *Obras*, Vol. 2, pp. 179–199.

173. Marcus, *Nicaragua*, p. 110.

174. Nolan, *Ideology of the Sandinistas*, pp. 17–18.

175. Vanden, "Carlos Fonseca," p. 110.

176. Marc Zimmerman, ed., *Nicaragua in Reconstruction and at War: The People Speak* (Minneapolis: MEP Publications, 1985), p. 53.

177. Wheelock Román, *Nicaragua: The Great Challenge*, p. 9.

178. Black, *Triumph of the People*, p. 90.

179. Víctor Tirado López, *El pensamiento político de Carlos Fonseca Amador* (Managua: Secretaría Nacional de Propaganda y Educación Política, 1979 or 1980), p. 2.

180. Marcus, *Nicaragua*, p. 126.

181. Fonseca Amador, *Obras*, Vol. 1, p. 334.

182. Pérez Bermúdez and Guevara, *El movimiento obrero*, pp. 3–4.

183. Ernesto Cardenal, *With Walker in Nicaragua and Other Early Poems, 1949–1954* (Middletown, Conn.: Wesleyan University Press, 1984), p. 10.

184. Sheldon B. Liss, *Marxist Thought in Latin America* (Berkeley: University of California Press, 1984), pp. 155–156.

185. Penny Lernoux, *Cry of the People* (New York: Penguin Books, 1982), p. 96.

186. Steven White, *Culture and Politics in Nicaragua: Testimonies of Poets and Writers* (New York: Lumen Books, 1986), pp. 69–70.

187. Ernesto Cardenal, *Vuelos de victoria* (Maryknoll, N.Y.: Orbis Books, 1985), pp. xiii-xiv.

188. Oleg Ignatiev and Genrykh Borovick, *The Agony of a Dictatorship: Nicaraguan Chronicle* (Moscow: Progress Publishers, 1980), pp. 51–52.

189. See Ernesto Cardenal, *The Gospel in Solentiname*, Vol. 1 (Maryknoll, N.Y.: Orbis Books, 1976).

190. Phillip Berryman, *The Religious Roots of Rebellion: Christians in Central American Revolutions* (Maryknoll, N.Y.: Orbis Books, 1984), p. 10.

191. Cardenal, *Gospel in Solentiname*, Vol. 4, p. 206.

192. Blase Bonpane, *Guerrillas of Peace: Liberation Theology and the Central American Revolution* (Boston: South End Press, 1985), p. 6.

193. Berryman, *Religious Roots*, p. 74.

194. Cardenal, *Gospel in Solentiname*, Vol. 1, p. 23.

195. Ibid., Vol. 3, p. 214.

196. Nolan, *Ideology of the Sandinistas*, p. 123.

197. Ernesto Cardenal, *Zero Hour* (New York: New Directions, 1980), p. 73.

198. Cardenal, *Gospel in Solentiname*, Vol. 1, p. 268.

199. Ibid., p. 11.

200. Ibid., Vol. 3, p. 211.

201. Ibid., pp. 206–207.

202. Ibid., pp. 212–214.

203. Ibid., Vol. 1, p. 49.

204. Ibid., Vol 2, p. 86.

205. Ibid., Vol. 3, p. 46.

206. Ibid., Vol. 1, p. 40.

207. Ibid., pp. 44–46.

208. Ibid., p. 262.

209. Alan Riding, "Revolution and the Intellectual in Latin America," *New York Times Magazine* (March 13, 1983):33, 36. Liss, *Roots of Revolution*, p. 205.

210. Teófilo Cabestrero, *Ministers of God, Ministers of the People* (Maryknoll, N.Y.: Orbis Books, 1983), p. 27.

211. Berryman, *Religious Roots*, p. 16.

212. Ernesto Cardenal, *In Cuba* (New York: New Directions, 1974), pp. 6–7.

213. Personal interview with Minister of Education Fernando Cardenal, Managua, Nicaragua, January 9, 1986.

214. Cardenal, *Gospel in Solentiname*, Vol. 3, pp. 25–27.

215. Ibid., Vol. 4, p. 85.

216. Nolan, *Ideology of the Sandinistas*, p. 74.

217. Cardenal, *Gospel in Solentiname*, Vol. 4, pp. 176–178.

218. White, *Culture and Politics*, pp. 73–74.

219. Kent Johnson, "Nicaraguan Culture: Unleashing Creativity," *NACLA Report on the Americas* 19 (5) (September–October 1985):10.

220. Cardenal, *In Cuba*, pp. 163–164.

221. Cardenal, *Gospel in Solentiname*, Vol. 2, p. 85.

222. Cabestrero, *Ministers of God*, pp. 31–32.

223. Cardenal, *Gospel in Solentiname*, Vol. 3, p. 44.

224. Ibid., Vol. 4, p. 58.

225. Ibid., Vol. 3, p. 79.

226. Hodges, *Intellectual Foundations*, pp. 287–288.

227. Ibid., p. 291.

228. Cardenal, *Gospel in Solentiname*, Vol. 1, pp. 21–22.

229. Bonpane, *Guerrillas of Peace*, p. 7.

230. Cardenal, *Gospel in Solentiname*, Vol. 4, p. 51.

231. Liss, *Marxist Thought*, pp. 283–285.

232. Ibid., p. 282.

233. Bonpane, *Guerrillas of Peace*, p. 8.

234. Berryman, *Religious Roots*, p. 230.

235. Cardenal, *With Walker*, p. 3.

236. White, *Culture and Politics*, pp. 64–65.

237. Cardenal, *Zero Hour*, p. ix.

238. Robert Márquez, ed., *Latin American Revolutionary Poetry* (New York: Monthly Review Press, 1974), p. 313.

239. Philip Zwerling and Connie Martin, eds., *Nicaragua: A New Kind of Revolution* (Westport, Conn.: Lawrence Hill, 1985), p. 43.

240. Cardenal, *Vuelos*, p. xviii.

241. Ernesto Cardenal, "Toward a New Democracy of Culture," in *The Nicaragua Reader: Documents of a Revolution Under Fire*, eds. Peter Rosset and John Vandermeer (New York: Grove Press, 1983), p. 352.

242. Marcus, *Nicaragua*, pp. 143–144.

243. Jaime Wheelock Román, *Raíces indígenas de la lucha anticolonialista en Nicaragua* (Mexico City: Siglo XXI, 1980), pp. 30–33.

244. Nolan, *Ideology of the Sandinistas*, p. 52.

245. Wheelock Román, *Raíces*, pp. 1–7.

246. Ibid., pp. 116–117.

247. Nolan, *Ideology of the Sandinistas*, pp. 52–54. Jaime Wheelock Román, *Nicaragua: Imperialismo y dictadura* (Havana: Editorial de Ciencias Sociales, 1980), pp. 191–192.

248. Wheelock Román, *Nicaragua: The Great Challenge*, p. 23.

249. Wheelock Román, *Nicaragua: Imperialismo*, pp. 192–193.

250. Ibid., pp. 193–194.

251. Ibid., p. 105.

252. Center for the Study of the Americas, *Listen Compañero: Conversations with Central American Revolutionary Leaders* (San Francisco: Solidarity Publications, 1983), pp. 103–104.

253. Ibid.

254. Marcus, *Nicaragua*, pp. 83–85.

255. Wheelock Román, *Nicaragua: The Great Challenge*, pp. 58–61.

256. Marcus, *Nicaragua*, p. 146.

257. Jaime Wheelock Román, "You Cannot Overthrow a People," *Contemporary Marxism* (8) (Spring 1984):205.

258. Ibid., p. 201.

259. Center for the Study of the Americas, *Listen Compañero*, p. 105.

260. Wheelock Román, "You Cannot Overthrow," p. 207.

261. Personal interview with Jaime Wheelock Román, Managua, Nicaragua, January 8, 1986.

262. Center for the Study of the Americas, *Listen Compañero*, p. 86.

263. Hodges, *Intellectual Foundations*, pp. 209–210.

264. Center for the Study of the Americas, *Listen Compañero*, pp. 94–95.

265. Wheelock Román, *Nicaragua: Imperialismo*, p. 194.

266. Jaime Wheelock Román, "Nicaragua's Economy and the Fight Against Imperialism," in *Sandinistas Speak*, ed. Bruce Marcus (New York: Pathfinder Press, 1982), p. 121.

267. Wheelock Román, *Diciembre victorioso*, p. 36.

268. Marcus, *Nicaragua*, p. 161.

269. Peter Rosset and John Vandermeer, eds., *Nicaragua: Unfinished Revolution* (New York: Grove Press, 1986), pp. 482–483.

270. Jaime Wheelock Román, *Entre la crisis y la agresión. La reforma agraria Sandinista* (Managua: Editorial Nueva Nicaragua, 1985), pp. 23–24.

271. Ibid., p. 106.

272. Thomas W. Walker, ed., *Nicaragua: The First Five Years* (New York: Praeger, 1985), p. 310.

273. Vilas, *Sandinista Revolution*, p. 205.

274. Personal interview with Jaime Wheelock Román, Managua, Nicaragua, January 8, 1986.

275. Marcus, *Nicaragua*, pp. 134–135.

276. Wheelock Román, *Nicaragua: The Great Challenge*, pp. 27, 32.

277. Ibid., p. 36.

278. Personal interview with Jaime Wheelock Román, Managua, Nicaragua, January 8, 1986.

279. Ibid. He told me, "if being a Marxist is to follow a rigid, prescribed line of thought, I would rather be a Mormon."

280. Wheelock Román, "You Cannot Overthrow," p. 202.

281. Ibid., p. 204.

282. Jaime Wheelock Román, *Nicaragua: El gran desafío* (Mexico City: Editorial Katún, 1984), pp. 45–50.

283. Wheelock Román, *Nicaragua: The Great Challenge*, p. 45.

284. Ibid., p. 49.

285. Wheelock Román, *Nicaragua: El gran desafío*, pp. 53–55.

286. Personal interview with Jaime Chamorro Cardenal, Managua, Nicaragua, January 8, 1986.

Chapter 7

1. Sheldon B. Liss, *Marxist Thought in Latin America* (Berkeley: University of California Press, 1984), pp. 273–274.

2. Miles L. Wortman, *Government and Society in Central America, 1680–1840* (New York: Columbia University Press, 1982), p. 77.

3. Sheldon B. Liss, *Roots of Revolution: Radical Thought in Cuba* (Lincoln: University of Nebraska Press, 1987), p. 206.

4. Noam Chomsky, *Turning the Tide: U.S. Intervention in Central America and the Struggle for Peace* (Boston: South End Press, 1985), p. 221.

5. Clive Y. Thomas, *The Rise of the Authoritarian State in Peripheral Societies* (New York: Monthly Review Press, 1984), p. 80.

Bibliography

Acosta, Oscar. *Rafael Heliodoro Valle: Vida y obra.* Rome: Instituto Italo-Latino Americano, 1981.

Adams, Richard N. *Crucifixion by Power: Essays on Guatemalan National Social Structure, 1944–1966.* Austin: University of Texas Press, 1970.

Aguilar Bulgarelli, Oscar. *Democracia y partidos políticos en Costa Rica (1950–1962).* San José: N.P., 1977.

Aguilera Peralta, Gabriel. "Terror and Violence as Weapons of Counterinsurgency in Guatemala." *Latin American Perspectives* 7 (2–3) (Spring–Summer 1980):91–113.

Alba, Víctor. *Historia del comunismo en América Latina.* Mexico City: Ediciones Occidentales, 1954.

——— . *Politics and the Labor Movement in Latin America.* Stanford: Stanford University Press, 1968.

Albízurez, Miguel Angel. "Struggles and Experience of the Guatemalan Trade Union Movement, 1976–June 1978." *Latin American Perspectives* 7 (2–3) (Spring–Summer 1980):145–159.

Aldana, Carlos, "Biografía de Ramón Amaya Amador: Apóstal de la liberación." *Pensamiento Económico* (Honduras) 1 (3) (July–September 1975):24–28.

Aldaraca, Bridget, Edward Baker, Ileana Rodríguez, and Marc Zimmerman, eds., *Nicaragua in Revolution: The Poets Speak.* Minneapolis: Marxist Educational Press, 1980.

Alegría, Claribel, and D. J. Flakoll. *Nicaragua: la revolución Sandinista: Una crónica política 1855–1979.* Mexico City: Ediciones Era, 1982.

Alexander, Robert J. *Communism in Latin America.* New Brunswick, N.J.: Rutgers University Press, 1957.

——— . *Organized Labor in Latin America.* New York: Free Press, 1965.

——— . *Trotskyism in Latin America.* Stanford: Hoover Institution Press, 1973.

Alvarado Martínez, Enrique. *El pensamiento político nicaragüense de los últimos años.* Managua: Artes Gráficas, 1968.

Alvarez Elizondo, Pedro. *El presidente Arévalo y el retorno a Bolívar.* Mexico City: Ediciones Rex, 1947.

Amaya Amador, Ramón. *El "Indio Sánchez." Síntesis biográfica de un revolucionario centroamericano.* San José: Editorial Borrasé, 1948.

Ameringer, Charles D. "Costa Rica." In *Political Parties of the Americas.* Robert J. Alexander, ed. Westport, Conn.: Greenwood Press, 1982.

_____ . *Democracy in Costa Rica.* New York: Praeger, 1982.

_____ . *The Democratic Left in Exile: The Antidictatorial Struggle in the Caribbean, 1945–1959.* Miami: University of Miami Press, 1974.

_____ . *Don Pepe: A Political Biography of José Figueres of Costa Rica.* Albuquerque: University of New Mexico Press, 1978.

Amurrio González, Jesús Julian. "El positivismo en Guatemala." Unpublished thesis, Facultad de Humanidades, Universidad de San Carlos de Guatemala, Guatemala City, 1966.

Andersen, Nicolás. *Guatemala, escuela revolucionaria de nuevos hombres.* Mexico City: Editorial Nuestro Tiempo, 1983.

Anderson, Thomas P. "El Salvador." In *Communism in Central America and the Caribbean.* Robert Wesson, ed. Stanford: Hoover Institution Press, 1982.

_____ . *Matanza: El Salvador's Communist Revolt of 1932.* Lincoln: University of Nebraska Press, 1971.

_____ . *Politics in Central America: Guatemala, El Salvador, Honduras, and Nicaragua.* New York: Praeger, 1982, 1988.

_____ . *The War of the Dispossessed: Honduras and El Salvador 1969.* Lincoln: University of Nebraska Press, 1981.

Anderson-Imbert, Enrique. *Spanish-American Literature: A History.* 2 vols. Detroit: Wayne State University Press, 1969.

Annunziata, Lucia. "Democracy and the Sandinistas." *Nation* 246 (13) (April 2, 1988): 454–456.

Antónov, Y. A., et al. *Los partidos comunistas de América Latina en la lucha por la unidad de las fuerzas antimperialistas.* Moscow: Editorial Progreso, 1983.

Araya Pochet, Carlos. *Historia de los partidos políticos: Liberación nacional.* San José: Editorial Costa Rica, 1968.

Arellano, Jorge Eduardo. *Contribuciones al estudio de Rubén Darío.* Managua: Dirección General de Bibliotecas y Archivos, 1981.

_____ . *Lecciones de Sandino.* Managua: Ediciones Distribudora Cultural, 1983.

_____ . *Panorama de la literatura nicaragüense.* Managua: Ediciones Nacionales, 1977.

Arévalo, Juan José. *Anti-Kommunism in Latin America.* New York: Lyle Stuart, 1963.

_____ . *Escritos pedagógicos y filosóficos.* Guatemala City: Tipografía Nacional, 1945.

_____ . *Escritos políticos y discursos.* Havana: Cultural, 1953.

_____ . *La filosofía de los valores en la pedagogía.* Buenos Aires: Instituto de Didáctica, Facultad de Filosofía y Letras de la Universidad de Buenos Aires, 1939.

_____ . *Guatemala: la democracia y el imperio.* Buenos Aires: Editorial Palestra, 1964.

———— . *La inquietud normalista: Estampas de adolescencia y juventud 1921–1927.* San Salvador: Editorial Universitaria de El Salvador, 1970.

———— . *Istmania, o la unidad revolucionaria de Centroamérica.* Buenos Aires: Editorial Indoamérica, 1954.

———— . *Memorias de aldea.* Guatemala City: Editorial Académica Centroamericana, 1980.

———— . *La pedagogía de la personalidad.* La Plata, Argentina: Facultad de Humanidades y Ciencias de la Educación de la Universidad de La Plata, 1937.

———— . *The Shark and the Sardines.* New York: Lyle Stuart, 1961.

———— . *Viajar es vivir.* Guatemala City: Tipografía Nacional, 1950.

Argueta, Mario. *Investigaciones y tendencias recientes de la historigrafía hondureña: un ensayo bibliográfico.* Tegucigalpa: Editorial Universitaria, 1981.

Arias Gómez, Jorge. "Agustín Farabundo Martí. Esbozo biográfico." *La Universidad* (San Salvador) (4) (July–August 1971):181–240.

———— . *Farabundo Martí: Esbozo biográfico.* San José: Editorial Universitaria Centroamericana, 1972.

Arias Sánchez, Oscar. *¿Quien gobierna en Costa Rica? Un estudio del liderazgo formal en Costa Rica.* San José: Editorial Universitaria Centroamericana, 1976.

Armstrong, Robert. "Nicaragua: Sovereignty and Non Alignment." *NACLA Report on the Americas.* 19 (3) (May–June 1985):15–21.

Armstrong, Robert, and Janet Shenk. *El Salvador: The Face of Revolution.* Boston: South End Press, 1982.

Armstrong, Robert, and Philip Wheaton. *Reform and Repression: U.S. Policy in El Salvador.* San Francisco: Solidarity Publications, 1982.

Arrocha, Angela Delli Sante. *Juan José Arévalo: Pensador contemporáneo.* Mexico City: Costa-Amic, 1962.

Arroyo Soto, Víctor Manuel, ed. *Carlos Luis Fallas.* San José: Ministerio de Cultura, Juventud y Deportes, Departamento de Publicaciones, 1973.

Augier, Angel. "Poet to Poet: Rubén Darío's Cult of José Martí." *Granma Weekly Review.* (May 19, 1985).

Aybar de Soto, José M. *Dependency and Intervention: The Case of Guatemala in 1954.* Boulder: Westview Press, 1978.

Bahbah, Bishara. *Israel and Latin America: The Military Connection.* New York: St. Martin's Press, 1986.

Baloyra, Enrique A. *El Salvador in Transition.* Chapel Hill: University of North Carolina Press, 1982.

Barahona Jiménez, Luis. *Apuntes para una historia de las ideas estéticas en Costa Rica.* San José: Ministerio de Cultura, Juventud y Deportes, Dirección de Publicaciones, 1982.

———— . *Ensayos.* San José: Ministerio de Cultura, Juventud y Deportes, 1985.

———— . *El gran incógnito.* San José: Editorial Costa Rica, 1975.

———— . *Las ideas políticas en Costa Rica.* San José: Departamento de Publicaciones de Ministerio de Educación Pública, 1977.

———— . *El pensamiento político en Costa Rica.* San José: Editorial Fernández-Arce, 1972.

Baran, Paul. "The Commitment of the Intellectual." *Monthly Review* 7 (13) (May 1961):8–18.

Barry, Tom. *Guatemala: The Politics of Counterinsurgency.* Albuquerque: Inter-Hemispheric Education Resource Center, 1986.

_____. *Roots of Rebellion: Land and Hunger in Central America.* Boston: South End Press, 1987.

Barry, Tom, and Deb Preusch. *AFILD in Central America: Agents as Organizers.* Albuquerque: Resource Center, 1986.

_____. *The Central American Factbook.* New York: Grove Press, 1986.

Barry, Tom, Beth Wood, and Deb Preusch. *Dollars and Dictators: A Guide to Central America.* Albuquerque: Resource Center, 1982.

Batista, Eugenio. *Ni imperialismo yankee ni comunismo.* San José: Editorial Aurora Social, 1955.

Bauer Paiz, Alfonso. *Cómo opera el capital yanqui en Centroamérica. El Caso de Guatemala.* Mexico City: Editora Ibero-Mexicana, S. de R. L., 1956.

Baylen, Joseph O. "Sandino: Patriot or Bandit?" *Hispanic American Historical Review* 31 (3) (August 1951):394–419.

Beals, Carleton. *Banana Gold.* Reprint. New York: Arno Press, 1970.

Beaud, Michael. *A History of Capitalism, 1500–1980.* New York: Monthly Review Press, 1983.

Becerra, Longino (pseud. Asdrúbal Ramírez). "The Early History of the Labor Movement." In *Honduras: Portrait of a Captive Nation.* Nancy Peckenham and Annie Street, eds. New York: Praeger, 1985.

_____. *Evolución histórica de Honduras.* Tegucigalpa: Baktún Editorial, 1982.

_____. *Leninismo y antileninismo en Américalatina.* Tegucigalpa: Ediciones Compol, 197?.

_____. *Línea general política del P.G.H.* Tegucigalpa: Ediciones El Militante, 1975.

_____. *El maoismo en Honduras.* Tegucigalpa: Ediciones Compol, 1974.

_____. *Los militares patriotas y la revolución hondureña.* Tegucigalpa: Ediciones Compol, 1972.

_____. *El problema agraria en Honduras.* Havana: Centro de documentación sobre América Latina, Juan F. Noyla, 1964.

_____. "Prólogo" of *Prisión Verde* by Ramón Amaya Amador. Tegucigalpa: Editorial Ramón Amaya Amador, 1974.

_____. *Síntesis de la historia de Honduras.* Tegucigalpa: Editorial Ramón Amaya Amador, 1979.

_____. "The Spaniards Capture Honduras." In *Honduras: Portrait of a Captive Nation.* Nancy Peckenham and Annie Street, eds. New York: Praeger, 1985.

Bell, John Patrick. *Crisis in Costa Rica: The 1948 Revolution.* Austin: University of Texas Press, 1971.

Bermann, Karl. *Under the Big Stick: Nicaragua and the United States Since 1848.* Boston: South End Press, 1986.

Bernstein, Richard J. *Praxis and Action: Contemporary Philosophies of Human Activity.* Philadelphia: University of Pennsylvania Press, 1971.

Berrocal Soto, Fernando. "Juan José Arévalo: El hombre y el político." *Revista de filosofía de la Universidad de Costa Rica* 5 (9) (January–June 1966):189–205.

Berryman, Phillip. *The Religious Roots of Rebellion: Christians in Central American Revolutions.* Maryknoll, N.Y.: Orbis Books, 1984.

Beverley, John, and Marc Zimmerman. *Literature and Politics in the Central American Revolutions.* Austin: University of Texas Press, 1990.

Biesanz, Richard, Karen Zubris Biesanz, and Mavis Hiltunen Biesanz. *The Costa Ricans.* Englewood Cliffs, N.J.: Prentice Hall, 1982.

Black, George. *Triumph of the People: The Sandinista Revolution in Nicaragua.* London: Zed, 1981.

Black, George, Milton Jamail, and Norma Stoltz Chinchilla. "Garrison Guatemala." *NACLA Report on the Americas* 17 (1) (January–February 1983):2–35.

———. *Garrison Guatemala.* New York: Monthly Review Press, 1984.

———. "Guatemala: The War Is Not Over." *NACLA Report on the Americas* 17 (1) (March–April 1983):2–38.

Blandón, Jesús M. *Entre Sandino y Fonseca.* Managua: Departamento de Propaganda y Educación Política del FSLN, 1982.

Blutstein, Howard I., et al. *Area Handbook for Costa Rica.* Washington, D.C.: Foreign Area Studies, American University, 1970.

———. *Area Handbook for El Salvador.* Washington, D.C.: Foreign Area Studies, American University, 1971.

———. *Area Handbook for Honduras.* Washington, D.C.: Foreign Area Studies, American University, 1971.

Bober, M. M. *Karl Marx's Interpretation of History.* New York: W. W. Norton, 1965.

Bodenheimer, Susanne. "The Social Democratic Ideology in Latin America: The Case of Costa Rica's Partido Liberación Nacional." *Caribbean Studies* 10 (3) (October 1970):49–96.

Boggs, Carl. *Gramsci's Marxism.* London: Pluto Press, 1976.

———. *The Two Revolutions: Gramsci and the Dilemmas of Western Marxism.* Boston: South End Press, 1984.

Bonilla, Abelardo. *Historia y antología de la literatura costarricense.* 2 vols. San José: Trejos Hermanos, 1957 and 1961.

Bonpane, Blase. *Guerrillas of Peace: Liberation Theology and the Central American Revolution.* Boston: South End Press, 1985.

Booth, John A. *The End and the Beginning: The Nicaraguan Revolution.* Boulder: Westview Press, 1982.

Booth, John A., and Thomas W. Walker. *Understanding Central America.* Boulder: Westview Press, 1989.

Borge, Tomás. *Carlos, the Dawn Is No Longer Beyond Our Reach.* Vancouver: New Star Books, 1984.

———. "Our Vengeance Toward Our Enemies Will Be the Pardon." In *The Nicaragua Reader: Documents of a Revolution Under Fire.* Peter Rosset and John Vandermeer, eds. New York: Grove Press, 1983.

———. *La paciente impaciencia.* Managua: Editorial Vanguardia, 1989.

———. *La revolución combate contra la teología de la muerte. Discursos (cristianos) de un comandante Sandinista.* Managua: N.P., 1982.

_____ . "Women and the Nicaraguan Revolution." In *The Nicaragua Reader: Documents of a Revolution Under Fire*. Peter Rosset and John Vandermeer, eds. New York: Grove Press, 1983.

Bracher, Karl Dietrich. *The Age of Ideologies. A History of Political Thought in the Twentieth Century*. New York: St. Martin's Press, 1984.

Brintnall, Douglas. "The Birth of Indian Political Activism in Western Guatemala." *Katunob* 9 (1) (March 1976):71–77.

Britton, John A. *Carleton Beals: A Radical Journalist in Latin America*. Albuquerque: University of New Mexico Press, 1987.

Brown, Jo Anne. "Professional Language: Words that Succeed." *Radical History Review* (34) (1986):35–51.

Browning, David. *El Salvador: Landscape and Society*. London: Oxford University Press, 1971.

Bulmer-Thomas, Victor. *The Political Economy of Central America Since 1920*. Cambridge: Cambridge University Press, 1987.

Burbach, Roger, and Patricia Flynn, eds. *The Politics of Intervention: The United States in Central America*. New York: Monthly Review Press, 1984.

Burns, E. Bradford. *At War in Nicaragua. The Reagan Doctrine and the Politics of Nostalgia*. New York: Harper & Row, 1987.

Busey, James L. *Notes on Costa Rican Democracy*. Boulder: University of Colorado, Studies Series Political Science, No. 2, 1962.

Bush, Archer C. *Organized Labor in Guatemala, 1944–1949: A Case Study of an Adolescent Labor Movement in an Underdeveloped Country*. Hamilton, N.Y.: Colgate University, 1950.

Caballero, Manuel. *Latin America and the Comintern, 1919–1943*. London: Cambridge University Press, 1986.

Cabestrero, Teófilo. *Ministers of God, Ministers of the People*. Maryknoll, N.Y.: Orbis Books, 1983.

_____ . *Ministros de dios, ministros del pueblo*. Managua: Ministerio de Cultura, 1983.

Cabezas, Omar. *Fire from the Mountain: The Making of a Sandinista*. New York: Crown Publishers, 1985.

Calvert, Peter. *Guatemala: A Nation in Turmoil*. Boulder: Westview Press, 1985.

Camacho, Daniel, ed. *Desarrollo de movimiento síndical en Costa Rica*. San José: Editorial Universidad de Costa Rica, 1981.

Camejo, Pedro, and Fred Murphy, eds. *The Nicaraguan Revolution*. New York: Pathfinder Press, 1974.

Camp, Roderic A. *Intellectuals and the State in Twentieth Century Mexico*. Austin: University of Texas Press, 1985.

Cantor, Daniel, and Juliet Schor. *Tunnel Vision: Labor, the World Economy, and Central America*. Boston: South End Press, 1987.

Cardenal, Ernesto. *The Gospel in Solentiname*. 4 vols. Maryknoll, N.Y.: Orbis Books, 1976.

_____ . *In Cuba*. New York: New Directions Books, 1974.

_____ . *Love*. New York: Crossroad, 1981.

_____ . *Nicaraguan New Time*. London: Journeyman Press, 1988.

_____. *To Live Is to Love*. New York: Herder and Herder, 1972.

_____. "Toward a New Democracy of Culture." In *The Nicaragua Reader: Documents of a Revolution Under Fire*. Peter Rosset and John Vandermeer, eds. New York: Grove Press, 1983.

_____. *Vuelos de victoria*. Maryknoll, N.Y.: Orbis Books, 1985.

_____. *With Walker in Nicaragua and Other Early Poems, 1949–1954*. Middletown, Conn.: Wesleyan University Press, 1984.

_____. *Zero Hour*. New York: New Directions Books, 1980.

Cardenal, Ernesto, et al. *La batalla de Nicaragua*. Mexico City: Bruguera Mexicana de Ediciones, 1980.

Cardenal, Fernando. Personal interview, Managua, Nicaragua, January 9, 1986.

Cardoza y Aragón, Luis. *Guatemala: las lineas de su mano*. Mexico City: Fondo de Cultura Económica, 1955.

_____. *La revolución guatemalteca*. Montivideo: Ediciones Pueblos Unidos, 1956.

Carvajal Herrera, Mario. *Actitudes políticas del costarricense. Análisis de opinión de dirigentes y partidarios*. San José: Editorial Costa Rica, 1978.

Caspi, Dan, and Mitchell A. Seligson. "Toward an Empirical Theory of Tolerance: Radical Groups in Israel and Costa Rica." *Comparative Political Studies* 15 (4) (January 1983):385–404.

Castello, Julio. *Así cayó la democracia en Guatemala. La guerra de United Fruit*. Havana: Ediciones Faro, 1961.

Caturla Brú, Victoria de. *¿Cuales son los grandes temas de la filosofía latinoamericana?* Mexico City: Editorial Novaro-México, 1959.

Cayetano Carpio, Salvador. "The Final Offensive." In *El Salvador: Central America in the New Cold War*. Marvin Gettleman et al., eds. New York: Grove Press, 1981.

_____. *Secuestro y capucha: En un país del "Mundo Libre."* San José: Editorial Universitaria Centroamericana, 1979.

_____. "Violencia popular, un preocupación central." In *Pueblos en armas*. Marta Harnecker, ed. Managua: Editorial Nueva Nicaragua, 1985.

Cayetano Carpio, Salvador, and Mélida Anaya Montes. *La guerra popular en El Salvador*. Mexico: Ediciones de la Paz, 1982.

Center for the Study of the Americas. *Listen Compañero: Conversations with Central American Revolutionary Leaders*. San Francisco: Solidarity Publications, 1983.

Cerdas Cruz, Rodolfo. "La conferencia del rector Facio sobre marxismo. Una respuesta." *Revista de la Universidad de Costa Rica* (20) (March 1960):23–127.

_____. *Costa Rica: problemas actuales de una revolución democrática*. Heredia, Costa Rica: Universidad Nacional, Instituto de Estudios Latinamericanos, 1977. Also in Chester Zelaya, et al. *¿Democracia en Costa Rica? Cinco opiniones polémicas*. San José: Editorial Universidad Estatal a Distancia, 1978.

_____. *La crisis de la democracia liberal en Costa Rica. Interpretación y perspectiva*. San José: Editorial Universitaria Centroamericana, 1978.

_____. *Farabundo Martí, la internacional comunista y la insurrección salvadoreña de 1932*. San José: El Centro de Investigación y Adiestramiento Político Administrativo (CIAPA), No. 7, September 1982.

———— . *Formación del estado en Costa Rica.* San José: Editorial Universidad de Costa Rica, 1967 and 1978.

———— . *Sandino, El Apra y la Internacional Comunista: Antecedentes históricos de la Nicaragua de hoy.* Lima: Comisión Nacional de Ideología y Doctrina del Partido Aprista Peruano, 1983.

Cersosimo, Gaetano. *Los estereotypos del costarricense.* San José: Editorial Universidad de Costa Rica, 1978.

Chacón León, Edwin. *El sindicalismo en Costa Rica: Ensayo histórico.* San José: Centro de Estudios Laborales CA, 1980.

Chamorro Cardenal, Jaime. Personal interview, Managua, January 8, 1986.

Chilcote, Ronald H. *Theories of Development and Underdevelopment.* Boulder: Westview Press, 1984.

Chinchilla, Norma Stoltz. "Class Struggle in Central America: Background and Overview." *Latin American Perspectives* 7 (2–3) (Spring–Summer 1980):2–23.

Chomsky, Noam. *The Culture of Terrorism.* Boston: South End Press, 1988.

———— . *On Power and Ideology: The Managua Lectures.* Boston: South End Press, 1987.

———— . *Turning the Tide: U.S. Intervention in Central America and the Struggle for Peace.* Boston: South End Press, 1985.

Comandancia General del FMLN. *Situación revolucionaria y escalada intervencionista en la guerra salvadoreña.* Morazán, El Salvador: Ediciones Sistema Radio Venceremos, 1984.

Conrad, Robert Edgar, ed. *Sandino: The Testimony of a Nicaraguan Patriot, 1921–1934.* Princeton: Princeton University Press, 1990.

Córdoba, Diego. "Personalidad, obra y paradigma de Juan José Arévalo." *Cuadernos Americanos* 114 (1) (January–February 1961):107–133.

Cortázar, Julio. *Nicaraguan Sketches.* New York: W. W. Norton, 1989.

Coto Romero, Rafael. *Visión de Centro América complejos interamericanos.* San Salvador: La Union, Dutriz Hermanos, 1946.

Cox, Harvey. *Religion in Secular City.* New York: Simon & Schuster, 1978.

Cruz, Vladimir de la. *Las luchas sociales en Costa Rica 1870–1930.* San José: Editorial Universidad de Costa Rica and Editorial Costa Rica, 1980.

Cuenca, Abel. *El Salvador: Una democracia cafetalera.* Mexico City: ARR–Centro Editorial, 1962.

Dalton, Roque. "Culture and Revolution in Central America." *World Student News* 28 (11–12) (1965):30–32.

———— . *Las enseñanzas de Viet-Nam.* California: Comités de Solidaridad "Cmdte Ernesto Jovel Funes" y "Roque Dalton," 1981.

———— . *Las historias prohibidas del pulgarcito.* Mexico City: Siglo XXI, 1974.

———— . *Miguel Mármol.* Willimantic, Conn.: Curbstone Press, 1987.

———— . *Miguel Mármol: Los sucesos de 1932 en El Salvador.* San José: Editorial Universitaria Centroamericana, 1972.

———— . "Notas sobre el sistema imperialista de dominación y explotación en Centroamérica." *Organización Continental Latinoamericana de Estudiantes* (Havana) (66) (June 1972):2–20.

———— . *Poemas clandestinos.* San Francisco: Solidarity Publications, 1984.

———. *Poetry and Militancy in Latin America*. Willimantic, Conn.: Curbstone Press, 1981.

———. *El Salvador*. Havana: Casa de las Américas, 1963.

———. *Taberna y otros lugares*. San Salvador: UCA/Editores, 1983.

Dalton, Roque, and Eduardo Bähr. *Guerra a la guerra*. Tegucigalpa: Editorial Universitaria, 1981.

Dalton, Roque, et al. *El intelectual y la sociedad*. Mexico City: Siglo XXI, 1969.

Danby, Colin, and Richard Swedberg. *Honduras: Bibliography and Research Guide*. Cambridge, Mass.: Central American Information Office, 1984.

Darío, Rubén. *Autobiografía*. Madrid: Editorial Mundo Latino, 1920.

———. *Crónica política*. Vol 11 of *Obras Completas*. Madrid: Biblioteca Rubén Darío, 1924.

———. "José Martí." *Granma Weekly Review*. May 19, 1985.

———. *Obras desconocidas*. Santiago: Prensas de la Universidad de Chile, 1934.

———. *Prosas políticas*. Managua: Ministerio de Cultura, 1983.

———. *Textos socio-políticos*. Managua: Ediciones de la Biblioteca Nacional, 1980.

Davis, Harold E., ed. *Latin American Social Thought*. Washington, D.C.: University Press of Washington, 1961.

———. *Latin American Thought: A Historical Introduction*. New York: Free Press, 1974.

Debray, Régis. *Las preubas de fuego*. Mexico City: Siglo XXI, 1975.

Denton, Charles F. *Patterns of Costa Rican Politics*. Boston: Allyn and Bacon, 1971.

d'Escoto, Miguel. "The Church Born of the People of Nicaragua." In *Revolution in Central America*, Stanford Central American Action Network, eds. Boulder: Westview Press, 1983.

Díaz Rozzotto, Jaime. *El carácter de la revolución guatemalteca: Ocaso de la revolución democrático-burguesa corriente*. Mexico City: Ediciones Revista Horizonte, 1958.

Dion, Marie-Berthe. *Las ideas sociales y políticas de Arévalo*. Santiago de Chile: Prensa Latinoamericana, 1958.

Dombrowski, John, et al. *Area Handbook for Guatemala*. Washington, D.C.: Foreign Area Studies, American University, 1970.

Dunkerley, James. "Class Structure and Socialist Strategy in El Salvador." In *Crisis in the Caribbean*. Fitzroy Ambursley and Robin Cohen, eds. New York: Monthly Review Press, 1983.

———. *The Long War: Dictatorship and Revolution in El Salvador*. London: Verso, 1983, 1985.

———. *Power in the Isthmus: A Political History of Modern Central America*. London: Verso, 1988.

———. "Rafael Menjívar." In *Biographical Dictionary of Marxism*. Robert A. Gorman, ed. Westport, Conn.: Greenwood Press, 1986.

———. "Roque Dalton García." In *Biographical Dictionary of Marxism*. Robert A. Gorman, ed. Westport, Conn.: Greenwood Press, 1986.

_____ . "Salvador Cayetano Carpio." In *Biographical Dictionary of Marxism*. Robert A. Gorman, ed. Westport, Conn.: Greenwood Press, 1986.

Edelman, Marc. "Lifelines: Nicaragua and the Socialist Countries." *NACLA Report on the Americas* 19 (3) (May–June 1985):33–53.

Edelman, Marc, and Joanne Kenen, eds. *The Costa Rica Reader*. New York: Grove Weidenfeld, 1989.

Ellis, Keith. *Critical Approach to Rubén Darío*. Toronto: University of Toronto Press, 1974.

English, Burt H. *Liberación Nacional in Costa Rica: The Development of a Political Party in a Transitional Society*. Gainesville, University of Florida Press, 1961.

EPICA Task Force. *Nicaragua: A People's Revolution*. Washington, D.C.: EPICA, 1980.

Espinoza, Francisco. "Experience of the Communists of Costa Rica." *World Marxist Review* 6 (7) (July 1963):36–38.

Etchison, Don L. *The United States and Militarism in Central America*. New York: Praeger, 1975.

Facio, Rodrigo. *Estudio sobre economía costarricense*. San José: Editorial Costa Rica, 1975.

Fagen, Richard R. *Forging Peace: The Challenge of Central America*. New York: Basil Blackwell, 1987.

Fagen, Richard R., Carmen Diana Deere, and José Luis Coraggio, eds. *Transition and Development: Problems of Third World Socialism*. New York: Monthly Review Press, 1986.

Fajardo, José. *Centroamérica hoy: Todos los rostros del conflicto*. Bogotá: Editorial La Oveja Negra, 1980.

Falla, Ricardo. *Quiché rebelde*. Guatemala City: Editorial Universitaria, 1978.

Fallas, Carlos Luis. *Mamita yunai*. Santiago de Chile: Editorial Nascimiento, 1949.

_____ . *Reseña de la intervención y penetración Yanki en Centro América*. Mexico City: Fondo de Cultura Popular, 1954.

Fallas, Carlos Luis, Eduardo Mora V., and Arnoldo Feretto S. *Calderón Guardia, José Figueres y Otillo Ulate: A la luz de los últimos acontecimientos políticos*. San José: N.P., 1955.

Feinberg, Richard E., ed. *Central America: International Dimensions of the Crisis*. New York: Holmes & Meier, 1982.

Feretto, Arnoldo. "The Lessons of a Strike." *World Marxist Review* 3 (8) (August 1960):91–93.

Fergusson, Erna. *Guatemala*. New York: Alfred A. Knopf, 1946.

Flora, Jan L. "Roots of Insurgency in Central America." *Latin American Issues* (5) (1987): 1–46.

Flora, Jan, and Edelberto Torres Rivas, eds. *Central America*. New York: Monthly Review Press, 1989.

Flores Valeriano, Enrique. *La explotación bananera en Honduras: Capítulos de deshonor nacional*. Tegucigalpa: Editorial Universitaria, 1979.

Fonseca Amador, Carlos. "Nicaragua: Zero Hour." In *Sandinistas Speak*. Bruce Marcus, ed. New York: Pathfinder Press, 1982. Also in *The Nicaragua Reader:*

Documents of a Revolution Under Fire. Peter Rosset and John Vandermeer, eds. New York: Grove Press, 1983.

_____ . *Obras*. Vol. 1. *Bajo la bandara del sandinismo*. Vol 2. *Viva Sandino*. Managua: Editorial Nueva Nicaragua, 1985.

Fortín Magaña, Romeo. *Democracia y socialismo*. San Salvador: N.P., 1983.

Fortuny, José Manuel. "Has the Revolution Become more Difficult in Latin America?" *World Marxist Review* 8 (8) (August 1965):38–45.

_____ . "The Political Situation and Revolutionary Tactics." *World Marxist Review* 10 (2) (February 1967):56–62.

_____ . *Lo que no se dijo en Quito*. Guatemala City: Departamento de Publicidad de la Presedencia de la República, 1949.

_____ . "Tendencias de la lucha actual en Guatemala." *Cuba Socialista* 3 (January 1963):58–75.

_____ . "Under the Banner of Proletarian Internationalism." *World Marxist Review* 7 (12) (December 1964):45–46.

Frank, Luisa, and Philip Wheaton. *Indian Guatemala: Path to Liberation*. Washington, D.C.: EPICA, 1984.

Fried, Jonathan, et al., eds. *Guatemala in Rebellion: Unfinished History*. New York: Grove Press, 1983.

Galeano, Eduardo. *Guatemala: Occupied Country*. New York: Monthly Review Press, 1969.

Galeano, Eduardo, José González, and Antonio Campos. *Guatemala: Un pueblo en lucha*. Madrid: Editorial Revolución, 1983.

Galich, Manuel, ed. "A ciento cincuenta años del congreso de Panamá: Bolivarismo y panamericanismo." *Casa de las Américas* 16 (96) (May–June 1976):4–17.

_____ . *Benito Juárez: Pensamiento y acción*. Havana: Casa de las Américas, 1974.

_____ ."The Dangers of Practicing Democracy." *United Nations World* 5 (1) (September 1951):43, 59.

_____ . *Del pánico al ataque*. Guatemala City: Editorial Universitaria, 1977.

_____ . "Guatemala 10 años de despojo y lucha 1954–1964." *Bohemia* 56 (June 26, 1964):88–89.

_____ . "La guerra anti-imperialista de 1855 en Centro América." *Historia y sociedad* (7) (Fall 1966):37–44.

_____ . *La historia a escena—3 evocaciones en un acto*. Guatemala City: Editorial del Ministerio de Educación Pública, 1949.

_____ . "Internal Reasons for the Defeat." *Tricontinental* (2) (1967):66–81.

_____ . *Por que lucha Guatemala, Arévalo y Arbenz: Dos hombres contra un imperio*. Buenos Aires: Elmer Editor, 1956.

García, Graciela A. *Páginas de lucha*. Tegucigalpa: Editorial Guaymuras, 1981.

_____ . *Páginas de lucha revolucionaria en Centroamérica*. Mexico: Ediciones Linterna, 1971.

_____ . *Personalidades célebres de América: Ensayos biográficos*. Mexico City: Costa-Amic, 1964.

_____ . *Por la superación de la educación en México*. Mexico City: Costa-Amic, 1971.

Gella, Aleksander. *The Intelligentsia and the Intellectuals: Theory, Method, and Case Study*. Beverly Hills: Sage Publications, 1976.

Gerassi, John. *The Great Fear in Latin America*. New York: Collier Books, 1965.

Gettleman, Marvin E., et al., eds. *El Salvador: Central America in the New Cold War*. New York: Grove Press, 1981.

Gilbert, Dennis. *Sandinistas: The Party and the Revolution*. New York: Basil Blackwell, 1988.

Gillespie, Richard. "Agustín Farabundo Martí." In *Biographical Dictionary of Marxism*. Robert A. Gorman, ed. Westport, Conn.: Greenwood Press, 1986.

Gilly, Adolfo. *Guerra y política en El Salvador*. Mexico City: Nueva Imagen, 1981.

———. "An Interview with Salvador Cayetano Carpio ("Marcial")." *Contemporary Marxism* (3) (Summer 1981):9–14.

Goldrich, Daniel. *Sons of the Establishment. Elite Youth in Panama and Costa Rica*. Chicago: Rand McNally, 1966.

González, Mike. *Nicaragua: Revolution Under Siege*. Chicago: International Socialist Organization, 1985.

González Casanova, Pablo, ed. *América Latina: Historia de medio siglo*. Vol. 2. Mexico City: Siglo XXI, 1981.

Gorman, Robert A., ed. *Biographical Dictionary of Marxism*. Westport, Conn.: Greenwood Press, 1986.

Gott, Richard. *Guerrilla Movements in Latin America*. Garden City, N.Y.: Anchor Books, 1972.

Gouldner, Alvin W. *The Dialectic of Ideology and Technology*. New York: Seaberry Press, 1976.

———. *The Future of Intellectuals and the Rise of the New Class*. New York: Seaberry Press, 1979.

———. "Prologue to a Theory of Revolutionary Intellectuals." *Telos* 26 (Winter 1975–1976):3–36.

———. *The Two Marxisms: Contradictions and Anomalies in the Development of Theory*. New York: Seaberry Press, 1980.

Grieb, Kenneth J. *Guatemalan Caudillo: The Regime of Jorge Ubico, Guatemala 1931–1944*. Athens: Ohio University Press, 1979.

Gualan, Alberto. "Years of Valiant Struggle (35 Years of the Communist Party of El Salvador). *World Marxist Review* 8 (6) (June 1965):64–71.

Guerín, Daniel. *Anarchism*. New York: Monthly Review Press, 1970.

Guerra, Tomás. *El Salvador en la hora de la liberación*. San José: Editorial Farabundo Martí, 1980.

Guillén, Fedro. *Guatemala: Prólogo y epílogo de una revolución*. Mexico City: Cuadernos Americanos, 1964.

Gunnell, John G. *Between Philosophy and Politics: The Alienation of Political Theory*. Amherst: University of Massachusetts Press, 1986.

Guzmán-Böckler, Carlos, and Jean-Loup Herbert. *Guatemala: una interpretación historico-social*. Mexico City: Siglo XXI, 1975.

Hagopian, Mark N. *Ideals and Ideologies of Modern Politics*. New York: Longman, 1985.

Hamilton, Nora, Jeffry A. Frieden, Linda Fuller, and Manuel Pastor, Jr., eds. *Crisis in Central America: Regional Dynamics and U.S. Policy in the 1980s.* Boulder: Westview Press, 1988.

Hampden-Turner, Charles. *Radical Man: The Process of Psycho-Social Development.* Garden City, N.Y.: Anchor Books, 1971.

Hándal, Schafik Jorge. "Interview by Mark Fried." *NACLA Report on the Americas* 20 (5) (September–December 1986):36–42.

————. "Un partido que supo ponerse a la altura de la historia." In *Pueblos en armas.* Marta Harnecker, ed. Managua: Editorial Nueva Nicaragua, 1985.

————. "Salvadoran Revolution on the Offensive." *Political Affairs* 60 (2) (February 1981):21–25.

Handy, Jim. *Gift of the Devil: A History of Guatemala.* Boston: South End Press, 1984.

Harnecker, Marta, ed. *Pueblos en armas.* Managua: Editorial Nueva Nicaragua, 1985.

Harris, Marvin, *Cultural Materialism: The Struggle for a Science of Culture.* New York: Vintage, 1980.

Harris, Richard L. "Economic Development and Revolutionary Transformation in Nicaragua." *Latin American Issues* 3 (1986): 1–68.

Harris, Richard, and Carlos M. Vilas. *Nicaragua: A Revolution Under Siege.* London: Zed, 1985.

Hartz, Louis. *The Founding of New Societies: Studies in the History of the United States, Latin America, South Africa, Canada, and Australia.* New York: Harcourt Brace and World, 1964.

Heliodoro Valle, Rafael. *Historia de las ideas contemporáneas en Centro-América.* Mexico City: Fondo de Cultura Económica, 1960.

Hodges, Donald C. *Intellectual Foundations of the Nicaraguan Revolution.* Austin: University of Texas Press, 1986.

Hopkins, Terence K., and Immanuel Wallerstein. *World-Systems Analysis: Theory and Methodology.* Beverly Hills: Sage Publications, 1982.

————, eds. *Processes of the World-System.* Beverly Hills: Sage Publications, 1980.

Horowitz, Irving Louis, et al., eds. *Latin American Radicalism: A Documentary Report on Left and Nationalist Movements.* New York: Vintage Books, 1969.

Hunter, Jane. *Israeli Foreign Policy: South Africa and Central America.* Boston: South End Press, 1987.

de Huszar, George B., ed. *The Intellectuals: A Controversial Portrait.* Glencoe, Ill.: Free Press, 1960.

Ignatiev, Oleg, and Genrykh Borovick. *The Agony of a Dictatorship: Nicaraguan Chronicle.* Moscow: Progress Publishers, 1980.

Immerman, Richard H. *The CIA in Guatemala: The Foreign Policy of Intervention.* Austin: University of Texas Press, 1982.

Inman, Samuel Guy. *A New Day in Guatemala: A Study of the Present Social Revolution.* Wilton, Conn.: Worldover Press, 1951.

Instituto de Estudio del Sandinismo. *Pensamiento antimperialista en Nicaragua. Antología.* Managua: Editorial Nueva Nicaragua, 1982.

Irvin, George, and Xabier Gorostiaga, eds. *Toward an Alternative for Central America and the Caribbean.* London: George Allen and Unwin, 1985.

Jamail, Milton, and Margo Gutierrez. *It's No Secret: Israel's Military Involvement in Central America*. Belmont, Mass.: Association of Arab-American University Graduates, 1986.

James, Daniel. *Red Design for the Americas: Guatemalan Prelude*. New York: John Day, 1954.

Jiménez, Jorge. "Progressive Juntas in Costa Rica." *World Marxist Review* 2 (5) (May 1959):69–70.

Jiménez, Liliam. *El Salvador: Sus problemas socio-económicos*. Havana: Casa de las Américas, 1980.

Jirón Terán, José. *Investigaciones en torno de Rubén Darío*. Managua: Dirección General de Bibliotecas y Archivos, 1981.

Johnson, Kent. "Nicaraguan Culture: Unleashing Creativity." *NACLA Report on the Americas* 19 (5) (September–October 1985):8–11.

Jonas, Susanne. "Guatemala: Land of Eternal Struggle." In *Latin America: The Struggle with Dependency and Beyond*. Ronald H. Chilcote and Joel C. Edelstein, eds. New York: Schenkman, 1974.

Jonas, Susanne, Ed McCaughan, and Elizabeth Sutherland Martínez, eds. *Guatemala: Tyranny on Trial*. San Francisco: Synthesis Publications, 1984.

Jonas, Susanne, and David Tobis, eds. *Guatemala*. New York: North American Congress on Latin America, 1974.

Jones, Chester Lloyd, *Guatemala: Past and Present*. Minneapolis: University of Minnesota Press, 1940.

Jrade, Cathy Login. *Rubén Darío and the Romantic Search for Unity: The Modernist Recourse to Esoteric Tradition*. Austin: University of Texas Press, 1983.

Jung, Harold. "Class Struggle and Civil War in El Salvador." *New Left Review* 122 (July–August 1980), as reprinted in *El Salvador: Central America in the New Cold War*. Marvin Gettleman, et al., eds. New York: Grove Press, 1981.

Karnes, Thomas L. *The Failure of Union: Central America, 1824–1925*. Tempe: Center for Latin American Studies, Arizona State University, 1976.

Kepner, Charles David, Jr. *Social Aspects of the Banana Industry*. New York: Columbia University Press, 1936. Reprint. New York: AMS Press, 1967.

Kepner, Charles David, Jr., and Jay Henry Soothill. *The Banana Empire: A Case Study of Economic Imperialism*. New York: Vanguard Press, 1935.

Kornbluh, Peter. *Nicaragua: The Price of Intervention: Reagan's Wars Against the Sandinistas*. Washington, D.C.: Institute for Policy Studies, 1987.

Krehm, William. *Democracies and Tyrannies of the Caribbean*. Westport, Conn.: Lawrence Hill, 1984.

Krusé, David Samuel, and Richard Swedberg. *El Salvador: Bibliography and Research Guide*. Boston: CAMINO (Central American Information Office), 1982.

Labastida, Jaime, et al. *Centroamérica: Crisis y política internacional*. Mexico City: Siglo XXI, 1982.

LaCharité, Norman A., et al. *A Case Study in Insurgency and Revolutionary Warfare: Guatemala 1944–1954*. Washington, D.C.: Special Operations Research Office, American University, 1964.

La Feber, Walter. *Inevitable Revolutions: The United States in Central America*. New York: W. W. Norton, 1984.

Laínez, Vilma, and Víctor Meza. "The Banana Enclave." In *Honduras: Portrait of a Captive Nation*. Nancy Peckenham and Annie Street, eds. New York: Praeger, 1985.

Lamperti, John. *What Are We Afraid Of? An Assessment of the "Communist Threat" in Central America*. Boston: South End Press, 1988.

Lancaster, Roger N. *Thanks to God and the Revolution: Popular Religion and Class Consciousness in the New Nicaragua*. New York: Columbia University Press, 1989.

Lapper, Richard, and James Painter. *Honduras: State for Sale*. London: Latin American Bureau, 1985.

Larín, Arístides Augusto. "Historical del movimiento sindical de El Salvador." *La Universidad* (San Salvador) 4 (July–August 1971):136–179.

Láscaris, Constantino. "Algunos pensadores centroamericanos." *Revista de filosofía de la Universidad de Costa Rica* 15 (41) (July–December 1977):281–307ff.

———. *Desarrollo de las ideas filosóficas en Costa Rica*. San José: Editorial Costa Rica, 1965.

———. *Historia de las ideas en Centroamérica*. San José: Editorial Universitaria Centroamericana, 1970.

Le Blanc, Paul. *Permanent Revolution in Nicaragua*. New York: Fourth Internationalist Tendency, 1984.

Le Moyne, James. "Testifying to Torture." *New York Times Magazine* (June 5, 1988):44–47, 66–67.

Leonard, Thomas M. *The United States and Central America, 1944–1949: Perceptions of Political Dynamics*. University: University of Alabama Press, 1984.

Lernoux, Penny. *Cry of the People*. New York: Penguin Books, 1982.

Liss, Sheldon B. *Diplomacy and Dependency: Venezuela, the United States, and the Americas*. Salisbury, N.C.: Documentary Publications, 1978.

———. *Marxist Thought in Latin America*. Berkeley: University of California Press, 1984.

———. "On Honduras: Exploring a Key Colonial Backwater." *Guardian*. November 26, 1986.

———. *Roots of Revolution: Radical Thought in Cuba*. Lincoln: University of Nebraska Press, 1987.

Liss, Sheldon B., and Peggy K. Liss, eds. *Man, State, and Society in Latin American History*. New York: Praeger, 1972.

López, Matilde Elena. "¿Masferrer socialista utópico, reformista o revolucionario?" *La Universidad* (San Salvador) 5 (September–October 1968):101–108.

López Larrave, Mario. *Breve historia del movimiento sindical guatemalteco*. Guatemala City: Editorial Universitaria, 1979.

Loveman, Brian, and Thomas M. Davies, Jr., eds. *Che Guevara: Guerrilla Warfare*. Lincoln: University of Nebraska Press, 1985.

Macauley, Neil. *The Sandino Affair*. Chicago: Quadrangle Books, 1967.

MacCameron, Robert. *Bananas, Labor, and Politics in Honduras, 1954–1963*. Syracuse: Foreign and Comparative Studies/Latin American Series, No. 5, Maxwell School of Citizenship and Public Affairs, Syracuse University, 1983.

McClintock, Michael. *The American Connection*. Vol. 2. *State Terror and Popular Resistance in Guatemala*. London: Zed, 1985.

McDonald, Ronald H. "El Salvador." In *Political Parties of the Americas*. Robert J. Alexander, ed. Westport, Conn.: Greenwood Press, 1982.

MacLeod, Murdo J. *Spanish Central America: A Socioeconomic History, 1520–1720*. Berkeley: University of California Press, 1973.

Marcus, Bruce, ed. *Nicaragua: The Sandinista People's Revolution. Speeches by Sandinista Leaders*. New York: Pathfinder Press, 1985.

—, ed. *Sandinistas Speak: Speeches, Writings, and Interviews with Leaders of Nicaragua's Revolution*. New York: Pathfinder Press, 1982.

Mariátegui, José Carlos. *Seven Interpretive Essays on Peruvian Reality*. Austin: University of Texas Press, 1971.

Marinello, Juan. "Cuba en Rubén Darío." *Bohemia* (Havana) (4) (January 26, 1968):16–21.

Márquez, Robert, ed. *Latin American Revolutionary Poetry*. New York: Monthly Review Press, 1974.

Marsal, Juan F., ed. *El intelectual latinamericano*. Buenos Aires: Editorial del Instituto, 1970.

Marshall, John, Peter Dale Scott, and Jane Hunter. *The Iran-Contra Connection: Secret Teams and Covert Operations in the Reagan Era*. Boston: South End Press, 1987.

Martí, José. *Our America: Writings on Latin America and the Struggle for Cuban Independence*. Philip S. Foner, ed. New York: Monthly Review Press, 1977.

Martin, Michael T. "On Culture, Politics, and the State in Nicaragua: An Interview with Padre Ernesto Cardenal, Minister of Culture." *Latin American Perspectives* 16 (2) (Spring 1989):124–133.

Martínez, José Francisco. *Honduras histórica*. Tegucigalpa: Imprenta Calderón, 1974.

Martínez B., Juan Ramón. *Historia del movimiento cooperativo*. Tegucigalpa: Instituto de Formación e Investigación Cooperativista, 1975 or 1976.

Martz, John D. *Central America: The Crisis and the Challenge*. Chapel Hill: University of North Carolina Press, 1959.

——— . *Communist Infiltration of Guatemala*. New York: Vintage Press, 1956.

Masferrer, Alberto. *Obras escogidas*. 2 vols. San Salvador: Editorial Universitaria, 1971.

Mayorga Quiros, Román. *La universidad para el cambio social*. San Salvador: UCA Editores, 1976.

Mejía, Medardo. *Don Juan Lindo: El frente nacional y el anticolonialismo*. Tegucigalpa: La Democracia, 1959.

——— . *Juan José Arévalo o el humanismo en la presidencia*. Guatemala City: Tipografía Nacional, 1951.

Melville, Thomas, and Marjorie Melville. *Guatemala—Another Vietnam?* Harmondsworth: Penguin Books, 1971.

——— . *Guatemala: The Politics of Land Ownership*. New York: Free Press, 1971.

Mendieta, Salvador. *Alrededor del problema unionista de Centro América*. Vol. 1. *El unionismo en la política transaccionista de Nicaragua*. Vol. 2. *Mundialidad del problema*. Barcelona: Tip. Maucci, 1934.

Menéndez Rodríguez, Mario. *El Salvador: Una auténtica guerra civil*. San José: Editorial Universitaria Centroamericana, 1980.

──────. *Voices from El Salvador*. San Francisco: Solidarity Publications, 1983.

Menjívar, Rafael. *Acumulación ordinaria y desarrollo del capitalismo en El Salvador*. San José: Editorial Universitaria Centroamericana, 1980.

──────. *Crisis del desarrollismo: Caso El Salvador*. San José: Editorial Universitaria Centroamericana, 1977.

──────. "El Salvador: The Smallest Link." *Contemporary Marxism* (1) (Spring 1980):19–28.

──────. "The First Phase of the General Offensive." *Contemporary Marxism* (3) (Summer 1981):18–22.

──────. *Formación y lucha del proletariado industrial salvadoreño*. San Salvador: UCA Editores, 1979.

──────. "Los problemas del mundo rural." In *Centro América hoy*. Edelberto Torres Rivas et al. Mexico City: Siglo XXI, 1976.

──────. *Reforma agraria: Guatemala—Bolivia—Cuba*. San Salvador: Editorial Universitaria de El Salvador, 1969.

Meza, Víctor, ed. *Antología de documentos sobre la situación y evolución del movimiento obrero en Honduras (1970–1979)*. Tegucigalpa: Editorial Universitaria, 1981.

──────. *Historia del movimiento obrero hondureño*. Tegucigalpa: Editorial Guaymuras, 1981.

──────. *Honduras: La evolución de la crisis*. Tegucigalpa: Editorial Universitaria, 1982.

──────. "The Military: Willing to Deal." *NACLA Report on the Americas* 22 (1) (January–February 1988): 14–21.

──────. *Política y sociedad en Honduras*. Tegucigalpa: Editorial Guaymuras, 1981.

──────. "Recent Developments in Honduran Foreign Policy and National Security." In *Honduras Confronts Its Future*. Mark B. Rosenberg and Philip L. Shepherd, eds. Boulder: Lynne Rienner Publishers, 1986.

Miliband, Ralph, et al., eds. *Socialist Register 1985/1986: Social Democracy and After*. London: Merlin Press, 1986.

Millá, José (pseud. Salomé Jil). *Historia de la América Central*. 2 vols. Guatemala City: Tipografía Nacional, 1937.

──────. "Problems of a United Democratic Front in Guatemala." *World Marxist Review* 7 (12) (December 1964):46–48.

Miller, Herbert J. "Positivism and Education in Guatemala." In *Positivism in Latin America, 1850–1900*. Ralph Lee Woodward, Jr., ed. Lexington, Mass.: D. C. Heath, 1971.

Millett, Richard. *Guardians of the Dynasty: A History of the U.S.-created Guardia Nacional de Nicaragua and the Somoza Family*. Maryknoll, N.Y.: Orbis Books, 1977.

Mills, C. Wright. *The Marxists*. New York: Delta, 1962.

Molina Arguello, Carlos. *La enseñanza de la historia en Nicaragua*. Mexico City: Pan American Institute of Geography and History, Pub. No. 165, 1953.

Monteforte Toledo, Mario. *Centro América: Subdesarrollo y dependencia*. 2 vols. Mexico City: Universidad Nacional Autónoma de México, 1972.

──────. *Guatemala: Monografía sociológica*. Mexico City: Instituto de Investigaciones Sociales, Universidad Nacional Autónoma de México, 1965.

Montes, César, et al. *Turcios Lima*. Havana: Tricontinental, 1970.

Montes, Segundo. *Estudio sobre estratificación social en El Salvador*. San Salvador: Universidad Centroamericana José Simeón Cañas, 1979.

Montgomery, Tommie Sue. "El Salvador." In *Central America: Crisis and Adaptation*. Steve C. Ropp and James A. Morris, eds. Albuquerque: University of New Mexico Press, 1984.

———. "Liberation and Revolution: Christianity as a Subversive Activity in Central America." In *Trouble in Our Backyard: Central America and the United States in the Eighties*. Martin Diskin, ed. New York: Pantheon Books, 1983.

———. *Revolution in El Salvador*. Boulder: Westview Press, 1982.

Mora Valverde, Eduardo. *Centro América en la integración económica latinoamericano*. San José: Ediciones Revolución, 1969.

———. *4 artículos en respuesta al revolucionarismo pequeño burgués*. San José: Editorial Rumbo, 1975.

Mora Valverde, Eduardo, and Alvaro Montero Vega. "Words and Deeds of the CPC Leaders." *World Marxist Review* 7 (6) (June 1964):56–59.

Mora Valverde, Manuel. *Discursos 1934–1979*. San José: Editorial Presbere, 1980.

———. *Imperialismo: Nuestra soberanía frente al Departamento de Estado*. San José: Partido Comunista de Costa Rica, 1940.

Morales Avilés, Ricardo. *La dominación imperialista en Nicaragua*. Managua: Secretaría Nacional de Propaganda y Educación Política del FSLN, 1980.

———. *Obras: No pararemos de andar jamás*. Managua: Editorial Nueva Nicaragua, 1983.

———. *El pensamiento vivo de Ricardo Morales Avilés*. Managua: Asociación de Estudiantes de Sociología, 1970s.

Morris, James A. "Honduras." In *Political Parties of the Americas*. Robert J. Alexander, ed. Westport, Conn.: Greenwood Press, 1982.

———. *Honduras: Caudillo Politics and Military Rulers*. Boulder: Westview Press, 1984.

Morris, James, and Steve C. Ropp. "Corporatism and Dependent Development: A Honduran Case Study." *Latin American Research Review* 12 (2) (1977):27–68.

Munck, Ronaldo. *Politics and Dependency in the Third World: The Case of Latin America*. London: Zed, 1984.

Muñoz, Alonzo. "The People of Honduras in the Fight Against Reaction and Imperialism." *World Marxist Review* 7 (6) (June 1964):24–28.

Munro, Dana G. *The United States and the Caribbean Republics 1921–1933*. Princeton: Princeton University Press, 1974.

Navarro Bolandi, Hugo. *La generación del 48*. Mexico City: Editorial Olimpo, 1957.

Nelson, Harold D., ed. *Costa Rica: A Country Study*. Washington, D.C.: Foreign Area Studies, American University, 1984.

Nolan, David. *The Ideology of the Sandinistas and the Nicaraguan Revolution*. Coral Gables: Institute of Interamerican Studies, University of Miami, 1984.

North, Lisa. *Bitter Grounds: Roots of Revolt in El Salvador*. Toronto: Between the Lines, 1982.

Nyrop, Richard F., ed. *Guatemala: A Country Study*. Washington, D.C.: Foreign Area Studies, American University, 1984.

Obando Sánchez, Antonio. *Memorias: la historia del movimiento obrero en este siglo*. Guatemala City: Editorial Universitaria, 1978.

Obregón Loria, Rafael. *Conflictos militares y políticos de Costa Rica*. San José: La Nación, 1951.

Ollman, Bertell, and Edward Vernoff, eds. *The Left Academy: Marxist Scholarship on American Campuses*. Vol. 3. New York: Praeger, 1984.

Ordóñez Argüello, Alberto. *Arévalo visto por América*. Guatemala City: Editorial de Ministerio de Educación Pública, 1951.

Osborne, Lilly de Jongh. *Four Keys to El Salvador*. New York: Funk and Wagnalls, 1956.

PACCA (Policy Alternative for the Caribbean and Central America). *Changing Course: Blueprint for Peace in Central America and the Caribbean*. Washington, D.C.: Institute for Policy Studies, 1984.

Palmer, Steven. "Carlos Fonseca and the Construction of Sandinismo in Nicaragua." *Latin American Research Review* 22 (1) (1988): 91–109.

Parenti, Michael. *The Anti-Communist Impulse*. New York: Random House, 1969.

Parker, Franklin D. *The Central American Republics*. London: Oxford University Press, 1964.

Partido Socialista Costarricense. *Programa de la nueva reforma social: Por un gobierno democrático popular hacia el socialismo*. San José: Ediciones Pensamiento Revolucionario, 1980.

Payeras, Mario. "Days of the Jungle: The Testimony of a Guatemalan Guerrillero, 1972–1976." *Monthly Review* 35 (3) (July–August 1983):19–94.

Payne, Walter A. *A Central American Historian: José Milla, 1822–1882*. Gainesville: University of Florida Press, 1957.

Pearson, Neale J. "Costa Rica, Honduras, and Panama." In *Communism in Central America and the Caribbean*. Robert Wesson, ed. Stanford: Hoover Institution Press, 1982.

————. "Nicaragua." In *Political Parties of the Americas*. Robert J. Alexander, ed. Westport, Conn.: Greenwood Press, 1982.

Peckenham, Nancy, and Annie Street, eds. *Honduras: Portrait of a Captive Nation*. New York: Praeger, 1985.

Peeler, John A. *Latin American Democracies: Colombia, Costa Rica, Venezuela*. Chapel Hill: University of North Carolina Press, 1985.

Pérez Bermúdez, Carlos, and Onofre Guevara. *El movimiento obrero en Nicaragua*. Managua: Editorial El Amanecer, S.A., 1985.

Persky, Stan. *America, the Last Domino: U.S. Foreign Policy in Central America Under Reagan*. Vancouver: New Star Books, 1984.

Petras, James, et al. *Latin America: Bankers, Generals, and the Struggle for Social Justice*. Totowa, N.J.: Roman & Littlefield, 1986.

Petrujin, A., and E. Churílov. *Farabundo Martí*. Moscow: Editorial Progreso, 1985.

Pierre, Andrew J., ed. *Third World Instability: Central America as a European-American Issue*. New York: Council on Foreign Relations, 1985.

Plant, Roger. *Guatemala: Unnatural Disaster*. London: Latin American Bureau, 1978.

Plantier, Basilio. "Comunismo Criollo." *Estudios Centroamericanos* 15 (148) (May 1960):197–205.

Pocock, J.G.A. *Politics, Language and Time: Essays on Political Thought and History.* New York: Atheneum, 1971.

Posas, Mario. *Conflictos agrarios y organización campesino: Sobre los orígenes de las primeras organizaciones campesinos en Honduras.* Tegucigalpa: Editorial Universitaria, 1981.

————. "Honduras at the Crossroads." *Latin American Perspectives* 7 (2-3) (Spring–Summer 1980):45–56.

————. "In the Jaws of the Standard Fruit Company." In *Honduras: Portrait of a Captive Nation.* Nancy Peckenham and Annie Street, eds. New York: Praeger, 1985.

————. *Lucha ideológica y organización sindical en Honduras (1954–65).* Tegucigalpa: Editorial Guaymuras, 1980.

————. *Luchas del movimiento obrero hondureño.* San José: Editorial Universitaria Centroamericana, 1981.

————. *El movimiento campesino hondureño: Una perspectiva general.* Tegucigalpa: Editorial Guaymuras, 1981.

————. "Política estatal y estructura agraria en Honduras (1950–1978)." *Estudios Sociales Centroamericanos* (24) (September–December 1979):37–116.

————. *Las sociedades artesanales y los orígines del movimiento obrero hondureño.* Tegucigalpa: E.S.P. Editorial, 1978.

————. "Tendencias ideológicas actuales en el movimiento obrero hondureño." *Anuario de Estudios Centroamericanos* (6) (1980):25–54.

Posas, Mario, and Rafael del Cid. *La construcción del sector público y del estado nacional de Honduras 1876–1979.* San José: Editorial Universitaria Centroamericana (EDUCA), 1981.

Pozzolini, Alberto. *Antonio Gramsci: An Introduction to His Thought.* London: Pluto Press, 1970.

Premio, Daniel L. "Guatemala." In *Communism in Central America and the Caribbean.* Robert Wesson, ed. Stanford: Hoover Institution Press, 1982.

Rabe, Stephen G. *Eisenhower and Latin America: The Foreign Policy of Anticommunism.* Chapel Hill: University of North Carolina Press, 1988.

Rama, Angel. *Rubén Darío y el modernismo.* Caracas: Universidad Central de Venezuela, 1970.

Ramírez, Sergio. "Sandinismo, Hegemony and Revolution." *Contemporary Marxism* (3) (Summer 1981):23–26.

Randall, Margaret. *Risking a Somersault in the Air: Conversations with Nicaraguan Writers.* San Francisco: Solidarity Publications, 1984.

Rarihokwats, ed. *Guatemala! The Horror and the Hope.* York, Pa.: Four Arrows, 1982.

Reding, Andrew, ed. and trans. *Christianity and Revolution: Tomás Borge's Theology of Life.* Maryknoll, N.Y.: Orbis Books, 1987.

Reglado Dueñas, Miguel, and José Salvador Guandique. *El repliegue político de la oligarquía cafetalera.* San Salvador: Tipografía Santa Anita, 1975.

Rey, Julio Adolfo. "Revolution and Liberation: A Review of Recent Literature on the Guatemalan Situation." *Hispanic American Historical Review* 38 (May 1958):239–255.

Richter, Ernesto. *Proceso de acumulación y dominación en la formación socio-política salvadoreña.* San Pedro de Montes de Oca, Costa Rica: Programa Centroamericano de Ciencias Sociales, 1976.

Ridenour, Ron. *Yankee Sandinistas.* Willimantic, Conn.: Curbstone Press, 1986.

Riding, Alan. "Revolution and the Intellectual in Latin America." *New York Times Magazine.* March 13, 1983, pp. 28–38.

Robinson, William, and Kent Norsworthy. *David and Goliath: The U.S. War Against Nicaragua.* New York: Monthly Review Press, 1987.

Rodríguez, Eugenio. *El pensamiento liberal: Antología.* San José: Editorial Costa Rica, 1979.

Rodríguez, Mario. *Central America.* Englewood Cliffs, N.J.: Prentice-Hall, 1965.

Ropp, Steve C., and James A. Morris, eds. *Central America: Crisis and Adaptation.* Albuquerque: University of New Mexico Press, 1984.

Romualdi, Serafino. *Presidents and Peons: Recollections of a Labor Ambassador in Latin America.* New York: Funk and Wagnalls, 1967.

Rosenberg, Mark B., and Philip L. Shepherd, eds. *Honduras Confronts Its Future: Contending Perspectives on Critical Issues.* Boulder: Lynne Rienner Publishers, 1986.

Rosset, Peter, and John Vandermeer, eds. *The Nicaragua Reader: Documents of a Revolution Under Fire.* New York: Grove Press, 1983.

_____, eds. *Nicaragua: Unfinished Revolution.* New York: Grove Press, 1986.

Ruchwarger, Gary. *People in Power. Forging a Grassroots Democracy in Nicaragua.* South Hadley, Mass.: Bergin and Garvey, 1987.

_____. *Struggling for Survival: Workers, Women, and Class on a Nicaraguan State Farm.* Boulder: Westview Press, 1989.

Rudolph, James D., ed. *Nicaragua: A Country Study.* Washington, D.C.: Foreign Area Studies, American University, 1982.

Ruiz, Henry, et al. *Carlos Fonseca siempre.* Managua: Departamento de Propaganda y Educación Política del FSLN, 1982.

Russell, Philip L. *El Salvador in Crisis.* Austin: Colorado River Press, 1984.

Ryan, John Morris, et al. *Area Handbook for Nicaragua.* Washington, D.C.: Foreign Area Studies, American University, 1970.

Sáenz, Vicente. *América hoy como ayer.* Mexico City: Editorial América Nueva, 1955.

_____. *Centro América en pie.* Mexico City: Ediciones Liberación, 1944.

_____. *Ensayos escogidos.* San José: Editorial Costa Rica, 1983.

_____. *Latin America Against the Colonial System.* Mexico City: Unión Democrática Centroamericana, 1949.

_____. *Martí. Raíz y ala del libertador de Cuba.* Mexico City: Editorial América Nueva, 1955.

_____. *Norteamericanización de Centro América.* San José: Talleres de la Opinión, 1925.

_____. *Nuestras vías interoceánicas.* Mexico City: Editorial América Nueva, 1957.

_____ . *Paralelismo de la paz y de la democracia.* Mexico City: Unión Democrática Centroamericana, 1946.

_____ . *Rompiendo cadenas: Las del imperialismo en Centroamérica y en otras repúblicas del continente.* Buenos Aires: Editorial Palestra, 1961.

_____ . *Vidas ejemplares hispanoamericanas.* Mexico City: Editorial América Nueva, 1959.

Sáenz, Vicente, et al. *Por qué lucha Centro América.* Mexico City: Unión Democrática Centroamericana, 1943.

Salazar Mora, Jorge Mario. *Política y reforma en Costa Rica 1914–1958.* San José: Editorial Porvenir, 1981.

Salguero, Miguel. *Tres meses con la vida en hilo: Crónicas y entrevistas (Manuel Mora—José Figueres).* San José: Editorial Universidad Estatal a Distancia, 1981.

Salisbury, Richard V. "Manuel Mora Valverde." In *Biographical Dictionary of Marxism.* Robert A. Gorman, ed. Westport, Conn.: Greenwood Press, 1986.

Sánchez, Ernesto Mejía, ed. *Estudios sobre Rubén Darío.* Mexico City: Fondo de Cultura Económica, 1968.

Sánchez, José. "Social Developments in El Salvador and the Policy of the Communist Party." *World Marxist Review* 8 (8) (August 1965):11–17.

Sánchez, José M. "Guatemala." In *Political Parties of the Americas.* Robert J. Alexander, ed. Westport, Conn.: Greenwood Press, 1982.

Sánchez, Luis. "Nicaraguan Communists in Van of the Liberation Movement?" *World Marxist Review* 2 (2) (February 1968):30–38.

Sánchez Vázquez, Adolfo. *The Philosophy of Praxis.* London: Merlin Press, 1977.

Sandino, Augusto C. *El pensamiento vivo.* 2 vols. Managua: Editorial Nueva Nicaragua, 1981.

_____ . *El pensamiento vivo de Sandino.* Havana: Casa de las Américas, 1980.

Sandino, Augusto C., Carlos Fonseca Amador, and FSLN. *Nicaragua: la estrategia de la victoria.* Mexico City: Editorial Nuestro Tiempo, 1980.

Sax-Fernández, John. "The Militarization of Costa Rica." *Monthly Review* (May 1972):61–70.

Schlesinger, Stephen, and Stephen Kinzer. *Bitter Fruit: The Untold Story of the American Coup in Guatemala.* Garden City, N.Y.: Anchor Books, 1982.

Schneider, Ronald M. *Communism in Guatemala, 1944–1954.* New York: Praeger, 1959.

Schware, Robert. *Quantification in the History of Political Thought.* Westport, Conn.: Greenwood Press, 1981.

Sedorsky, David, ed. *The Liberal Tradition in European Thought.* New York: G. P. Putnam's Sons, 1970.

Seligson, Mitchell A. *Peasants of Costa Rica and the Development of Agrarian Capitalism.* Madison: University of Wisconsin Press, 1980.

Selser, Gregorio. "Presencia de la internacional socialista en América Latina y el Caribe." In *Centroamérica crisis y política internacional.* Jaime Labastida, et al. Mexico City: Siglo XXI, 1982.

_____ . *Sandino.* New York: Monthly Review Press, 1981.

Silvert, Kalman H. *Essays in Understanding Latin America.* Philadelphia: Institute for the Study of Human Issues, 1977.

_____ . *A Study in Government: Guatemala*. New Orleans: Middle American Research Institute, Tulane University, 1954.

Simon, Jean Marie. *Guatemala: Eternal Spring—Eternal Tyranny*. New York: W. W. Norton, 1987.

Slutzky, Daniel, and Esther Alonso. *Empresas transacionales y agricultura: El caso del enclave bananero en Honduras*. Tegucigalpa: Editorial Universitaria, 1982.

Soler, Ricuarte. *Estudio sobre historia de las ideas en América*. Panama City: Imprenta Nacional, 1960.

Solórzano Martínez, Mario. "La constitución de un nuevo bloque histórico en Guatemala." *Política y Sociedad* 2 (5) (January–June 1978):67–127.

Soto Hall, Máximo. *Nicaragua y el imperialismo norteamericano*. Buenos Aires: Artes y Letras Editorial, 1928.

Spell, Lota M. "Rafael Heliodoro Valle (1891–1959)." *Hispanic American Historical Review* (obituary) 65 (3) (August 1960):424–430.

Stabb, Martin S. *In Quest of Identity: Patterns in the Spanish American Essay of Ideas, 1890–1960*. Chapel Hill: University of North Carolina Press, 1967.

Stanford Central American Action Network. *Revolution in Central America*. Boulder: Westview Press, 1983.

Stokes, William S. *Honduras: An Area Study in Government*. Madison: University of Wisconsin Press, 1950. Reprint. Westport, Conn.: Greenwood Press, 1973.

_____ . "The Pensadores of Latin America." In *The Intellectuals: A Controversial Portrait*. George B. de Huszar, ed. Glencoe, Ill.: Free Press, 1960.

Stone, Samuel. *La dinastía de los conquistadores: La crisis del poder en la Costa Rica contemporánea*. San José: Editorial Universitaria Centroamericana, 1975.

_____ . *The Heritage of the Conquistadores: Ruling Classes in Central America from Conquest to the Sandinistas*. Lincoln: University of Nebraska Press, 1990.

Sundaram, Anjali, and George Gelber, eds. *A Decade of War: El Salvador Confronts the Future*. New York: Monthly Review Press, 1991.

Sunshine, Catherine A. *The Caribbean: Survival, Struggle and Sovereignty*. Washington, D.C.: EPICA, 1985, 1988.

Swedberg, Richard. *The Honduran Trade Union Movement, 1920–1982*. Cambridge, Mass.: Central American Information Office, 1983.

Therborn, Göran. *The Ideology of Power and the Power of Ideology*. London: Verso, 1980.

Thomas, Clive Y. *The Rise of the Autoritarian State in Peripheral Societies*. New York: Monthly Review Press, 1984.

Tirado López, Víctor. *El pensamiento político de Carlos Fonseca Amador*. Managua: Secretaría Nacional de Propaganda y Educación Política, 1979 or 1980.

Toriello Garrido, Guillermo. *¿A donde va Guatemala?* Mexico City: Editorial Nueva, 1956.

_____ . *La batalla de Guatemala*. Mexico City: Ediciones Cuadernos Americanos, 1955.

_____ . *Guatemala, mas de 20 años de traición*. Caracas: Editorial Ateneo de Caracas, 1980.

_____ . "Introduction." In *Guatemala in Rebellion: Unfinished History*. Jonathan L. Fried et al., eds. New York: Grove Press, 1983.

_____ . "Message from the Central American and Caribbean Anti-Imperialist Tribunal." St. George's, Grenada, March 13, 1982.

_____ . "On the Role of the United States and Israel." In *Guatemala: Tyranny on Trial*. Susanne Jonas, Ed McCaughan, and Elizabeth Sutherland Martínez, eds. San Francisco: Synthesis Publications, 1984.

_____ . *A Popular History of Two Revolutions: Guatemala and Nicaragua*. San Francisco: Synthesis Publications, 1985.

_____ . *Tras la cortina de banano*. Havana: Editorial de Ciencias Sociales, 1981.

Torres-Rioseco, Arturo. *Rubén Darío: casticismo y americanismo*. Cambridge: Harvard University Press, 1931.

Torres, Edelberto. *La dramática vida de Rubén Darío*. Havana: Editorial Arte y Literatura, 1982.

_____ . "Francisco Morazán and the Struggle for a Central American Union." In *Honduras: Portrait of a Captive Nation*. Nancy Peckenham and Annie Street, eds. New York: Praeger, 1985.

_____ . Personal interview, Managua, Nicaragua, January 7, 1986.

_____ . *Sandino y sus pares*. Managua: Editorial Nueva Nicaragua, 1983.

Torres Rivas, Edelberto. "Central America Today: A Study in Regional Dependency." In *Trouble in Our Backyard: Central America and the United States in the Eighties*. Martin Diskin, ed. New York: Pantheon Books, 1983.

_____ . "The Central American Crisis and the Common Market." In *Crisis in Central America: Regional Dynamics and U.S. Policy in the 1980s*. Nora Hamilton, Jeffry A. Frieden, Linda Fuller, and Manuel Pastor, Jr., eds. Boulder: Westview Press, 1988.

_____ . "The Central American Model of Growth: Crisis for Whom?" *Latin American Perspectives* 7 (2–3) (Spring–Summer 1980):24–43.

_____ . *Centroamérica: La democracia posible*. San José: Editorial Universitaria Centroamericana, EDUCA, 1987.

_____ . *Las clases sociales en Guatemala*. Guatemala City: Universidad de San Carlos, 1962.

_____ . *Crisis del poder en Centroamérica*. San José: EDUCA, 1981.

_____ . "Guatemala: Medio siglo de historia política." In *América Latina: historia de medio siglo*. Vol. 2. Pablo González Casanova, ed. Mexico City: Siglo XXI, 1981.

_____ . *Interpretación del desarrollo social centroamericano*. San José: Editorial Universitaria Centroamericana, 1981.

_____ . "The Nature of the Central American Crisis." In *Towards an Alternative for Central America and the Caribbean*. George Irvin and Xabier Gorostiaga, eds. London: George Allen and Unwin, 1985.

_____ . "Notas para comprender la crisis política centroamericana." In *Centroamérica: Crisis y política internacional*. Jaime Labastida et al. Mexico City: Siglo XXI, 1982.

_____ . "The Origins of Crisis and Instability in Central America." *Contemporary Marxism* 14 (Fall 1986):49–58.

_____ . "Presentation by the Prosecutor." In *Guatemala: Tyranny on Trial*. Susanne Jonas, Ed McCaughan, and Elizabeth Sutherland Martínez, eds. San Francisco: Synthesis Publications, 1984.

_____ . "Problemas de la contrarevolución y la democracia en Guatemala." *Nueva sociedad* 53 (March–April 1981):97–112.

_____ . *Procesos y estructuras de una sociedad dependiente (Centroamérica)*. Santiago de Chile: Ediciones Prensa Latinoamericana, 1969.

_____ . "Refleciones en torno a una interpretación histórico-social de Guatemala. *Revista Mexicana de Sociología* 34 (1) (January–May 1972):115–131.

_____ . *Repression and Resistance: The Struggle for Democracy in Central America*. Boulder: Westview Press, 1989.

_____ . "Seven Keys to Understanding the Central American Crisis." *Contemporary Marxism* (3) (Summer 1981):49–61.

Torres Rivas, Edelberto, and Julio César Pinto S. *Problemas en la formación del estado nacional en Centroamericana*. San José: ICAP, 1983.

Torres Rivas, Edelberto, et al. *Centro América hoy*. Mexico City: Siglo XXI, 1976.

Trejos S., Juan Diego. *Costa Rica: Economic Crisis and Public Policy, 1978–1984*. Miami: Occasional Papers Series, Latin America and Caribbean Center, Florida International University, 1985.

Tünnerman B., Carlos, ed. *Pensamiento universitario Centroamericano*. San José: Editorial Universitaria Centroamericana, 1980.

Turcios Lima, Luis Augusto. "Carta abierta del Movimiento Revolucionario 13 de noviembre." In *Turcios Lima*. Havana: Instituto del Libro, 1969.

Valle, Rafael Heliodoro. *Historia de la cultura hondureña*. Tegucigalpa: Editorial Universitaria, 1981.

Vanden, Harry E. "Carlos Fonseca Amador." In *Biographical Dictionary of Marxism*. Robert A. Gorman, ed. Westport, Conn.: Greenwood Press, 1986.

_____ . "The Ideology of the Insurrection." In *Nicaragua in Revolution*. Thomas W. Walker, ed. New York: Praeger, 1982.

_____ . "Tomás Borge Martínez." In *Biographical Dictionary of Marxism*. Robert A. Gorman, ed. Westport, Conn.: Greenwood Press, 1986.

Vega Carballo, José Luis. *La crisis de los partidos políticos tradicionales de Costa Rica*. Costa Rica: Ediciones Academia Costarricense de Bibliografía, 1978.

_____ . *Democracia y dominación en Costa Rica*. San José: Instituto de Investigaciones Sociales, Facultad de Ciencias Sociales, Universidad de Costa Rica, 1981.

_____ . *Estado y dominación social en Costa Rica: Antecedentes coloniales y formación del estado nacional*. San José: Instituto de Investigaciones Sociales, Facultad de Ciencias Sociales, Universidad de Costa Rica, 1980.

_____ . "Estapas y procesos de la evolución sociopolítica de Costa Rica." *Estudios Sociales Centroamericanos* 1 (1) (January–April 1972):45–72.

_____ . *Hacia una interpretación del desarrollo costarricense: Ensayo sociologico*. San José: Editorial Porvenir, 1981.

_____ . *Orden y progreso: La formación del estado nacional en Costa Rica*. San José: Instituto Centroamericano de Administración Pública, 1981.

_____ . *Poder político y democracia en Costa Rica*. San José: Editorial Porvenir, 1982.

Vega Carballo, José Luis, Elena Gil, and Walter V. Costanza. *Tres temas en la América Latina hoy: Consideraciones en torno al cambio social, la mujer en el mundo del trabajo, el militarismo en América Latina.* San José: Centro de Estudios Democráticos de América Latina, 1970.

Ventura, José. *El poder popular en el Salvador.* Mexico City: Mex Sur, N.D.

Verzi, H. G., ed. *Recopilación de textos sobre Roque Dalton.* Havana: Ediciones Casa de las Américas, 1986.

Vilas, Carlos M. *The Sandinista Revolution: National Liberation and Social Transformation in Central America.* New York: Monthly Review Press, 1986.

Volk, Steven. "Honduras: On the Border of War." *NACLA Report on the Americas* 15 (8) (November–December 1981):2–37.

Waggoner, George R., and Barbara Ashton Waggoner. *Education in Central America.* Lawrence: University Press of Kansas, 1971.

Walker, Thomas W. *Nicaragua: The Land of Sandino.* Boulder: Westview Press, 1981 and 1986.

———, ed.*Nicaragua in Revolution.* New York: Praeger, 1982.

———, ed. *Nicaragua: The First Five Years.* New York: Praeger, 1985.

———, ed. *Reagan Versus the Sandinistas: The Undeclared War in Nicaragua.* Boulder: Westview Press, 1987.

Wallace, Mike. "Interview with Nicaraguan Historians," *Radical History Review* (33) (September 1985):7–20.

Wallerstein, Immanuel. *The Capitalist World-Economy.* London: Cambridge University Press, and Paris: Editions de la Maison des Sciences de l'Homme, 1979.

——— . *The Modern World-System.* Vol. 1. *Capitalist Agriculture and the Origins of the European World-Economy in the Sixteenth Century.* Vol. 2. *Mercantilism and the Consolidation of the European World-Economy, 1600–1750.* New York: Academic Press, 1974 and 1980.

Watland, Charles D. *Poet-Errant: A Biography of Rubén Darío.* New York: Philosophical Library, 1965.

Weber, Henri. *Nicaragua: The Sandinist Revolution.* London: Verso, 1981.

——— . "Nicaragua: The Sandinist Revolution." In *Crisis in the Caribbean.* Fitzroy Ambursley and Robin Cohen, eds. New York: Monthly Review Press, 1983.

Weeks, John. *The Economies of Central America.* New York: Holmes and Meier, 1985.

——— . "An Interpretation of the Central American Crisis." *Latin American Research Review* 21 (3) (1986):31–53.

Wells, Henry, ed. *Costa Rica Election Factbook.* Washington, D.C.: Institute for Comparative Study of Political Systems, February 6, 1966.

———, ed. *Costa Rica Election Factbook Number 2 Supplement.* Washington, D.C.: Institute for Comparative Study of Political Systems, February 1, 1970.

Wesson, Robert, ed. *Communism in Central America and the Caribbean.* Stanford: Hoover Institution Press, 1982.

Wheaton, Philip E. *Inside Honduras: Regional Counterinsurgency Base.* Washington, D.C.: EPICA, 1982.

Wheelock Román, Jaime. *Diciembre victorioso.* Managua: Editorial Nueva Nicaragua, 1982.

_____ . *Entre la crisis y la agresión: La reforma agraria Sandinista*. Managua: Editorial Nueva Nicaragua, 1985.

_____ . *Frente Sandinista: Hacia la ofensiva final*. Havana: Editorial de Ciencias Sociales, 1980.

_____ . "Interview." *Latin American Perspectives* 6 (1) (Winter 1979):121–127.

_____ . *Nicaragua: El gran desafío*. Mexico City: Editorial Katún, 1984.

_____ . *Nicaragua: Imperialismo y dictadura*. Havana: Editorial de Ciencias Sociales, 1980.

_____ . *Nicaragua: The Great Challenge*. Managua: Alternative Views, 1984.

_____ . "Nicaragua's Economy and the Fight Against Imperialism." In *Sandinistas Speak*. Bruce Marcus, ed. New York: Pathfinder Press, 1982.

_____ . Personal interview, Managua, Nicaragua, January 8, 1986.

_____ . *Raíces indígenas de la lucha anticolonialista en Nicaragua*. Mexico City: Siglo XXI, 1980.

_____ . "You Cannot Overthrow a People." *Contemporary Marxism* (8) (Spring 1984):201–207.

Whetten, Nathan L. *Guatemala: The Land and the People*. New Haven: Yale University Press, 1961.

White, Alastair. *El Salvador*. New York: Praeger, 1973.

White, Steven. *Culture and Politics in Nicaragua: Testimony of Poets and Writers*. New York: Lumen Books, 1986.

Wiarda, Howard J., Mark Falcoff, et al., eds. *The Communist Challenge in the Caribbean and Central America*. Washington, D.C.: American Enterprise Institute for Public Policy Research, 1987.

Woodward, Ralph Lee, Jr. *Central America: A Nation Divided*. New York: Oxford University Press, 1976, 1985.

_____ , ed. *Positivism in Latin America, 1850–1900*. Lexington, Mass.: Heath, 1971.

Wortman, Miles L. *Government and Society in Central America, 1680–1840*. New York: Columbia University Press, 1982.

Yanes, Gabriela, Manuel Sorto, Horacio Castellanos Moya, and Lyn Sorto, eds. *Mirrors of War: Literature and Revolution in El Salvador*. New York: Monthly Review Press, 1985.

Ydígoras Fuentes, Miguel. *My War with Communism*. Englewood Cliffs, N.J.: Prentice-Hall, 1963.

Zaldívar Guzmán, Raúl. *Liberalismo en Honduras*. Tegucigalpa: Imprenta Bulnes, 1964.

Zamora, Rubén. Personal interview, Managua, Nicaragua, January 9, 1986.

Zea, Leopoldo. *El pensamiento latino-americano*. 2 vols. Mexico City: Editorial Pormaca, 1965.

Zelaya, Chester, et al. *¿Democracia en Costa Rica? Cinco opiniones polémicas*. San José: Editorial Universidad Estatal a Distancia, 1978.

Zimmerman, Marc, ed. *Nicaragua in Reconstruction and at War: The People Speak*. Minneapolis: MEP Publications, 1985.

Zwerling, Philip, and Connie Martin, eds. *Nicaragua: A New Kind of Revolution*. Westport, Conn.: Lawrence Hill, 1985.

About the Book and Author

Central American *pensadores* have interpreted the theories of Marx and other scholars of revolution in diverse ways. In this book Sheldon Liss examines the political theory and ideology of some of Central America's most important radical thinkers, including non-Marxists, and demonstrates how they have challenged the tenets of imperialism and capitalism.

Chapters on individual Central American countries begin with brief historical introductions that emphasize the rise of radical activities and organizations. Individual essays based on published writings, interviews, and scholarly analyses of their works then establish each writer's personal ideology, social and political goals, and theories of society, state, and institutions of power. Liss also examines their relationship to social and political movements and contributions to the national intellectual life of the past and present. In addition, Liss discusses the writers' understanding of the role of the United States in the Americas and beliefs about national struggles for independence. By focusing on political and social theory and on intellectual history, this book also provides the background critical for understanding recent developments and changes in Central America.

Sheldon B. Liss is professor of Latin American history and politics at the University of Akron.

Index